AMERICAN IDENTITIES

A BREAD LOAF ANTHOLOGY

The Bread Loaf Anthology of
Contemporary American Poetry,
edited by Robert Pack, Sydney
Lea, and Jay Parini, 1985.

The Bread Loaf Anthology of
Contemporary American Short
Stories, edited by Robert Pack
and Jay Parini, 1987.

The Bread Loaf Anthology of
Contemporary American Essays,
edited by Robert Pack and
Jay Parini, 1989.

Writers on Writing, edited by
Robert Pack and Jay Parini, 1991.

Poems for a Small Planet:
Contemporary American Nature Poetry
edited by Robert Pack and
Jay Parini, 1993.

American Identities: Contemporary Multicultural Voices
edited by Robert Pack
and Jay Parini, 1994.

EDITED BY

Robert Pack

Jay Parini

American Identities

Contemporary Multicultural Voices

Middlebury College Press

Published by University Press of New England

Hanover and London

MIDDLEBURY COLLEGE PRESS

Published by University Press of New England,

Hanover, NH 03755

© 1994 by the President and Fellows of Middlebury College

Printed in the United States of America   5   4   3   2   1

CIP data appear at the end of the book

Acknowledgments for previously published pieces appear on page 371.

CONTENTS

Introduction

The movement broadly known as "multiculturalism" has moved to the center of American intellectual life in the last decade. Indeed, it has become embroiled in the larger argument over what critics call "the canon"—that variable list of works considered valuable by editors, teachers, and critics in a position to promulgate taste and articulate a version of "the tradition." That debate, which increased in intensity in the mid-1980s, has tapered off in this decade as it has become generally accepted that literary merit is to be found in an ever widening range of writers coming from many regions and backgrounds.

The debate over what constitutes Western civilization will no doubt continue as long as there are people eager to argue their preferences, but what seems inevitable is that any curriculum is bound to broaden as writers who associate themselves with a given "minority" produce work of undeniably imaginative power and complexity. It is now clear that the metaphor of the American melting pot is obsolete as groups within the society refuse to merge but insist on a multiplicity of well-maintained identities. Rubrics such as "African-American," "Jewish-American," and "Native American" emerge as specific categories, even though the individual voices within each category often will conflict.

Writers have always sought an identity of one sort or another, so there is nothing new here. Regional identity was an early allegiance, with New England proudly maintaining its cultural hegemony in writers like Emerson, Thoreau, Whittier, Longfellow, and Dickinson. Certain institutions such as *The Atlantic Monthly* and Harvard University became centers of cultural power and points of transmission. William Dean Howells, an ambitious writer coming from the Midwest, left for Boston as soon as he could, aware that to establish himself as a national writer he would have to identify consciously with that region. Indeed, one of the important cultural moments of the later nineteenth century occurred with the shift of power from Boston to New York.

The South did have its own strong cultural identity from early on, but it took the synthetic power of William Faulkner to invent that region in a way that allowed future writers to take full possession of their heritage as specifically "Southern" writers. A vast range of authors from Robert Penn Warren, Flannery O'Conner, and Walker Percy to Toni Morrison and Alice Walker owe something to Faulkner's vision of the South. The same may be said for more recent writers like Sam Pickering, Larry Brown, Pinkney Benedict, Robert Houston, and Ted Perry, all of whom are represented in this volume by new work.

It should quickly be added that few writers hope to be identified solely by a specific tag, such as "Southern" or "Jewish" or "gay." A literary identity is blessedly complex. No one can escape his or her class, sex, race, or a host of other contingent factors, but each writer is free to choose his or her own emphasis in shaping a literary style. One can, like Scott Fitzgerald, aspire to a different class. One might spend a whole career redefining one's ethnic or social origins, but especially in recent years, writers have often sought to lay claim to their actual pasts, to participate in their cultures of origin, assuming that one does not go *around* one's identity but *through* it, accepting and working with the complexity that results from having specific allegiances.

In *American Identities*, we have sought to move the argument over multiculturalism in a slightly different direction by assuming that writers are empowered to acknowledge and explore their individual points of origin—religious, racial, class, sexual—and to freely identify, if they so choose, with other identities. Writers create a literary *persona* that is as much a voluntary construction as an inherited fate, working with a vast array of materials at hand. Quite often, the essays, poems, and stories in this volume deal with the different ways in which writers work to create that *persona*.

Julia Alvarez, for example, writes about the conflicted process of assuming an identity within the English language after having spent her childhood in the Spanish-speaking world of the Dominican Republic: "When I was ten, we emigrated to New York. How astonishing, a country where everyone spoke English! These people must be smarter, I thought. Maids, waiters, taxi drivers, doormen, bums on the street, garbage men, all spoke this difficult language. It took some time before I understood that Americans were not necessarily a smarter, superior race."

A number of these selections might be considered adventures in the genre of autobiography. Erica Jong, Ron Powers, Paul Mariani, Louise Erdrich, Robert Stepto, Michael Dorris, Ishmael Reed, Gary Soto, Terry Tempest Williams, and Gore Vidal, for example, deal frankly with their own ethnic (Jewish, Italian, Hispanic, Mormon, African-American, Native American) or socioeconomic class origins as part of the ongoing process of defining selfhood, of coming into adulthood with a sense of achieved presence. Sam Pickering, in "Gathering an Identity," centers himself almost entirely in the present, attempting to construct an identity from the materials of his daily life, while Robert Houston plumbs a dark moment in his past to examine aspects of his present self. Larry Brown writes about his own "late start" as a writer in northern Mississippi: "I've been writing for about twelve years," he says. "I didn't start until I was twenty-nine. I figure most people who write start a lot younger than that. Most people who want to make something out of their lives probably take control of them a lot earlier than that."

Not infrequently, the writers in this anthology begin a troubled meditation on identity by focusing on one or more forebears, a parent or grandparents, as in "Ningyo," a poem by Lee Ann Roripaugh:

> She took me everywhere
> in my crocheted
> lace dresses,
> embroidered initials.
> It pleased her
> I could say
> hippopotamus
> so I said it
> in the supermarket.
> After hot baths,
> laid out on the counter,
> my hair floating
> in the sink
> like seaweed,
> she would hand me
> a mirror. *See!*
> *Tako-chan, the octopus*
> *has left his ink.*

Similarly, Garrett Hongo in his memoir, "Kubota," writes about his Japanese-American grandparents, who were caught in their own specific racial/national identities at the wrong place and time: "On December 8, 1941, the day after the Japanese attack on Pearl Harbor in Hawaii, my grandfather barricaded himself with his family—my grandmother, my teenage mother, her two sisters and two brothers—inside of his home in La'ie, a sugar plantation village on Oahu's North Shore. This was my maternal grandfather, a man most villagers called by his last name, Kubota. It could mean either 'Wayside Field' or else 'Broken Dreams,' depending on which ideograms he used."

An identity might, as James Atlas and Lynne Sharon Schwartz imply, have developed by living in an urban environment. Atlas invokes Chicago as a place that had as much a symbolic as literal appeal as a backdrop to his identity formation as an "intellectual." He writes about walking home from the Art Institute as a teenager: "On the way home, I wandered through the slush-filled streets of the Loop beneath the elevated tracks. Trains trundled overhead, showering sparks through the dusk; a Salvation Army band played 'Good King Wenceslas.' I was looking for the sort of cafeteria I had read about somewhere—in *The Adventures of Augie March*? Anyway, some place where intellectuals gathered and had animated conversations, scraping their chairs back and pounding the table, smoking and gesturing with frantic hands. A place where Roquentin, the hero of Sartre's *La Nausée* (as I called it, though I had read a translation), might have whiled away dull afternoons."

Not infrequently, the writers included here attempt to understand the way they see themselves in contrast to the way their community regards them. John Preston, for example, meditates on his gay identity and the reactions of some men from his home town. "That I am a writer," he says, "apparently is more important to these men than the fact that I write about gay themes. My family's that way, too. For someone in our hometown to have ended up writing books is such a high achievement in the community's estimate that it overwhelms what they think of the content."

Many of the writers here, such as Michelle Taigue, focus movingly on the complex issue of denial. Some identities, such as hers as a Native American, may be more difficult to lay claim to than others. "To exist as a family," she writes, "we had to continually construct who were who. We learned how not to be ourselves. Around strangers, words were spoken carefully or not at all. Silence became a strategy for survival. But we had to comprehend its subtle complexity, recognize its disguises. We came to understand silence as a powerful rhetorical tool which cuts and gives shape to sound and meaning—not to confuse it with the inarticulate and illiterate, or the inchoate place of nonbeing, the silence of suppression, a void which lends itself to shame and insecurity."

Most of these essays, poems, and stories turn on a moment of recognition, a point where one's past or present suddenly coheres, and the notion of "identity" becomes relevant to the continuous process of self-definition. That moment may have to do with a willingness to accept an aspect of oneself constructed in the past and then suppressed, or it may have to do with choosing to ally oneself with a movement, such as feminism in Nancy Mairs' essay, or with a profession, as in William H. Pritchard's piece about himself in the role of a teacher.

American Identities does not plead for any special sense of what it means to construct an identity in America today. The collection, rather, is meant to reflect an issue that concerns contemporary writers. Certain key questions emerge: Who am I? Where have I come from? To what degree am I determined by race, class, or gender? How does one construct a "self" from the materials of life in our contentious and often incoherent culture? The writers in this volume necessarily arrive at different answers to these questions, which are addressed in highly distinct ways in the diverse essays, poems, and stories that we have included here. What all of these authors share is a commitment to their art as a mode of expression which assumes that communication across differences is both possible and desirable.

AMERICAN IDENTITIES

JULIA ALVAREZ

Homecoming

When my cousin Carmen married, the guards
at her father's *finca* took the guests' bracelets
and wedding rings and put them in an armored truck
for safekeeping while wealthy, dark-skinned men,
their plump, white women and spoiled children
bathed in a river whose bottom had been cleaned
for the occasion. She was Uncle's only daughter,
and he wanted to show her husband's family,
a bewildered group of sunburnt Minnesotans,
that she was valued. He sat me at their table
to show off my English, and when he danced with me,
fondling my shoulder blades beneath my bridesmaid's gown
as if they were breasts, he found me skinny
but pretty at seventeen, and clever.
Come back from that cold place, Vermont, he said,
all this is yours! Over his shoulder
a dozen workmen hauled in blocks of ice
to keep the champagne lukewarm and stole
glances at the wedding cake, a dollhouse duplicate
of the family *rancho*, the shutters marzipan,
the cobbles almonds. A maiden aunt housekept,
touching up whipped cream roses with a syringe
of eggwhites, rescuing the groom when the heat
melted his chocolate shoes into the frosting.
On too much rum Uncle led me across the dance floor,
dusted with talcum for easy gliding, a smell
of babies underfoot. He twirled me often,
excited by my pleas of dizziness, teasing me
that my merengue had lost its Caribbean.
Above us, Chinese lanterns strung between posts
came on and one snapped off and rose
into a purple postcard sky.
A grandmother cried: *The children all grow up too fast.*
The Minnesotans finally broke loose and danced a Charleston
and were pronounced good gringos with latino hearts.
The little sister, freckled with a week of beach,

her hair as blonde as movie stars, was asked
by maids if they could touch her hair or skin,
and she backed off, until it was explained to her,
they meant no harm. *This is all yours,*
Uncle whispered, pressing himself into my dress.
The workmen costumed in their workclothes danced
a workman's jig. The maids went by with trays
of wedding bells and matchbooks monogrammed
with Dick's and Carmen's names. It would be years
before I took the courses that would change my mind
in schools paid for by sugar from the fields around us,
years before I could begin to comprehend
how one does not see the maids when they pass by
with trays of deviled eggs arranged in daisy wheels
—It was too late, or early, to be wise—
The sun was coming up beyond the amber waves
of cane, the roosters crowed, the band struck up
Las Mañanitas, a morning serenade. I had a vision
that I blamed on the champagne:
the fields around us were burning. At last
a yawning bride and groom got up and cut
the wedding cake, but everyone was full
of drink and eggs, roast pig, and rice and beans.
Except the maids and workmen,
sitting on stoops behind the sugar house,
ate with their fingers from their open palms
windows, shutters, walls, pillars, doors,
made from the cane they had cut in the fields.

Queens, 1963

Everyone seemed more American.
than we, newly arrived,
foreign dirt still on our soles.
By year's end, a sprinkler waving
like a flag on our mowed lawn,
we were melted into the block,
owned our own mock Tudor house.
Then the house across the street
sold to a black family.
Cop cars patrolled our block

from the Castellucci's at one end
to the Balakian's on the other.
We heard rumors of bomb threats,
a burning cross on their lawn.
(It turned out to be a sprinkler.)
Still the neighborhood buzzed.
The barber's family, Haralambides,
our left side neighbors, didn't want trouble.
They'd come a long way to be free!
Mr. Scott, the retired plumber,
and his plump midwestern wife,
considered moving back home
where white and black got along
by staying where they belonged.
They had cultivated our street
like the garden she'd given up
on account of her ailing back,
ailing legs, poor eyes, arthritic hands.
She went through her litany daily,
politely my mother listened,
Ay, Mrs. Scott, que pena!
her Dominican good manners
still running on automatic.
The Jewish counselor next door,
had a practice in her house;
clients hurried up her walk
ashamed to be seen needing.
(I watched from my upstairs window,
gloomy with adolescence,
and guessed how they too must have
hypocritical, old world parents.)
Mrs. Bernstein said it was time
the neighborhood opened up.
(She remembered the snubbing she got—
the first Jews on the block—
a few years back from Mrs. Scott.)
But real estate worried her,
our houses' plummeting value.
She shook her head as she might
at a client's grim disclosures.
Too bad the world works this way.
The Irish girl playing piano
down the street abruptly stopped

in the middle of a note.
I completed the tune in my head,
as I watched *their* front door open:
a dark man in a dark suit
and a girl about my age
walked quickly into a car.
Driving by, the girl looked up.
My hand lifted but fell before
I could make a welcoming gesture.
On her dark face beyond glass
I had seen a look I remembered
from the days before we melted
in the United States of America:
It was hardness mixed with hurt.
It was knowing we never could be
the right kind of Americans.
A police car followed their car.
Down the street, curtains fell back;
blinds, slanted opened, closed.
Mrs. Scott swept her walk
as if it had just been dirtied.
Then the Irish piano commenced
downward scales as if tracking
the plummeting real estate.
One by one I imagined the houses
sinking into their lawns,
the grass grown wild and tall
in the past tense of this continent
before the first foreigners owned
any of this free country.

Chicago Highbrow

Sun poured through the double glass doors, but the air-conditioned lobby of the Piser Memorial Chapel chilled my skin as I came in out of the heat of a Chicago June. I had flown in the night before, home from a year away at Oxford. The services for my grandmother, I learned from a placard on a wooden easel, would be held in Parlor One. Mourners pushed through the doors: my mother's cousin Minna, dough-faced and heavy, a spinster librarian at the Belmont Avenue branch; Sylvia, my grandmother's niece, who lived in a western suburb and enclosed a mimeographed letter about her children with every Christmas card; Agnes, my surviving grandmother's maid, inconceivably old behind her walker, clutching the bars with tremulous spotted hands like a tottering baby in its crib. Gigantic women folded me in their arms; dry-skinned men with tufts of white hair that drifted over their heads like snow blown across a road pumped my hand. Since both my parents were only children, I could never figure out why we had so many relatives. But we did, a Homeric catalogue of them. They showed up at weddings, family parties, funerals. "You remember Grisha," said my mother, posted vigilantly at my side. "Your father's uncle; his wife is Grandma Rya's sister. And this is my cousin Rose." A high-bosomed woman with down on her cheeks had come up to us. "Her mother is married to Grandpa's brother." But despite her prompting, I couldn't hide the bafflement on my face.

A man in sunglasses and a seersucker suit hurried in; he had the tanned look of an athletic coach. His cuff links, two gold plaques, glittered in the sunlight. "Leon!" my father cried, embracing him. They had been classmates at Carl Schurz High School, neighbors on the Northwest Side; they had gotten married the same year and gone with their wives to Mackinac Island.

Leon had prospered; his face had the rosy tinge of the rich. With his brothers, he had founded a glassware empire and become a millionaire at forty. He was a figure in Chicago: chairman of the board of Roosevelt University, president of his North Shore synagogue. He had raised millions for a new temple and commissioned a Japanese architect to build it. He read *The New Republic,* subscribed to the classical-music station WFMT, and was a patron of the Chicago Symphony. He had commissioned a painting by Chagall for his wife and had spent an afternoon with the painter in Vence.

My father hated rabbis—we were liberals, free-thinkers—and had prevailed upon his old friend to deliver the eulogy. In the kitchen that morning, he had stood beside the sink in his robe and dictated the details of my grandmother's life over the phone to Leon in his Mercedes. Pacing up and down while his old friend crept through rush-hour traffic on Lake Shore Drive, he tried to remember how old she was, the name of the town where she was born. "Leon, are you there?" he shouted when a light changed and he heard the car move off amid angry horns.

We filed into a wood-paneled auditorium with movie-theater seats and recessed lights in the ceiling. Leon strode up to the podium and adjusted the microphone. He cleared his throat. "We have come here today to mourn the passing of Rya Atlas, beloved mother of Donald, grandmother of James and Stephen," he began. "It is hard for me to be standing here before you mourning the death in old age of a woman I remember from my own childhood. She was a young woman then, preparing lunch for Donald and me in the kitchen of their apartment above the drugstore on Peterson Avenue. I remember her standing at the sink, the light coming through the window." There was wonder in his voice. "There were always books in Rya's home. They were people of culture. Herman"—my grandfather, long since dead—"was a man of profound learning. When he was a young engineering student in Moscow, he graduated first in his class, and he could read five languages. And Rya"—Leon paused, allowing emotion to collect—"Rya loved opera, literature, art. She loved the finer things in life and passed that love on to her son." He sipped from a glass of water. "It was Rya who wanted Donald to become a doctor. The day he was accepted by Northwestern Medical School was the happiest day of her life."

In the front row, my father wept; my mother, dry-eyed, held his hand. "She was like a mother to me," Leon was saying. I thought of the last time I had seen her, in a North Side nursing home. She had had a stroke and sat oblivious in a wheelchair, her toothless mouth open, hair sprouting from her chin. My father bustled about the room. "Here's James, Mother. Say hello to James." He straightened the flowers in a vase. My grandmother's eyes were like cloudy marbles. I stared at the slack webbed skin between her fingers. There was a sour smell in the room. "Would you like the television on?" my father said in a cheerful voice. Tears started from my eyes. I ran out the door and down the corridor, past old women sitting with their hands in their laps. Out on the street, it was summer, and the odor of roses in a flower bed on the lawn mingled with a spew of bus exhaust. I pounded down the sidewalk toward the lake, a block away, and collapsed on a bench. There was no one on the beach but a mother and her two children; it was nine in the morning, and the sand was damp, the grass dew-sodden. The air was tropical, moist, like Florida. Out on the water, a sailboat rode against the horizon. I could feel my heart still leaping, but exhilaration swept over me: the pleasure of feeling anything deeply, even death.

"It has been a long journey for Rya Atlas," Leon was saying. "From a Lithuanian village to the shores of New York, and then on to the community our people made here in Chicago. That world is disappearing before my very eyes, in the march of generations, but we remember it in our hearts. Was it T. S. Eliot who said, 'They are all gone into the world of light'?" Donne, I thought to myself. (It was Vaughan.) Leon dabbed his eyes with a linen handkerchief. "So, Rya," he said in a faltering voice, "we'll miss you." Then he said some words in Hebrew and walked away from the podium.

An attendant hurried up and led us to a private room with Kleenex dispensers on the end tables. My father sank down on a sofa, holding a handkerchief to his face as if it were an oxygen mask. "That was fantastic," he murmured. "How could he remember so much?" Sweltering in a brown nubbled suit, he seemed uncomfortable, like a child dressed up in his Sunday best. He blotted his face, and we made our way through the crowd of relatives to the limousine that waited out front for the immediate family: my father and mother, my mother's mother, Liz—my last surviving grandparent—my brother and me.

It was a long drive to Woodlawn Cemetery, on the far West Side. The sun flashed like foil on the hoods of cars as we glided through red lights, past gas stations and used-car lots, bowling alleys and tuxedo-rental outlets, drive-ins and dry cleaners. My grandmother, in sunglasses and a black shawl, was excited; the nearness of death made her talkative. She told me how the Cossacks had lunged on their horses through the snow when she was a girl in Ekaterinoslav, bursting into the kitchen and dragging her brother out into the yard, where they beat him in sight of the family at the window. "He was the smart one," she said. "Always politics, politics, politics. Every other word was revolution."

I had seen a photograph of this brother, standing beside his father and grandfather—my great-great-grandfather—the three of them dressed in soft hats and thick woolen coats, mufflers wound about their necks like swaddling clothes. An ample, Tolstoyan beard flows down from the oldest one's chin like a river dividing his tunic. The Social Register families in Lake Forest weren't the only ones with an ancient lineage.

We were at the cemetery now, winding through the monument-crowded grounds until we came to a plot where men in denim overalls leaned on their shovels beside an apparatus with pulleys poised over the grave. We put on the gray gloves distributed by a Piser employee and dragged the casket from the hearse: my brother and I, Leon and my father, and two men from Piser. When we reached the plot, the grave-diggers lifted it off our shoulders and slid it onto the scaffold. My father had wanted no text; he flung his gloves into the trough, murmured "Goodbye, Mama," and walked away, sobbing, to the limousine. A small engine started up, whirring in the dead heat of the day, and the casket disappeared into the ground.

We retrieved our car, and dropped my brother off at the airport. He worked for Ralph Nader, and had to get back to Washington. He was always going somewhere, I brooded as he unloaded his hanging bag and briefcase. Five years older than I, he had gone off to college when I was thirteen, and had lived in South America for three years after graduation. I hung around with my parents while he traveled the globe; it was no different now from what it had ever been. Handsome in his khaki suit, Steve leaned down and kissed my mother, then vanished inside the terminal.

We drove through the deserted North Side to Ashkenaz's delicatessen on Morse, beneath the elevated tracks. Nothing had changed; there was the same middle-aged cashier, her streaked blonde hair swept up in a hive, crescents of blue mascara beneath her eyes, a cigarette in the ashtray beside the rubber-bristled change pad. Behind the counter were bins crammed with sides of corned beef and slabs of tongue in white-enameled trays. It was the middle of the afternoon, and the restaurant was empty.

My parents looked tired. I noticed the gathered folds of skin beneath my mother's chin, the blue veins in her hands; my father's moist eyes reflected the knowledge that he had no parents left. He picked at his smoked fish and studied the menu while the two women talked.

Death had brought them no closer. "Will you stop cracking chicken bones with your teeth?" my mother said. "And don't lean over your soup like that. Bring the soup to your mouth." My grandmother glanced up from her plate with a sly look; embarrassing my mother was a good game. Remember, her bright shawls and antique jewelry proclaimed, your ancestors were peasants, bohemians, foreigners.

"Oh, Mother, spare us this pushcart-and-peddler talk, will you?" my mother said. My grandmother had been recalling the first time she met my grandfather, who traveled around the Midwest hawking postcards out of a suitcase—" 'Pos'l cards,' he called them."

"Mother, we know from 'pos'l cards' already. You've told the boy about it a hundred times."

But I was curious; I found this lore exotic, vivid. Besides, three of my grandparents were dead; my cousins were in Kew Gardens and Florida; my parents had sold their home in Evanston and moved to California the year before, during my last semester of college. I felt like an anthropologist among the Nambikwara; if I didn't study these people now, it would be too late. The old generation was virtually gone; whenever I showed up at my grandmother's residential hotel in downtown Evanston, her last surviving friend, an old woman named Jenny, would prop herself up in her chair and grip my hand, uttering my name in a hoarse croak: "Jeehmy, how wahnderful to see you." Cradling my chin in her spotted hand, my grandmother would scrutinize my face with the ecstatic zeal of an archaeologist happening on a find—only the artifact was new, its discoverer old.

"Mother, finish your borscht and let's go," my mother was saying. My father leafed through his fat wallet and pulled out a twenty; I wondered if I would ever carry around such a wad of bills. Out on Morse, the mica-speckled sidewalk shone like a riverbed.

I dropped my grandmother off, then my parents—they were staying with my mother's cousin in Winnetka—and drove off in their rented Pinto. I hadn't been back in a year and I was eager to look around.

On County Line Road, I pulled into a gas station and got out of the car; it was something I had seen my father do when I was a child, and for some reason the gesture had impressed me. Perhaps the image of my mother sitting in the car while my father asked the attendant to check the oil in some way explained their marriage. It had taken me years to emulate him; in high school I had stayed in the car and rolled down the window, afraid that I would seem too young—lacking the authority even to buy gasoline. But lately I had found myself pulling up in front of gas pumps and leaping from the car. Thus did heredity assert itself.

I breathed in the fumes, listening to the clang of the bell whenever a car drove up. The attendant came over, a boy about sixteen with a head of bedraggled blond curls. The stitched red signature on his shirt pocket gave his name: Eddie. He pulled the hose over to the tank and cranked up the pump. The numbers whirred. I could feel the warm air against my skin, and sensed the lake a mile away. I left Eddie counting a roll of bills in his grease-blackened hand and headed through town toward Evanston.

On the far side of the northwestern tracks the larger homes began: colonial, Tudor, neo-Georgian, they were set back from landscaped lawns and graveled driveways. On Sheridan Road, hidden behind hedges and walls, were estates that fronted on Lake Michigan; I glimpsed a few mansions through wrought-iron gates. Then I was driving past the Wilmette boat basin and the Baha'i temple, a soaring white edifice in the shape of an orange-juice squeezer, just beyond it was Laurel Avenue, where my mother's parents had lived. The houses, built in the prosperous years after World War I, when the middle class moved north from the city, were of burgundy-colored brick and had white sun porches.

Laurel came to a dead end by the golf course. I pulled up before the last house, stunned; it was so small. I had remembered a sprawling estate with french doors thrown open to a lawn that sloped down to the fairway, a long driveway where my grandfather parked his Lincoln, a garden with a latticed gate and beds of tulips. "Are you growing, or is it just that I'm shrinking?" my father had said when he picked me up at the airport the night before. I had the reverse thought as I stood before this bungalow, with its weed-seamed walk and red-brick staircase flanked by giant urns.

At least the blackberry bush seemed no smaller. I had loved to reach up and gather the blackberries off the branch; they were shaped like miniature bunches of grapes, and when I put them in my mouth they left their inky traces on my hands. I recalled the Fourth of July parties: every year my grandparents invited over a crowd of Russians from Chicago and served dinner on the lawn. Japanese paper lamps were strung between the front porch and a giant elm in the front yard. Aluminum tables were hauled upstairs from the basement, slid from their cardboard cartons, and set up on the lawn. My father and I brought up the folding chairs while my grandmother unfolded the heavy linen tablecloths. Agnes, in a white uniform, carried out platters of blintzes and *peroshke*, pastry stuffed with dry shreds of meat.

They were lavish, these grandparents; they served champagne and caviar beneath the gaudy lamps. Tidy and white-haired, the Russians sweltered in their winter suits; their accents were full of soft consonants. "*Bozhe moy!*" they would cry, squatting down beside me. "*Sheyn punim.*" I fingered their gold ornaments: cuff links, watch fobs, heavy rings. There was one, I remembered, a man named Morris, with a cloud of silken hair, who smoked his cigarette underhanded, the ash pointed toward the palm.

The house was out of another time: in the garage my grandmother's bachelor brother, Benny, made ornate bronze clocks; upstairs, in a sunwarmed attic, Grandma worked at one of her giant looms, weaving rugs and wall hangings. In the living room hung a portrait of my mother by Nikolai Remisoff, a White Russian who had been a satirical artist for *Krokodil* and had known Diaghilev and Mayakovsky. (He was an old man now, sitting by a pool in Palm Springs with a transistor radio in his hands—a gift from Frank Sinatra for his work as a set designer on *Ocean's Eleven.*) Once, returning from a day spent idling by the canal that ran beside the golf course, I had encountered a tall, angular man with a fierce look on his face escorting a woman down the walk: it was Frank Lloyd Wright, I later learned, who had courted his third wife in my grandparents' home.

When it got dark on those summer nights, the older people would sit around card tables on the sun porch and play pinochle or settle down, coffee cups in hand, on the plush old sofas. Sprawled on the carpet with a book, I noticed the women's marbled legs, the way the men hiked up their trousers to reveal bony ankles. Through the screen door I could hear the slap of cards.

Then there were the elaborate rituals of departure. "In this family, you have to start your good-byes an hour before you're ready to leave," my father used to say. The leftovers were wrapped up in casseroles covered with waxed paper and carried out to the cars, where the men sat impatient at the wheel, staring across the lawn at the cluster of women huddled beneath a yellow lamp aswarm with bugs. Finally, Mother slid in beside the platters of hors d'oeuvres and turned around to make sure I was there.

On the way home, lying on the cool, vinyl-covered seat, I looked up through the rear window at the elms canopied over Sheridan Road and listened to my parents talking. My mother commented on various relatives' health. "Sylvia has aged," she would begin; or, "Don't you think Gladys looked awful? I wonder what's the matter with her." To which my father invariably had the same reply: "Too fat." (Weight was an obsession of his; I was always being told to "maintain a thin edge of hunger" and warned that fat people were "candidates for coronary.") "I've never seen Grisha looking so unhappy," she persisted. "I could see it in his eyes." My father grunted; it was people's waistlines that interested him, not their faces.

In the back seat, I was eager to hear more. I hadn't noticed any unhappiness in Grisha's eyes. How did my mother know this? What was her evidence? Frustrated by my father's indifference to these matters, I spoke up: "What do you mean, Mom?"

She turned and draped her elbow over the back seat; here was an audience. Then a story would unfold: Sylvia's son Joey was threatening to drop out of high school and join the Marines; Gladys had finally been forced to put her mother in a nursing home; Sarah's husband, Harry, a professor of engineering at the University of Wisconsin, had quarreled with the chairman of his department.

In the back seat, beneath the car's dark dome, I brooded on these dramas. Rivalry, betrayal, disappointment: it was hard for me to reconcile the ominous events my mother spoke of with the prim, balding men in their gold-rimmed spectacles and dark suits, the plump women in their flowered-print dresses, their gray hair springy as lichen, who had just been gathered in my grandmother's living room. As we pulled into our driveway and the electric garage door clattered up, I still had many questions; but I was half-asleep, blinking in the harsh garage light and inhaling the sweetish odor of the oil patches on the concrete floor. "Why does Joey want to join the Marines?" I said, desperate to tie up loose ends before it was too late.

"He just does. You're stalling."

"But I have to know why."

"I'll give you why," my mother said, raising a hand to spank me. But I knew she never would, and danced away down the narrow aisle between the two cars, whining, "I have to know *why*."

Why? Why? Why? I still had to know. I leaned against the Pinto's hot metal hood, staring down at the smears of fallen blackberries on the sidewalk. Beyond the house, two women in pleated skirts and golf caps trudged toward the green, wheeling their carts before them. Somehow I could imagine people dying one by one, but it was harder to think of a generation simply vanishing from the earth. Gone. Lowered like my grandmother into the ground, commemorated with as little ceremony as my father's "Good-bye, Mama" and the gray gloves tossed in the grave.

But could I really say I missed her? "With a mother like that, it's a miracle I'm not in some institution somewhere, drooling in a padded cell," my father used to say. Newly married, he couldn't persuade his wife to come upstairs when he visited on Sundays; she sat in the car and smoked. When he tried to leave, my grandmother would throw herself down in front of the door and lie there weeping. My father had to nudge her with his foot to get by.

Still, he was a dutiful son. After my grandfather died, we drove to Rogers Park every Sunday and had dinner in his mother's apartment. Grandma Rya lived in a new building with cinderblock walls, but otherwise it was the same as above the drugstore on Peterson Avenue: a cut-glass chandelier, a mahogany sideboard where the silver was kept in velvet pouches, a sofa with silk pillows and roped fringe, a glass-topped coffee table cluttered with silver nut bowls and photographs of relatives propped up in easel-like frames. On a corner table stood the samovar, a bronze globe with a spigot.

The drugstore had been sold and my grandmother had money now, but according to her it wasn't enough. She was suspicious of her broker—"that Mr. Klein who's always telling me to buy Stanford."

"Standard, Mother. And his name is Cohen."

"A *goniff*, that Klein. I haven't had a dividant in months."

Stocks, bonds, dividends: these discussions infuriated my mother, who sat picking at her boiled chicken while I went off to watch *The Ed Sullivan Show* in the "library"—so called because of the row of paperbacks on a shelf above the television set. There was nothing for me to read; they were mostly blue Penguin editions of Nietzsche, Schopenhauer, and Rousseau. My grandmother had enrolled in the same introductory philosophy course at the YMCA night school downtown for eleven years, until the harried instructor begged, "Please, Mrs. Atlas, not again!"

I got back in the car and drove off down Laurel, but the tears that came to my eyes weren't for the dead; they were for the living—for my parents, getting older, and for me, the somber face in the rearview mirror. It had been easier to be a child in the back seat listening to my mother go over the evening while my silent father drove.

I turned the dial to WFMT, the fine-arts station. The voice of Ray Nordstrand—or was it Norman Pellegrini?—spoke in the familiar, lucid tones I had been hearing for a decade. Their identical voices reminded me of T. S. Eliot reciting *The Waste Land* on the Caedmon album I had been given for my twelfth birthday. They were so reasonable; they managed to read even advertising copy as if they were delivering a lecture on art history. "The Gregorian Brothers have been in business since 1948," the precise voice said. "They have traveled the world, from the deserts of Baluchistan to the markets of Kabul, in search of fine rugs. Why not stop in to examine these lovely wares? The showroom is open from noon until eight every day of the week." Bertolli's Wine Shop; Kroch's & Brentano's; the Scandinavian Furniture Mart; Toad Hall, for the finest in stereo equipment: a familiar, civilized litany more moving to me than the Beethoven piano concerto that followed it.

I was in Evanston now, driving past the clay-colored neo-Gothic buildings of Northwestern and the Garrett Theological Seminary, where my father had boarded as an undergraduate. "Your grandmother couldn't stand it that I moved away from home," he had once told me. "She used to drive over on Sundays with a dinner of boiled chicken and a bowl of soup on the front seat of the car."

"She came alone?"

"My father had to mind the store."

Not that there was much to mind. The store had an abandoned look: dusty placards advertising Sealtest and Squibb in the window, grime-coated beach balls in metal bins, and a rack of curling, faded Classic Comics. It was dark in the back; no one ever sat in the booths.

My grandfather liked it that way; he wanted no customers. He sat by the cash register leafing through pharmaceutical journals or cleaning his old-fashioned gold-rimmed spectacles with a handkerchief. "He was brilliant," my father was always reminding me, "a physics wizard. He had a diploma from the czar. When he came to this country, he got a job right away, building the Chicago Bridge." (During the Depression he was laid off, acquired the drugstore cheap, and got by during the leanest years selling grain alcohol to bootleggers.) By the time I came to know him he had already had a stroke, and shuffled around the apartment above the store in a bathrobe and slippers, the leather seamed and cracked. On Saturday afternoons he sat in a bristly armchair beside the radio, a wooden Magnavox with a speaker in the shape of a cathedral arch, and listened to the live broadcast from New York of the Metropolitan Opera, sponsored by Texaco and narrated by Milton J. Cross.

His favorite was *La Traviata*. When Cross's baritone voice, dropping low in murmurous sorrow, came to the final scene, my grandfather's eyes shone with tears. "Violetta tries to rise from her bed," Cross would announce with agonizing deliberation, "but it is too late." At this disclosure, my grandfather would grimace and stare out the window, as if silently denouncing the injustice of a world in which such a travesty could occur. "Comforted by the presence of Alfredo, she sings," and then, in the wooden, inflectionless Italian of a tourist in Rome, " '*Ah! io ritorno a vivere!*'—'I shall live after all!'—only to fall back lifeless on her couch." After an ominous pause, broken by the sound of a pot simmering on the kitchen stove or a car accelerating up the street, Milton J. Cross would declare: "A moment later, she is dead."

What a catastrophe! One more disquieting for my grandfather, I imagine, than whatever events had conspired to erode the promise of his youth. Applause came through the speaker like static, the curtain descended, and Cross renewed his grim narrative: "And now Renata Tebaldi emerges for a second curtain call while the orchestra stands to applaud. She beckons to the conductor, Fausto Cleva, who bows; and now she summons the whole supporting cast from the wings." With an abrupt surge of energy, my grandfather would rise from his chair and switch off the radio, then lapse back in his chair. Beside him on the carpet, I was fascinated by a wooden doll—a Russian peasant woman in the shape of an egg—that unscrewed to reveal identical, ever smaller dolls within.

He nudged me playfully with his soft old slipper; my father had felt a sharper prod. Doing his homework at the dining-room table as a high school boy, he was reprimanded for using a slide rule. "You should be able to do it in your head," my grandfather insisted.

"But he *wants* us to use a slide rule."

"What does he know? If he had any brains, he wouldn't be teaching physics in a school."

I was in my old neighborhood now, coasting down streets that hadn't changed since my father was a student; there were the same turreted, bay-windowed Victorian homes encircled by porches, the same elm-lined boulevards. Beside the lake were parks separated from the beach by a seawall of bleached boulders. Idling at a light, I heard a click inside the aluminum post on the curb; five blocks away, an elevated train clattered by. An ice-cream truck's metallic nursery rhyme played over and over as I turned down the street where I had lived for eleven years.

We had moved here when I was twelve, from Highland Park, a rich suburb an hour north of Chicago. In the 1950s one lived in the suburbs, so that was where my parents had gone to live—until the day my father arrived home from work after an hour's drive through rush-hour traffic and stood out on the back porch, briefcase in hand, surveying the yard. It needed mowing, and the hedge was overgrown. I had forgotten to move the sprinkler; the lawn was as sodden as a rice paddy. My father's collar was damp with sweat. "We're moving," he said. "I didn't go to medical school to become a gardener."

A week later, he bought a plot of land in Evanston, just north of Chicago and only a few yards from Lake Michigan, across from a row of wine-colored-brick apartment houses that curved around the crescent shape of Sheridan Square. A local architect was commissioned to design and build a house, a split-level with walls of purple brick and a sloping pebbled roof. Instead of a front yard, my parents installed a Japanese garden: bonsai, an Oriental lamp, a bamboo gate, and boulders strewn about. The living room was beige nubbled couches, teakwood coffee tables, a Herman Miller chair beside the slate fireplace. There were skylights in the stippled ceiling, and the floor was parquet. Everything was neutral, barren, spare—from the gaunt sculpture of Joseph clutching seven thin stalks in one hand and seven fat stalks in the other to the collages of rubble-strewn cities done by my mother's cousin Si, who had escaped from Germany during World War II.

Our house was like a Bennington dorm: in the basement, my brother practiced *Für Elise* on the piano; in the dining room, my mother sat with a French primer open in front of her, muttering, *"Dis donc, Paul, où est la bibliothèque?"* In the laundry room behind the garage, my father crouched over a Formica counter among the sheets and towels hung out to dry, a pair of magnifying glasses strapped to his head, making oboe reeds. Knives and thread, minute cylinders of cork, and strips of fish skin were scattered about among the socks and underwear. He pared away at wedges of bamboo for hours; upstairs in my room at the other end of the house, I could hear a high, shrill whine as he put a reed to his lips and tested it.

Music dominated my father's life. He had lost interest in medicine by then, and spent most of his time playing along with Music Minus One albums—recordings by an orchestra lacking one instrument. I would come home from school to find him planted before a metal music stand in the living room, earphones on his head, his face scarlet, swaying like a snake charmer as he struggled to keep up with a Telemann concerto. "What is it about this music?" he would cry, pulling the earphones off his head. "It lifts up the soul. It has the power to intoxicate."

My father considered himself one of Stendhal's "happy few," that ardent band of outcasts who made their way alone, who lived and felt on a more exalted plane than ordinary people. Not that they were so happy; prominent among their number were Dostoevsky, Proust, and above all, Kafka, whose sense of imprisonment, of thwartedness, was so familiar to my father. When I came home bitter over some childish disappointment, a poor grade or a bruised knee, he would reassure me: "You're a sensitive boy; you'll suffer your whole life. Look at Kafka."

He found his own experience "Kafkaesque"—one of his favorite adjectives until *Time* magazine began to use it—and marveled at Kafka's *Letter to His Father*. "This is me," he would gloat nervously, reading aloud the passage where Kafka complains that his father controlled him by means of "abuse, threats, irony, spiteful laughter, and . . . self-pity." And when *Irrational Man*, William Barrett's popular introduction to existentialism, appeared in the late fifties, he was so enthralled by its theme of brooding anguish that he even brought it along to a baseball game in Comiskey Park, absorbing disquisitions on Heidegger and Sartre as I sat beside him filling out my scorecard.

Like Kafka, my father awaited punishment for some unknown sin—which must have been why his favorite album was Bruno Walter conducting the Columbia Symphony Orchestra in a live rehearsal. Walter, a histrionic German, stormed at his musicians like a teacher faced with a room full of unruly children. Bullying and pleading, unctuous and severe, he could change moods in mid-sentence; he had an actor's sense of timing. My father was fascinated by the conductor's imperious manner, especially when he rebuked the lagging oboist. "Please," (pronounced to rhyme with *fleece*) "Mr. Bloom," Walter would cajole, "*can't* you come in just a little sooner?" Then, decisively—"Again."

I think my father must have identified with Mr. Bloom; he was, after all, a persecuted man himself. He felt embattled, a guardian of high culture during the barbaric Eisenhower years. Philistinism was rampant in the land. My father raged against the bland décor of restaurants, gigantic American cars, those who read best sellers. He was contemptuous of his colleagues at Mount Sinai Hospital who had never heard of Rilke. He couldn't bear Muzak, and derided people who whistled in elevators as "empty-headed." He was furious when Arthur Miller married Marilyn Monroe; "He has a responsibility to the intellectuals in this country," my father stormed. "We'll lose credibility." When Dwight Macdonald's famous essay "Masscult and Midcult" was published in *Partisan Review*, he exclaimed over it for days, reading it aloud, gloating over Macdonald's assault on the pretensions of those contemptible middlebrows Thornton Wilder and Archibald MacLeish.

In our house, though, learning would go on; ignorance would be kept at bay. I had to be prepared to answer difficult questions at any moment— even while picking at the meat loaf or pot roast my mother had slaved over in the kitchen all afternoon. "What's wrong with this?" my father said one night, waving a form letter from a pharmaceutical company in front of my nose.

"Donald, let the boy eat," my mother objected.

"It'll just take a minute. This is important." I studied the letter. "Well?" my father said.

"Dinner is getting cold." There was an edge of nervous anger in my mother's voice.

I glanced down at the lima beans I had tried to hide beneath a lettuce leaf, and scanned the cheerful sales pitch again, hunting for a mistake.

"It's near the top," my father hinted.

"I give up," I said at last, hungry for the brownies my mother was removing from the oven.

"Come on," my father prompted, then snatched away the letter. "Listen to this: 'No physician can afford to be disinterested in the therapeutic benefits of Tylenol . . .' *Disinterested* means objective, impartial; the word they want here is *uninterested*." He wiped his plate with a slice of rye bread. "That is known as a *catachresis*, otherwise a *solecism*—a grammatical lapse."

"Why do you need two words for the same thing?" I asked.

"Well, they're not *exactly* the same," my father said. "Let's look 'em up." He pushed aside his chair and beckoned me to follow.

"Donald!" My mother's voice rang out in a sharp reprimand. "Why can't you finish dinner before rushing off to the dictionary?"

But he was already out of his seat and heading for the living room, where the one-volume *OED* stood open on a metal stand, exhibited as proudly as if it were the Book of Kells. I fled my mother's reproachful gaze and hurried off to join my father. We stood side by side, feeding at the trough of knowledge. "Let's see," he muttered, running his finger down the page. "Ca-ta-*chre*-sis. Here." He read the definition aloud: " 'Improper use of words; application of a term to a thing which it does not properly denote; abuse of a trope or metaphor.' And a so-le-cism," he said, drawing out the word while he searched for it, "is . . . 'impropriety or irregularity in speech or diction.' " He slammed the volume shut. "So there *is* a subtle difference," he said. "Words are like snowflakes: no two are exactly alike." We trotted back to the kitchen, where my mother, in a furious mood, had started to clear the dishes.

"Do you have to leap up from the table like that?" she said tearfully, bending over the sink and scraping dishes into the disposal. "You're just showing off for the boy." And she hurried out of the room, her shoes clacking on the parquet floor.

"Mom's not an intellectual like us," I volunteered.

My father blew on his instant coffee, wrinkling the surface. "Being an intellectual isn't everything," he said.

No, but my mother's failure to measure up to our high scholarly standards troubled me all the same. For a woman who had a degree from the Medill School of Journalism, she was surprisingly unlettered; she hadn't read *Ulysses*, she hadn't read *Death in Venice*, she failed to identify lines from *The Waste Land* that I recited at the dinner table. " 'Datta. Dayadhvam. Damyata,' " I chanted while she hurried back and forth with steaming plates of food. "Come on, Mom. What's it from?"

"I really haven't the faintest idea, dear." She dipped down to straighten my knife and spoon. "Would you please take your elbows off the table?"

My elbows! I was quoting T. S. Eliot—and in a foreign language, yet! "Just guess, Mom. It has to be modern, right? I'll give you a hint," I nagged. "It's twentieth-century. That ought to narrow it down."

"I told you, dear," she said, a hint of impatience in her voice. "I really don't know."

My father knew. He gave me a sly smile. "It's Eliot, Mom," I announced. "*The Waste Land*."

" 'I grow old, I grow old,' " my father said in a sonorous voice. " 'I shall wear the bottoms of my trousers rolled.' "

I was puzzled. "Is that from *The Waste Land*?"

"It's from *Prufrock*. 'Do I dare to eat a peach?' " In his late forties then, my father adored this poem of old age; it evoked a time in life that I think he looked forward to, a time when he could walk along the beach himself and not have to think about getting old because he would *be* old.

Why couldn't my mother quote Eliot? I fumed. It never occurred to me to imagine what my life would have been like if she *had* been an intellectual. What if I had come home from school every afternoon to find her, in faded jeans and a flannel work shirt, a Gauloise smoldering beside her, reading *Being and Nothingness* at the kitchen table? Who would have driven me to the Varsity Shop to pick out my back-to-school wardrobe? Who would have sorted out my laundry and left it in tidy stacks on the bed, the socks piled up like cannonballs on a New England green? But I was oblivious of the impeccable service at 647 Sheridan Square, the meals on the table and such minor amenities as the "after-school snack"—a glass of milk, already poured, that stood in the refrigerator beside a plate of Oreo cream cookies. I was oppressed by my mother's trivial demands. "What do you mean, my nails are dirty? Come on, Mom. Did Verlaine's mother complain that his nails were dirty?"

"Who?"

"Verlaine, Mom, Verlaine. The great French *symboliste*." (I gave it the French pronunciation: *sambo-least*.)

And finally, on a day when I refused to tuck in my shirt: "You're just a housewife, Mom"—upon which she fled to her bedroom in tears and slammed the door. I sat at my desk reading H. G. Wells's *The Outline of History*, but some primal fear gathered within me. Had I gone too far?

Too nervous to concentrate, I slammed my book shut and ran to her room. "Mom?" I called, pressing my ear against the door. "Mom, I'm sorry about what I said." Silence. "Mom?" The house was so still I could hear the refrigerator hum in the kitchen below. I had never known such terror. "Mom, please answer."

On the other side of the door, she blew her nose. "What?" Her voice seemed cold, remote. "What is it?"

"Forgive me, Mom. I know you go to French class and everything. And you liked *The Stranger*, right?" There was no reply. How could I have said that? I felt as if an evil spirit had spoken through me: The debbil made me do it! Oh, Mother, please come out; please say something. Please!

"It's all right, dear," she said through the door in a shaky voice. "It doesn't matter."

"Mom, come out. I want to see you." A sob rose in my throat.

"Go away now. I'll be all right."

In my room, I could hardly read for the tears that streamed down my face.

After that, I concentrated my demand for intellectual rigor on my eighth-grade teacher, Mr. Sensenig, a thin, sallow, fortyish man with a head of tight curls, a Prussian tenseness of posture, and small, furious eyes that darted about behind thick glasses. Proud of his ability to keep a roomful of defiant thirteen-year-olds at bay, he strode among our desks, tapping them with a ruler while he discoursed in a grim voice on the principles of grammar. When he asked us to subscribe to *Reader's Digest*, I raised my hand. "But Mr. Sensenig, isn't *Reader's Digest* a mediocre magazine for ignorant people?" I enumerated its failings: the trite, optimistic "Life in These United States" feature; the banality of the "Toward More Picturesque Speech" column; the pathetic efforts at self-improvement catered to by their vocabulary lists. "Why don't we subscribe to something more stimulating?" I proposed. "Like *The Nation* or *The Christian Science Monitor*?"

Mr. Sensenig blinked in annoyance, like an owl disturbed in daylight. When I reported the episode over dinner that night, my father was proud.

I tried to keep up; I played the flute until it became evident that despite the private lessons, despite practicing two hours a day, I had no promise. For my fourteenth birthday, I was given a set of expensive oil paints, fine brushes, an easel, and enough canvas for *Guernica*. I set up shop down in the basement, and within a week had completed my first work, a gaudy web of blotted shapes, the paint squeezed on so thick it refused to dry—and in the center, a white square. What this enigmatic composition represented I wasn't sure; but it was rushed off to the framers and hung in the front hall.

I soon tired of painting and put away my tubes and brushes among old board games and athletic equipment in a downstairs closet. It was poetry that absorbed me now. I subscribed to *Writer's Digest* and studied the poetry markets. *Lucifer's Lamp*, a journal in Los Angeles, advertised a "national poetry contest," so I sent off three poems, and was informed a week later that all three had been accepted. I was ecstatic—even though the editors informed me that no free copies could be given out; I would have to order them, at $12.95 apiece. Eager to present copies to my grandmothers and my parents, I ordered three.

A month later, I arrived home from school to find a parcel from *Lucifer's Lamp*. I rushed upstairs and tore it open; my first appearance in print! The magazine had a curious format, though; instead of a compact, book-size periodical like *Partisan Review*, I held in my hands an assemblage as thick as a telephone book, loosely bound by plastic rings. The cover consisted of a sheet of blue paper with the legend *Lucifer's Lamp: A Magazine of Verse* typed across it. There was no index, but the poems were arranged alphabetically by author, and I quickly found mine—just after the work of Leonard Atkinson, of Butte, Montana, and before poems by Melissa Atwater, of Baltimore, Maryland, and R. W. Auty, of Eureka, California. There were nine poems on the page, in miniscule print—or rather, typed out on a typewriter with minuscule characters. The page was smudged, as if it were a faint mimeographed copy. I put my three copies of *Lucifer's Lamp* on a shelf in the closet, beside my baseball glove.

But I persisted in my "work," and when my poems were returned by *Poetry* and *The New Yorker* with printed rejection slips, I wondered what was wrong with them. One day I came across an advertisement in *Writer's Digest* from a "Poetry Consultant" in Nacogdoches, Texas, and wrote soliciting his services. A few weeks later, I received a mimeographed manifesto for *Cyclops*, "Songs of the Last Frontier." "Commercialism, propaganda, and ignorance roil the waters of literature," it began. "Only gradually are men being enjoined away from provincial pride—Abaddon—The Destroyer. Will they depart the abyss in time?" Hunched over my desk, a Tensor lamp trained on the page, I pursed my lips. This manifesto was heavy going; who was Abaddon? He wasn't listed in my *Dictionary of Mythology*. My eye drifted up to the built-in book-shelves—a row of Freddy the Pig books; *Charlotte's Web*; *The Phantom Tollbooth*. I tried again to focus on the fierce argument of Raymond Winkley, *Cyclops*'s editor-publisher: "Poetry can find hope in an age that seems hopeless, can begin the reconstruction before the ruin is visited. Today, especially, those monolithic axioms that have been thought to be Truth Absolute are scaling and crumbling to reveal the shapes of more enduring cores." It was that enduring core I was after, and I was glad to find enclosed a "checklist of common errors." "Check your own poems for these errors," read the directions, "and if you want us to aid you, submit one poem for a detailed criticism, plus $1.00 for a consultant's time and years of training, writing, publishing, and personal interest in all sincere poets." Eagerly, I submitted a poem with my dollar.

Within a week, I had a reply:

Mr. Jim Atlas, your poem will be held 10 days pending the arrival of a SASE for its return. The ethic of sending return postage with a submitted manuscript is so well established that it would seem unnecessary to remind anyone of this.

Humiliated, I sent Mr. Winkley a stamped, self-addressed envelope, and waited.

The response was again prompt: of the twenty-one failings listed under the category "Avoid," only one had been checked off, but there was a terse comment in the margin: "A good start in 'Summer in Maine' ends up in landscape rambling. Poetry asks 'So What, So Why, So Whither.'" I was wounded by Mr. Winkley's rebuke, but at least my work had been read. I submitted another poem—too soon, as it happened. Under the category "How to Submit a Manuscript," Mr. Winkley had checked off "Wait sixty days after a poem is rejected or published to resubmit"—and in the margin of my second evaluation sheet he scrawled: "Sir, we are busy." The size of the envelope ("approximately 4" × 10"") was under-lined; "Note how *stuffed* your small one is," scolded the consultant. Under "Avoid," two errors were noted: "Ideas not fresh or original, far removed from our own age"; and "Literalism, not imagery, the soul of poetry." A disheartening indictment. There was, however, a hopeful mes-sage from Mr. Winkley: "Although she would be more critical of crafts-manship in a sonnet, I would like to have Miss Lorraine see 'A Painting.' Try to give the title more force—like 'Captured Awareness,' 'The Senses Bound,' or other."

But I never heard from Miss Lorraine—apparently she was unim-pressed with 'A Painting'—and by the time the stipulated sixty days had passed, I had found another mentor: Marie Claire Davis, the creative-writing teacher at Evanston Township High School. A gaunt, hectic woman with a big blade of a nose, she would read aloud from *The Oxford*

Book of English Verse and fix us with a glad stare. "That is art," she would declare, slamming the book down on the table. "Read 'em and weep." Not only were these poets great, her command implied, but they had somehow trumped us; their greatness was our defeat.

Yet she was far from contemptuous of our efforts. Indeed, her expectations were unrealistic. In our private conferences, she addressed us as if we had a high literary calling. "Your greatest enemy is intellectualization," she once advised me. "You need to work to your own internal music and word-joy." She sat up straight at her desk, staring across the room and drumming her bony fingers on my manuscript. "Find that spontaneous well of emotion, and *use* it."

One afternoon Mrs. Davis turned off the fluorescent lights, flicked on a projector, and showed us a documentary about Theodore Roethke. A fat, sweating man with a sorrowful face, he muttered his poems with tense, incantatory fervor, standing awkwardly before the camera in a rumpled suit. When he spoke about his life in response to the questions of an invisible interlocutor, he was shy, morose, inaudible; his mouth worked nervously, his eyes were full of pain. And when he recited the poem that begins "I knew a woman, lovely in her bones," he seemed on the verge of tears. He was the only poet I had ever seen.

One Saturday in my junior year, Mrs. Davis drove me down to the Chicago campus of the University of Illinois, in a decaying Greek neighborhood on the near West Side, for the statewide poetry contest. As we walked across the new concrete-paved campus, windswept and deserted beneath an iron sky, she coached me. "Now, remember, if they ask for a Petrarchan sonnet, it's ABBAABBA, then a six-line coda. And you know what a sestina is." In the classroom, while Mrs. Davis hovered in the hall, a nun scrawled our assignment on the blackboard: "A sonnet on the theme of seasons." We had one hour.

The other contestants—seventeen girls and a wild-haired boy in a lumber jacket—opened their notebooks and started to write, while I sat there without a thought in my head. I could see Mrs. Davis through the door, pacing up and down in her worn fur coat. Finally, a line occurred to me, then another:

> As a November day, desolate calm,
> My own irretrievable, missing loves
> Are preserved, impenetrable, embalmed—
> Eternal as rhythms of flying doves,
> That remain immortal in memory,
> Enhanced by the fact that they ne'er shall be.

When the hour was up, I glanced over my lines; I had gotten the rhyme scheme wrong! I rushed from the room and buried my head in

Mrs. Davis's musky lapel. "You are a poet," she assured me when I had blurted out my tale of failure, "but you must remember what Joyce says about going forth to forge in the smithy of his soul the uncreated conscience of his race. No one said it would be easy." And we walked back to the car in silence, wrapped up in our separate perceptions of my destiny.

I needn't have despaired, for I placed second in the poetry contest, and thus acquired another certificate to affix to what my father called "the honor board"—a cork bulletin board covered with memorabilia of my accomplishments: a yellow ribbon commemorating the occasion when I came in fourth in the 100-yard dash at the Ravinia School Field Day in 1958; a crumbled photograph from the *Evanston Review* that showed me doing push-ups at a tennis clinic when I was twelve; a medal from Camp Shewahmegon in Drummond, Wisconsin, for second place in Arts & Crafts; a letter from Senator Everett Dirksen congratulating me for an editorial on school spirit that had appeared in the *Nichols School Newsletter*; and a photostat of my high school aptitude tests.

My room was a museum of self-improvement. On the shelves, lodged among my collection of paperbacks—*The Sun Also Rises*, *Tortilla Flat*, *Of Mice and Men*, *Portrait of the Artist as a Young Man*, *Rhinoceros*, *Long Day's Journey into Night*, *Heart of Darkness*, *On the Road*—stood my tennis trophies. On the wall above my bed was a framed copy of the Declaration of Independence on crisp imitation parchment, brought back from a field trip to the nation's capital in seventh grade, and a reproduction of *The Old Guitarist*. From the ceiling dangled a mobile I had purchased at the Old Town Art Fair. In the record rack were my albums: Miles Davis, Herbie Mann, Pete Seeger, the Kingston Trio, Joan Baez, Odetta.

Yet why was it, I often wondered as I lay on my bed and listened to Mozart or Vivaldi through the wall, that all this striving, this accumulation of culture, this rage for self-expression, made me so melancholy? Taken by my parents downtown to the Goodman Theatre to see Morris Carnovsky in *King Lear*, I shifted in my seat, bored by the old man's long-winded speeches; with his lavish mannerisms and madly waving arms, he seemed like a vaudeville actor. *Crime and Punishment*, which I had first come across in a Classic Comics edition in my grandfather's drugstore, I put down after I had read a hundred pages; I could make nothing of Raskolnikov's guilt, and the style seemed overwrought.

Loitering in the Art Institute one winter afternoon when I should have been in school, I stood in front of the huge Impressionist canvases for hours, unmoved. Contemplating Seurat's *A Sunday Afternoon on the Island of La Grande Jatte*, I was impatient with the placid scene, stirred only by the boats offshore, their white sails mirrored on the pointillist surface—and then only because they reminded me of summers on Lake

Michigan. I was more conscious of a vast emptiness, an ache of solitude touched off by the echo of my own footsteps in the vast, empty halls.

On the way home, I wandered through the slush-filled streets of the Loop beneath the elevated tracks. Trains trundled overhead, showering sparks through the dusk; a Salvation Army band played "Good King Wenceslas." I was looking for the sort of cafeteria I had read about some-where—in *The Adventures of Augie March*? Anyway, some place where intellectuals gathered and had animated conversations, scraping their chairs back and pounding the table, smoking and gesturing with frantic hands. A place where Roquentin, the hero of Sartre's *La Nausée* (as I called it, though I had read a translation), might have whiled away dull afternoons.

In DeMar's Coffeeshop I glanced up from an article by Lionel Trilling on literature and neurosis, and I looked around at the topcoated derelicts and pensioners warming their hands against their coffee cups. The windows were fogged over, the counter exuded a sudsy damp. It occurred to me: I hated art.

PINCKNEY BENEDICT

Bank Examiners

"A lot of people are having themselves frozen," Ron says to me. "It's a stab at immortality, I guess." Ron is a big solid guy, an ex-Marine. It's getting late and I'm drinking water to rehydrate, but Ron is still going, shot and a beer, shot and a beer. He's a bank examiner from Roanoke, Virginia, trying to entertain himself in a motel bar. He's wrapped too tight for the time and place, and alcohol doesn't seem to relax him at all. I met him about an hour ago.

"It's a thing that wasn't possible fifty years ago. That's what you call the exponential curve of technological development," Jocko says. Jocko was in the Air Force. He has pushed his chair about three feet away from the table, into the shadows. His voice is quiet. His words sound like they're coming to us from far away. He's a bank examiner from Roanoke as well; the two of them won't say what they're doing in West Virginia. It seems sinister to me, but I don't know much about the banking business.

"It's called cryonics," Jocko says. "Walt Disney did it. He was one of the first. He pioneered the thing."

"Frozen," I say.

"Like a popsicle," Jocko says.

"There's a whole group of them in California that's got a pact," Ron says. "When they check out, it's into the freezer, one by one. I saw it on a show. They've got a date to play tennis in a hundred and fifty years. They figure they'll be young again and cured of whatever disease it was that killed them, and ready to hit the courts."

"They can play tennis with Walt Disney," I say. "Imagine a world where a thing like that is possible."

"And Hitler," Jocko says. "I hear they've got his brain in a jar down there in Argentina."

"That's nothing but a movie," Ron says. "Hitler died in a bunker in Berlin. They've got photographic evidence. He's never coming back."

"Just a brain," I say. "You wonder where the harm could be in that. What would they do with Hitler's brain and no Hitler to put it in?"

"That's the only part they need, these cryonics guys," Ron says. "The minute you die they cut your head off your body with this little electric saw and dip it into a vat full of liquid nitrogen. Hundreds and hundreds of degrees below zero."

"Absolute zero," Jocko says. "Put a banana in there, you can use it for a hammer. Put your hand in and shake it, your fingers will drop off."

"It stops all the processes that go on in the cells," Ron says. "Preserves them without letting any more damage happen."

"Jesus Christ," I say. "I bet it does."

"They've done it with animals and made it work," Ron says. "They can bring the head of a cat back to life for hours at a time. It looks around the room like it's alive and blinks if you shine a bright light in its eyes. One guy even has his head in a vat with five animal heads: two dogs, two cats and a monkey."

"Wake up to that," Jocko says.

"Does he know it?" I ask. "Did he plan for that situation?"

"Who could figure a thing like that?" Ron says. "Maybe he died unexpectedly and they had no place else to put him. He won't complain."

"Not for a time, anyway," Jocko says.

"Or maybe it was cheaper that way. One price to get put in with animal heads, another to get people. It's an expensive proposition, waiting until your youth comes around again."

"The pharaohs in Egypt had a similar idea," Jocko says. "Look how it turned out for them. You see them in museums all the time and they're just coming apart."

"I saw a movie with something like what you describe in it," I say. "It was called *Bring Me the Head of Alfredo Garcia*."

"I saw that one too," Jocko says. "A guy is counting some things when he gets his head cut off, and the head keeps counting when it rolls on the ground. It doesn't even know it's dead."

"That's not part of it," I say. "Not that I remember."

"I know the one you're talking about," Ron says. "Warren Oates has this head that came off a gigolo. He carries it around in a bag."

"That's the one. He keeps it fresh with dry ice," I say. "That's what made me think of it."

Ron turns to Jocko. "You remember. I rented it on tape one time. We watched it over at my house and you thought it was pretty funny. It had that Mexican girl in it that you liked."

"Oh, yeah," Jocko says. He doesn't sound convinced. "That one."

"Some people I know have a hunting camp in Montana that they go to every year," Ron says. "A beautiful place in the mountains. It's right near where Warren Oates and what's-his-name, the director—Sam Peckinpah—had their places."

"Did your friends know these guys?" I ask.

"Sure they did," Ron says. "Everybody knows everybody up in those mountains. They said Oates was a regular guy like you might meet on the street, but Peckinpah was a son of a bitch. He'd about crap if you crossed the line onto his place. He'd make you go around even if you were carrying a goddamn elk carcass out. Oates didn't mind much, but that's the kind of guy Peckinpah was." Ron stubs his cigarette in the ashtray, grinds the butt.

"They're both dead now," I say.

"Yeah," Ron says. "Dead and gone. They call Peckinpah's place by his first name now. They call it Sam. Like they say, 'Think I'll go over to Sam now,' and they mean the ranch where he lived. Strange." We sit in silence for a while. Ron continues to wreck the cigarette in the ashtray.

"Tell me," I say, when the lack of conversation gets to be uncomfortable. "When they wake these guys up, these frozen heads, how will they get around? I mean, just a head, it seems inconvenient."

"Clones," Ron says. "Or they'll make robots for them. It's the future. Who can tell exactly?"

"I guess," I say. "It's just hard to imagine how they'll fit in."

"Probably they won't," Jocko says. It's the most excited he's sounded all evening. "Probably they'll just use them for cheap slave labor. What kind of rights would a person from the past have? Would they have the vote? I don't think so." He leans forward. "They'll just wake them up and stick them on some starship and send them out to a mining colony on another planet. Wire them up and use their brains for energy. Nothing to stop it." He leans back again.

"Not a single solitary thing," Ron says, and he glares at me. His look makes me feel like I should argue with him and Jocko, but I can't imagine what my argument would be. After he stares at me like that for a minute, Ron pushes his chair away and joins Jocko in the shadows.

"What are you two guys doing here?" I ask. "Bank examiners and all."

"Nothing," Ron says. "No big thing. Just checking some records is all."

"We need to see some people about some things," Jocko says.

"Cheaters?" I say. "You're on the trail of tax evaders."

"No," Ron says. "We're not from the government. We don't do anything like that. We're privately employed."

"No big deal then," I say. "I don't have to try to get my money out of the bank before you shut it down."

"Negative," Jocko says. "Our company sent us up here. We're just doing a routine job."

"Leave your money where it is," Ron says. Like Jocko's, his voice now seems to come from a long way off. I take a drink of water and decide that, in a minute or two, I'm going to get up and get out of here.

LARRY BROWN

A Late Start in Mississippi

I've only been writing for about twelve years. I didn't start until I was twenty-nine. I figure most people who write start a lot younger than that. Most people who want to make something out of their lives probably take control of them a lot earlier than that.

I live at a little place called Yocona in North Mississippi, in Lafayette County, an area whose history and people have already been well documented by Mr. Faulkner, a writer I hold a great respect for. Some comparisons have been made by reviewers holding my work up to his, and this is something I didn't want that I knew was going to happen anyway. I also knew there wouldn't be anything I could do about it. There's already been a good bit written about the handing down of some sort of symbolic literary torch. People just naturally expect a lot out of me as a writer because I was born in Oxford. But I try not to worry much about it, and just go on and do my work.

One of the questions about human nature that interests me most is how people bear up under monstrous calamity, all the terrible things that can befall them, war, poverty, desperation. As a writer, it bothers me to be accused of brutality, of cruelty, of hardheartedness, of a lack of compassion. Only a few reviewers of my work have lodged these complaints. But more than a few seem to register a certain uneasy feeling, and I wonder if this is because I make them look a little too deeply into my characters' lives. Maybe I make them know more than they want to about the poor, or the unfortunate, or the alcoholic. But a sensible writer writes what he or she knows best, and draws on the material that's closest, and the lives that are observed. I try to write as close as I can to the heart of the matter. I write out of experience and imagination, toward blind faith and hope.

Flannery O'Connor, who I'm happy to admit is one of my idols, said that a writer didn't need to have much happen to him after age twenty-one. She said by that time, there was plenty to write about. And even though I'd had plenty of material for a long time, just like everybody else, I didn't know that I needed it or was ever going to want to use it until I was almost thirty. When I was twenty-nine, I stopped and looked at my life and wondered if I was ever going to do anything with it. I had been a firefighter for six years, and on my off days I had set out pine trees, done carpentry work, cleaned carpets, cut pulpwood, deadened timber, you name it. I'd built those chain-link fences for Sears & Roebuck, and painted houses, and I'd hauled hay. I knew what it was like to pick up heavy bales and stack them on a truck all day under the sun, and then unload it and stack it in some hot old barn full of red wasps. I had done all these things to support my wife and my two little boys, to make ends meet. When I was in high school I never gave a thought to more education. I did poorly in school, especially English, and I paid so little attention to that course that I was obliged to attend summer school after my senior year just to get my diploma. I loved reading, and had all my life, but I didn't see how English was going to help me get a job after I got out of school, which was all I wanted to do.

But standing just short of thirty I suddenly realized that if I didn't find something else to do with my life, I was never going to amount to anything. When I had gotten married, I hadn't looked too far into the future. I guess what I thought for most of my life was that I'd just let one day take care of the next. I'd made it that way okay for a long time, had some good times, some beautiful babies. But those babies were going to grow up. They were going to want things, and I wanted things to be better for them than they had been for me. I didn't want mine to start out like I did, working in a factory.

The proposition of writing came on me slowly. I had been wondering how this process evolved, how these books and stories came to be written. I knew that people sat down and wrote them, but it seemed almost impossible that people could actually do something like that. I wondered what it took to be a writer, and I wondered if just anybody could do it. I wondered if it might be like learning how to build houses, or lay brick, or even fight fires, for that matter. I knew that some writers made a lot of money. I was a big fan of Stephen King, and I knew that his books sold well. The main question was, could a person teach himself how to do it by doing it? It seemed a logical question to me. I had absolutely no idea of the odds against me when I decided to try it.

My wife had an old portable Smith-Corona electric, and I went out and bought a box of typing paper and sat down in our bedroom one night and started writing a novel. It was about a man-eating bear in Yellowstone National Park, a place I'd never been to, and it had a lot of sex in it. I thought sex sold, because of the Harold Robbins novels I'd read. I was wrong. Nobody in New York wanted it. I know because I almost wore that novel out sending it around. It took me five months to write it and I couldn't understand why nobody wanted it. The main reason they didn't want it, I know now, is because it was horrible. You would not believe how horrible. Just imagine. It was 327 single-spaced pages of sex and man-eating.

That was my first acquaintance with a thing called the Apprenticeship Period, but it got me hooked on writing, on telling a story, putting down words on paper. After that I decided I'd try my hand at short fiction, so I wrote a few horrible short stories. Nobody wanted them either. Nobody would even write anything on a rejection slip. I decided pretty quick that nobody in New York knew his ass from a hole in the ground about fiction, but I decided that I would forge gamely on, in spite of them. I was working at a place called Comanche Pottery on my days off then. We poured liquid plaster into rubber molds shaped like pottery, Indian heads, leopards, and elephants, let them harden, then stripped the molds off. One night the whole place burned down and I was out of a part-time job for a while, but that was okay. It gave me more time to write.

Also during this time I tried to sell some stuff to *Outdoor Life*, some nonfiction pieces about things I'd seen and done while I was hunting. The first person who ever showed me any kindness was a girl who worked there named Jeannie Jagels. She wrote me a letter back about one of my early efforts, telling me why they couldn't publish it, telling me, gently and kindly, why it wasn't good enough. She was the first saint I met in the publishing business, and the publishing business is full of saints. Later on she turned another story of mine over to a guy named Rich LaRocco, who was a field editor for *Outdoor Life*. He read my piece, which was pretty horrible and illogical, and used a lot of words in a lot of ways they didn't need to be used, and he wrote a cryptic note: "Write the way you'd write a letter to a friend." Mr. LaRocco will probably never know how much good that little piece of advice did me. What it did was cause me to look at my own work and actually try to evaluate it with an objective eye, which was something I'd never done before. I'd always thought I'd just send it off and they'd buy it and publish it. Up to that point it had never occurred to me that I still had a lot to learn.

I decided that it might be a good idea to go to the library and find some books on writing and start learning more about my craft. So that's what I did. I checked out books on writing by the armload and read them from cover to cover. I also started reading work by better writers. I had been reading Faulkner since I was about sixteen, but not with any regularity or sense of purpose. I started rereading him and other novelists, and I started reading the collections of short stories that appear every year, books like the *O. Henry Awards* and the *Pushcart Prize* and the *Best American Short Stories*. I began to see how weak and pitiful my own work was, and it was a depressing thing to see. I saw that there was a great gulf between what I was writing and what I wanted to write. But I still had the belief that if I hung in there long enough and wrote enough, I would eventually learn how. So I started another novel. This one was about a couple of old boys in Tennessee who were going to plant a big patch of marijuana and make a lot of money. It had a lot of sex in it, too, but I'm a slow learner. I think that one took about seven months, and when I finished it I knew it was a lot better than the first one, and I sent it off knowing it would be a hit. The same thing happened, nobody wanted it. I sent it out enough times to realize that it wasn't going to be taken, and after a while I shelved it, and chalked it up to experience, and apprenticeship. I did that for years, and I kept writing, and reading.

It was only later that I learned to write about what I knew, which was Mississippi. I wasted a lot of time writing about things I didn't know anything about, instead of using my natural home and the landscape that creates the lives that are lived here, and the characters who live in my fiction. I didn't think too much about the dirt roads, or the vast forests and the creeks and rivers that run through them. I didn't know back then that I would eventually learn to listen to people talking and look at their lives or wonder what caused them to do the things they did.

You don't know when you start out that there's plenty of life around you, no matter where you live. It took me years to follow Miss Flannery's advice, or anybody else's. I didn't know how rich I was with material. I didn't know how many characters I could summon out of my imagination and Lafayette County and put them into a place other people would recognize without ever seeing it. I guess I didn't think there was anything here worth writing about, but you don't know a lot of things when you start. You don't know that what's inside the heart of a human is the only story you have to tell, or the vast millions of acres of imagination that door opens when you find it. You don't know that you can make a story out of absolutely anything, or that the things you know best are the easiest things to tell. What you *know*. But nobody can tell you this stuff. You have to find out, slowly and painfully, over a long period of time and failure. You write, and fail, and you write, and you fail. The main thing is that you don't give up hope and stop writing. You learn to reach back into your memory and take what you see around you and combine it with your imagination and you learn to build your stories and novels out of that and make it all real. And once you can do that, the reader will follow you as far as you care to take him.

I see stories around me constantly now, but I didn't use to. I can see a story now just driving down the road, or watching some people fishing, or cutting up in a beer joint, or working in a field. Loggers and housewives and children and drunks and farmers and mailmen and lawyers and widowed old ladies and mechanics and cowboys and bums and preachers, every one of them has a story, and I know now that the little place I live in is full of stories. I know what the woods look like in winter, and how a hawk sails over the grass looking for rabbits in the spring, and how the rain marches across the land at the end of a dry spell in summer, and the way the leaves on the ridges start turning brown in the fall. All these things are worth writing about because they're a part of my life, and I never tire of looking at them. I don't think I'll ever tire of writing about them. There's too much beauty in the world that I know, about ten miles out of Oxford, Mississippi.

In the early years I read a lot of essays on writing by fiction writers. The things they had to say about their own early careers could be tremendously heartening. I knew that I was a late starter and I figured the answer to that was to write even more, as much as possible, every chance I had, and compress the years of learning into a shorter period of years. That's what I did. My children were small then, and whenever I was home I could usually lock myself away in a room, sometimes for ten or twelve hours, sometimes for as much as five or six thousand words.

By that time I had realized there wasn't going to be any money made any time soon off writing, but I decided to go on anyway, for as long as it took. Two other things had happened to me. One was that I was enjoying what I was doing enormously, and the other was that I was teaching myself, without knowing it, to become a better reader. I had started reading the best writing by the best writers, and I began to find out it was what they called literature. I couldn't write it yet, but at least I knew what it was. I finally knew what I was aiming for. And that was Mr. Faulkner's advice all along: read all you can by the best writers. What he meant was read literature, and maybe that's still the best advice young writers can get.

It took me a long time to understand what literature was, and why it was so hard to write, and what it could do to you once you understood it. For me, very simply it meant that I could meet people on the page who were as real as the people I knew in my own life. They *were* real people, as far as I was concerned, not just characters. Even though they were only words on paper, they were as real to me as my wife and children. And when I saw that, it was like a curtain fell away from my eyes. I saw that the greatest rewards that could be had from the printed page came from literature, and that to be able to write it was the highest form of the art of writing.

From that time on that's what I've tried to write, and in the past few years I've been lucky enough to see some of my stories published in literary magazines. I've seen that distant dream come true, a book with my name on it. It hasn't been easy and I doubt if it ever will be. I don't think it was meant to be easy. I think that from the first it was meant to be hard for the few people who came along and wanted to write it, because the standards are so high and the rewards so great, in my case, making readers look into the hearts of the people I've chosen to write about.

All of my work comes out of Mississippi, out of the dirt roads and the woods and the fields I drive my truck by. The people who live in this land are the people I've known best throughout my life, and together with the country we live in, they form a vast well that will never run dry.

JUDITH ORTIZ COFER

Advanced Biology

As I lay out my clothes for the trip to Miami to do a reading from my recently published novel, then on to Puerto Rico to see my mother, I take a close look at my travel wardrobe—the tailored skirts in basic colors easily coordinated with my silk blouses—I have to smile to myself remembering what my mother had said about my conservative outfits when I visited her the last time—that I looked like the Jehovah's Witnesses who went from door to door in her pueblo trying to sell tickets to heaven to the die-hard Catholics. I would scare people she said. They would bolt their doors if they saw me approaching with my briefcase. As for her, she dresses in tropical colors—a red skirt and parakeet-yellow blouse look good on her tan skin, and she still has a good enough figure that she can wear a tight, black cocktail dress to go dancing at her favorite club, *El Palacio*, on Saturday nights. And, she emphasizes, still make it to the 10 o'clock mass on Sunday. Catholics can have fun and still be saved, she has often pointed out to me, but only if you pay your respects to God and all His Court with the necessary rituals. She has never accepted my gradual slipping out of the faith in which I was so strictly brought up.

As I pack my clothes into the suitcase, I recall our early days in Paterson, New Jersey, where we lived for most of my adolescence while my father was alive and stationed in Brooklyn Yard in New York. At that time, my mother's views on everything from clothing to (the forbidden subject) sex were ruled by the religious fervor that she had developed as a shield against the cold foreign city. These days we have traded places in a couple of areas since she has "gone home" after my father's death, and "gone native." I chose to attend college in the United States and make a living as an English teacher and, lately, on the lecture circuit as a novelist and poet. But, though our lives are on the surface radically different, my mother and I have affected each other reciprocally over the past twenty years; she has managed to liberate herself from the rituals, mores, and traditions that "cramp" her style, while retaining her femininity and "Puertoricanness," while I struggle daily to consolidate my opposing cultural identities. In my adolescence, divided into my New Jersey years and my Georgia years, I received an education in the art of cultural compromise.

In Paterson in the 1960s I attended a public school in our neighborhood. Still predominantly white and Jewish, it was rated very well academically in a city where the educational system was in chaos, deteriorating rapidly as the best teachers moved on to suburban schools following the black and Puerto Rican migration into, and the white exodus from, the city proper.

The Jewish community had too much at stake to make a fast retreat; many of the small businesses and apartment buildings in the city's core were owned by Jewish families of the World War II generation. They had seen worse things happen than the influx of black and brown people that was scaring away the Italians and the Irish. But they too would gradually move their families out of the best apartments in their buildings and into houses in East Paterson, Fairlawn, and other places with *lawns*. It was how I saw the world then; either you lived without your square of grass, or you bought a house to go with it. But for most of my adolescence, I lived among the Jewish people of Paterson. We rented an apartment owned by the Milsteins, proprietors also of the deli on the bottom floor. I went to school with their children. My father took his business to the Jewish establishments, perhaps because these men symbolized "dignified survival" to him. He was obsessed with privacy, and could not stand the personal turns conversations almost always took when two or more Puerto Ricans met casually over a store counter. The Jewish men talked too, but they concentrated on externals. They asked my father about his job, politics, his opinion on Vietnam, Lyndon Johnson. And my father, in his quiet voice, answered their questions knowledgeably. Sometimes before we entered a store, the cleaners, or a shoe-repair shop, he would tell me to look for the blue-inked numbers on the owner's left forearm. I would stare at these numbers, now usually faded enough to look like veins in the wrong place. I would try to make them out. They were a telegram from the past, I later decided, informing the future of the deaths of millions. My father discussed the Holocaust with me in the same hushed tones my mother used to talk about God's Mysterious Ways. I could not reconcile both in my mind. This conflict eventually led to my first serious clash with my mother over irreconcilable differences between the "real world" and religious doctrine.

It had to do with the Virgin Birth.

And it had to do with my best friend and study partner, Ira Nathan, the acknowledged scientific genius at school. In junior high school it was almost a requirement to be "in love" with an older boy. I was an eighth grader and Ira was in the ninth grade that year and preparing to be sent away to some prep school in New England. I chose him as my boyfriend (in the eyes of my classmates, if a girl spent time with a boy that meant they were "going together") because I needed tutoring in biology—one of his best subjects. I ended up having a crush on him after our first Saturday morning meeting at the library. Ira was my first exposure to the wonders of an analytical mind.

The problem was the subject. Biology is a dangerous topic for young teenagers who are themselves walking laboratories, experimenting with interesting combinations of chemicals every time they make a choice. In my basic biology class, we were looking at single-cell organisms under the microscope, and watching them reproduce in slow-motion films in a darkened classroom. Though the process was as unexciting as watching a little kid blow bubbles, we were aroused by the concept itself. Ira's advanced class was dissecting fetal pigs. He brought me a photograph of his project, inner organs labeled neatly on the paper the picture had been glued to. My eyes refused to budge from the line drawn from "genitals" to a part of the pig it pertained to. I felt a wave of heat rising from my chest to my scalp. Ira must have seen my discomfort, though I tried to keep my face behind the black curtain of my hair, but as the boy-scientist, he was relentless. He actually traced the line from label to pig with his pencil.

"All mammals reproduce sexually," he said in a teacherly monotone.

The librarian, far off on the other side of the room, looked up at us and frowned. Logically, it was not possible that she could have heard Ira's pronouncement, but I was convinced that the mention of sex enhanced the hearing capabilities of parents, teachers and librarians by one hundred percent. I blushed more intensely, and peeked through my hair at Ira.

He was holding the eraser of his pencil on the pig's blurry sexual parts and smiling at me. His features were distinctly Eastern European. I had recently seen the young singer Barbra Streisand on the Red Skelton show and had been amazed at how much similarity there was in their appearances. She could have been his sister. I was particularly attracted to the wide mouth and strong nose. No one that I knew in school thought that Ira was attractive, but his brains had long ago overshadowed his looks as his most impressive attribute. Like Ira, I was also a straight A student and also considered odd because I was one of the few Puerto Ricans on the honor roll. So it didn't surprise anyone that Ira and I had drifted toward each other. Though I could not have articulated it then, Ira was seducing me with his No. 2 pencil and the laboratory photograph of his fetal pig. The following Saturday, Ira brought in his advanced biology book and showed me the transparencies of the human anatomy in full color that I was not meant to see for a couple more years. I was shocked. The cosmic jump between paramecium and the human body was almost too much for me to take in. These were the first grown people I had ever seen naked and they revealed too much.

"Human sexual reproduction can only take place when the male's sperm is introduced into the female womb and fertilization of the egg takes place," Ira stated flatly.

The book was open to the page labeled "The Human Reproductive System." Feeling that my maturity was being tested, as well as my intelligence, I found my voice long enough to contradict Ira.

"There has been one exception to this, Ira." I was feeling a little smug about knowing something that Ira obviously did not.

"Judith, there are no exceptions in biology, only mutations, and adaptations through evolution." He was smiling in a superior way.

"The Virgin Mary had a baby without . . ." I couldn't say *having sex* in the same breath as the name of the Mother of God. I was totally unprepared for the explosion of laughter that followed my timid statement. Ira had crumpled in his chair and was laughing so hard that his thin shoulders shook. I could hear the librarian approaching. Feeling humiliated, I started to put my books together. Ira grabbed my arm.

"Wait, don't go," he was still giggling uncontrollably, "I'm sorry. Let's talk a little more. Wait, give me a chance to explain."

Reluctantly, I sat down again mainly because the librarian was already at our table, hands on hips, whispering angrily: "If you *children* cannot behave in this *study area*, I will have to ask you to leave." Ira and I both apologized, though she gave him a nasty look because his mouth was still stretched from ear to ear in a hysterical grin.

"Listen, listen. I'm sorry that I laughed like that. I know you're Catholic and you believe in the Virgin Birth (he bit his lower lip trying to regain his composure), but it's just not biologically possible to have a baby without . . . (he struggled for control) . . . losing your virginity."

I sank down on my hard chair. "Virginity." He had said another of the forbidden words. I glanced back at the librarian who was keeping her eye on us. I was both offended and excited by Ira's blasphemy. How could he deny a doctrine that people had believed in for 2,000 years? It was part of my prayers every night. My mother talked about *La Virgen* as if she were our most important relative.

Recovering from his fit of laughter, Ira kept his hand discretely on my elbow as he explained in the seductive language of the scientific laboratory how babies were made, and how it was impossible to violate certain natural laws.

"Unless God will it," I argued feebly.

"There is no God," said Ira, and the last shred of my innocence fell away as I listened to his arguments backed up by irrefutable scientific evidence.

Our meetings continued all that year, becoming more exciting with every chapter in his biology book. My grades improved dramatically since one-celled organisms were no mystery to a student of advanced biology. Ira's warm, moist hand often brushed against mine under the table at the library, and walking home one bitter cold day, he asked me if I would wear his Beta Club pin. I nodded and when we stepped inside the hallway of my building where he removed his thick mittens which his mother had knitted, he pinned the blue enamel B to my collar. And to the hissing of the steam heaters, I received a serious kiss from Ira. We separated abruptly when we heard Mrs. Milstein's door open.

"Hello, Ira."

"Hello, Mrs. Milstein."

"And how is your mother? I haven't seen Fritzie all week. She's not sick, is she?"

"She's had a mild cold, Mrs. Milstein. But she is steadily improving." Ira's diction became extremely precise and formal when he was in the presence of adults. As an only child and a prodigy, he had to live up to very high standards.

"I'll call her today," Mrs. Milstein said, finally looking over at me. Her eyes fixed on the collar of my blouse which was, I later saw in our hall mirror, sticking straight up with Ira's pin attached crookedly to the edge.

"Good-bye, Mrs. Milstein."

"Nice to see you, Ira."

Ira waved awkwardly to me as he left. Mrs. Milstein stood in the humid hallway of her building watching me run up the stairs.

Our "romance" lasted only a week; long enough for Mrs. Milstein to call Ira's mother, and for Mrs. Nathan to call my mother. I was subjected to a lecture on moral behavior by my mother, who, carried away by her anger and embarrassed that I had been seen kissing a boy (understood: a boy who was not even Catholic), had begun a chain of metaphors for the loss of virtue that was on the verge of the tragi/comical:

"A *perdida*, a cheap item," she said trembling before me as I sat on the edge of my bed, facing her accusations, "a girl begins to look like one when she allows herself to be *handled* by men."

"Mother . . ." I wanted her to lower her voice so that my father, sitting at the kitchen table reading, would not hear. I had already promised her that I would confess my sin that Saturday and take communion with a sparkling clean soul. I had not been successful at keeping the sarcasm out of my voice. Her fury was fueled by her own bitter litany:

"A dirty joke, a burden to her family . . ." She was rolling with her Spanish now, soon the Holy Mother would enter into the picture for good measure. "It's not as if I had not taught you better. Don't you know that those people do not have the example of the Holy Virgin Mary and her Son to follow and that is why they do things for the wrong reasons. Mrs. Nathan said she did not want her son messing around with you— not because of the wrongness of it—but because it would interfere with his studies!" She was yelling now. "She's afraid that he will (she crossed herself at the horror of the thought) make you pregnant!"

"We could say an angel came down and put a baby in my stomach, Mother." She had succeeded in dragging me into her field of hysteria. She grabbed my arm and pulled me to my feet.

"I do not want you associating any more than necessary with people who do not have God, do you hear me?"

"They have a god!" I was screaming now too, trying to get away from her suffocating grasp: "They have an intelligent god who doesn't ask you to believe that a woman can get pregnant without having sex!" That's when she slapped me. She looked horrified at what she had instinctively done.

"Nazi," I hissed, out of control by then too, "I bet you'd like to send Ira and his family to a concentration camp!" At that time I thought that was the harshest thing I could have said to anyone. I was certain that I had sentenced my soul to eternal damnation the minute the words came out of my mouth: but my cheek was burning from the slap and I wanted to hurt her. Father walked into my room at that moment looking shocked at the sight of the two of us entangled in mortal combat.

"Please, please," his voice sounded agonized. I ran to him and he held me in his arms while I cried my heart out on his starched white shirt. My mother, also weeping quietly, tried to walk past us, but he pulled her into the circle. After a few moments, she put her trembling hand on my head.

"We are a family," my father said, "there is only the three of us against the world. Please, please . . ." But he did not follow the "please" with any suggestions as to what we could do to make things right in a world that was as confusing to my mother as it was to me.

I finished the eighth grade in Paterson, but Ira and I never got together to study again. I sent his Beta Club pin back to him via a mutual friend. Once in a while I saw him in the hall or the playground. But he seemed to be in the clouds, where he belonged. In the fall, I was enrolled at St. Joseph's Catholic High School where everyone believed in the Virgin

Birth, and I never had to take a test on the human reproductive system. It was a chapter that was not emphasized.

In 1968, the year Paterson, like many U.S. cities, exploded in racial violence, my father moved us to Augusta, Georgia, where two of his brothers had retired from the army at Fort Gordon. They had convinced him that it was a healthier place to rear teenagers. For me it was a shock to the senses, like moving from one planet to another: where Paterson had concrete to walk on and gray skies, bitter winters, and a smorgasbord of an ethnic population, Georgia was red like Mars, and Augusta was green—exploding in colors in more gardens of azaleas and dogwood and magnolia trees—more vegetation than I imagined was possible anywhere not tropical like Puerto Rico. People seem to come in two basic colors: black and blond. And I could barely understand my teachers when they talked in a slowed-down version of English like one of those old 78 speed recordings played at 33. But I was placed in all advanced classes and one of them was biology. This is where I got to see my first real fetal pig which my assigned lab partner had chosen. She picked him up gingerly by the ends of the plastic bag in which it was stored: "Ain't he cute?" she asked. I nodded, nearly fainting from the overwhelming combination of the smell of formaldehyde and my sudden flashback to my brief but intense romance with Ira Nathan.

"What you want to call him?" My partner unwrapped our specimen on the table, and I surprised myself by my instant recall of Ira's chart. I knew all the parts. In my mind's eye I saw the pencil lines, the labeled photograph. I had had an excellent teacher.

"Let's call him Ira."

"That's a funny name, but OK." My lab partner, a smart girl destined to become my mentor in things Southern, then gave me a conspiratorial wink and pulled out a little perfume atomizer from her purse. She sprayed Ira from snout to tail with it. I noticed this operation was taking place at other tables too. The teacher had conveniently left the room a few minutes before. I was once again stunned—almost literally knocked out by a fist of smell: "What is it?"

"*Intimate*," my advanced biology partner replied smiling.

And by the time our instructor came back to the room, we were ready to delve into this mystery of muscle and bone; eager to discover the secrets that lie just beyond fear a little past loathing; of acknowledging the corruptibility of the flesh, and our own fascination with the subject.

As I finish packing, the telephone rings and it's my mother. She is reminding me to be ready to visit relatives, to go to a dance with her, and, of course, to attend a couple of the services at the church. It is the feast of the Black Virgin, revered patron saint of our home town in Puerto Rico. I agree to everything, and find myself anticipating the eclectic itinerary. Why not allow Evolution and Eve, Biology and the Virgin Birth? Why not take a vacation from logic? I will not be away for too long, I will not let myself be tempted to remain in the sealed garden of blind faith; I'll stay just long enough to rest myself from the exhausting enterprise of leading the examined life.

WILLIAM C. COOK

Hudson Hornet

My father preached full, powerful;
Raised heavenly thunder as he roared,
Salvation sang,
Sang holy, phallic, masterful
Till sisters big and hallelujah
Danced out their locked-in passion.

Locked big with mastering they live,
Queens to whom small husbands cower
Drowned in vastness, female greed—
I want, I want—
Small husbands never could supply;
But heavenly and phallic deity
Drawn from my father's book and dreams—
Full-muscled, steel-loined deity
Could move them from their frigid thrones
Could set their hips and legs to life
And holy dance them to orgasm.
How shall a mere man satisfy
What has been moved to shouting joy
By such complete priapic might?
No man for Leda after Zeus.

My father home, without the robes,
The pulpit or the book, came down
Shrunk small—to bullying the weak.
The child could never plan resistance,
Never dared defend or lodge complaint.
Despite my prayers that he would grow
And tower pulpit-like at home,
My father never rose above his times.
Behind the news he hid himself;
Beneath the used car ads he crept
And did not fix on that great Hudson Hornet
A massy chariot fit for more than god;
But meekly in my mother's sound advice,

The humble Ford for gelded men
Androgynous and weak he chose.

God save the Sundays where he rode.

Maternity

For Frances Cook who died singing.

I

"The last night that she lived,"
She had a baby.
Cradled on her right arm
He lay
And did not cry
Protected by the arching mother "S"
Her body made.
And we were not her children.
How could she mother anyone
So old and knowing in the world?
    "Fool! You better look where you set down!
    Don't put that package on this bed!
    Go get a chair from out the hall.
    And watch out for the child."
The shattered right arm and the cast
She did not answer to.
Pain that cut our voices off
Had altered hers into a rasp-like croon
As she instructed her now restless child
We meant no harm. She'd see to that.
He would not grow beyond her need to nourish
Who now lay cradled on her arm.
She had a baby
That last night that she lived.
We were too old to see or say good-bye.

II

We were too big to silence on a youthful arm;
No need to comfort or to pity what we seemed.
Under my sister's neatly patterned braids

Her thoughts knit and unknit
(Were we there too?)
But shielding was the only text she read,
And so she blinked the text we held before her eyes.
She let confusion briefly knit her face;
Then like a swimmer breaking surface, treading water
She shook her head, refused our claim.
And, turning unresponding eyes on our maturity,
Our pleas to be remembered and our willingness to pay,
She smilingly erased the fear that we could be.

III

She was at home and young away from us;
Hospital beds were birth or death to her.
She was not sick.
The poor are sick or well always at home.
She turned her condescending head
Toward the curtains that shut out the ward
Sure in her meaning after so much doubt.
Old men and women, we stood silent;
Too old to be her friends or visit her.
She silently denied the grandchildren
Hushed by the smell of age and sickness,
. Attendants of the snack machine
Their pennies in their hands.
Her final stare was puzzled and indignant
And was full.
She sang to her restless, whimpering child
And with a quiet sigh closed out her day.
There was no need to comfort or to pity us
Who were too big to silence on a youthful arm.
We were too old to say good-bye.

Translations

For Cleve Cook

446 North Ninth Street
Philadelphia or North Philly
"Checkaah!" meant "Shut Up!"
and "hatburn" was a euphemistic way

a private code
"Goddamn!"

That private code
Almost a foreign language
Is souvenir
For me.
I turn the words
When I come down to words
To find a crack
In their hard cover.

We could not bother you
When you were resting
And at home;
No one could ask you
For translation then.

You had a language for us
And it hurt where it
Caressed
Like biting kisses
I remember.

Times Square Hotel
—Basement Floor

Sunday mornings
Around the corner and underneath the meat rack and the flesh strip
The old men
With the pensioned women
Who
Bless Jesus for the quiet of old age
Sing.

The old men
With the wrinkled women
Who
Are glad at decent skirts again
Bless Jesus for their freedom.

No legs thrown back
As did not fit their dignity—
The boiling tumble
When
A fatal sense of duty raises legs.

Make no responding moves
You are no women of the streets
He can just go and get that somewhere else.
Bless Jesus
At the final thrust and gasp
Eyes left or right
Visions of dogs and water buckets
And sigh the wrinkled clothing smooth.
Sing.

Around the corner upstairs on the strip
"You going out?"
"Want to have some fun?"
The flaming swords for old men exiled from the youthful garden
Who
Walk slowly as they stalk.
The price of fantasy bulges in their pants
They shop for water sports
Discipline
Or reamed on all fours
Kneeling in their holy penitence
Their trembling shanks and road map legs
Do obeisance to the gods of platform shoes
Who advertise their holy icons
In their hustling dress.

Stripes for the sin of age and wrinkles;
The lash.
The cold-eyed adolescent gods
Lay on their scourges
And take their offerings
Granting pain
Pain and a dream of unity:
Flat bellies, narrow waistlines
Pain
And the little children bleed them.

First Baptist Church: Princeton, New Jersey

A long black hearse, Hughes Funeral Company,
And at its sleek, mortician door
Mortician Hughes or else his minions.
Reflected in its clean black sides
A neighborhood stands paused in time.
Black men and women walk soft-shoed
To sidewalk's edge to see the . . . . what?
And through the silence sober-edged,
With sharp and sudden alarm-clock ring,
The scream high-pitched, trailed to a moan,
Rides out into the noonday air.
And we are stilled before such ringing grief
And turn shamefaced that we beheld.

Some inside mourner in black grief
Felt full at that moment full the loss
And out of all that loss and all
Flew sharp the scream that shook our brooding.

Flew out against the shortness
Flew out against the hardness
Flew out against the sameness of our days.
Drew us from neutral corners,
Bar room corners,
Juke joint corners.
Drew us to share its love lost love.

And sharing all we sent a cry
That tolled our clipped and darkened days,
That broke the gloss of noonday polish,
That dulled the sheen of Hughes and Company;
And wiped away their practiced smile.

MELVIN DIXON

The Boy with Beer

I t was Friday night and crowded. He stood alone outside the club, trying to see into the front window, where his breath clung to the tinted
glass and people were blurred shapes of rising and falling colors. He left
the window and returned to it. The doubt in him was as real as the cold
outside. He approached the window again, then the front door, shoving a
course notebook into his coat pocket as he went. He held it there. Maybe
next weekend, he thought. He felt the night air on his neck and knew
it would be warm inside. For the third time he told himself, "I have to,"
but the voice questioning inside him was cautious.

—*What if Mama finds out?*
—She won't know anything about it, I'm sure.
—*And Larry?*
—Larry. He's gone.
—*And she won't know?*
—I won't tell them who I am.
—*They already know.*
—I'm going in anyway.
—*No, you're not.*
—I have to.
—*Do you remember the words?*
—I'm going in anyway.

People laughing somewhere behind him brought his attention back to
the street. Suddenly his neck felt wet. The air on his sweat made him
aware of a cool emptiness growing inside him. Real voices came from
the laughter behind.

"Ha, ha, chile, I'm a little too tired tonight. And you all sure are some
crazy folks, I swear! Dragging me out of my house in this cold. Humph!
Just being with you crazy children is too much. Ha, ha, I swear."

"Well, honey," another one said, "we'll just leave you behind then. I been sitting home all week, let me tell you, waiting for that man to call. That's right. *All week.* And that bum ain't called yet. Bet you I ain't sitting home for nobody no more. I ain't about to rot for nobody."

A third one joined the group. "Yeah, but you said he was worth waiting ten years for."

"That was last week, darling. I'm in the market for something better-looking tonight," the second one answered.

"Whooooo, for days, chile," the third one said.

"Quit running your mouths," said the first, "so we can get one good drink before the night's through."

The voices came toward him. He moved quickly away from the entrance, relieved that the three hadn't noticed him. He watched the red front door open for the new guests, and he listened as the sounds of black night life flew out into the street. Then quietly he followed the trio inside.

—It ain't easy, girls, it ain't easy
   It ain't easy, girls, it ain't easy . . .

He recognized the song from the jukebox. Its rhythm made him feel more of a willing captive to the smoke, the wine, the music, and the solitary bodies. Several heads turned in his direction, and he felt a dull pain in his chest. One by one, the heads turned back to their drinks as if he was not the one they expected.

As he walked farther inside the bar, he thought again of what she would say if she saw him. But she's far away from me now, he thought. Far away. But her voice returned to him, and his legs went stiff.

—You're Mama's little man. That's who you are.
—Yes, Mama.
—Now don't you look nice?
—I guess so.
—Sure you do.
—Mama?
—I know you're going to like church today. Youth Choir singing?
—Yes.
—Should I sit near the front to hear your solo?
—I don't have a solo.
—No?
—Mama?
—Yes, son. Oh, is my hat on straight? Here, zip me up quick. We can't be late.
—Mama?
—What is it, son?
—I don't feel well.
—You'll be all right. Reverend Jones preaches a fine sermon. He'll make you feel real good.

—Mama!
—Come on now. We're going to be late. Watch your step.
—Mama!

All the way inside the bar colors danced around him in pink knits, tailored orange sharkskins, and burgundy velvets. The burgundy velvet blew its cheap wine breath across the glossy dance floor to meet him. A forest-green jacket and a pair of chartreuse shoes slid into action in front. But instead of joining them he moved beyond the dancers, the empty beer bottles, the cigarette fog, and settled in a booth near the door to the back kitchen.

Order a beer. "That's not too expensive," he told himself. "What with the little change I brought." Drink it slowly. Nurse each swallow. Make it last.

But he was afraid.

"Ballantine, please."

No response.

Then louder, deeper. "Ballantine, please!"

"Comin'." The response was electric.

He returned to his seat with a glass, hugging the neck of the brown bottle and jiggling with his walk. He thought for a moment that he would not be able to stay the whole night. Fear danced inside him and voices kept coming to his mind. They warned him to leave. "No, not yet," he said to himself. He tried to focus on the bar, the Ballantine, the thirst, but the voice of his father reached into him and chilled.

—Willis! What the hell you doing in here making a damn cake! And with your mother's apron, on too! Come on out here and help me clean up the yard.
—He's helping me.
—Helping you nothing, Sarah. He should be out doing some man's work like the other boys his age. Not laid up in some damn kitchen!
—If he wants to bake a cake, let him.

The first gulp of beer was so icy it numbed his insides. Willis looked around him at the rows of laughing faces and bodies, the people in couples, some standing alone, watching. He wondered what he should say to them. What he should do. Maybe Larry would know. He remembered asking:

—Larry, will you be my friend!

and asking him again, but Larry had gone.

—Willis!

Someone else was calling.

—Wwwwwwiiiiilllliiissssss. Come home!

Her voice calling was not like his father's voice, which was tender only after collard greens and three cups of pot liquor. He often forgot birthdays and, once, even Christmas. Willis remembered his own birthdays, twelve of them, passing unnoticed. He was six when he received his last gift from his father, a battery racing car that fell apart after three days.

His father used to scare away friends. Like Larry when they listened to records, read comic books, and sometimes played catch outside. His father said they made too much noise, so Larry could never stay long. Yes, he and Larry were friends. Good friends. Until.

—Larry?
—Yeah.
—We're still friends, aren't we?
—Sure. Good friends. Yeah.

Larry. The green house across the street. Larry. A year older. They went to the same school, and every day they would shine shoes for a quarter downtown until Willis was fourteen and Larry spent the night. Willis felt awkward. Larry's hands were cold and hard. Willis had warm fingers, and that night they touched, fumbled nervously, and shook. He remembered what they said about his hands.

—Sarah, what firm, wide hands your son has.
—He used to play the piano.
—That's so nice.
—He practiced every day.
—That's so nice.

And Larry, who was his friend.

—But listen, Willis.
—You do understand, don't you?
—Naw, I don't think so.
—Larry?
—Look, Willis, man, I don't think we can be friends anymore. Not that way. Understand? You understand?
—I guess so.
—Look, man, don't act like you're gonna cry.

Larry. The face and the voice came too sudden. Harsh. Willis tried to blur the memory. He swallowed hard and concentrated on the drops of water forming on the beer bottle. He took another swallow and rinsed his gums before dropping it deep into his throat. He looked at the men and the few women around him.

He remembered Sandy, who was the color of cinnamon with short bristly hair and agile enough for the girl's track team at Eastern High.

All the girls moved like athletes then, he thought. Willis took her to the Sophomore-Junior Prom, where they drank from the quart of Calvert L.B. had hidden under his dinner jacket. Nothing mattered then; he was with Sandy. He remembered her body growing warm against his as they danced. In the morning they drank the last of the whiskey.

—*Willis!*
—*Yes.*
—*Why do you drink so much? You know it's wrong.*
—*I don't know.*
—*I don't like you to drink like this. It's not good.*
—*All right.*
—*You know, Willis, I feel so lucky.*
—*Why?*
—*All the girls in my homeroom are jealous because we're going together.*
—*Oh! But I just took you to the prom.*
—*And I like you because you're not like the other boys. You're different, and for me that's special.*

Her voice vanished quickly from his mind when Willis saw a figure come near his booth. He held the beer bottle tighter and shifted in his seat. He saw a black satin gown, streams of costume pearls flowing about a thick brown neck, a blond bouffant wig covering the head. When he saw that it was a man Willis shivered, but his eyes remained glued. The man glided past like a ghost, catching him in the perfume lagging behind. Out of the mist an angry face loomed near. Imaginary, but its voice was menacing.

—*What took you so long in there?*
—*I was brushing my teeth.*
—*You know I got to shave.*
—*Sorry.*
—*And take a shower.*
—*I'm sorry, Daddy.*
—*Hey, come here, Willis.*
—*Yes?*
—*Closer. What's that black mess around your eyes? And that red on your cheeks?*
—*Nothing.*
—*Nothing, huh! Boy, you better get away from me looking like that.*

The summer after high school, Willis remembered, had been lonely. He'd sit in the park. Watch people. He wondered why they didn't respond to his looking. Why they didn't sense the doubt inside him. He wanted to ask someone, anyone, if he was always to be lonely. Or could he face the steady torture in his father's eyes? Should he leave home? Where could he go? He had measured his misery by the blankness of the faces passing him and wondered why he was even there. If he could have remembered the words, maybe the emptiness would have gone away:

The Lord is my shepherd; I shall not want.
And Sandy?
I shall not want. He maketh me to lie down in green pastures. He leadeth me.
Sandy, I love you.
He leadeth me beside the still waters. I shall not want. He restoreth my soul.
Sandy, we can't anymore.
He leadeth me in the paths of righteousness for his name's sake, for his name.

How would he welcome the funeral of his body and the touching, the steady touching of him? To lie alone like a corpse in an abandoned field without flowers, where on top of his body the grass grows yellow and the sky above is empty? Is empty.

Willis thought of last summer when the neighbors talked of nothing but the two boys caught fondling each other in the bushes near the park's pond.

Yea, though I walk through the valley . . .

The bar was too crowded now, and the night was continuing. Willis participated in the funeral not yet welcomed. He repeated to himself

of the shadow of death, I will fear no evil. No evil. For Thou art with me; I shall not want . . . he leadeth me . . . I shall not want.

His back felt the stiffness of the pewlike booth, but there were no altars here. He could not pray; but he could remember. And he remembered the Church School Children's Day Program, the deacons who shook his hand, the church mothers who kissed him when he recited the verses in his clearest voice.

Suddenly a hand brushed against his thigh. He turned sharply and searched the crowd. Did he just imagine the touch? Was it his own hand and fingers that crept so often to his groin and pulled and pulled until he had released himself to sleep? His body sank into the pew-booth again and the recitation grew louder, louder inside him.

Thou preparest a table before me in the presence of mine enemies though anointest my head with oil my cup runneth over and over and over and over and surely goodness and mercy shall follow me all the days all the nights in the night of my life and I will dwell in the house in the bar of the house of the Lord forever and ever and ever

The journey into him was taking too long. "Don't touch me!" The words choked him inside.

—Reverend Jones preaches a fine sermon in his way. You listen to Mama. Join the church, son. Mama knows. Baptism will help you.

The coldness of the water then made his chest feel empty. He felt the bottom of the pool until his toes couldn't touch anymore. Willis folded his arms across the chest as if he were dead and went down. When the preacher lifted him up, he broke the water with his cheeks puffed out. His mother saw him and she believed. Still he couldn't answer when she asked,

—*Willis, why are you looking at those boys like that?*
—*I'm not, Mama.*
—*You are, son. You are.*
—*No, Mama.*
—*They're wearing the same white robes you are. They have the same thing you have.*
—*I know, Mama.*
—*They're just as wet as you are.*
—*But I'm not. I'm not looking at their legs or their thighs.*
—*Here, take this towel and dry yourself good.*
—*I'm not looking at them.*
—*Hurry up now before you catch cold.*

What had the preacher said? Willis tried to remember when a girl in a short blue dress staggered to his booth and was sick and falling near him. Willis wanted to leave the booth, and he couldn't leave the booth, and he was afraid to stay. The door to the back kitchen flapped open and a man came out to take the girl away. The preacher said he would be safe.
The waters of grace shall set you free. Repent, brethen, repent!
His glass of beer dropped to the floor. Cold liquid oozed down his leg and dripped into his shoe. The chill filled him inside. Willis was too embarrassed to ask for a napkin. He let the wetness stay.
Black shapes and colors dancing and melting into fuzzy silhouettes made him want to laugh, and he did. He touched his wet leg and laughed again. People around him were laughing and singing with the music and sharing each other's secrets. No one knew Willis's secret, but still the people laughed.
Then a hand on his shoulder. A man's voice. Willis stopped laughing, stopped breathing, stopped thinking, stopped living. Could not die. Was it his father's voice?

—*Willis?*
—*Yes, Daddy.*
—*Be strong, hear. You hear me?*

No, don't move, Willis thought. Hold on to the hand. But he did nothing. He said nothing; he listened.
"Hi."
It didn't sound like his father.
"I said *hello* there."
The voice was not his father's voice. Still he was afraid to answer. After a moment Willis spoke.

"Oh, I didn't quite hear you."

"May I join you?"

"No, no, I don't mind at all."

"You sound nervous."

"I was hoping it wouldn't show. Well, not that much anyway."

"Can I get you a drink?"

"No, thanks."

"No?"

"I'm still on this one."

"Been here before?"

"No."

"No?"

"Actually, I was on my way home from—"

"Yes?"

"Well, from class. We had this evening lecture that—"

"Still in school, huh? That's good."

School. His mother's voice found him again.

He was always such a good student, my son. You know my son, don't you? Willis? They call him Willie sometimes, but his name is Willis.

The man, sitting opposite, looked straight into him. "You like school?" And Willis shuddered to forget what had happened there.

—*I'm gonna kick your skinny ass all the way home, chump. You hear?*

—*But why, Jake?*

—*I can get an A, too, chump. An A right upside your head. You cheated on the test anyway.*

—*I didn't, Jake. And I haven't done anything to you.*

—*Just be by the playground gate, I'll show you who's smartest.*

—*I won't be there.*

—*Yes, you will.*

Willis watched the man and listened again. He noticed the smooth skin, the moustache neatly trimmed and moving up and down with his words, calm, like his eyes; the eyes shining like coal from the clear brown face, the face moving gracefully toward his.

"I bet you're a science major. Probably going to be a doctor, huh? We need doctors."

"No."

"Maybe a lawyer, then? You look like a lawyer."

"I like music."

"Music?"

"And I might teach." As Willis spoke and tried to smile, the voices inside him rang together like a bell, stiffening him and hollowing him and emptying him of his troubled song.

—*He's my son. I was the proudest mother on Parent's Night.*
—*Larry, will you be my friend?*
—*Shadow of death and valley, comfort me. I am wanting, I am wanting*

Then silence. Silence inside him and out. The jukebox finished. Feet shuffled off the dance floor. The cigarette fog rose up again and blurred the crowd. With his eyes Willis reached deep into the face before him for the music he could share. He was sure now, if only for a few hours until the voices reached for him again.

"Your glass is empty," the man said. "Here, let me get you another beer."

"Thanks."

"What are you drinking—Schlitz?"

"No, Ballantine."

"By the way, I'm Jerome."

"My name is Willis."

MICHAEL DORRIS

Home

In contemporary America, where we come from is rarely our ultimate destination. We accept as natural the notion that the future follows from and is supposed to improve upon the past in a never-ending trajectory. "What do you call home?" is a question for which we may provide many different answers in the course of our lifetimes; in some cases we've relocated so frequently and so dramatically in ambition for betterment that the only possible response is: "Nowhere." "New" is the adjective usually slapped on brand name products that need a pick-me-up in sales, and "old" is what gets traded in the moment we can afford to do so.

This attitude, pervasive and, some would argue, necessary to an industrialized society, is in fact a particularly Western fad. Among out not so distant ancestors and in much of the world today, the connection between a person and a specific place has traditionally been intimate and consistent over time—in many respects one of the primary characteristics of both individual identity and group-definition. In such contexts, the significant and enduring social truths are considered to have been discovered and tested long ago. Remembered history is both instructor and revered guide, and common practice, that over-arching product of repeated trial and error, is the benchmark against which every novel idea must be measured.

Naturally enough, the arbiters of these systems are generally those who have functioned within them the longest. The presence in daily intercourse of elders—keepers of the hearth-fire—protects stability, continuity, perspective, all highly valued. Men and women who have been through the seasons of life are honored as the segment of a population who can, by reference to their own experience and longevity, simultaneously take pleasure in the exuberance of a child, remember the confusion of an adolescent, empathize with the adult emotions of love and jealousy, grief and disappointment, anger and passion. Out of the fray, they alone can ideally attain the serenity of calm vision, offer advice without the suspicion of personal profit. They are, in a literal and figurative sense, "grounded."

Ambiguity about "home" simply does not arise for members of many cultures, because their locus is inflexible, often coterminous with family membership. In a matrilocal kinship system, a woman remains a resident in the household of her birth, and passes on the privilege to her own daughters and granddaughters. (A man does the same in a patrilocal schema.) To be apart from extended family is an almost incomprehensible hardship, a deprivation so ego-diminishing that it is avoided even in death: the ghosts of ancestors and the proximity of their remains persist in exerting influence within the limits of their former abodes. They must daily be recalled, invoked, and consulted. Belongingness is a continuum, a process stretching backward and forward in time, a landscape whose contours are framed in stone, bounded by rivers too wide to contemplate crossing. Entitlement is inseparable from birthright, and only tangentially—through marriage or formal adoption—do outsiders gain lateral access to the sanctum.

Casual mobility changes all guidelines, producing that amazing oxymoron: a *new home.* When approved custom dictates that a young person "leave the nest," never to return as a full-fledged inhabitant, the creation of a place of one's own immediately becomes both a goal and a directive. But of what qualities should this domicile consist? Is it realistically attainable? Will it satisfy? Nurture? Fulfill expectations? Upon whose criteria is it based? And, perhaps most pertinent of all, is it portable? Does it travel with its creator or must it be re-established afresh with each transfer?

Most of these questions are not explicitly addressed in the heat of pursuit. Rather, in taking for granted the normalcy of change, though we generally hope for the best, we are not surprised at disappointment, at falling short of perfection. We harbor in our mythology a vague notion of an ideal ambiance even if we've never directly experienced it. We know or think we know how the sense of rightness would feel, believe we'll recognize and cherish it when we find ourselves within its embrace, judge all else against its hypothetical standard, presume that more fortunate or astute adults possess the secret of harmonious settlement, and castigate the universe, the economy, the perversity of others or even ourselves for our failure to achieve tranquility.

The sad truth is that when home is deemed synonymous with permanence it is always illusionary. The pictures whose match we seek—the Norman Rockwell *Saturday Evening Post* cover of several generations gathered around a Thanksgiving table, the "family values" neighborhood of our second grade reading book, the two-dimensional simplicity of the euphemistic good old days—have more to do with cherished fictions than with actual historical realities. Human life is, by its very nature, complex and dynamic. It requires frequent re-adjustment, compromise, and ingenuity. Moments, friezes, occur when empirical experience and fantasy align, but they are transitory, appreciated more often in anticipation or retrospect than in process.

Identifying home is then in essence an act of ongoing imagination. The trick lies in our own willingness to bestow recognition, to caption an agreeable situation with an affirming ascription. Home is not necessarily—though it surely could be—on the range or where the heart is, but it clearly *is* a mental state that bespeaks relative contentment. When we're home we don't pine to be anywhere else, we don't feel out of place or a stranger. We not only know the rules of conduct, we subscribe to them. There's no frustrating separation between desire and fulfillment, no chasm of distance or years dividing nostalgia and satisfaction.

But to settle, to take root, to be of one spot, means to release the promise of all other possibilities. Home entails commitment, the arguably irrational allegiance to a condition *known* over all other potentialities. Like every other self-imposed absolute, it works only by foregoing hypothetical future alternatives.

Personally, I've lived in and cared deeply for many disparate settings. As the child of a single parent with a small income, I was often a guest in the house of a more established blood-relation. While growing up, I had, variously, a room with my grandmother in Tacoma, a couch at my uncle's in Miami, a bed in the basement of a government duplex on an Indian reservation in eastern Montana, an alcove, kept private by quilts hung from clotheslines, in my other grandmother's house in Louisville. I was, it seemed to me at the time, perpetually the new kid in school, the outsider looking in, the embarrassed, untested last-pick in a choose-up-sides ball game. The sole offspring of an ethnically mixed marriage, I was either the wrong color or the wrong attitude, the wrong accent or the wrong religion, wherever I happened to land.

What attachments I formed were to books—library books, to be precise—that described faraway locales. Being from no town or state in particular, I was free to imagine myself a citizen of any land, and before sleep each night I took to reciting a shifting litany: Egypt, Java, Greece, Afghanistan, New Mexico.

Thanks to the good services of the International Friendship League, still operating in Boston, I had access to the world. For twenty-five cents I could request a pen pal from any country I chose, and for an extra dollar I received a map, an "international passport," and an official certificate attesting to my participation in the adventure of cross-cultural communication. I exchanged my first overseas letter with Michael Lythgoe of London, England—we were both eleven, liked geography and astronomy, and had unusual family stories: his mother was in a wheelchair as a result of the blitz.

Loneliness and the low cost of making exotic friends made me greedy, and by the time I was fourteen I had fifty-seven regular correspondents: Masoud in Iran, Reiko in Japan, Ingrid in Sweden, Mohammed in Sierra Leone, José in Brazil, Veronica in New Zealand, Eileen in Dublin, Marta in Colombia, Helen in Australia, Pansy in Hawaii, Margot in Uganda, Hamid in Syria, Dan in Indonesia, Paule in France—and those are just the ones I eventually, in the course of the next thirty years, met in person.

Throughout my youth and adolescence, as I criss-crossed America with my mother in pursuit of our next stop, these faraway friends came along, never more than a forwarding address away, a community of determined shared interests and colorful stamps. Wherever I went, the ritual of waiting for the mail was my substitute for more immediate peer-bonding, and what this habit lacked in immediacy was compensated for by feelings that combined control, acceptance, and exclusivity. I was a full member in a club so secret that no one but me even knew it existed!

I went away to college at seventeen, away from there to graduate school four years later, and three years after that to a small Athapaskan-speaking fishing village in Alaska to do field work in anthropology. Chance and a teaching job brought me to northern New England in 1971, and while it was "like" at first sight, I had no notion that, as things turned out, I at last had found my way home.

Primary home, to me, is where the formative adventures of my life have taken place, and, to my great surprise, that happened for twenty years to be in New Hampshire. There exist ten acres in the town of Cornish where every worn outcrop of granite, every tree and stump, every structure, every pattern of weather or light resonates with association. There, beneath two old willows, my wife and I married each other. There, one son tipped over his bicycle without getting hurt. There, three daughters spent their initial nights on earth, their breath quick and marvelous against my chest, their weight light as a summer blanket. There, in one chilly corner of a very old house, I wrote the first and last lines of the books that changed the direction of my life. There, I often exulted in pleasure and there, superimposed on that happy image, I occasionally dragged through grief.

I know that oddly shaped plot of land as I know nowhere else, and with knowledge comes the pleasure of ease, the gratitude for bounty. I've dug its soil, reaped its harvest. I've sunk into the quiet, almost undecipherable rhythm of accumulating snow, shifting leaves, renewing grass, the smell of July sunlight on the tangle of wild raspberry with which I annually compete for space in the back yard. Its limited vistas are imprinted upon my brain, reassuring as family portraits in an album. It's the territory for which the only map I require is internal, a map whose roads and pathways lead through time and space, all ultimately rejoining into interlinking circles. It's the place I leave with the surety of return, the destination that does not preclude an expanded itinerary, the safe box where I store memory. It's the part of the earth that I miss constantly when I'm not there, the topography I can least do without. It informs my perception of anywhere else because it's beyond my capacity to forget. Cornish doesn't compete for my affection, for it abides in its own unassailable category. As long as that small, rocky terrain is in the world, wherever I go a part of me is securely at home.

To the objective eye there are sceneries more beautiful, houses far more grand, arrangments more convenient, neighbors more predictably congenial. To a real estate developer the property falls within that standard early-nineteenth-century classification: too big for a modern family, too hard to heat, too small to make a profit as a working farm. It lacks town plumbing or an artesian well; instead it receives all water from an underground stream, part of which, after a disproportionate amount of rain, temporarily flows through a worn channel in the earthen cellar. Three times in two decades, usually at the worst possible moment of late summer, the spring has run dry for weeks at a time, causing, shall we say, a lover's quarrel between the land and me: threats of divorce, of the importation of outside intervention, accusations of betrayal. But always before an enduring rupture has occurred the spring refinds itself, returns fresh and fragrant. Recriminations are put aside, appeased if not completely forgotten.

There are cracks in the house's foundation so old that they've been naturally refilled with packed dust, and the attic ceiling is insulated against the winter sky not with blown chemical foam but with layers of hundred-year-old weeklies; the paper has turned yellow but the type is still readable and the events of town—the pattern of births and of accidents, the doings of the church, the visitations of strayed sons and daughters, the marvel at the extremities and fickleness of weather—were much the same then as they are today.

The floors of the downstairs are laid with hand-hewn white pine planks, wider than any contemporary tree could yield, thick enough to sustain countless resandings. They fit together poorly, those boards, their seams as haphazard and ambling as the rivulets of a downpour upon a dirt incline, and a round object placed at the eastern quadrant of any room will slowly, with gathering momentum, find its way west.

The exterior landscape abounds with projects begun by one owner and abandoned by the next: barbecue pits of stacked fieldstone, unpruned apple orchards, tough gooseberry bushes, hand-dug wells dry eleven months of the year. Far from the gravel road that bisects the property can be found the wreck of a 1944 Ford, the doors still wedged open, the trunk stuck shut and secret. White stone posts mark the boundaries of fields no longer subdivided, and a small pond, once carefully shaped and tended, has become shallow with silt, the dark green amphitheater of frogs and crickets, an environment ideal for dragonflies and curious children.

We have never yet systematically researched the human history of our land, but in conversation with town clerks and road agents, with the dispensers of baked beans at town hall suppers, with John McCauley, the man who has delivered mail to our box for thirty years, we learn the odd fact or rumor. A suicide. A wedding predating our own by almost a hundred years to the day. An eccentric recluse.

Our house was at one time or another a turkey farm, the regional poor house, the residence of the minister. It gave long shelter to three siblings, two sisters and a brother, who never married and rarely socialized. There has been a peculiar pattern of proprietorship: every other deed for the past six has belonged to a different family named Smith. Indeed, in 1972 I bought from a Smith. To be consistent, we should someday sell to one as well.

But not soon. Not before we fulfill our store of legend to the place. To the normal run of marriages, births, deaths, we've added the creation of books. My wife, Louise Erdrich, finished her first volume of poetry, *Jacklight*, in the parlor one late spring afternoon. It was a decent hideaway for writing because it was the room least inhabited. I recall standing in the doorway, the breeze through the propped-open windows disturbing the precious, reworked pages, the look of fear and amazement on her face that at last this task was done. By the time she wrote her novel, *Love Medicine*, we had cleared the summer kitchen, and day after day she sat in solitude, perched on a green painted bar-stool—found at a yard sale—before a door laid horizontal and used as a table. I read parts of the manuscript in a hammock strung between two trees in the side yard and I can hear the bang of the door as I rushed inside to sing praises of the words, to make my little suggestions, to see her afresh with each unexpected line. In tandem we took turns at a typewriter set on the kitchen table, pounding out draft after draft in those endless days before word processing.

Months later, we were piled together in the car, halfway to the limit of our land and on the way to Hanover for a prenatal visit in anticipation of our first-born child, when John McCauley, coming from the opposite direction, honked his horn to make us stop. Through the rolled-down windows he handed over the fat brown envelope that held the galley set in real type, with a peach cover, soon to be out on its own in the world. We left the motor idling, remained there turning the pages, incredulous and terrified and proud all at the same time.

After *The Beet Queen*, after *A Yellow Raft in Blue Water*, after *Tracks*, after the birth of another daughter and amidst the expectation of a third, Louise moved across the street to a small house we had previously leased in exchange for child care. Actually, "house" doesn't do the story justice. The Smiths immediately previous to us had a firecracker of a scheme—a hotdog stand for snowmobilers. Before they ran out of capital and sold us the property, they had poured a concrete foundation, run in wiring, and secured a variance for the installation of the largest septic tank in Cornish—old timers, twenty years later, still pause their trucks and point out the sight to visitors as part of the standard tour of town.

We finished the building, dividing the structure into three rooms, and over the years an unforgettable array of tenants occupied the premises: a woman who drove a L'Eggs van had her driver's license suspended for D.W.I. She was succeeded by a man who operated a Pepsi truck, and then by a couple seized by a succession of, as they put it, "$100,000" schemes: a car repair operation in our falling-down barn, dog breeding kennels for their mongrel pack, and finally a book about how a small rental home could be "beautified" with ingenuity but practically no cash outlay on the part of the owner.

The single common trait shared by all these people was unapparent during our initial interviews with them, but ultimately, in all cases, surfaced within weeks of occupancy: a passion for motorcycles. Perhaps it was the frustrated spirit of snowmobiles, still haunting the environs, but sooner or later, a morning always came when we were startled out of sleep by the proud rev of an unthrottled engine, the hacking cough of a chrome tail pipe, the haughty snap of a kickstand preparatory to lift-off. Would this obsession infect Louise, we worried, when at last we were financially able to survive without supplementary income and converted the house into her studio? Would the drive to write be replaced by the drive to drive, the call of the tarmac? Would her wardrobe suddenly run to black leather? Would she henceforth insist that our children address her as "Pretty Mama" instead of "Mom"?

Not yet, anyway, and with peace and quiet restored, animals ventured forth from the surrounding woods—wild turkeys, woodchucks, ravens, deer, foxes, and porcupines. A placid skunk established residence beneath the entrance and a blue heron began to fish the shallow pond. Tiny birds built nests in every eave. Within the garland of their song, Louise's second book of poetry, *Baptism of Desire*, was completed and a series of nature essays—to be eventually published as *The Blue-Jay's Dance*—begun.

It was in Cornish we learned, reluctantly and painfully, that our three older adopted children, two sons and a daughter, were each crippled to one degree or another by the lifelong effects of prenatal exposure to alcohol. I recorded our dawning sorrow and frustration in *The Broken Cord*, a book that somehow refused to be written during daylight. I would rise each morning at three or four, release my mind to recollection until the sun rose, and then reread the pages before bed at night.
As with most FAS or FAE victims, the successes of our older children's lives peaked early, around age ten. The family reveries guarded before that invisible marker are happy: beautiful, trusting, loving boys and girl, full of enthusiasm and energy, their futures brimming with promise. And then we watched helpless as, one after the other, they were overtaken, as the balance of their respective lives narrowed toward limiation, veered toward trouble. Their development either plateaued or regressed, their anger and resentment grew at a world that became increasingly incomprehensible to them in its expectations and demands. Now, the resonation of their youthful exuberance—free, hearty, brief as the hour of a mayfly—reverberates through the apple trees around our house like the echo of music.
It was to Cornish that our beloved aunt came to stay, two years past, while receiving daily radiation treatments at a nearby hospital. During those months of uncertainty, of necessary hope and repressed anxiety, Louise and I completed the final drafts of *The Crown of Columbus*, a book we tried to infuse with laughter and optimism as well as meaning. At the end of each day we would retreat to Louise's little house, become Vivian Twostar and Roger Williams for an hour or two, lose ourselves in words and fictions, in the foibles of intellectual geometry and romance.

Home is an ongoing character in our lives. It serves as elder, as friend, as reference, as point of both origin and return, as haven. We absorb its solace even though we pass through it as silently, ultimately as anonymously, as those who preceded us. We leave behind no bronze statues, no markers, only the scars we've made, only the trees we've planted. Three years ago, my grandmother Federal-Expressed from Washington State a branch from her oldest cherry tree, according to her my father's favorite source for pies as a child. One end came swathed in wet paper towels encased in a plastic bag tied with a rubber band. We stuck it in our ground. It rooted. Someday it will drop seeds.

Conversions

O n the road to Damascus, Saint Paul of Tarsus was struck with blinding light and converted to belief in one true God. In more humble and hometown circumstances, I, too, was the victim of a bolt. Only mine occurred in 1961, on the Ninth Street sidewalk on the way to Zimmerman School in Wahpeton, North Dakota, and the bolt itself was unhurled, which meant it hung over me a good many years.

It is impossible to remember back and calculate the order of ideas going through my seven year old brain in order to produce the thought that stopped me cold on that threatening, overcast morning. Whatever they were, I suddenly wondered if God, about whom I'd heard so much, was real. There were already ominous rumors adrift on the Indian School Campus, where my family worked and lived, regarding Santa Claus, the Easter Bunny. So far, however, no one had mentioned God.

I stood for a long moment, before a deep pink house upon which a small white sign was hung advertising the services, within, of a licensed Swedish masseuse. Times were innocent. People went there and just got their shoulders kneaded. I looked up into the sky, regarded the darkening assembly of clouds, and then my heart beat fast. I knew I was about to say something aloud, and I did. When the words came out, I awed myself.

"You're not really up there!" I whispered.

I expected a jag of lightning, a bolt of thunder, some sign of outrage, if not an immediate sizzling direct hit that would, as my cousin convinced me lightning did to humans, turn me to hamburger. But absolutely nothing broke the stillness except, from a distance, the electrical jangle of the first bell.

I was just a year short of making my first confession and receiving Holy Communion, about which I mainly remember the struggle not to lose balance and become overwhelmed by the yellow spots that danced before my eyes, not to faint into the aisles of Saint John's church. For by then I had begun to swoon at every Mass that I attended, always right after the congregation shuffled to the front and received the Host on their tongues. In that hush of suspension, when the priest muttered to himself and everyone was silent and reflective around me, I seemed to feel the clouds pressing down. The ornate chandeliers hung, fragile and immense, above me on linked chains and I would try to keep certain thoughts from entering my mind: How were the lightbulbs changed? What ladders could reach that high? Who in the world had the courage to climb them?

If I visualized a climber on the spindly and impossible rungs, the golden haze would spread, the strength would flood from my limbs, and I would collapse. So over time, and with the help of ordinary events, the days of school and summer that came and went, the warmth of my busy parents, the necessities of fitting in among my classmates, I controlled my fantasies. I stopped thinking things that made me dizzy. I grew up. Years went by and I grew increasingly adept at this, until, finally, at the other end of my undistinguished school career, which was mainly a struggle to fit somehow, anyhow, into the ornate schemata of female social alliances, I could almost congratulate myself on not having thoughts at all.

How else to explain the zeal and determination with which, a decade later as a high school senior, I tried to become the Queen of the Wops?

There are confessions I make, even now, late at night, only to those who love me for myself. The first is the name of my hometown team, the Wahpeton Wops; the second is my short but unforgettable reign as their homecoming queen.

At the time, the fall of 1971, I was terribly proud, ecstatic even when my name was announced over the school P.A. system along with the other members of the Royal Court. It did not occur to me that, should I actually win the title, I'd be queen of an ethnic slur.

Of course, to Wahpetonians, the Wop was a mascot of rather undeterminate smurflike nature. A friend of mine had even constructed a costume to represent the Wops at games. It consisted of a dark purple bedsheet into which eyeholes were cut. Years later, an Italian friend visiting the community was astonished and then pained to hear the words of our defiant song issue from a passing schoolbus . . . *We are the Wops, the mighty mighty Wops, everywhere we go, people want to know, who we are, so we tell them, WE ARE THE WOPS!*

I could tell by the bewildered look in his eyes, the shamed anger, that the word didn't just amuse people but could actually hurt.

I was a long shot for the title because I didn't belong to the popular group of girls, the ones who swung their hair, stood in clumps, slept at each other's houses and vacationed in "DL" (short for Detroit Lakes), and partied. Our school was carefully stratified, relationships between girls were calibrated and maintained. My friends and I were those whom hard work drew together—the yearbook editor, the newspaper columnists, those who took advanced typing, set up scenery for school plays, joined Chemistry Club, and decorated the gym for prom—the serious girls.

These were the days before girl's sports were organized; indeed, we were not allowed to do the splits lest our virginity suffer. Every gym day, we stood in line, and those who had their periods stepped out and, sheepishly, said the word "observing" as though menstruation were a thing happening to our bodies, not ourselves. "Observers" were permitted to sit on the stage and gossip, and the word itself was a euphemism known throughout the school, snickered at when teachers used it in a lecture. Because we girls had no athletic teams or activities to democratize us, as boys did, we were forced to rely for status solely on our grooming, our clothing, and the cultivation of something that I never got the hang of—cuteness.

Cute was a combination of things, not just a certain look, not just money or a quick wit or self-confidence. It also involved, as I now realize, the final suppression of every original thought. Still, after years of trying, I had come no closer to cuteness than that fluke nomination, which, however, decided me in my aspirations. Desperately, wholly, and with a passion beyond myself, I wanted to be elected the Queen.

"This is the greatest challenge of my life," I wrote solemnly in my journal, never realizing that the very act of keeping a journal, of having secret thoughts, was what barred me from cuteness in the first place and made the whole enterprise so difficult. Later in that notebook I meditated on the word "popular" and it came as a kind of revelation that the definition meant, simply, having lots of friends. Lots and lots! Then it also dawned on me that there were many potential friends (voters) in Wahpeton High School that the designated popular girls did not notice in their daily pre-class perambulations through the hallways. So I did notice them. Homecoming candidates did not campaign with posters, with slogans. They were never so crass. Instead, charm was used, constantly applied, full pressure. But where my opponents ricochetted it mainly off each other, I spread around whatever charm I could muster.

The young, for instance: Those innocent ninth graders who did not understand the subtleties of senior class distinctions might welcome a little attention. And how about the wild-eyed junior botanists who discovered North Dakota ditchweed before the widespread use of herbicides? They had a vote apiece, if they remembered to cast it. And the guys who only cared to work on their cars? I'd admire their lifters, their fancy grills. The members of the chess club? I knew (embarrassing admission for a girl at the time) how to play chess. And the choir members, the piano accompanists, the doggedly but somehow unsuccessfully "cute," the earnest "personality girls"—would I, could I, win their votes?

I tried. I became the first populist homecoming candidate, even if nobody else was aware of it. I brought my campaign to the masses and gave up for lost those elite few who would vote for other members of their group no matter what.

I did have one ally on the court, a surprise nominee, like me, but predictable also since she was absolutely gorgeous—tall, with dreamy blue eyes, a rose and cream complexion. Her problem, the reason she was not in the in-group, was that she was somehow too nice to be cute. She blushed constantly and her figure stunned grown men in their tracks. I'd seen it happen on Dakota Avenue, during Krazee Daze, a man dropping a drumstick right out of his hand at the barbecued chicken feed, when she walked past him. But this friend was so nice that she wouldn't have believed it, too kind to have any vaulting ambitions.

Other problems: Royal courtesans required a boy on their arms, and I was thwarted in my first escort idea. I wanted my brother Mark, a junior, to walk down the floodlit aisle with me on Homecoming Night, before the big football game. He was handsome, about my height, too, and a lettered cross country runner. But he did not play football and so was automatically vetoed by the contest organizers, who were strict on protocol.

On the rebound, I chose the person with the broadest based support imaginable. An eagle scout. If I couldn't have a blood relation for support, I would get the whole pack's vote.

I make my plans sound thoroughly premeditated, energetic and ridiculous, but in a way I think of this whole time of my social life as sad. The proof is in my journal, filled with words of angst, of conviction that the prettier and nicer you are, the better the world will treat you, of absolute reliance on female cunning, a learned response that, later in life, would cause me to set my hair with electric steam rollers during the very first stages of labor.

I assumed that if I "looked nice" while delivering my daughter, I would be treated better in the hospital. Perfectly styled hair would dispel pain. Yes, absurd. By the time I was panting and pushing, no one was the slightest bit interested in the upper end of me, least of all myself. I had quickly become so absorbed that I did not even get the chance to comb out my curls. My hair is lumpy in the first pictures of mother and daughter, but I look like I am having thoughts all over the place, and so does she.

As homecoming inexorably neared, the royal gowns were constructed with insane amounts of wrangling. Purple velvet was the material of choice, the style Empire, decorated at the bodice with tiny purple ruffles and a band of hotly contested silver braid. I bought silver lamé bedroom slippers, and planned my coif like an architect. I also began to overeat from nervousness so that, on The Night, the zipper burst and my mother had to sew me into my dress by hand. And then there followed a claustrophobic, blank, uncertain hour in which I wished all of this had never taken place. Standing in the girl's locker room, looking at myself in the mirror, I hardly recognized or much liked the young woman who pushed at her lacquered ringlets.

God should have struck me then, having saved His chance for all those years. It had occasionally crossed my mind that He might have held back because He was, by my own reasoning, All Merciful. At this moment, however, I really deserved no mercy. In a frenzy of ambition I had denied everything but victory. I kept such ideas at a distance by humming Pomp and Circumstance as I walked down the aisle and stood before the dias that my own hardworking friends had lovingly decorated. The stage was all tin foil, purple streamers, and for the royalty, antique wooden chairs made to resemble actual thrones. The auditorium blurred, my parents and sisters and brothers were somewhere out there, and a hush fell as the world waited for the fateful announcement.

There was a strange moment, when it happened, as I felt the crown descend and fit onto my skull. What was happening to me was not completely wonderful, as I had imagined, but rather in a faint way, it was a push to the edge of some unexpected boundary. A proof. If I tried hard enough I could garner things I craved, but I wouldn't be the same once I got them. Nothing, nothing is quite as untarnished as one imagines, except the actual and true exchange of love.

In a photograph of that night, taken by our school photographer and given to me by his daughter, a member of the Wopanin Yearbook staff, I am screaming, "No, no, no!" This is not the picture of a person proud of what she's done, or even very pleased with what's happening. It's an image of a young woman afraid of her own power, soon to be surprised that the crown, which looked so glittery from below the stage last year, is welded from scrap metal and glued with bits of blue glass. The longstem roses, thrust into her arms, bristle now, but by morning they'll be deader than nails.

I should have put the roses in water. I should have done a lot of things. The thorns scratched, but I clutched them as I approached the microphone, and said:

"I'd like to thank the other members of the Royal Court, to say to the football team, 'We're Gonna Win!', to thank my teachers and thank everyone, my family, my friends, and especially the members of the high school band and those of you parents who will be observing . . . (here I stop, in horror, swallow and retrieve myself) . . . the game."

GARRETT HONGO

Kubota

On December 8, 1941, the day after the Japanese attack on Pearl Harbor in Hawaii, my grandfather barricaded himself with his family—my grandmother, my teenage mother, her two sisters and two brothers—inside of his home in La'ie, a sugar plantation village on Oahu's North Shore. This was my maternal grandfather, a man most villagers called by his last name, Kubota. It could mean either "Wayside Field" or else "Broken Dreams," depending on which ideograms he used. Kubota ran La'ie's general store, and the previous night, after a long day of bad news on the radio, some locals had come by, pounded on the front door, and made threats. One was said to have brandished a machete. They were angry and shocked, as the whole nation was in the aftermath of the surprise attack. Kubota was one of the few Japanese Americans in the village and president of the local Japanese language school. He had become a target for their rage and suspicion. A wise man, he locked all his doors and windows and did not open his store the next day, but stayed closed and waited for news from some official.

He was a *kibei*, a Japanese American born in Hawaii (a U.S. territory then, so he was thus a citizen) but who was subsequently sent back by his father for formal education in Hiroshima, Japan, their home province. *Kibei* is written with two ideograms in Japanese: one is the word for "return" and the other is the word for "rice." Poetically, it means one who returns from America, known as the Land of Rice in Japanese (by contrast, Chinese immigrants called their new home Mountain of Gold).

Kubota was graduated from a Japanese high school and then came back to Hawaii as a teenager. He spoke English—and a Hawaiian creole version of it at that—with a Japanese accent. But he was well liked and good at numbers, scrupulous and hard working like so many immigrants and children of immigrants. Castle & Cook, a grower's company that ran the sugarcane business along the North Shore, hired him on first as a stock boy and then appointed him to run one of its company stores. He did well, had the trust of management and labor—not an easy accomplishment in any day—married, had children, and had begun to exert himself in community affairs and excel in his own recreations. He put together a Japanese community organization that backed a Japanese language school for children and sponsored teachers from Japan. Kubota boarded many of them, in succession, in his own home. This made dinners a silent affair for his talkative, Hawaiian-bred children, as their stern *sensei*, or teacher, was nearly always at table and their own abilities in the Japanese language were as delinquent as their attendance. While Kubota and the *sensei* rattled on about things Japanese, speaking Japanese, his children hurried through their suppers and tried to run off early to listen to the radio shows.

After dinner, while the *sensei* graded exams seated in a wicker chair in the spare room and his wife and children gathered around the radio in the front parlor, Kubota sat on the screened porch outside, reading the local Japanese newspapers. He finished reading about the same time as he finished the tea he drank for his digestion—a habit he'd learned in Japan—and then he'd get out his fishing gear and spread it out on the plank floors. The wraps on his rods needed to be redone, gears in his reels needed oil, and, once through with those tasks, he'd painstakingly wind on hundreds of yards of new line. Fishing was his hobby and his passion. He spent weekends camping along the North Shore beaches with his children, setting up umbrella tents, packing a rice pot and hibachi along for meals. And he caught fish. *Ulu'a* mostly, the huge surf-feeding fish known on the mainland as the jack crevalle, but he'd go after almost anything in its season. In Kawela, a plantation-owned bay nearby, he fished for mullet Hawaiian-style with a throw net, stalking the bottom-hugging, gray-backed schools as they gathered at the stream mouths and in the freshwater springs. In an outrigger out beyond the reef, he'd try for *aku*—the skipjack tuna prized for steaks and, sliced raw and mixed with fresh seaweed and cut onions, for *sashimi* salad. In Kahaluu and Ka'awa and on an offshore rock locals called Goat Island, he loved to go torching, stringing lanterns on bamboo poles stuck in the sand to attract *kumu'u*, the red goatfish, as they schooled at night just inside the reef. But in Lai'e on Laniloa Point near Kahuku, the northernmost tip of Oahu, he cast twelve- and fourteen-foot surf rods for the huge, varicolored, and fast-running *ulu'a* as they ran for schools of squid and baitfish just beyond the biggest breakers and past the low sand flats wadable from the shore to nearly a half mile out. At sunset, against the western light, he looked as if he walked on water as he came back, fish and rods slung over his shoulders, stepping along the rock and coral path just inches under the surface of a running tide.

When it was torching season, in December or January, he'd drive out the afternoon before and stay with old friends, the Tanakas or Yoshikawas, shopkeepers like him who ran stores near the fishing grounds. They'd have been preparing for weeks, selecting and cutting their bamboo poles, cleaning the hurricane lanterns, tearing up burlap sacks for the cloths they'd soak with kerosene and tie onto sticks they'd poke into the soft sand of the shallows. Once lit, touched off with a Zippo lighter, these would be the torches they'd use as beacons to attract the schooling fish. In another time, they might have made up a dozen paper lanterns of the kind mostly used for decorating the summer folk dances outdoors on the grounds of the Buddhist church during O-Bon, the Festival for the Dead. But now, wealthy and modern and efficient killers of fish, Tanaka and Kubota used rag torches and Colemans and cast rods with tips made of Tonkin bamboo and butts of American-spun fiberglass. After just one good night, they might bring back a prize bounty of a dozen burlap bags filled with scores of bloody, rigid fish delicious to eat and even better to give away as gifts to friends, family, and special customers.

It was a Monday night, the day after Pearl Harbor, and there was a rattling knock at the front door. Two FBI agents presented themselves, showed identification, and took my grandfather in for questioning in Honolulu. He didn't return home for days. No one knew what had happened or what was wrong. But there was a roundup going on of all those in the Japanese-American community suspected of sympathizing with the enemy and worse. My grandfather was suspected of espionage, of communicating with offshore Japanese submarines launched from the attack fleet days before war began. Torpedo planes and escort fighters, decorated with the insignia of the Rising Sun, had taken an approach route from northwest of Oahu directly across Kahuku Point and on toward Pearl. They had strafed an auxiliary air station near the fishing grounds my grandfather loved and destroyed a small gun battery there, killing three men. Kubota was known to have sponsored and harbored Japanese nationals in his own home. He had a radio. He had wholesale access to firearms. Circumstances and an undertone of racial resentment had combined with wartime hysteria in the aftermath of the tragic naval battle to cast suspicion on the loyalties of my grandfather and all other Japanese Americans. The FBI reached out and pulled hundreds of them in for questioning in dragnets cast throughout the West Coast and Hawaii.

My grandfather was lucky; he'd somehow been let go after only a few days. Others were not as fortunate. Hundreds, from small communities in Washington, California, Oregon, and Hawaii, were rounded up and, after what appeared to be routine questioning, shipped off under Justice Department orders to holding centers in Leuppe on the Navaho reservation in Arizona, in Fort Missoula in Montana, and on Sand Island in Honolulu Harbor. There were other special camps on Maui in Ha'iku and on Hawaii—the Big Island—in my own home village of Volcano. Many of these men—it was exclusively the Japanese-American men suspected of ties to Japan who were initially rounded up—did not see their families again for more than four years. Under a suspension of due process that was only after the fact ruled as warranted by military necessity, they were, if only temporarily, "disappeared" in Justice Department prison camps scattered in particularly desolate areas of the United States designated as militarily "safe." These were grim forerunners of the assembly centers and concentration camps for the 120,000 Japanese-American evacuees that were to come later.

I am Kubota's eldest grandchild, and I remember him as a lonely, habitually silent old man who lived with us in our home near Los Angeles for most of my childhood and adolescence. It was the fifties, and my parents had emigrated from Hawaii to the mainland in the hope of a better life away from the old sugar plantation. After some success, they had sent back for my grandparents and taken them in. And it was my grandparents who did the work of the household while my mother and father worked their salaried city jobs. My grandmother cooked and sewed, washed our clothes, and knitted in the front room under the light of a huge lamp with a bright three-way bulb. Kubota raised a flower garden, read up on soils and grasses in gardening books, and planted a zoysia lawn in front and a dichondra one in back. He planted a small patch near the rear block wall with green onions, eggplant, white Japanese radishes, and cucumber. While he hoed and spaded the loamless, clayey earth of Los Angeles, he sang particularly plangent songs in Japanese about plum blossoms and bamboo groves.

Once, in the mid-sixties, after a dinner during which, as always, he had been silent while he worked away at a meal of fish and rice spiced with dabs of Chinese mustard and catsup thinned with soy sauce, Kubota took his own dishes to the kitchen sink and washed them up. He took a clean jelly jar out of the cupboard—the glass was thick and its shape squatty like an old-fashioned. He reached around to the hutch below where he kept his bourbon. He made himself a drink and retired to the living room where I was expected to join him for "talk story," the Hawaiian idiom for chewing the fat.

I was a teenager and, though I was bored listening to stories I'd heard often enough before at holiday dinners, I was dutiful. I took my spot on the couch next to Kubota and heard him out. Usually, he'd tell me about his schooling in Japan where he learned judo along with mathematics and literature. He'd learned the *soroban* there—the abacus, which was the original pocket calculator of the Far East—and that, along with his strong, judo-trained back, got him his first job in Hawaii. This was the moral. "Study *ha-ahd*," he'd say with pidgin emphasis. "Learn read good. Learn speak da kine *good* English." The message is the familiar one taught to any children of immigrants: succeed through education. And imitation. But this time, Kubota reached down into his past and told me a different story. I was thirteen by then, and I suppose he thought me ready for it. He told me about Pearl Harbor, how the planes flew in wing after wing of formations over his old house in La'ie in Hawaii, and how, the next day, after Roosevelt had made his famous "Day of Infamy" speech about the treachery of the Japanese, the FBI agents had come to his door and taken him in, hauled him off to Honolulu for questioning, and held him without charge for several days. I thought he was lying. I thought he was making up a kind of horror story to shock me and give his moral that much more starch. But it was true. I asked around. I brought it up during history class in junior high school, and my teacher, after silencing me and stepping me off to the back of the room, told me that it was indeed so. I asked my mother and she said it was true. I asked my schoolmates, who laughed and ridiculed me for being so ignorant. We lived in a Japanese-American community, and the parents of most of my classmates were the *nisei* who had been interned as teenagers all through the war. But there was a strange silence around all of this. There was a hush, as if one were invoking the ill powers of the dead when one brought it up. No one cared to speak about the evacuation and re-location for very long. It wasn't in our history books, though we were studying World War II at the time. It wasn't in the family albums of the people I knew and whom I'd visit staying over weekends with friends. And it wasn't anything that the family talked about or allowed me to keep bringing up either. I was given the facts, told sternly and pointedly that "it was war" and that "nothing could be done." "*Shikatta ga nai*" is the phrase in Japanese, a kind of resolute and determinist pronouncement on how to deal with inexplicable tragedy. I was to know it but not to dwell on it. Japanese Americans were busy trying to forget it ever happened and were having a hard enough time building their new lives after "camp." It was as if we had no history for four years and the relocation was something unspeakable.

But Kubota would not let it go. In session after session, for months it seemed, he pounded away at his story. He wanted to tell me the names of the FBI agents. He went over their questions and his responses again and again. He'd tell me how one would try to act friendly toward him, offering him cigarettes while the other, who hounded him with accusations and threats, left the interrogation room. Good cop, bad cop, I thought to myself, already superficially streetwise from stories black classmates told of the Watts riots and from my having watched too many episodes of *Dragnet* and *The Mod Squad*. But Kubota was not interested in my experiences. I was not made yet, and he was determined that his stories be part of my making. He spoke quietly at first, mildly, but once into his narrative and after his drink was down, his voice would rise and quaver with resentment and he'd make his accusations. He gave his testimony to me and I held it at first cautiously in my conscience like it was an heirloom too delicate to expose to strangers and anyone outside of the world Kubota made with his words. "I give you story now," he once said, "and you learn speak good, eh?" It was my job, as the disciple of his preaching I had then become, Ananda to his Buddha, to reassure him with a promise. "You learn speak good like the Dillingham," he'd say another time, referring to the wealthy scion of the grower family who had once run, unsuccessfully, for one of Hawaii's first senatorial seats. Or he'd then invoke a magical name, the name of one of his heroes, a man he thought particularly exemplary and righteous. "Learn speak dah good Ing-rish like *Mistah Inouye*," Kubota shouted. "He *lick* dah Dillingham even in debate. I saw on *terre-bision* myself." He was remembering the debates before the first senatorial election just before Hawaii was admitted to the Union as its fiftieth state. "You *tell* story," Kubota would end. And I had my injunction.

The town we settled in after the move from Hawaii is called Gardena, the independently incorporated city south of Los Angeles and north of San Pedro harbor. At its northern limit, it borders on Watts and Compton, black towns. To the southwest are Torrance and Redondo Beach, white towns. To the rest of L.A., Gardena is primarily famous for having legalized five-card draw poker after the war. On Vermont Boulevard, its eastern border, there is a dingy little Vegas-like strip of card clubs with huge parking lots and flickering neon signs that spell out "The Rainbow" and "The Horseshoe" in timed sequences of varicolored lights. The town is only secondarily famous as the largest community of Japanese Americans in the United States outside of Honolulu, Hawaii. When I was in high school there, it seemed to me that every *sansei* kid I knew wanted to be a doctor, an engineer, or a pharmacist. Our fathers were gardeners or electricians or nurserymen or ran small businesses catering to other Japanese Americans. Our mothers worked in civil service for the city or as cashiers for Thrifty Drug. What the kids wanted was a good job, good pay, a fine home, and no troubles. No one wanted to mess with the law—from either side—and no one wanted to mess with language or art. They all talked about getting into the right clubs so that they could go to the right schools. There was a certain kind of sameness, an intensely enforced system of conformity. Style was all. Boys wore moccasin-sewn shoes from Flagg Brothers, black A-1 slacks, and Kensington shirts with high collars. Girls wore their hair up in stiff bouffants solidified in hairspray and knew all the latest dances from the slauson to the funky chicken. We did well in chemistry and in math, no one who was Japanese but me spoke in English class or in history unless called upon, and no one talked about World War II. The day after Robert Kennedy was assassinated, after winning the California Democratic primary, we worked on calculus and elected class coordinators for the prom, featuring the 5th Dimension. We avoided grief. We avoided government. We avoided strong feelings and dangers of any kind. Once punished, we tried to maintain a concerted emotional and social discipline and would not willingly seek to fall out of the narrow margin of protective favor again.

But when I was thirteen, in junior high, I'd not understood why it was so difficult for my classmates, those who were themselves Japanese American, to talk about the relocation. They had cringed, too, when I tried to bring it up during our discussions of World War II. I was Hawaiian-born. They were mainland-born. Their parents had been in camp, had been the ones to suffer the complicated experience of having to distance themselves from their own history and all things Japanese in order to make their way back and into the American social and economic mainstream. It was out of this sense of shame and a fear of stigma I was only beginning to understand that the *nisei* had silenced themselves. And, for their children, among whom I grew up, they wanted no heritage, no culture, no contact with a defiled history. I recall the silence very well. The Japanese-American children around me were burdened in a way I was not. Their injunction was silence. Mine was to speak.

Away at college, in another protected world in its own way as magical to me as the Hawaii of my childhood, I dreamed about my grandfather. Tired from studying languages, practicing German conjugations or scripting an army's worth of Chinese ideograms on a single sheet of paper, Kubota would come to me as I drifted off into sleep. Or I would walk across the newly mown ball field in back of my dormitory, cutting through a street-side phalanx of ancient eucalyptus trees on my way to visit friends off campus, and I would think of him, his anger, and his sadness.

I don't know myself what makes someone feel that kind of need to have a story they've lived through be deposited somewhere, but I can guess. I think about *The Illiad, The Odyssey, The Peloponnesian Wars* of Thucydides, and a myriad of the works of literature I've studied. A character, almost a *topoi* he occurs so often, is frequently the witness who gives personal testimony about an event the rest of his community cannot even imagine. The sibyl is such a character. And Procne, the maid whose tongue is cut out so that she will not tell that she has been raped by her own brother-in-law, the king of Thebes. There are the dime novels, the epic blockbusters Hollywood makes into miniseries, and then there are the plain, relentless stories of witnesses who have suffered through horrors major and minor that have marked and changed their lives. I myself haven't talked to Holocaust victims. But I've read their survival stories and their stories of witness and been revolted and moved by them. My father-in-law, Al Thiessen, tells me his war stories again and again and I listen. A Mennonite who set aside the strictures of his own church in order to serve, he was a Marine codeman in the Pacific during World War II, in the Signal Corps on Guadalcanal, Morotai, and Bougainville. He was part of the island-hopping maneuver MacArthur had devised to win the war in the Pacific. He saw friends die from bombs which exploded not ten yards away. When he was with the 298th Signal Corps attached to the Thirteenth Air Force, he saw plane after plane come in and crash, just short of the runway, killing their crews, setting the jungle ablaze with oil and gas fires. Emergency wagons would scramble, bouncing over newly bulldozed land men used just the afternoon before for a football game. Every time we go fishing together, whether it's in a McKenzie boat drifting for salmon in Tillamook Bay or taking a lunch break from wading the rifles of a stream in the Cascades, he tells me about what happened to him and the young men in his unit. One was a Jewish boy from Brooklyn. One was a foul-mouthed kid from Kansas. They died. And he *has* to tell me. And I *have* to listen. It's a ritual payment the young owe their elders who have survived. The evacuation and relocation is something like that.

Kubota, my grandfather, had been ill with Alzheimer's disease for some time before he died. At the house he'd built on Kamehameha Highway in Hau'ula, a seacoast village just down the road from La'ie where he had his store, he'd wander out from the garage or greenhouse where he'd set up a workbench, and trudge down to the beach or up toward the line of pines he'd planted while employed by the Work Projects Administration during the thirties. Kubota thought he was going fishing. Or he thought he was back at work for Roosevelt, planting pines as a windbreak or soilbreak on the windward flank of the Ko'olau Mountains, emerald monoliths rising out of sea and cane fields from Waialua to Kaneohe. When I visited, my grandmother would send me down to the beach to fetch him. Or I'd run down Kam Highway a quarter mile or so and find him hiding in the cane field by the roadside, counting stalks, measuring circumferences in the claw of his thumb and forefinger. The look on his face was confused or concentrated, I didn't know which. But I guessed he was going fishing again. I'd grab him and walk him back to his house on the highway. My grandmother would shut him in a room.

Within a few years, Kubota had a stroke and survived it, then he had another one and was completely debilitated. The family decided to put him in a nursing home in Kahuku, just set back from the highway, within a mile or so of Kahuku Point and the Tanaka Store where he had his first job as a stock boy. He lived there three years, and I visited him once with my aunt. He was like a potato that had been worn down by cooking. Everything on him—his eyes, his teeth, his legs and torso—seemed like it had been sloughed away. What he had been was mostly gone now and I was looking at the nub of a man. In a wheelchair, he grasped my hands and tugged on them—violently. His hands were still thick and, I believed, strong enough to lift me out of my own seat into his lap. He murmured something in Japanese—he'd long ago ceased to speak any English. My aunt and I cried a little, and we left him.

I remember walking out on the black asphalt of the parking lot of the nursing home. It was heat-cracked and eroded already, and grass had veined itself into the interstices. There were coconut trees around, a cane field I could see across the street, and the ocean I knew was pitching a surf just beyond it. The green Ko'olaus came up behind us. Somewhere nearby, alongside the beach, there was an abandoned airfield in the middle of the canes. As a child, I'd come upon it playing one day, and my friends and I kept returning to it, day after day, playing war or sprinting games or coming to fly kites. I recognize it even now when I see it on TV—it's used as a site for action scenes in the detective shows Hollywood always sets in the islands: a helicopter chasing the hero racing away in a Ferrari, or gun dealers making a clandestine rendezvous on the abandoned runway. It was the old airfield strafed by Japanese planes the day the major flight attacked Pearl Harbor. It was the airfield the FBI thought my grandfather had targeted in his night fishing and signaling with the long surf poles he'd stuck in the sandy bays near Kahuku Point.

Kubota died a short while after I visited him, but not, I thought, without giving me a final message. I was on the mainland, in California studying for Ph.D. exams, when my grandmother called me with the news. It was a relief. He'd suffered from his debilitation a long time and I was grateful he'd gone. I went home for the funeral and gave the eulogy. My grandmother and I took his ashes home in a small, heavy metal box wrapped in a black *furoshiki*, a large silk scarf. She showed me the name the priest had given to him on his death, scripted with a calligraphy brush on a long, narrow talent of plain wood. Buddhist commoners, at death, are given priestly names, received symbolically into the clergy. The idea is that, in their next life, one of scholarship and leisure, they might meditate and attain the enlightenment the religion is aimed at. "*Shaku Shūchi*," the ideograms read. It was Kubota's Buddhist name, incorporating characters from his family and given names. It meant "Shining Wisdom of the Law." He died on Pearl Harbor Day, December 7, 1983.

After years, after I'd finally come back to live in Hawaii again, only once did I dream of Kubota, my grandfather. It was the same night I'd heard HR 442, the redress bill for Japanese Americans, had been signed into law. In my dream that night Kubota was "torching," and he sang a Japanese song, a querulous and wavery folk ballad, as he hung paper lanterns on bamboo poles stuck into the sand in the shallow water of the lagoon behind the reef near Kahuku Point. Then he was at a work table, smoking a hand-rolled cigarette, letting it dangle from his lips Bogart-style as he drew, daintily and skillfully, with a narrow trim brush, ideogram after ideogram on a score of paper lanterns he had hung in a dark shed to dry. He had painted a talismanic mantra onto each lantern, the ideogram for the word "red" in Japanese, a bit of art blended with some superstition, a piece of sympathetic magic appealing to the magenta coloring on the rough skins of the schooling, night-feeding fish he wanted to attract to his baited hooks. He strung them from pole to pole in the dream then, hiking up his khaki worker's pants so his white ankles showed and wading through the shimmering black waters of the sand flats and then the reef. "The moon is leaving, leaving," he sang in Japanese. "Take me deeper in the savage sea." He turned and crouched like an ice racer then, leaning forward so that his unshaven face almost touched the light film of water. I could see the light stubble of beard like a fine, gray ash covering the lower half of his face. I could see his gold-rimmed spectacles. He held a small wooden boat in his cupped hands and placed it lightly on the sea and pushed it away. One of his lanters was on it and, written in small neat rows like a sutra scroll, it had been decorated with the silvery names of all our dead.

Reconstruction

I t's been almost twenty-five years since I wrote the following story, or essay, or confession. It was complete then, but it no longer is. After you've read it, I'll try to explain what I mean by that. It's called "Nigger Knocking."

It is an odd truth that most anything that *is* in one's childhood is accepted as the natural order of things. A chuck-hole in the street is there because it is supposed to be there, and to think of it as a accident, as a piece of carelessness by your elders, is out of the question. Causality is assigned only in retrospect. And so I suppose the varieties of nigger-knocking should be remembered as they were, and as I accepted them—and I must be left to attempt to absolve my guilt in private insurrections.

Nigger-knocking, like fighting to bring blood, was a phenomenon of my freshman year in high school. In that larger world after grammar school, my social inadequacies were mercilessly revealed: Success and status, with a kind of Alabama populism, were denied to both ends of all spectrums. The rich and the poor, the liberal and the klansman, the hood and the intellectual—none thrived in a pseudo-genteel world that suspected any distinct shape. So with a terrible new fear of distinction, I resolved to become invisible. One could not be a Baptist, I discovered right away, and be a success. Baptistism was too conspicuous, too raw and reminiscent of the too recent immigration of one's grandparents into Birmingham from the mining camps. I was willing enough to change, and there was at least no problem of alternatives. Catholicism was unheard of; Episcopalianism was an affectation; Presbyterianism was alien and Tennesseeish. Methodism, the middle ground, was the only choice. So I converted, covering as best I could my other inadequacies: My father wasn't a professional man—a fireman, mailman, draftsman, clerk, or the like—my mother smoked Camels, worked, and didn't plant flowers, and I had never been nigger-knocking.

But no matter, all that. Since nigger-knocking, the initiation ceremony, was a regular Sunday night ritual after Methodist Youth Fellowship, it was a problem whose solution was implied in conversion, and the others I could lie about. Having been nigger-knocking, I would have proven myself, and would become a true good old boy, my ticket to invisibility.

The connection between Methodism and nigger-knocking was, it seems now, a reasonable enough one. Birmingham Sunday nights were nightmares of boredom. Baptist fervor could spend at least enough energy to make them tolerable, but Methodist restraint was only a catalyst. At nine o'clock on a summer Sunday evening, with a father's car on hand (Methodist fathers had cars), seduced by the pulpy Southern night and keyed up from a weekend of dates with don't-even-french-me Methodist girls, some sort of action was a gut necessity. And since everything in town was blue-lawed, and the quarters were near, and nigger-knocking had about it the air of Cause as well as excitement, it was a logical choice of outlets. Not that there was any real danger involved, of course, since we were always near enough to a white section for easy refuge, and few blacks had cars anyway. But there was the joy of the hunt about it.

Southerners have always enjoyed hunts, as both literature and fact witness. And nigger-knocking, the urban adaptation of this instinct, enjoyed quite the same universality, complexity of weapons, and ingenuity as hunting. Methodism, nigger-knocking, and I enjoyed only a brief partnership, but one that lasted long enough to allow me to learn most of the refinements of the art (although I never did learn the religion, being driven away for drinking beer in public before I even had the chance to memorize all of the Apostles' Creed). As best I can recall, the equipment and techniques of a typical Sunday night foray were roughly as follows.

We would gather behind the church, usually in a group of four or five—four being the ideal number, since everyone could then have his own window and no one would feel slighted. The most basic and available ammunition, rocks, could be laid in on the spot from around the unpaved parking lot, so that before we left, each of us had his own reserve stores. But the more sophisticated weapons were what we were really after, and these demanded more careful shopping.

There were, for instance, clay pots to be swiped from the florist's yard on Seventy-seventh Street, as a start. These had the ballistic advantage of throwing well and shattering loudly, so that even if there were no direct hits, the target was sufficiently terrified for us to feel the sally successful. (The image of three black girls, neat in white starched Sunday dresses, leaping and screaming and covering their faces as the pots shattered all around them, distills itself from one particularly success- ful run. And as we sped away, whooping, we thought it all the better when, vanishing behind us, the biggest girl screamed, "You motherfuck- ers, you motherfuckers, you rotten motherfuckers . . ." Methodist girls would never say that; it was proof of white superiority.) Pots *could* be used to smash windshields, too, but rocks would do as well and were more popular, since even if we missed the windshield a rock could still leave a good dent.

Next to rocks and pots, water balloons were probably our most popu- lar munition. They were relatively harmless—or at least not potentially fatal—and they admitted to interesting variations. They could, when thrown from a car at forty miles an hour, stun with a direct hit, and produce a grand fallout area even with a miss. For Panama suits there were balloons with ink in the water, and for girls, the ultimate: piss in the water. If it were a water night, in fact, one of the more daring raids could involve luring a black man to the window to ask directions, then opening up on him with water guns full of pure piss or ink. (Again an image: an old man with a cane, alone, caught from behind as he walked past a weedy vacant lot. With rebel yells and unusual accuracy, three out of four balloons direct hits, and the old man toppling slowly and stiffly, like a radio tower in a storm, into the weeds. And with no look of sur- prise at all on his face, before the distance and dust behind us on the dirt road wiped him out of sight.)

But probably the subtlest, most accurate and imaginative weapon of all was the simplest and easiest to use. Automobile radio aerials were no trouble to steal, and could be carried in a ready position almost in- visibly, and discarded instantly if need be. Usually the honor of their use was accorded the hunter riding shotgun, since he could conceal one most easily by holding it against the car in the roof drain channel, and still leave it untelescoped and ready for use.

The only problem with aerials was finding proper quarry. The object, of course, was to locate game walking close enough to the street, since the aerial's reach was a bit limited. And one had to be accurate enough to avoid necks and faces, since that would be *too* cruel at forty or fifty miles an hour. At any rate, when a target was found, all that was needed was a wrist movement, and the aerial would be extended perpendicular to the car, back high, and would hit with a resounding splat that could draw blood from a bare back, and raise, we were sure, fine welts on a covered one. It would, as I remember from one expedition, even stagger a large male protected by a leather jacket.

There were, of course, other refinements, though for the most part they were only serendipitous variations on the major traditions. Becoming too visionary in seeking new methods could in fact often do more harm than good—as I remember from the night we decided to add psychological nuance to our hunt. Police sirens, we all knew, tended to produce immediate and varied responses from blacks. So that evening we cruised through the downtown quarters strewing the usual balloons, pots, and rocks, but jazzing things up by doing our best siren imitations all the while. It was an effective thing to do, granted, but stupid. We were stepping at last on forbidden turf.

They had apparently kept us in sight for some time, and as we pulled into an alley behind the Thomas Jefferson Hotel to take a piss, they caught us, literally, with our pants down—or at least unzipped. Their white car hissing suddenly around the building left us with no choice but to freeze. "Oh, God," one us moaned. "Oh, God. Shit creek."

"Y'all boys stay where you are," came the driver's voice from behind the headlights, with a voice as deep and authoritative as the Methodist God's must be.

The lights went out, two doors slammed, and the cops, both as tall and slow as fathers, sauntered over to us. They hitched their gun belts up and, with terrifying flashlights, silently gave us a once over.

"Zip them pants up," the driver ordered.

We complied, fumbling.

"You boys pretty good at sirening, ain't you," the other cop said.

"Having a good time," the driver rumbled. "We seen it all."

"Yessir," I finally said, doing my best to look sheepish. "I guess."

"Bout to get your asses in a sling for it, I'll tell you that for one thing," the driver said. "We been keeping up with you."

"Yessir."

"Yessir, hell. Y'all ever one disgust me, you know that? Damn flat disgust me."

None of us answered him. "Yessir," I said just before it was too late to. He still waited. "Why's that, sir?"

"Why? Goddamn, boy. How'd you like your mama to walk by and see somebody pissing on the street like that? Like a animal!"

"Disgusting," his partner said.

Later, churches were bombed, and there were assassinations.

In the late 1960s, I could count on a gallery of images to help me tell that story. When the name Birmingham was mentioned, almost everyone in my audience could summon black-and-white TV pictures of police dogs, water hoses, a bombed-out church holding the bodies of four little girls in Sunday dresses. Or even more currently, color images of a hotel walkway in Memphis, of the chaos surrounding a dying Martin Luther King.

On one level, that's why it—let's call it an essay—is incomplete now: The images have fuzzed and faded with time, like pictures of dead relatives you never knew in an old scrapbook. Millions of people in this country can't even call them up at all, unless they might have run across them as brief clips in a PBS documentary, or have seen Hollywoodized versions of them. The essay is a body without clothes. To finish it, I'll have to redress some things—and, yes, the pun is intended.

On another level, the essay is incomplete because it raises a question it doesn't answer: how I got from taking part in the events it describes, to writing about them in a way that, I hope, exposed not only their intrinsic horror, but their even more horrible potential. In answering that question, I might well be describing a journey that some others took with me. In its largest sense, however, the essay—and the journey—will never be finished, not by me, in my lifetime.

In the 1950s, Birmingham was still the largest company town in America, kept that way by U.S. Steel and other like companies, who knew that encouraging different industries to move in meant increasing competition for workers. The city had no history other than that, no traditions that didn't somehow involve punching a time clock in a steel mill or a foundry or a mine. Perhaps precisely because of that, it became the most fiercely Southern city of them all, even though it hadn't even existed until after the Civil War.

Because it was a new city, and it was in the deep South, and it was primarily working class, it grew up as an anomaly. From the terrible poverty of the post Civil War South, hundreds of thousands of white dirt farmers and ex-slaves fled into it as, years later, they would flood into Detroit and Los Angeles after another war. Segregation, therefore, could be included as part of every pattern in every fabric of life in the city: Black and white immigrants began as strangers to each other, and could be kept that way. When huge tracts of housing for workers were built, you simply built black tracts, and off someplace else, white tracts. When you built changing houses in the new mines and mills, you built black ones and white ones. When you divvied up the jobs in those mines and mills, you created white jobs (which paid more) and black jobs. When unions at last worked their ways into town, you organized white unions and black ones—from the start. When you built new churches, you didn't build them the old way, with balconies for blacks in the rear, you had the luxury of building all white and all black churches.

It was supposedly the New South. It was the Old South—with a vengeance.

I don't know what black children learned in school: I was never in a black school, nor was a black child in mine. I know that we were taught that most whites had been good masters to their slaves, and that the reason many blacks had the same last names as ours was that, out of loyalty to their masters after the War, the ex-slaves had simply adopted their master's names. We learned all of Stephen Foster's songs, put on mistrel shows, and when we needed to learn the tune to "The Battle Hymn of the Republic," we sang it to these words:

> I'm a lover of the Southland, living down in Alabam,
> In the fairest of her counties, in her favored Birmingham
> Garden spot of dear old Dixie, she has made me what I am,
> And Birmingham's my home!
>
> Dixie, Dixie, how I love you!
> Dixie, Dixie, how I love you!
> Dixie, Dixie, how I love you!
> And Birmingham's my home!

Lincoln's birthday wasn't a holiday; Jeff Davis's was. We still heard stories from our grandparents of Sherman's monstrous legions, and knew well the excesses of the depraved carpetbaggers and their black factotums during Reconstruction. Once, in the sixth grade, our teacher had us all stand up according to our Protestant denomination: No one stayed seated.

Garden spot of dear old Dixie, she had made most of us what we were as teenagers in the 1950s, and had done it well. Birmingham had created a natural order for us that, so far as we could tell, no one except a few misled blacks and Yankee agitators questioned. And in one sense we weren't far off the point.

Why should the owners of the mines and mills object to all that cheap black labor, especially when its threat helped keep white wages down, too? Why should white workers object to unions and job classifications that kept their wages higher than blacks'? Why, we were asked, should blacks object to jobs that gave them a princely living compared to what they would make picking cotton, especially given the meager range of their natural talents and ambition? Who was to tell us different?

We knew no blacks our own age: That had been carefully arranged by Birmingham's seamless segregation. Would old George at the Pure Oil station on the corner, who called my sister and me Miss Nancy and Mr. Bobby, and himself a "poor old nigger," tell us? Would the preachers at our white churches? Would Betty Davis, who walked the five miles to our house to feed us and clean while our parents worked, tell us? What books could we go to, when none that would have questioned our certainties were in the libraries we used, much less our schoolrooms?

It was a closed system, not populated by evil church-bombers but by hard-working people for the most part, people who had fought the Nazis and helped liberate concentration camps, who gave to charities, loved their children, did well by their parents. When I was in the eighth grade, on his way from work my father saw a black teenager hit by a train, "knocked right out of his shoes," my father said. He picked the bleeding boy up in his arms and rushed him to the hospital, saving his life, he was later told. Yet until my father's death a couple of years ago, he felt certain that mixing of the races was unnatural.

As a good man, he had saved one black child's life, but he, and for a time I, too, supported a system whose consequences were the deaths of other black children. He abhorred those deaths. He, like millions of others of his time, simply missed the connection.

He was the kindest man I ever knew. I could go to him for moral guidance on every subject save one.

Less than ten years after the time I wrote about in "Nigger Knocking," I stood in the muddy schoolyard of St. Jude's Academy in Montgomery, Alabama, with several hundred other people. It was the last night of the Selma-to-Montgomery march, which still stands as the emblem of the civil rights movement in the South, and a black friend had invited me to come to the closing rally with him.

I wish I could say that some blinding vision, some road-to-Damascus conversion, had brought me there. That would provide considerably more drama than the facts. But in truth the road had been longer and not terribly dramatic, and millions of other white Southerners took it with me. What had happened between nigger-knocking and St. Jude's was hardly blinding, but it did involve enlightment, a slow process of bringing light into darkness.

For me, the "natural order" had fallen apart, and all around me in the South its racial prescriptions and restrictions were literally falling apart, too. The destruction of it in my own life seemed to have been almost startling simple, in one respect. I went away to school—a still segregated one, but where there were people who said it shouldn't be. I sat on a bus beside a black man, and nothing bad happened. I ate in the same restaurants with black people, and nothing bad happened. I went into the Air Force, lived with black people, took orders from black people, and nothing bad happened. I *talked* with black people, and good things happened.

The "natural order" had simply revealed itself to be a fraud, ipso facto, self-evidently and completely. It was based on fraudulent assumptions, used fraudulent logic, proclaimed fraudulent truths. Not much of a revelation, I know, to someone raised outside Birmingham's closed system, though a few ex-seminarians and a South African have told me they understand.

By the closing night of the Selma march, in the summer of 1965, I had long come to accept that utterly bogus nature of everything I had been taught to believe about race, and had, I hoped, exorcised it from my life. But I had done so privately; my family, I knew, would see me as betraying "my own people." A few wrenching, pointless arguments with my parents had shown me in which wilderness direction attempts at conversion would lead.

I was still in the Air Force that summer, having been sent to a small base in Montgomery from overseas to mark time for the few months until my enlistment was up. So while I was *in* Alabama, I wasn't *of* it anymore, I thought; I had special status. As my friend and I walked up to the school past charter buses, newsvans, and cars with mostly out-of-state plates, I felt at ease knowing that the harried, college-aged men, black and white, who were moving constantly around the perimeter of the school talking gravely into walkie-talkies weren't guarding against *me*. They were *like* me; I was one of them, of the good guys.

It had been raining almost constantly since the marchers had left Selma days before, and the mud in the schoolyard was deep enough to suck up good-sized children without a ripple. In its middle, floodlights lit a platform stage, and as we worked through the crowd, I spotted Harry Belafonte near the front of it, fiddling with a microphone. I recognized Martin Luther King in a group farther back on the stage, then Peter, Paul, and Mary, then Dick Gregory, as relaxed as people who weren't even famous. All around the stage, stretching to the edge of the light, campfires burned low and sleeping bags littered the mud. Inside a few of them were muddy people. In a yellow schoolbus, we found Floyd Patterson, sprawled along the back seat and looking exhausted, all alone.

In spite of the mud and the weariness, however, the atmosphere was one of energy at rest, at peace with itself for the job it had done, and ready to move on to the next one. There was confidence in the speeches, in the music, in the faces of the people. Great God, I remember thinking as the night deepened, have I ever been part of anything more . . decent than this?

Then, near the end of the rally, as the speeches and music were winding down, my friend ran across someone he knew, a local black guy about our age. He introduced us by campfire light, first names only, and we smiled and shook. I asked him what his last name was.

"Oh, just Frank's enough," he said.

"Hey," I said, and nodded toward my friend. "I'm with him. It's OK."

His smile slowly disappeared, and he looked away from me. "Just Frank."

My friend touched my shoulder. "Dr. King's starting to speak," he said in a voice as flat as his eyes were. "Let's get closer." He turned to Frank. "Catch you, man."

Frank met his eyes only for a moment, mumbled, "Right," and walked off toward the darkness. My friend and I worked our way through the crowd toward the platform. We didn't look at one another or speak.

I don't remember what Martin Luther King said that night. I remember instead the awkwardness of standing next to my friend while King spoke, and I remember feeling both shocked and fatuous–both accurate. How stupid, I thought, to make the easy assumption that because I had changed, everything had changed. Those guys with walkie talkies had a *reason* to be out there. Frank had a *reason* not to trust me. Maybe, only a few years ago, he'd caught a rock, a flower pot, a water balloon from a carload of white kids—not redneck crackers who blew up churches, but clean-cut kids in a reasonably new Chevy or Olds. Kids who could have been me, who didn't even have to hate him.

While King spoke, and the reverberations of his voice, bouncing from loudspeakers and brick walls, filled that pulpy Alabama night, I thought how hard the trip here had been for all those muddy marchers, and how easy for me. There were dues to pay, and these people around me had been paying them. And would continue to. I hadn't even finished filling out an application yet.

When he finished talking, King asked all of us to link arms, and as a close to both the evening and the march, join him in singing "We Shall Overcome." Though I knew the words from all those black-and-white images on TV, I'd never sung them. That night I did, surrounded beyond the schoolyard by the same Alabama darkness that had invited me out nigger-knocking once, an invitation I'd accepted. On one side of me, our arms joined, was a black woman about my mother's age, who would have been given food in our house, but would have had to eat it in the kitchen. On the other side was my friend, who could not have been my friend ten years before. I felt an immense sense of gratitude to both of them.

The choruses seemed to go on for a very long time, as we swayed together with the rhythm. And each time the slow, dignified, sure music brought us back around to the words,

> We shall overcome, we shall overcome,
> Deep in my heart, I do believe,
> Oh, we shall overcome, someday,

I knew very clearly, very precisely, that my definition of *we* was changing forever.

Not too long after that, I could, and had to, write "Nigger Knocking." And now have come back to it. And will again, until my dues are paid up, until we do overcome that old Birmingham lie, someday.

ERICA JONG

How I Got to Be Jewish

News of America travelled quickly around the European shtetls. Word was that even if the streets of the "Golden Land" weren't paved with gold, at least a Jew had a chance. —Jeff Kisseloff, You Must Remember This (1989)

The older we get, the more Jewish we become in my family. My mother's father declared himself an atheist in his communist youth, so we never belonged to a synagogue or had *bat mitzvahs*. But we wind up in Hebrew homes for the aged and in cemeteries with Hebrew letters over the gates. Thus does our heritage claim us—even in America, our promised land. In my family, if you're still protesting you're Unitarian, you're just not *old* enough. (I refer, of course, to one of my ex-husbands, who having married a *shiksa*, worships at the local Unitarian Church. That will change, I predict.)

My father, on the other hand, sends money to Israel and carries around a card that supposedly will expedite his admission to Mt. Sinai Hospital, and after that Heaven, identifying him as a Big Donor. This is the sort of thing he would have done riffs on in his vaudeville days. Now my daughter *Molly* does those riffs. The young are cruel. They *have* to be to supplant the old. The old are such a burden, so territorial, so inclined to hold on to their money. The young have to be tough to make it at all.

After all, what does the ritual of circumcision say to a Jewish son? "*Watch out. Next time I'll cut off the whole thing.*" So Jewish boys are horny, but also full of fear about whether their cocks will survive their horniness. Alexander Portnoy is the archetypal good Jewish boy. The good Jewish boy and the bad Jewish boy inhabit the same skin—if not the same foreskin. Jewish girls are luckier. Their sexuality is less damaged—whatever those jokes about dropping emery boards may imply. Girls are allowed to be sexual as long as they keep it in inside the family. Marriage is sacred as long as you marry an oedipal stand-in. Jewish adultery is an oxymoron. We read Updike for that. Jewish men who cheat end up like Saul Wachler or Woody Allen. In big trouble. Even Jewish lesbians are required to have silverware and bone china from Tiffany's. Jewish lesbians are required to fall in love with women who remind them of their mothers. And, in today's feminist times, are doctors or lawyers.

How did I get to be Jewish?—I with no religious training? Jews are made by the existence of anti-Semitism—or so says Jean-Paul Sartre, who knew. And despite myths to the contrary, there is *plenty* of anti-Semitism in America (otherwise we'd be saying "Next year in Oyster Bay or Grosse Pointe" instead of "Next year in Jerusalem"). But American anti-Semitism takes the clever form of class snobbery. Let me show you what I mean.

We say that America is a classless society, but really it is not. It's just that our class distinctions are so much subtler than those of other countries that sometimes we don't even see them as class distinctions. They are uniquely American class distinctions and they follow us all our lives. We go happily into the Hebrew Home for the Aged, having learned that where aging and death are concerned, only our own kind *want* us. When we're young and cute, we can hang out with *goyim*—but as the sun goes down, we revert to *knishes* and *knaydlach*. We do *mitzvahs*—of the sort that I have done by getting my aunt into the Hebrew Home.

When I was growing up in a New York that seemed dominated by Jews whose parents or grandparents had fled from Europe, I never consciously thought about Jewishness. Or about class. And yet invisible barriers ruled my life—barriers which still stand.

Even in childhood I knew that my best friend Glenda Glascock, who was Episcopalian and went to private school, was considered classier than me. We lived in the same gloomy Gothic apartment house near Central Park West. We both had parents who were artists. But Glenda's name ended with *cock* and mine did not. I knew that names ending in *cock* were intrinsically classier.

What was my name anyway?

My father was born Weisman and became Mann. My mother was called Yehuda by her Russian Jewish parents when she was born in England, but the intransigent Englishman in the registry office had changed it first to Judith and then to Edith ("good English names")—leaving the resultant impression that Jews were not even allowed to keep their own names. The dominant culture around our (mental) ghetto required names that did not *sound* Jewish or foreign. That left a strong impression too.

There were categories of Americans in our supposedly egalitarian country and I did not belong to the better (as in "better dresses") category.

Glenda did. Her last name bespoke this. Even her nickname—Jewish girls did not have nicknames like Glennie then—bespoke this. And yet we were close as twins, best buddies, in and out of each other's apartments—until we took a bath together one day and she accused me of making peepee in the bathwater because that was "what Jews did." I was outraged, having done no such thing. (Unless my memory censors.)

"Who says they do that?"

"My mother," said Glennie confidently.

So I reported this conversation to my parents and grandparents and mysteriously my friendship with Glennie cooled.

She went off to private school. I did not. I was in some "Intelligently Gifted Program" at P.S. 87 on 77th Street and Amsterdam Avenue—a great Victorian pile in those days, with girls' and boys' entrances. There I discovered other class stratifications. The closer you lived to Central Park West and the "better" your building, the more classy you were. Now I had status. Below me were poorer Jewish kids whose parents had fled the Holocaust and lived in lesser buildings further west, Irish kids who lived in tenements side streets, and the first sprinkling of Puerto Rico kids to arrive in New York. They lived in other tenements on West Side Storyish side streets. In the forties, New York was far from being racially integrated. I did not meet black kids from Harlem until I went to the High School of Music and Art where talent, not neighborhood, was the qualification. The only African-Americans we met—called Negroes then—were servants. In childhood, my world was Jewish, Irish, Hispanic—with Jews lording it over everyone else.

The WASP kids were, by this time, off in private school meeting their own kind so they could run the CIA, go to Yale, and rule the world (like George and Barbara Bush). Jewish kids did not go to private school in *that* New York—unless they were superrich, had disciplinary problems, or were orthodox.

I figured out pretty soon that in my school I was high class, but that in the world I was not. The kids on television shows and in reading primers did not have names like Weisman, Rabinowitz, Plotkin, Ratner, or Kisseloff. Certainly not Gonzales or O'Shea. There was another America out there in televisionland and we were not part of it. In that other America, girls were named things like Gidget and boys were named things like Beaver Cleaver. Our world was not represented—excepted when the credits rolled by.

Kept out of this *proper* America, we learned to control it by reinventing it (or representing—as in agent). Some of our parents already did this as actors, producers, or writers, so we knew this was a possible path for us. Others were businessmen, or artists-turned-businessmen—like my father. The point was: We were outsiders longing to be insiders. In those days, we knew that Princeton and Yale might not want us unless we were rich enough. We knew our initials were ICM, not CIA. We knew we were not born into the ruling class, so we invented our own ruling class. Mike Ovitz, not George Bush. Swifty Lazar, not Bill Clinton.

How much the world has changed since the forties! And how *little*! Except for Henry Kissinger, who has changed these laws of class and caste? Not even Mike Ovitz. What you see your parents do is what you think *you* can do. So are we defined, designed. Since my father was a songwriter-musician turned importer, my grandfather a portrait-painter, my mother a housewife and portrait-painter, I just *assumed* that I would do something creative. I also just *assumed* that I would graduate from college, and live in a "good building" forever. I also assumed that I would never turn out to be anything like those American families I saw on TV.

My family was fiercely proud to be Jewish, but not religious—unless our religion was buying new English Maryjanes at Saks and English leather-leggings, and velvet-collared Chesterfield coats at de Pinna. We were dressed like little English princesses and I understood that this was the class to which we aspired.

Dress tells you everything about aspiration. I hated the damned leather leggings but had to wear them because Princess Elizabeth and Margaret did. How did *they* get to be Princesses of the Jews? Better not ask. It was tacitly understood just as it was understood that Glascock was a better name than Weisman (or even Mann).

I smile writing all this. I am trying (clumsily, I fear) to re-enter that world of 1940s New York with its "air-cooled" movie palaces (complete with towering matrons and wrapper-strewn children's sections, its striped awnings on apartment buildings in summer, its bus transfers, its candy stores, its big marble lunch counters that sold the most delicious bacon lettuce and tomato sandwiches and fresh-dipped ice cream cones).

Gone, gone forever. But just as sunlight on a series of paving stones or the taste of tea-soaked cake returned Proust* to his halcyon childhood, I sometimes stop on a streetcorner in New York and am taken back to the forties. The smells do it. The mouths of the subway stations still, on occasion, blow a blast of cotton candy/bubble gum breath, mixed with sweat and popcorn, with piss and (its precursor) beer—and inhaling deeply I am taken back to being six years old, standing in the subway, staring at a forest of knees. In childhood, you feel you'll never grow up. And the world will always be incomprehensible. First you are all mouth, then you have a name, then you are a member of a family, then you begin to ask the hard questions about better/worse which are the beginnings

* Note to reviewer. Of course I am not comparing myself to Proust. I know my place. If I don't, I'm sure you'll remind me.

of class-consciousness. Human beings are naturally hierarchical beasts. Democracy is not their native religion.

It was in Junior High that my world opened up beyond 77th Street and the West Side. Because my parents and I were both terrified of the violence of the local junior high, I went to private school—a deliciously comic place where the paying students were mostly Park Avenue Jews and the scholarship students mostly WASPs from Washington Heights whose parents were professors, clergy, missionaries.

The teachers were genteel and Waspy like the scholarship students, and they had proper American-sounding names like the TV people. The school had been started by two redoubtable New England ladies named Miss Birch and Miss Wathen who were probably lovers—but in those days we called them spinsters. One of them looked like Gertrude Stein, the other like Alice B. Toklas. They pronounced "shirt" as if it had three i's in the middle, and they pronounced poetry as if it were poy-et-try. I knew this was classy. I knew this was WASP.

At Birch-Wathen, most of the Jewish kids were wealthier than me. They lived on the East Side in apartments hung with expensive art and some of them had German names. They went to Temple Emmanuel—my nephews now call it Temple Episcopal—and took dancing and deportment—what an old-fashioned word!—at Viola Wolf's. Again my sense of class was up for grabs. With my Russian grandparents and my West Side bohemian home, I didn't fit in with these kids either. And the scholarship kids all stuck together. I thought them snotty—though now I realize they must have been scared to death. The paying students got bigger allowances—and some of them came to school in chauffeured Cadillacs, Lincolns, or Rollses. That must have seemed daunting to kids who rode the subway. It seemed daunting to me. Cliques splintered us. The Park Avenue kids stuck with their own kind. The scholarship kids did the same.

I floated between the two groups, never knowing where I belonged, now shoplifting at Saks with the rich kids (the richer the kids, I learned, the more they shoplifted), now wandering up to Columbia with one of the scholarship kids (whose parents were professors).

I felt I belonged nowhere. Ashamed that my father was a businessman, I used to wish he were a professor. If you couldn't have a name that ended with cock, you ought to have a Ph.D. at least.

When High School began, I joined still another new world—a world that was racially mixed and full of kids from the ghetto. Chosen for their talent to draw or sing or play an instrument, these kids were the most diverse I'd ever met. Their class was talent. And like all insecure people, they shoved it in your face.

It was in high school that I began to find my true class. Here the competition was not about money or color or neighborhood but about how well you drew or played. At Music & Art, new hierarchies were created, hierarchies of virtuosity. Was your painting in the semi-annual exhibition? Were you tapped to perform in the orchestra, or on WQXR? By now we all knew we did not belong in televisionland America—and we were *proud* of it. Being outsiders was a badge of merit. We had no teams, no cheerleaders, and the cool class uniform was early beatnik: black stockings, handmade sandals, and black lipstick for the girls; black turtlenecks, black jeans, black leather jackets for the boys. Stringy hair was requisite for both sexes. We experimented with dope. We cruised the Village hoping to be mistaken for hipsters. We had found our class at last.

Many of us rose to the top of it. I count among my high school classmates pop singers, television producers, actors, painters, novelists. Many are household names. A few earn tens of millions of dollars a year. Most went to college—but it was not finally a B.A. or a Ph.D. that defined our status. It was whether or not we stayed hot, were racing up the charts with a bullet, were going into syndication, on the bestseller list, into twenty-five languages. Even the professors envied *this* status: money and name-recognition level all classes in America. Hence the obsession with celebrity. Even in Europe you can pass into the "best" circles, though the rules of class are quite different there.

Having done my time with the Eurotrash set, I'm always amazed at how an aristocratic name still covers a multitude of sins in Europe. In England, in Germany, a lord or ladyship, a gräf or gräfin, a von or zü, still carries weight. Italians are more cynical about titles. The classiest friends I have in Italy may be *contesse, marchesi,* or *principi,* but they're too cool to advertise it. They'd rather be famous for a hit record, or a big book. But, go to the chic watering spots—St. Moritz, for example—and membership in the best clubs still goes by family, not by individual achievement. Walk into the Corviglia Club and say you're Ice T. or Madonna. Honey—you won't get in, while any old Niarchos or von Ribbentrop will.

Many of my European friends still inhabit a world where name and old money can become a positive *bar* to achievement. There is so much *more* to do than merely work. If you have to be in Florence in June, in Paris in July, in Tuscany in August, in Venice in September, in Cologne in October, in New York in November, in St. Bart's in January, in St. Moritz in February, in New York in March, in Greece in April, in Prague in May—how on earth can you take (*let alone* hold) a job? And the fittings. And the balls. And the spas. And the dryings out! As a husband of Barbara Hutton's once asked: "When would I have *time* to work?" True class means never even having to *talk* about it. (Work, I mean).

Americans are intrinsically unclassy—so the Jews almost fit in. All we talk about is our work. All we want to do is make our first names so recognized we don't even *need* a last (Ms. Ciccone is the ultimate American here). We believe in change as fervently as Europeans believe in the status quo. We believe that money will buy us into heaven (with heaven defined as toned muscles, no flab at the chin, interest on interest, and a name that cows maitre d's). Once that's accomplished, we can start to save the world: plow some money into AIDS research, the Rain Forest, political candidates. Maybe we can even run for office ourselves! (Witness Mr. Perot.) In a society where pop name recognition means everything, celebrities are more equal than everyone else. But celebrity status is hell to keep in shape (just like an aging body). It needs a host of trainers, P.R. experts, publishers, media consultants. Plus you have to keep turning out new product—and new scandal. (Witness Woody Allen.) Maybe the reason celebrities marry so often is simply to keep their name in the news. And maybe—whether they know it or not—they create scandal to hype their movies. (Again, witness Woody Allen, né Alan Konigsberger.)

Ah—we are back to the question of Jews and names. Can we keep our names? As long as we keep them *hot*. Otherwise, we also have to change them. We may have, as political theorist Benjamin Barber says, "an aristocracy of everyone," but not everyone can be hot at once. Thus, the drive for class becomes as relentless and chronic in America as the diet. No matter how hot you are, you're always in danger of growing cold.

It's a lot like mortality, isn't it? No wonder *carpe diem* is our motto. This is what makes America such a restless country and her top-class celebrities so insecure.

Ah friends, I long to be born into a membership in the Corviglia Club. But I suspect I never would have written any books.

Did you ever wonder why Jews are such relentless scribes? You may have thought it was because we are people of the book. You may have thought it was because we come from homes where reading is stressed. You may have thought it repressed sexuality. Yes, yes—all that is true. But I submit the *real* reason is our need to constantly define our class. By writing, we reinvent ourselves. By writing we create pedigrees. Some of my heroines are West Side, New York Jewish girls like me. But the heroines I love the best—*Fanny* in *Fanny Hackabout-Jones*, and Jessica in *Serenissima*—are to the manor born, good little equestriennes, and you can bet they have high cheekbones. Fanny grew up at Lymeworth, Lord Bellars' country seat. Jessica grew up on the Upper East Side of Manhattan, in the Golden Rectangle. Her pedigree was very gin and country club. Why does a West Side kid like me invent such heroines? Am I trying to escape from my *schmearer-klesmer* class? Interestingly enough, my heroines always escape too. Fanny runs away from her aristocratic upbringing, becomes a highway woman, a whore in a brothel, and a pirate-queen. Jessica leaves the Upper East Side for Hollywood! And both of them come to regret it, and find their final happinesses back in their own backyards. The heroines who are *apparently* more like me—Isadora Wing and Leila Sand—change their status, or else establish it, through creative work. I guess my writing tells me something that I didn't even consciously know about myself: I write to give myself a class, to invent my name, and then to leave myself a country seat!

I suspect the process is not so different with other writers—however uninvolved with class their books may seem. Saul Bellow's heroes start out as drifters and end up professors. But his very best picaresque hero, Henderson the Rain King, is a WASP to the manor born who goes to Africa and embraces his multiculturalism, thereby finding his true identity. Philip Roth's heroes are equally concerned both with questions of class and with questions of Jewishness. Though they themselves are almost always Jewish, they aspire to fuck their way into WASPdom—a familiar gambit for American Jewish (male) creators. We could call it the Annie Hall Syndrome. Surely Woody Allen defined it forever when his autobiographical hero, sitting at Annie Hall's midwestern dinner table, amid the WASPs, suddenly sprouts *payess* and a big black hat.

The archetypical Jewish American fear! If we eat *trayfe*, we may suddenly grow payess! Perhaps the reason Jews in America have adopted Thanksgiving as their own special holiday is that we hope by claiming the Pilgrims as our fathers, we will fool the rest of America too!

Howard Fast is a perfect example here. His best books, the fictional *April Morning* and nonfictional *The Jews*, are oddly connected. They both chronicle rootless people. They testify to the fact that Americans, like Jews, must constantly define themselves.

A Jew may wander from Egypt to Germany to America to Israel, picking up different languages and hair and eye color, but he remains a Jew. And what is a Jew? A Jew is a person who is safe *nowhere* (i.e., always in danger of growing *payess* at inopportune times!) A Jew is a person who can convert to Christianity from now to Doomsday, and still be killed by Hitler if his mother was Jewish. This explains why Jews are likely to be obsessed with matters of identity. Our survival depends upon it.

Americans, too, are obsessed with defining identity. In a melting pot culture, where aristocratic titles are considered laughable (witness Count Dracula or Count Chocula, as kids are introduced to him—a breakfast cereal), we must constantly test the limits of identity. Andy Warhol's remark that in the future everyone will be famous for fifteen minutes, delineates the quintessential American dilemma. We can become famous, but perhaps not *stay* famous. And once having known that fame, how will we live out the rest of our lives? More to the point, how will we ever get into the Hebrew Home for the Aged?

Many American lives seem doomed by Warhol's definition. Remember George Bush struggling to stay president against the historical tide? Or Stephen King aspiring to top all three bestseller lists at once? Or Bill Clinton wiring the White House to become its own media network? American can never rest. They can never join the Corviglia Club and amuse themselves skiing down into the picturebook village. The grace of their skiing is *never* enough in itself enough. They must always climb back on the chairlift and do it again, do it again, do it again.

I see that the Corviglia Club has become my symbol of aristocratic *sprezzatura*—a lovely Italian word which means the art of making the difficult look easy. Perhaps I select that image because it evokes a world of blessed people who do not have to *do* anything, they only have to *be*. I long for such status as only an American Jew can. How nice to have an entrée into the world that cannot ever be revoked. How nice to be *born* into an identity.

My yearning is real even though I know dozens of people born into such identities who use them as excuses to become drug addicts and drifters. I know it is not easy to be noble and rich. Yet, like F. Scott Fitzgerald, something in me insists: "The very rich are different from you and me." Fitzgerald tested that hypothesis in Gatsby, showing the carelessness of the very rich to life, limb, and love. And yet the longing *remains* in American writers. Perhaps that's why that this rather slight, beautifully written American novel has become a bona fide classic. It embodies the American dream of identity and class.

The jumped-up bootlegger, Jay Gatz, dreams of a world where he wouldn't have to *work* to be Gatsby. And that is still the primal American dream. Even lotteries play to it, promising houses and yachts. Rootless by definition, we dream of roots.

American novelists are usually good examples of this. The first thing they do after a bestseller is to buy a house and land. Alex Haley bought a farm in the south. He didn't become a slave-owner, of course, but he became a landowner. Gore Vidal settled in a villa in Ravello fit for an Italian aristocrat. Arthur Miller bought a Connecticut farm for a Connecticut Yankee. So did Philip Roth.

I'm no different. After *Fear of Flying*, I bought a house in New England. Believing that when writers died and went to heaven, heaven was Connecticut, I bought a piece of that literary state. To a writer, used to making up the world with ink and a blank piece of paper, roots and gentrification are the same thing. And you get them both with *words*.

Rootless people always gravitate to those fields of endeavor where class has to be repeatedly self-created. Perhaps that's also why creativity flowers during periods of great social turmoil and often among former underclasses. Perhaps that's what draws Jews to the word and the image. If you think of the vitality of Jewish-American writing in the fifties and sixties, the vitality of women's writing in the seventies and eighties, the vitality of African-American writing in the eighties and nineties, you see that there is a clear connection between change of status and productivity. As a group becomes restless and angry, it produces writers.

I may dream of what I would have done with my life if I had been born on a plantation with plenty of coupons to clip, but probably my literary ambitions would have never blossomed. Perhaps I would have written inscrutable poetry, readable only by advanced graduate students. But most likely the anxiety and aggression needed to finish a whole book would have been denied me. For writing is not just a question of talent with words, but of drive and ambition, of restlessness and rage. Writing is hard. The applause never comes at the end of the paragraph. The rotten tomatoes often come at publication time. And given the hours put in, the money isn't all that good. Counting taxation and time spent, most writers make less than dental hygienists.

But we don't do it for the money. We do it to give ourselves a class.

When I finished college at Barnard, I went on to graduate school, simply because I couldn't think of what *else* to do. I knew I wanted to be a writer, but I wasn't yet sure I had the *zitsfleish* to sit down and write a whole book. While I waited to mature a little, I studied English literature. Somehow I knew it would come in handy.

But the period I studied—the rollicking eighteenth century engraved by Hogarth—was the one that saw the birth of America, of women's rights, and of the novel. The novel started as a low-class form, fit only for serving maids, and it has been the only literary form where women distinguished themselves so early with such excellence that even the rampant misogyny of literary history cannot erase them. Ever wonder about women and the novel? Women, like any underclass, depend for their survival on self-definition. The novel permitted this—and pages could still be hidden under the embroidery hoop.

From the writer's mind to the reader's there was only the intervention of printing presses. You could stay at home, yet send your book abroad to London—the perfect situation for women. In a world where women are still the second sex, many still dream of becoming writers so they can work at home, make their own hours, nurse the baby. Writing still fits into the interstices of a woman's life. Through the medium of words, we have hopes of changing our class. Perhaps the pen will not always be equated with the penis. In a world of computers, our swift fingers may yet win us the world. One of these days we'll have class. And so we write as feverishly as only the dispossessed can. We write to come into our own, to build our houses and plant our gardens, to give ourselves names and histories, inventing ourselves as we go along.

YUSEF KOMUNYAKAA

Monticello

Beverly, Harriet, Madison,
    & Eston, all with sandy red hair
        & listed in Jefferson's

Farm Book. The deepest doors
    open in the soil & flesh, rooms
        designed to lead into others

& alcoves where a kiss
    is stolen. The man's fingers
        flash through chenille

like Virginia rails into November
    afternoons. Their wet sighs
        seethed into poems by Thomas

Moore & William Cullen Bryant.
    Black Sal, Monticellian Sally,
        a ditty sang to Yankee

Doodle. This dome-shaped
    room, did they kiss & hug
        here, gazing out over

luteous fields, whose round windows
    changed their world? Did lies
        coagulate to the roof

of the mouth like stalactites
    of blood? This architect,
        a central protagonist

in the passion that tiptoed & turned
    glass doorknobs at the midnight hour.
        How about the whispered

disagreements, the cries
    that made everyone flesh,
        where did they go,

are they still spiralling
    around the aurora borealis?
        Words: *I advance it,*

therefore, as a suspicion
    only, that the blacks . . .
        are inferior to the whites

in the endowments of body
    & mind. As he talked & dined,
        did the women ever face

each other like Philomela
    & Procne, a nightingale
        & swallow on some forked

branch in their minds? If
    we try hard enough, he's still
        at his neo-classical desk

musing, but we know his hands
    are touching a breast,
        brushing away abstractions.

Rendezvous

Her fingertips touch his
    left palm, her grin
        like an image stolen

from Fellini's *La Strada.*
    "Don't you ever wonder
        where the Chinese

were in the '60s, when you
    & Chavez were out there facing
        dogs & billyclubs,

don't you wonder?" Her voice
        is somewhere between Atlanta
                & Boston. Her blue eyes

linger on his Ibo features. "Family
        is what makes them so strong,"
                he says, smoothing out

the napkin. "They've been here
        since the early railroad days,
                maybe longer. I don't

know." The waitress brings their
        chardonnay. Before she turns
                to leave, he notices the dragons

on her green silk jacket
        in some tussle of light
                across her breasts.

"I'm fascinated by all this
        Chinese stuff. *Instructions*
                for Court Ladies,

Du Fu, I read what I can
        get my hands on, anything,"
                she says. A tiger fish

kisses the aquarium with its dark
        nose, eyes like two bulbous
                bloodstones. On a wall

to the right is a representation
        of Yan Liban's *The Emperor Wu*
                of the Northern Zhou.

"Have you ever seen a black
        waitress in places like this?" She's always
                so quiet at the office—

does he really know her, can the night
        go anywhere? "I like your dress,"
                he says. She nods & smiles.

The waitress serves their sweet
        & sour prawns, snow peas,
                & curry chicken. Blue

bowls of steamed rice. "At Mount Zhiju
        there's an inscription about black-haired
                people. Oh, well, I don't

know what I'm thinking about
        these days." She pops
                a prawn into her mouth.

The hot curry tingles
        his tongue. A cube of onion
                tastes like something sinful.

"Have you ever heard of Ah
        Coy & Sam Gin?" He shakes
                his head, knitting his brows.

"I'm just fooling. Just
        being silly tonight."
                He notices the poster

of *Monkey Creates Havoc*
        in Heaven tacked beside the kitchen door
                where ginger & garlic

steam up from hot sesame oil
        like ghosts. "I used to come here
                last year. Every Friday.

The place hasn't changed.
        We used to sit right here
                in this booth. Paul

& me." He wishes she'd stop
        talking. Those flowers
                beside the cash register

are too damn red to be
        real. "That was before he
                started dating a Chinese girl.

I think her family has money."
The waitress refills their water
glasses. "Are you sure

you want to talk about this?"
he says. She picks at
the snow peas with her fork.

"They come in here all the time.
But I bet he'd just die if he
saw us here."

Anthony, Isabella . . .

Sunny or cloudy, Blue
Monday or Fat Tuesday, the afternoon
still stunk like a bloated whale

on Chesapeake Bay as Captain Jope
& his English pilot Marmaduke
steered that Dutch man of War

into Jamestown. This prefiguration of Ahab
hijacked & looted a Spanish ship
of Africans on the high seas,

& was in port to trade twenty women,
men & children for food. August heat
lulled cormorants on the hemp-laced

rigging. But even in hell, after cancer
began to take root & eat the air,
there was still a love story,

an Anthony & Isabella, someone
just hurting to birth
a William Tucker—

a tobacco planter's name,
some promise to heal the earth
beneath their feet.

Henry the Navigator

He dreamt of latitude, his mind
    on constellations & astrolabes,
        some maritime lodestar

jostling the magnetic field
    & mystifying the sextant,
        pulling him beyond

the sight of land. Carvels
    piled with a mapmaker's desire
        & atlases blessed by God,

he pushed on till they could
    taste the salty lustre
        of precious metals,

till the sea vultures
    turned around at midday
        to backtrack their hunger

to Portugal. The seamen
    spoke to the sky & crossed
        themselves. Gold

drew the ships onward, beyond
    the brain's dark continent
        that no tallow lantern

or prayer could throw light upon.
    Shadows of towering sails
        like monsters across

the grassy dawn. They dropped
    anchors . . . tiptoed. Suddenly
        the whole village bloody

& moored to a pagan sky. Against
    bruised horizon the day
        looked like two hundred

& thirty-five silhouettes
    shackled to the earth,
        durable as twilight on iron.

Other Worlds

Hair & skin damp with holy water
    & blood, we slouched to the Algarve
        like yoked oxen. Money

& religion etched our faces along
    every trampled path as far north
        as Lisbon. We made love

& died to transfuse Spain & Portugal.
    Ringed inside like trees, our new names
        tumored under another language.

We were no longer Sudanese, Ibo,
    or Senegalese. Only field workers,
        stevedores & masters of every other

maddening curse. Our wide-hipped women
    pulled muted voices out of lusty
        soil, but somehow we shouldered

the night with names like Pedro
    Alonso Niño & Estevanico. We were
        footsteps alongside Cortes, Pizarro,

Balboa, Menendez, & DeSoto. Back then
    you could look at us & see the naked
        stare of the enemy beneath

our eyelids. We trekked virgin forests
    as if to force blood to sing forbidden
        chants, to outrun the power of sugar.

MICHAEL KRAUS

Prague: A Poem Reappearing

Though it is often said that Prague's ambiance and culture reflect the coexistence and mutual influences of three cultures, Czech, German, and Jewish, the word coexistence does not tell the whole story. To be sure, before the Second World War, on Prague's cobbled streets and inside apartment houses German was spoken nearly as often as Czech. And the interplay of those cultures defined the cultural milieu that shaped Franz Kafka's life and work in the first two decades of this century. But today his work is widely read at least in part because his art anticipated the horrors of twentieth century totalitarianism. My home, Prague of the nineteen fifties and sixties, was a place that had already lived through those horrors.

While Hitler destroyed much of the European Jewry, including nearly 200,000 of Czechoslovakia's Jews, he also put an end to the Czech-German cohabitation. Because in 1938 the vast majority of Czech Germans rallied behind Berlin and demanded unification with Germany, and most ardently embraced his wartime causes, the Czechs decided after the war to let their Germans have their way. Spurred on by German atrocities and humiliations directed against the Czechs in the course of 1938–45, the Prague government carried out a sweeping wave of mass deportations, expelling nearly 3 million Sudeten Germans from Bohemia into Germany.

There was, however, a close connection between the plight of the Germans, deemed collectively guilty, and the fate of the postwar democracy. By backing what was euphemistically called the "population transfer," Stalin saw to it that the Czech Communists were put in charge of distributing the formerly German property among their own loyalists and, largely as a result, were firmly ensconced in power by 1948. Though this version of ethnic cleansing enjoyed the support of the Great Powers, it also rendered the Czechs, much like the Poles across the border, dependent on Moscow's deadly embrace to protect them from the neighboring Germans.

So by the time I was born in the last week of the decade of the nineteen forties, Bohemia's capital was, thanks to Hitler, equally devoid of Jews and Germans, including, of course, Prague's German Jews, like Kafka. Just as the physical demise and the forcible exit of the peoples who for many decades coexisted within Prague's walls, more or less peacefully, would irretrievably change the city's nature, it was bound to change the survivors as well.

My parents were survivors in more ways than one. My father, a five-year veteran of half a dozen German concentration camps, was one of a few thousand Jews remaining. Strangely enough, for a long time, neither myself, nor my siblings, knew he was Jewish. I say strangely enough because his parents, his brother, and countless relatives perished in Auschwitz, and that was no secret. On the contrary, growing up, the five kids in our family felt surrounded by places like Neungamme, Dachau, Terezienstadt, or Buchenwald, the concentration camps where father was held during the war, and we knew a lot about these things, or so we thought, if only because in 1946 he wrote *The Death Factory*, one of the first books about Auschwitz. Besides, all of his friends came from "there," wearing proudly those numbers tattooed in blue on their arms. "It's a number to heaven," father would explain, smiling, as if referring to some kind of a cosmic phone directory.

The truth was that his friends, almost exclusively, were fellow inmates, survivors from hellholes, and their shared horrors created bonds that cemented their friendship. Whenever they gathered, which was about once a week, they talked behind closed doors, beyond our reach. Theirs was a world truly beyond anyone's reach. So it happened that I assumed most of my youth that what Czeslaw Milosz has called the "concentration universe" was more or less part of every Czech adult's experience, indeed of every European's, since we felt quite European. So I never associated my grandparents' one-way transport to Auschwitz as being caused by anything other than the war, and concluded that wars were terrible, and were best to be avoided. And since my government spent a lot of time speaking out against war, I felt secure in the 1950s that we, the "people's democracy" of Czechoslovakia, were on the right side of things, though I did not confide my feelings about this to anyone.

While there were several reasons in the 1950s why my father's Jewish roots were understated in our home, the chief among them was probably the Communists, or, more precisely, their officially sponsored anti-Semitism. On Stalin's mad orders in the waning years of the dictator's paranoia, they turned harshly anti-Israeli and anti-Semitic. In November

1952, just before my third birthday, Prague Communists hanged a dozen of their own top leaders, nearly all Jewish, including Rudolf Slansky, the party's General Secretary, singling out their Jewish, "uprooted cosmopolitan" heritage as the main source of their putative treachery. And to drive the anti-Semitic message of terror home, they broadcast the trial live on the radio, so that the entire nation could witness and appreciate "people's justice" in action.

While I don't remember listening to it, I would not rule out that I sat on my grandfather's lap, as I often did, taking it in on some deeper level. My grandfather, a tall, upright man, was a farmer and a devout Catholic. When in September 1938 my mother wanted to marry outside her faith, she needed his blessing, and he gave it on the condition that the children would be brought up in the Church. September 1938 was not a good time to get married. Earlier that summer, my father was called up into the army to defend the country, but returned home soon along with the rest of the Czechoslovak army, which never got to fire a shot. As far as most Czechs were concerned, the Second World War started with the Munich Agreement of September 1938, which gave Hitler the Sudentenland, the border regions largely populated by the Germans. What made Munich all the more bitter to the Czechs was that the deathblows were administered by France and Great Britain, the supposed allies and democracies.

But my parents got married anyway. Their honeymoon did not last long, for Hitler, in violation of the Munich Agreement, occupied the country in March 1939, and in May 1940, my father was arrested for supplying a shortwave radio transmitter to the resistance. And while his subsequent five years as a prisoner of the Gestapo did not inspire any faith in him, father kept his part of the bargain after the war, accepting that his children would grow up as Catholics. So that was the other reason why his own Jewish roots remained hidden from the consciousness of our childhood. Moreover, because he came from an assimilated family, and because he was arrested on account of his resistance activities, rather than his Jewish origin, his own roots may have receded from his consciousness as well.

My mother, already with child, and barely having enough sustenance for herself, spent the war years sending food packages to him and his parents, to places like Auschwitz, which was rumored to be sulfur mines. Most of such supplies would not reach him, though from some camps he was allowed to write a postcard. The only formulation permitted was something like: "I am well, and don't need anything." I recall how my parents would, quite absurdly, argue years later as to whether the packages were a waste or not. They were, my father claimed, but mother wondered why he didn't let her know. But he did let her know, father insisted, he wrote postcards, and meant what they said. "Next time you had better make it clear," mother would say. This was my parents' way of treating war like a normal phenomenon.

Thinking that war is something everyone could experience, that you might end up in a concentration camp, and that the choice you make in your profession is what could determine whether you survive, is how we grew up. There was a hierarchy of careers in terms of survival prospects, and you should think ahead. Some professions were definitely out: Lawyers, for example, died first in Auschwitz, and if law is what you were thinking about, you were as good as dead. What you needed was something practical, a profession that would make you strong, and, if possible, exposed to bad weather, so you'd get used to it while you could. Being a locksmith or a farm hand was more promising. Father's ability to persuade was quite meager, for both my brothers became actors, and both sisters were destined to be teachers. In his survival scheme actors and college teachers were near the bottom. So what we became was mostly mother's influence.

While being Jewish was nothing to brag about in Prague of the 1950s, being Catholic was not a winning proposition either. After all, we were growing up in a land that already had an official religion, communism, which was, quite logically, intolerant of other religions. That was why our religious ties were kept subterranean. I learned to read and write by way of copying passages from the Bible during the summers we spent in the country under the tutelage of my staunchly Catholic aunt, whose husband was killed in May 1945 by one of the last bullets the Nazis fired. She insisted that I be an altarboy in my spare time, and while I had my communion and even confirmation, this was something one never talked about, even to one's friends. On the contrary, in Prague mother instructed us, as she dressed us for church in the best clothes we had on Sunday mornings, to be prepared to lie about our destination. We were going to visit our uncle, she explained we should reply, in case our neighbors wanted to know why we were all spiffed up. I never was bothered by the tension embedded in my mission—going to church to learn to respect the truth, but to lie about it, if I had to. Obviously, there were truths and higher truths, and the highest ones were defined by my mother.

The Sunday masses were followed by Wednesday sessions of the Young Pioneers, a youth organization for grade schoolers, which taught us to celebrate Lenin and his friends. Two photographs preserved in my album tell the story of my early youth. One shows an eleven year old after his first communion, a big candle in his hand, his face appropriately tuned to the weightiness of the occasion; the other shows a nimbler figure in a white shirt and a red scarf, smiling in front of a statue of Lenin, this being obviously a ceremony to celebrate one's induction into the happy world of Young Pioneers. Both are photographs of me.

The wars, hot and Cold, scattered our family across the globe. Of my father's relatives, everyone perished except for four cousins, and three of them had soon left for America. My mother's brother ran away to Bogotá, Colombia, when the Communists took over. From the point of view of the ruling authorities, people who chose to abandon the land of socialism were traitors, and a cloud of suspicion descended upon their relatives in Prague. So the story of the family diaspora was yet another realm we tried to protect against the outside world. Here, we could succeed only up to a point. Invading our realm, Communist bureaucrats produced countless questionnaires on the subject of family profiles, which they would use to decide such matters as access to higher education or who deserved a better apartment. I saw my mother agonize over them late into night, finding ways of having a brother abroad, but giving him the right niche. From time to time, a package would come from Bogotá or New York, and as we assembled to open it, finding chewing gum and second-hand clothes, a delicious aura of exotic foreign lands would spread through our home and, despite the closed borders, take us away on a dreamy journey to New York.

Growing up in the Communist world, where parents are kept in check by the Party, which controls their children's future, one is taught early to distinguish what is for private and for public consumption. My parents spoke German whenever they needed to make sure we couldn't understand. How ironic it seems in retrospect that they spoke the language of their tormentors to deny us the knowledge of things that could harm us all. So whispers behind the closed doors, family confidences camouflaged in German, the chain of secrets we were taught to keep from the outside world, the domain of confidences our parents hid from us to preclude us from divulging them to the Party, all these provided a protective shield in the face of the biggest secrets of them all—those kept from us by the Party. Periodically one would find out something or other one was not supposed to know, some delicious crumb falling one's way, making life immediately exciting, if not dangerous. These chains of confidences comprised the world of my childhood, a fast track in learning about the subtleties of the human predicament.

Given how easy it was in the early 1950s to rub out people like Slansky, it was not too difficult to try to rub culture bare as well. Since Communism was not only a system of power, but also an attempt to create a new man, it had its important culture-transforming aspirations. Though never realized in full, the culture-molding impulse was an important, if not central, aspect of Communist schooling and education. And if the goal was the creation of a new society based on new values, it was essential that the old ways of doing things be unlearned, the established values undone, and the cultural heritage of my parents eradicated. Libraries were purged of books, like Kafka's, containing nefarious influences, writers had to be re-educated, and those that couldn't be, silenced, the educational system redesigned in accordance with Soviet norms. Cities and streets were renamed to reflect the new heroes embraced by the Party.

In this fashion, Stalin and his Czech followers in the 1950s attempted a cultural cleansing, designed to rid the residents of all bourgeois influences, including Czech democratic traditions and indigenous cultural influences. So it happened, that while the rest of the world admired Kafka's prescient, if depressing, tales of modernity, the Czech literati "discovered" Kafka only in the mid-1960s, when an official writers' gathering dared to advocate the radical view that Kafka had a place in modern literature.

The Prague of my childhood was a huge laboratory for the Communist revolution being played out on the desolate landscape left by the failure of the Nazi experiment. Yet this city of mourners and avid Kafka-hunters was in some essentialways invisible to my young eyes. Living in an elegy, my parents sheltered us from many of the torments they knew only too well, to spare us the grief they had just experienced.

So while I grew up quite aware of the horrors man was capable of inflicting upon fellow human beings, I felt fortunate about narrowly escaping them. And my childhood was happy, idyllic, in fact, and largely free of worry. I felt rather secure about my life and my place in the world—even though, as I learned later, few of the adults around me did. All that was to change in the mid-sixties, with the arrival of glasnost and perestroika, Czech style.

By 1968 when the Prague Spring erupted, we had felt the thaw for some time. Cracks in the unity of the Communist leadership had brought about a gradual loosening of censorship, which in turn had lifted the curtain on the Party's dirty secrets. And when the Communist reformers admitted, for example, that the Slansky conspiracy was nothing but a judicial murder, they brought into question the Party's own myths and, ultimately, its right to rule. In 1968, Alexander Dubcek's quest for "socialism with a human face" was as much an admission of the failure of the previous two decades as it was an attempt to reform Communism to make it work better.

Having just turned eighteen, I was completely captivated by Dubcek's vision, unaware of the underlying reality. In the course of the eight months of the Prague Spring, like many in my generation, I became intensely politicized, attending every public gathering I knew of, questioning our teachers, our parents, our leaders. Now that the Party had opened itself to scrutiny, there was a palpable sense of excitement in the air, the chain of secrets being broken at last at the source. And while the government spokesmen abandoned the self-congratulatory language of Communist Newspeak to identify problems by proper names, my parents no longer felt compelled to resort to speaking German in front of us. Glasnost Czech-style opened up many family archives as well.

On the night of August 20–21, 1968, our world was turned upside down, once again. As half a million Soviet-led troops poured in to snuff out the reforms and the reformers, I was one of those bewildered Prague youths, running among Soviet troops, demanding an explanation. Thanks to my competence in Russian, I met many equally bewildered Russian boys of my age, unable to provide any such explanation. Later that morning, like most of my compatriots I went to work, as our government, in choosing passive resistance, had asked us to do. Holding a summer job at the post office next to the Ministry of Interior, we watched from our windows as a circle of tanks surrounded the ministry and us.

Shortly, the last Czech radio station still on the air announced that they, too, were surrounded, and when they played the national anthem, it meant it was over. Soon it was. As the first notes of the anthem mixed in with the sounds of the tanks' gunfire coming from outside the radio building defended by hapless pedestrians, I looked around, only to see the shattered faces of other mail carriers, mostly women of my mother's generation. When they sang the opening lines, "Where is my home? Where is my home?" tears rolling down their lips, for the first time in my life I felt truly lost in the world.

In the wake of the tanks came what the new Party leadership called, quite prosaically, "normalization." But there was nothing normal about Prague of the seventies and eighties when "normalization" reigned supreme. A return to orthodoxy was epitomized by the notion, born within a year, that the Soviet invasion constituted an act of "fraternal assistance," and whoever could not see it that way was unfit to hold his job. Accordingly, about half a million people had to be purged from the Party, and more from their jobs. Dubcek was replaced by Gustav Husak, whom Milan Kundera has aptly called the President of Forgetting. And once again, libraries were purified of books, including my father's, writers had to be re-educated, and those that couldn't be, like Vaclav Havel, silenced. The educational system had to be revamped in accordance with the new norms, and some streets were renamed after Brezhnev's friends. Unfortunately for Kafka, he was out again.

And so was I. That I did not stick around to witness all this was my mother's doing. She had seen enough in her lifetime to want me out of the country, "for the time being," she thought. And while my parents remained in Prague, I was followed by three siblings, in a new wave of the family diaspora. Though I did not know about it at the time, in 1977 the normalizers sentenced me to prison for being abroad. My mother's "for the time being" turned out to be fourteen years, for I did not dare to go back without an American passport in my trembling hand.

In 1987, when Gorbachev made his first visit to Prague—then still in the throes of one of the most hard-line Communist regimes still headed by Husak—his spokesman was asked about the difference between perestroika and the Prague Spring of 1968. "Nineteen years," he replied, thus attesting to the chronicles of wasted time. It took that long before Moscow embarked on the same type of changes, but by then, it was too late. Under the impact of Moscow's Spring, the regime of normalization that had extinguished the Prague Spring became completely exposed, collapsing like a house of cards in November 1989.

My mother used to say well into the 1980s that in Central Europe, the war had never come to an end in 1945. For her generation, no peace in the pre-Munich sense returned to Prague, no stable order emerged, no justice was done. Instead, the hot war had merely changed into the Cold war, bringing no respite from endless campaigns against the "enemies." That is why, as far as my mother is concerned, 1989 was the year when the war, hot and Cold, had finally ended. As for me, I see with greater clarity today that the study and teaching of politics at an academic institution in the United States were not my first choice. In fact, they were not my choice at all. Rather, politics thrust themselves upon me, and would not let go.

Back in the days of normalization when Prague was becoming one of Europe's backwaters, Kundera wrote an essay, "Prague: A Disappearing Poem," which mourned the city's fate of "gradually fading away into the mists of Eastern Europe, to which it has never really belonged." Kundera lamented the loss of Prague's thousand year culture to Europe as Europe's loss, all the greater, because Europe was blind to see it. Today, Prague is a city upside down, but it is for the first time in more than fifty years the right side up. Prague is a poem reappearing. But when I return to my home town now I can no longer see it through the same innocent eyes of my youth, without the mists, for I know too much about the torments that caused the poem to be written.

LESLIE LI

Empty Bamboo

The soggy square of cardboard wedged between the two crates read "5 for $2 (45¢ each)." Tangelos are my favorite citrus fruit: half tangerine, half grapefruit; half sweet, half sour. The grizzled vendor saw where my wandering eyes had settled, peeled a pink plastic bag emblazoned with "Thank you for your patronage—Have a nice day" from the thick stack hanging from a meathook overhead and, with a practiced snap of the wrist, ballooned the sack with air.

"That's for the tangelos, right?" I asked, pointing to the sign. "Not the mandarin oranges?"

There it was again: the turtlelike retraction of the head, the momentary hardening of the irises. He grunted in indifference or dismissal. Unwilling or unable to answer me, he turned away. Right before I did the same, he nodded just perceptibly. I held up one hand, my fingers outspread.

Across the street in a tiny curio shop presided over by a chain-smoking elder, I considered two bamboo flutes. I was refurbishing my apartment feng-shui style—that is, I was moving my furniture around for maximum harmony with the natural order, maximum energy, and maximum profit in the New Year. The bamboo flutes would cost me 99 cents apiece. Within my redecorating budget and worth every penny, I thought, since my Greenwich Village one-bedroom has a beam bisecting the living-room ceiling which, according to Chris, my long-term but not live-in companion and a sometime student of Taoism, causes a kind of psychic compression that thwarts both business acumen and personal development. The flutes placed on the oppressive beam, he assured me, would pump ch'i, or vital energy, around the room. "You really believe in that stuff?" I asked him.

"The Chinese know." He pointed an index finger heavenward, nodded his shaggy blond head and opened his blue eyes wide as if to offset the skepticism implied by my narrowed ones.

I laughed and gave him a playful punch in the arm. "The only thing Chinese about you is *me!*"

"*Juk sing.*"

I looked up at the chain-smoker. "I beg your pardon?"

He smiled with his mouth but not his eyes and nodded not to me but himself.

"You. *Juk sing.* Same as them." He pointed at the two bamboo flutes I'd just paid for. "*Juk sing* mean hollow bamboo. Bamboo with nothing inside. *Juk sing* also mean a Chinese who don't speak Chinese, who look Chinese but don't act Chinese. Don't have the culture inside. You like them." He tapped my flutes with a nicotine-yellowed finger. "*Juk sing.*"

I thought of asking for my money back but instead threw the bamboo flutes in with the tangelos. Just before I let myself out, I gave the red tassels that I couldn't make my mind up about and that still beckoned beside the door a nonchalant and final flick.

I was early and it was cold, so I ducked into the bank on the corner of Mott and Canal. Although I was the only one waiting inside the vestibule, I constantly had to shift my position not to be bumped or jostled by people coming and going, opening and closing the inner set of doors, their sights set unswervingly—like the straight line evil spirits are constrained to travel—on their money and therefore oblivious of me.

There they came, at precisely the appointed hour, he holding her elbow as he guided her chivalrously across the street, for lately her knee was stiff with arthritis; she with her black Persian lamb toque tilted saucily to one side. If they had been younger, they could have been in love; if they had been older, they could have been the proverbial "old partners," a "whole" couple to whom destiny had been kind and had blessed with many sons and grandsons. As it was, they were separated and parents of a single daughter who was single. I pushed against the thick glass door. Because of the angle at which the sunlight struck it, they hadn't seen me waving inside, only their own reflection.

My father slipped a large cardboard tube into my pink plastic bag. What's this? my eyes asked. My father frowned and shook his head, gesturing, Nothing of importance. We walked along Mott Street, my bag of tangelos, flutes, and long cardboard tube thumping clumsily against my leg and taking up so much of the sidewalk that I had to walk behind my parents. I smiled to myself. The proverbial dutiful daughter. My father looked over his shoulder at me. "I have so many," he said, finally. "I thought I'd get rid of one."

Inside the doorway of the second-floor restaurant, a man my father's age with an unlined oval face the color of old ivory and just as smooth greeted him. "This is my friend—an old high school classmate from China," my father said. "And this is my wife and my daughter."

No names. Merely our relationship to the speaker. Friend. Wife. Daughter. Typical.

My Chinese grandmother had no name—merely a number denoting her rank in the family hierarchy, thus her duties and responsibilities to her immediate and extended family—until she married my Chinese grandfather. It was he who gave her her name. It was marriage which gave her her personhood and a fresh set of duties and responsibilities to her husband's immediate and extended family.

All the tables in the restaurant were taken, so while we waited for one to become vacant I unzipped my knapsack and took out the latest issue of *Preventive Medicine*. My illustrations occupied a full eight pages, including a pull-out centerfold. I had sent my parents color photocopies of the article, but the colors hadn't produced true. Too reddish and too dark. I wanted my mother and father to see the actual pictures and the place they occupied—smack dab in the middle of the magazine.

But my father was inattentive as usual or otherwise engaged. He was saying, now in Mandarin (a few words of which I could understand), now in Cantonese (not a word of which was comprehensible to me), something to his old schoolmate who responded in the same Mandarin-Cantonese mix, then, with a quick nod to my mother and me, fled down the stairs. Perplexed and irritated, my mother and I looked at each other. "He went to find an emptier restaurant," my father explained.

Just then four people got up, their chair legs groaning against the floor. A harried young woman at the back of the restaurant and carrying a pot of tea screeched something to us and held up four fingers of her free hand. Again, my mother and I looked at each other, this time a weary and knowing glance. Musical dim sum, our eyes said simultaneously. We should have expected this. The two of us started towards the table, but my father hung back. "I'll go find him," he yelled over the cacophony of voices and clatter of dishes, "and bring him back. Grab the table before someone else gets it. Did you know?" He strained his head forward and wagged his index finger as if it should be a lesson to me. "My friend has a daughter who's a professor. At Cal Tech. Physics." He disappeared down the stairs.

"It's amazing how proud he is of the accomplishments of other people's children," I said once he was gone, "particularly if it underscores the failings of his own." My mother ignored my remark by asking a passing waiter for a pot of jasmine tea.

When I was a junior at Bronx High School of Science my father decided that I would be a doctor. So when I was accepted at Duke University on early decision, I wrote down pre-med as my area of matriculation. By the end of my freshman year, I had earned C's in my science courses, an A in my life-drawing course, wore djellabas, guayaberas, parejos (but nothing close to a cheongsam), and ban-the-bomb buttons, and hung out wit students majoring in painting and sculpture or the models who posed for them.

My first summer home from college I asked my father if I might transfer from pre-med to art school. He told me that if I did I could pay for my schooling as well as my living expenses. A doctor made good money and was respected. An artist led a dissolute life and was hounded by the CIA. After a few tearful and angry scenes (the tears were mine, the anger my father's) followed by a sophomore year where I was just squeaking by with a two-point grade average, we arrived at a compromise, a Middle Way that combined both art and medicine. It must have cost my father considerable face to have to tell his friends to whom he had boasted in the humble, self-negating fashion unique to proud Chinese parents that I was studying to be a doctor, a surgeon no less, that now I was going to be a medical illustrator, drawing human bodies for a living instead of saving human lives. I interpreted the hopeless shake of his head (for he expressed his disappointment with my career choice only in gesture) as saying, What kind of field is this medical illustration, and what kind of girl was I to want to spend most of my college days, the happiest days of one's life, in the company of cadavers, scrutinizing and reproducing their every tissue and organ in the minutest detail?

"I found him!" he called out. My father and his long-lost schoolmate sat down while my mother took up the teapot and poured them both some tea.

"Did you see how nicely they. . . ." But my father's interest quickly shifted from the magazine I held out to him to the approaching trolley whose conductor was droning in indifferent nasal syllables the names of the dishes she wheeled from table to table: *har gow, lo bak go, siu mai, char siu bao.*

It's been said that Chinese food is the world's most refined cuisine and that among Chinese the act of eating is also an act of nonverbal communication. But the eloquence of such a language escapes me. We consumed our dim sum in a silence punctuated every so often by a discreet burp or two and wild bursts of Cantonese or Mandarin chatter from my father or his friend which my mother and I, understanding neither, could only ignore, retreating into the wordless spearing of dumplings with our chopsticks and balancing of tea pot lid between spout and rim, signaling to whichever waiter was passing by that a fresh brew was needed.

My father pointed to his friend with his chopsticks, an impropriety which made my mother purse her lips. "Did you know? My friend's five daughters support him and his wife." My mother and I raised our eyebrows and nodded as if on cue.

My mother, too, was one of five daughters, all of whom were working by the time they were four years old, singing, dancing, and bending themselves into pretzels in kiddie reviews. With what they earned—and as children, no less—they supported not only their parents but their baby brother as well. Dutiful daughters if ever dutiful daughters existed. And they weren't even Chinese.

As for me, it was only after college, my previous summers having been spent in sleep-away camps, summer schools, or our summer home on Long Island, that I had my first taste of earning power. With my college roommate I moved to Boston where I worked for a firm that published medical textbooks. But after less than a year I was bored, restless, and frustrated. Not knowing what I would do there and caring even less, I took off for Paris "for two months." Two months became four years. The first year I supported myself by working *au pair* and giving private English lessons. When I graduated to runway model at prêt-à-porter houses (I was tall, slender, and looked "exotic"—Chinese but not Chinese), my father's reply to my mother concerning my good fortune was a disdainful, "That's (*that* meaning the willingness to exhibit oneself) from *your* side of the family."

A telling remark, I thought, since unless my father is a psychic, his initial attraction to my mother was not because she was brainy, though brains she surely has, but because she was beautiful. An undergraduate at Stanford during the Second World War when he first saw her up on the stage of George White's Scandals in San Francisco, my father was, literally, at her feet. His marrying her—a *guailou*, and a performer to boot—had enraged his father, an unredeemable Confucianist and a renowned calligrapher. Only after I was born did my Chinese grandfather forgive my father his dereliction to duty and bring him back to the land of the living by no longer considering him dead. "You don't know what it meant for your father, a Chinese man, to defy his father and marry me," my mother once told me. "You just don't know."

My mother has always been the go-between for my father and me, the interpreter of my father's feelings and my own, the smoother of ruffled feathers, the blunter of sharp words. It was she who had arranged my first encounter with him after my four "wasted" years in Paris, a meeting which, like today, took place in Chinatown over numerous dishes of dim sum and a starvation diet of meaningful dialogue. She had been present on that occasion, too, along, as it were, for the ride—arbitrator and referee. But, then as now, nothing happened. We ate dumplings; we drank tea; we spoke in platitudes; and, when we weren't speaking or eating, we maintained a strained silence.

The ways my father and I saw life, the ways we lived our lives, were as different as our mother tongues, a gap of miscommunication and incomprehension that my mother tried to bridge with the language of experience, wisdom, compassion, and mostly well-timed silences. Even now my father could not understand why I didn't want to work for a big pharmaceutical company whose name everybody knew, why I was a freelancer, loyal to no company at all. To him, being freelance was tantamount to being unemployed. Though his father had temporarily relegated him to the land beyond Dog Mountain, my father had never quite considered me dead, though he could not understand how I could live the way I did. I could just about support myself. I worked when I needed money. When I had it, I spent it, sometimes taking refuge on a tiny, spare, virtually uninhabited island off the coast of Maine, living in a one-room log cabin with electricity but no plumbing. ("Why not go back to the ancestral village?" my father had teased me mercilessly. "There's no plumbing there either.") It was where I was happiest. It was where I was most me.

"Why does she want to do that for?" my father would ask my mother, and she relay to me later, to learn I had taken off again for my all-to-myself island. He'd shake his head at my strange ways, his eyes darting away from hers to conceal his anxiety. When I think of my father, it is this expression—of incomprehension and anxiety—and this feeling—of shame for his failure to have taught me what I should know, of his grudging but helpless love for his wayward child—that most often comes to mind. When I try to summon an image of my Chinese grandfather whom I hardly knew, it is quite the same vision—shaking his head and brooding over my father.

What Chinese fear most is to be alone in life. They love their family and friends and want them around, along with the *renao* they bring, the heat and noise of human relationships. After being alone, Chinese fear being cold. My father must think: What kind of woman is this daughter of mine who longs for solitude and a log cabin in arctic Maine? She should stay put, get married and have children. She should give me a son-in-law and grandsons. She should think of her happiness in the present and her security in her old age. A woman needs her family and her people around her. It is the proper way to live. Each generation is a link in the great chain of life. No one can drop out without breaking it.

We had come to the egg noodles topped with slices of beef and scallion, the culinary announcement to the end of our meal. But my father's friend, with a glance at his watch, had to leave. He was accompanying his wife who needed to be fitted for a hearing aid, a device which only now I noticed my father was wearing in both ears, not just the left one. I looked at my mother who returned my glance and nodded. When the nameless man, my father's friend, had gone, the three of us shared the last course but not a word.

Noodles mean long life. Long life. Prosperity. Many sons. These three are what Chinese dream of. The heaven on earth that occurs only in the world of the living. The happiness that humans experience only in the here and now.

"Daddy." The word erupted our silence. I pulled the magazine out of my knapsack and yelled into his formerly good ear. "Did you see what a nice job they did with the article I illustrated?" This time he took the magazine and turned the eight pages of my illustrations. They weren't the kind of images one cares to ponder after eating a big meal, but he looked at them because they were my illustrations and because I was proud of them.

"The photocopies you sent me—terrible!" He frowned and shook his head. His cheeks were lower than the last time we ate dim sum in Chinatown. And looser. Empty pouches that sagged and flapped like a turkey's gullet and did not even try to resume their former place close to the bone. "So dark! I couldn't even tell what I was supposed to see." He laughed, then frowned and shook his head and jowls again. Over forty years in this country, I thought, and his English pronunciation is worse than ever. *This country.* It was how he always referred to these United States. Alien territory. Never really home. "But these illustrations—you draw very well."

"You really think so?"

When he handed the magazine back to me, my mother pursed her lips. "Take it, Leo," she said in a flat voice. "She's giving it to you."

He blinked at her, then retrieved the magazine. "Thank you."

"My pleasure," I answered, the words partially lost in the scraping of our chair legs against the floor as we rose to go.

We walked to Mulberry Street: my parents legally separated but physically side by side, my mother hobbling almost imperceptibly, my father's hand gently yet firmly cupping her elbow, and me behind and between them, my left hand about my father's arm, my right curled around my mother's—not so much three links in the chain of life but, rather, a human triangle. The triangle I had learned at Bronx Science is the most stable of geometric shapes. The eternal triangle I now discovered isn't the romantic configuration but the familial one.

I left them on Mulberry Street after having kissed them both on the cheek, a non-Chinese practice which I had long ago repudiated and now resumed. At this stage of my life, and theirs, I wanted and needed to touch them.

Back in my apartment I put four of the tangelos in the refrigerator. I made tassels from a spool of red silk string which I bought at the notions store around the corner from me and tied them around the two bamboo flutes. These I hung at angles to each other in the middle of the beam where they might free up the blocked ch'i and bring me prosperity and personal development. Then I drew out the cardboard tube my father had dropped in the plastic bag. Inside was a hanging Chinese scroll. It wasn't the usual brush-and-ink painting but a rubbing. My father had shown it to me once a long time ago.

"Your grandfather was a master calligrapher. He drew this picture on the side of a mountain. Then an anonymous stone cutter carved it out of the stone. You could say this scroll is the third generation of the original image."

The subject of the scroll was a pliant white bamboo sapling, but it was the black emptiness around it, delineating and defining it, that held my attention and gave the print life. I remembered reading in an art history book which was required for a Chinese landscape painting course I took—a style of painting as spontaneous as medical illustration was meticulous—that Chinese painters left large areas of the picture empty not so that the viewer could complete it in his imagination but because the very idea of completion is alien to the Chinese mind. I went to my bookshelves, found the volume, and thumbed through it until I located the passage.

"The Chinese painter deliberately avoids a complete statement," it read, "because he knows that we can never know everything, that what we can describe, or 'complete,' cannot be true except in a very limited sense. All he can do is to liberate the imagination and set it wandering. . . . His landscape is not a final statement, but a starting point. Not an end, but the opening of a door."

I peeled myself the tangelo I'd left out on the kitchen counter the way my father peels the mandarin oranges he prefers: so that the orange remains whole and connected at its source, the stem, and the peel forms both the petals of a flower and a little cupped dish to hold the exposed fruit. I ate each segment slowly, savoring the half-sweet, half-sour taste as I looked at the scroll's empty space that gave both substance and support to its bamboo subject.

Juk sing, I said in my mind.

"Juk sing." I said it loudly, as though by saying it I could dispel the implication of my unspoken words and the accusation when they were spoken by someone else. I looked up at my flutes, my hollow bamboos, the red tassels suspended from them shimmering a little in the fading daylight and the slight updraft from the floor grate. They hung on my beam at equal but opposite angles to each other. At cross purposes to each other. In counterbalance of each other.

Then in the stillness, from their very emptiness, I heard them issue forth their soundless song.[*]

[*] This story is a revised version of one that originally appeared as "Juk Sing" in the November 1990 issue of the Hong Kong magazine, *The Peak*, in memory of her father who died on Qing Ming, The Grave Sweeping Festival.

NANCY MAIRS

Voice Lessons

The question I am most often asked when I speak to students and others interested in writing is, "How did you find your voice?" I have some trouble with this locution, because "find" always suggests to me the discovery, generally fortuitous, of some lack or loss. I have found an occasional four-leaf clover. I have found a mate. I have, more than once, found my way home. But is a voice susceptible of the same sort of revelation or retrieval? Hasn't mine simply always been there, from my earliest lallation to the "I love you" I called after my husband on his way to school several hours ago?

But of course, I remind myself, the question doesn't concern *my* voice at all but the voice of another woman (also named Nancy Mairs, confusingly enough) whose "utterances" are, except for the occasional public reading, inaudible: not, strictly speaking, a voice at all but a fabrication, a device. And when I look again at the dictionary, I see that "find" can indeed also mean "devise." The voice in question, like the woman called into being to explain its existence, is an invention.

But of whom? For simplicity's sake, we assume that the voice in a work is that of the writer (in the case of nonfiction), or one invented by her (in the case of fiction). This assumption describes the relationship between writer (the woman in front of a luminous screen) and persona (whoever you hear speaking to you right now) adequately for most readers. And maybe for most writers, too. Until that earnest student in the second row waves a gnawed pencil over her head and asks, timidly as a rule because hers is the first question, "How did you find your voice?"

As though "you" were a coherent entity already existing at some originary point who has only to open her mouth and agitate her vocal chords—or, to be precise, pick up her fingers and diddle the keys—and call the world she has in mind into being. Not just a writer: an Author.

But I've examined this process over and over in myself, and the direction of this authorial plot simply doesn't ring true. In the beginning, remember, was the *Word*. Not me. And the question, properly phrased, should probably be asked of my voice: How did you find (devise, invent, contrive) your Nancy?

On the day I was married (actually, a few days beforehand, since I got rather caught up in last-minute preparations), I stopped writing. These two events (one event and one nonevent, to be precise) might have been purely coincidental, but I suspect that they weren't. Although, thirty years later, I can see that that day marked a beginning, which like a healthy rootstock has burgeoned over time into beginning after beginning after beginning, I had no such sense then. On that day something came to an end, which I might call my artistic youth.

I was nineteen then, and I had been writing for at least eleven years. And I mean writing: not just dutiful school assignments, though I did plenty of those, but sheaves of poems and short stories scribbled in time stolen from school assignments, the very opposite of dutiful, downright subversive of duty. What was different about married life, I wonder, that made it resistant to subversion of this sort? Or—and I think this is the same question in different guise—what did I think writing was that my married state seemed to debar it?

One easy explanation refuses itself: My husband was not responsible for my silence. As anyone who's read Charlotte Perkins Gilman's "The Yellow Wallpaper" will recall, some husbands, wary of the way artistic endeavor resists control, will suppress it, if not outright then by ignoring, deprecating, even ridiculing it. But George always liked my writing, and he urged me to continue it. In the years since I've established myself as a writer, we've both been happier, in part, I think, because I'm doing what we've both always believed I should be doing. So, although I tend to blame George for everything from lost teaspoons to the colonies of blue mold sprouting at the back of the refrigerator, and it would be both convenient and credible to blame him for the fatal consequences to my writing of its collision with marriage, I'll have to look elsewhere.

I had no explicit reason, back in 1963, to believe that a married woman could not be a writer. In fact, my aunt was one—a married woman writer, that is—although the way my grandmother referred to her daughter's poetry and her psychoanalysis in the same shuddering breath was, I'll admit, unnerving. But, Aunt Jane aside, I didn't have any particular reason to believe that a married woman could—or should—write more than grocery lists and thank-you notes for the christening presents. In high school I'd had a passion for historical romances, many written by women, but as an English major in college I'd been assigned virtually no works by women, married or otherwise, so women's literary legitimacy seemed dubious. Both in classes and on my own I'd read plenty of works about women, of course. Most of them weren't married, though they were generally trying to get that way, and the book ended when they finally made it. Those who were married seemed to have few creative options: They could knit, sometimes with powerful consequences; they could commit adultery, but then they were likely to heave themselves under the wheels of a train or gobble fistfuls of arsenic; childbirth was all too often fatal; and if they got really out of hand, there was always the attic.

Thus, I encountered few enough figures to suggest how to function happily as a wife, much less a writing wife. But the absence of models was only one strand in an elaborate knot. Another, perhaps even more important, was spun by the need that sent me hurtling into marriage while I was still, in every way, a girl, and here both literature and psychoanalysis are again, at least partially, implicated. From the age of four on, I had no father. The figurative lack that at once underwrites and undermines human expression* was accompanied, in my case, by a more literal hole, a wound even, and I desired, above everything else, to stop it up. Whatever I wrote, I wrote out of that pain, and whatever I wrote assuaged the pain a little but never enough. Everything I saw and read informed me, assured me, that what I needed to fill that void was a man. Maybe it also told me what to do with him, and with our life together, after I got him, but I neglected that part. I just wanted to get him, and plug him in, and ease the pain. Since I had written entirely out of yearning, and now I yearned no more, I had neither the motivation nor the material to keep on writing.

Does this sound far-fetched? Probably it does. I'm writing about "prefeminist" experience in an era that labels itself, more wistfully than accurately, "postfeminist." You'll just have to take my word for it: Once I was married, nothing in my life seemed worth writing about. I was, perhaps, unusually naive. I favored the surfaces of poems by Sara Teasdale and Edna St. Vincent Millay. I'd been given the *Sonnets from the Portuguese* but never, of course, *Aurora Leigh*. Sylvia Plath was still alive on my wedding day (though not for long thereafter), but I'd never heard of her and didn't read her work for almost a decade. Anne Sexton was still alive, too, but I hadn't heard of her. Or of Adrienne Rich. Or of Carolyn Kizer. As a college freshman I did hear May Sarton read, my diary records, but obviously I didn't "hear" her. For some reason (not hard now to fathom, but then I didn't even wonder), the only painting

*For we (mis)speak only out of irredeemable loss: of the infantile "imaginary harmony with the mother and the world," in the words of Toril Moi, *Sexual/Textual Politics: Feminist Literary Theory* (London and New York: Routledge, 1988), p. 101.

by Georgia O'Keeffe in my art text was of the Brooklyn Bridge, not the secret spaces of shells or bones or flowers. Not one work in my yearlong music course was composed by a woman.

Maybe if I'd gone to Radcliffe or Smith, my experience would have been different, but my little women's college was playing it safe. A few of the writers and artists we studied were still alive, but they were mostly men, and what they were depicting wasn't going on in my life. Later, I got a job as a technical editor, and then I read Carl Sagan on the greenhouse effect on Mars and Venus and Ursula Marvin on the composition of moon rocks, but what they were depicting wasn't going on in my life or anybody else's, for that matter. I did read *The Feminine Mystique*, and later *The Golden Notebook*, and later still *The Second Sex*, but for a long time I couldn't (or, I now see, I wouldn't, didn't dare) discern how these might be about what was going on in my life.

Here's what was going on in my life after I was married. A final year of college. A brief, unhappy stint of grade-school teaching. The birth of a daughter. A job. An episode of depression so debilitating as to require six months of confinement in a state mental hospital. After my release, the same job for another year. The birth of a son. A different job. Also weekly sessions with a psychiatrist, summer vacations in New Hampshire, season tickets to the Charles Playhouse, occasional concerts by the Chorus Pro Musica and visits to museums and to zoos, increasing involvement in the antiwar movement. Yearnings? Yes, but not the sort I knew how to articulate and none I'd have counted as art if I had been able to speak.

After about eight years, I started committing adultery, and again at long last I had something to write about: sexual arousal masked as a troubled heart, which was more fruitful, I found, than my interminably troubled mind. The poems started coming reliably enough in number and quality to get me into graduate school. Luckily, I refrained from throwing myself under an MBTA car (the railroads being by this time pretty well defunct), and arsenic in quantity is hard to come by nowadays. All the same, adultery proved increasingly unsatisfactory. For one thing, no matter how discreetly it's handled, it's awfully hard on a marriage. And increasingly I knew myself committed to George and the children. I couldn't have both commitment and independence: not what I meant by commitment; not what I meant by independence. For his own reasons, George never forced—never even asked—me to choose. He let me travel to the point of choice on my own.

I chose him. But did I choose only him? On my wedding day I seemed to have chosen between marriage and writing, not consciously but firmly nonetheless. I believed that choice necessary, and so I suppose it was, even though now I perceive the dilemma as false. The choice I made nearly twenty years later—the one to remain actively married rather than frittering away my emotional energies—circumvented the dilemma by breaking my reliance on romance for inspiration. The dilemma was beside the point. I could have both marriage and writing. The price was labor, an awful lot of it: grinding, occasionally wearisome, often scary, and absolutely without end. I had to change my intellectual and aesthetic beliefs about the world, and about what I was doing in it, and I had to keep on changing them as the world changed, and I changed in it, forever. The reward: well, who knew?

The fact is that adultery had been hard on more than my marriage. It was fixing me in amber. The golden aromatic resin was thickening. I could feel its sticky pressure in my nostrils, down my throat. I was sucked in by love and loss. I had to get out. But how? What else could rouse me to write? What else did I know? *There were the babies, and the blood, the way bread yields and sighs like flesh under your fist, the death of the little dog, so sudden, unlooked for, and the way your tears choked you as you folded him into the pillowcase and heaped dirt over the linen, and then too your body, its betrayal sudden also but its diminishment protracted so that grief, you learn, will actually never end, and the babies gone, and soon the blood as well.* These were the sorts of things I knew, or was learning, and so I tried some of them out on the guys (it was just them and me that year) in a poetry workshop. "Yech," they said.

And kept on saying. That was a bad time for me, alone with the guys, who knew what writing was because they were doing it, who knew that what I was doing, to the extent that they weren't doing it, wasn't writing, not the real thing (muscular, tough-minded, penetrating, gritty), and who didn't mind telling me so. One or another has gone on telling me so ever since. "Stop squandering your time on this feminist stuff," Edward Abbey told me for years, and after he died a reviewer for the New York Times caught up the tune before it faded away: "a waste of a 'talented voice.'" I don't think any man has ever suggested I give up writing. It's just that a lot of them want me to write something *else*. (My mother does too, by the way, so I'm using the word *man* pretty loosely.)

Whether some of us like it or not, men (in the loose sense of the word) have determined and continue to dominate our culture, and that still (though who knows for how long) includes the arts. It's been men senators ranting about queer photographers and crucifixes in piss and the need to protect the taxpayers' hard-earned pennies from being squandered on obscenities (environmental degradation and the deaths of people with brown or red or yellow or black skin being something other than obscene). It was a man director of the National Endowment for the Arts who, lashed by the senators' tongues, scurried around demanding pledges of sanitation before doling out his meager funds. Women (white heterosexual middle-class educated ones, anyway) may more frequently succeed at grabbing men's goodies—the directorship of the National Endowment for the Arts among them—and call themselves postfeminist when they do, but they're still men's goodies and will be as long as men determine what they are, what you must believe and do in order to get them, and what they're worth.

As the feminist theologian Rosemary Radford Ruether points out, "It is almost impossible for an individual alone to dissent from this culture. Alternative cultures and communities must be built up to support the dissenting consciousness." * If I'd been trapped forever by some evil genie in that poetry workshop with all those guys doing the polite equivalent of sticking their fingers down their throats in response to my writing, I can't imagine what would have become of me, but it might have warranted my enshrinement as the tragic heroine of some "real" work of art, along the lines of Hedda Gabler, maybe, or Blanche DuBois. As luck would have it, however, I found myself in another poetry workshop altogether, gathered under the pear trees outside a very old farmhouse in New Hampshire on summer Mondays, listening to, reflecting upon, discussing, and celebrating the poems of a small but diverse group of women.

And when, around the time I began my doctoral work, my poems began to turn to essays about a woman's life, the life of a woman's body, the life of a crippled woman's body, no one at Skimmilk Farm moved to banish me from the Monday workshop. In the Ivory Phallus of academia, I had found, where poets hardly speak even to fiction writers, let alone to essayists, literary critics, and the like, the genres are like armed camps, and transgressing their boundaries can result in swift expulsion. If I'd started reading an essay in my poetry workshop there, I'd have been cut off and told to register for the nonfiction workshop meeting down the hall. At the Farm, the women simply listened to my essays very hard, and laughed in all the right places. Although I have not seen many of them for years now, I still think of them as my audience. They, and all the others like them whom I've never met, are the ones I write for.

And really, what more can we—as writers, as artists, as human beings —do for one another? When, in the middle of a sentence I'm having trouble with, my attention strays and I find myself cringing in anticipation of the next inevitable *yech* (and I do cringe; old habits die hard), I say: Let the masters of the written word cling to their bodiless principles. Let them pronounce what is interesting and what is not, what is a poem and what is not, what merits their grudging praise and what

*Rosemary Radford Ruether, *Disputed Questions: On Being a Christian* (New York: Orbis Books, 1989), p. 128.

does not. For myself, I want another model. I want to hear *this* poem by *this* woman on *this* muggy August morning under the pear trees. I want to know what it is doing in the life of her work, and in my life as well. I want to give her the courage to say the next hard thing, without fear of ridicule or expulsion if she strays across the borders of good taste, good sense, good judgment demarcated by a tradition she has had no part in forming. I want her to do the same for me. This is what we can all do to nourish and strengthen one another: listen to one another very hard, ask hard questions too, send one another away to work again, and laugh in all the right places.

2. The Groves of Academe

In fact, the autobiographical pitch and timbre distinguishing this voice that utters me developed unconsciously but not spontaneously during the years after finding community under the pear trees when, as a doctoral student, I began at last to attend seriously to the words and intonations of women as women. I found my writing voice, and go on finding it, in precisely the same way that I came to my first utterances: by listening to the voices around me, imitating them, then piping up on my own, timidly at first, making plenty of mistakes, being corrected, correcting myself, listening some more. . . . Up until this point, my writing had been rooted in fertile but decidedly uneven emotional ground, and now I began to tap intellectual sources instead. No, that implicit split between ardor and intellect is the very opposite of what I mean: Ideas now erupted into and became indistinguishable from my emotional and even my corporeal life. I could feel them in my flesh, quickening my breath, itching my fingers, spilling out through the nib of the black Parker fountain pen my husband gave me as an anniversary present appropriate to a writing wife. I can trace this development, as I entered, inhabited, and then slipped out of the academy, from my earliest attempts at articulating a deliberately, if sometimes falteringly, feminist vision onward: a kind of archaeology of voice.

By the time I established myself as a doctoral student in English literature with a particular interest in works by women, I was pushing forty. I'm no longer sure why I started to work on a doctorate—and probably never was. I certainly didn't burn with ambition either to "get" or to "be" a Ph.D. I'd come to like the classroom, however, and the Catholic high school where I'd been teaching after I finished my M.F.A. fired me. I lacked credentials for the public schools, which I could acquire while I worked on a Ph.D. in English education, teaching freshman composition in the bargain. The fact that I happen to like teaching freshman composition, both because I believe it the most important course in the university curriculum and because I feel an inarticulate passion for the mute helplessness of freshmen, signaled my unsuitability for doctoral work (no true scholar would so abase himself), but fortunately no one took it seriously. By 1979, I'd completed the course work for a Ph.D. in English education, all but the required course in advanced sadistics. Then, after a summer of those workshops at Skimmilk Farm, where I also devoured a shelf of books by Virginia Woolf, I had returned to Tucson with permission to speak.

I came to feminism in my characteristic fashion: late. Trailing a good decade or more behind the vanguard of feminist scholars, I discovered women writers and began writing a woman's life myself. While other women had been, rumor had it, burning their bras, I was still strapping myself into mine, even though my breasts are so small that it routinely rode up and threatened to strangle me. Later, arriving in Tucson on an August morning when the temperature was a hundred three in the shade, I stripped it off. My conversions, like all my acts, are experientially rather than theoretically grounded. I didn't object to my bra on principle; I just couldn't stand the grip of wet elastic around my neck.

Similarly, although I wasn't entirely unaware of feminist issues, I could never quite see how they applied to my life and thus why I should act on them. And in truth, for a number of reasons, they may have impinged on me less than on some others. I had spent my formative years in a household of self-sufficient women: my grandmother, divorced long before my birth, supported herself as a bank teller, and my widowed mother worked as a school secretary until her remarriage when I was eleven. I attended a college where, even in those prefeminist days, female competence was taken for granted under the stage lights, in the chemistry lab, on the hockey field, and definitely at the bridge table. My husband took part in running our household and rearing our children without the fuss and fanfare that many men make to call attention, like toddlers assisting mommy, to their "helpfulness."

Small wonder, perhaps, that such privileged circumstances had obscured other women's pain, not to mention my own. For I had been, in spite of my good fortune, inexplicably and often bitterly unhappy for reasons that feminist readings of my experience were at last enabling me to scrutinize and then even to manage. In the spring semester of 1980, I entered my first explicitly feminist gathering: a graduate seminar entitled "Woman As Sign." The setting turned out to be extraordinary, because the professor, having lost one baby and in danger of losing another, was put to bed just a week or so into the semester, and instead of canceling the course or turning it over to someone else (even if there had been anyone else equipped to teach it, as really there wasn't), she moved it to her home. Every week, then, in place of the plastic and fluorescence to which we'd grown inured, we gathered in an airy space around Susan's couch: a dozen or so women, one (rather brave, as I think on it) man, and Alden, humping up higher and rounder each week, her mute presence bespeaking the knowledges our books and seminar papers refused us until, just a couple of weeks before the semester's end, she showed up in tiny but thriving person to set a kind of seal on the proceedings.

In this company, embarrassed by my stunted growth, wary, curious, and curiously afraid, I began to learn to read again and to try my hand at formal feminist criticism, straining after a tone of subtle irony. ("Subtlety" struck me as a great virtue in those days: I didn't want to mark myself as ingenuous by explaining some point that everyone who knew anything took for granted. But I couldn't figure out just what "everyone" knew, except that it was obviously more than I did. I still can't, and it still is, but I forgive myself for bafflement more readily now.) This voice—arch and insiderly—was not my own.

In the same semester that the "Woman As Sign" seminar awaited Alden Carroll's arrival, a departure yanked me into another opportunity for growth. I admire people who leap into larger selves with the élan of skydivers entering the ether, but I grow only if yanked, I'm afraid, and then only under protest. In this case, my reluctance was born as much of sadness as of timidity. I had known and admired Sally Perper for eight years, since first coming to the University of Arizona, and when pancreatic cancer forced her to give up teaching just days before the spring 1980 semester began, I assumed her Composition Through Literature without the joy I'd have felt otherwise at being permitted to teach the course.

Today I remember with pleasure every detail about that class except for a model I wrote to prepare my students for their major assignment, a documented essay about a literary work of their own choosing. The structure of my piece was clear; the ideas were accessible; the mechanics of documentation were correct; but the tone was all wrong, designed to baffle and discomfit the ordinary reader. Bafflement and discomfiture are much of the point, if not quite the whole of it, in the academy. The Haves and Have Nots of general society are paralleled there by the Knows and Know Nots. The same principle of exclusion operates, but on a linguistic rather than a material basis. To belong, you need a word hoard, as the Anglo-Saxons would say: linguistic currency, in both senses of the phrase. Unfortunately, thanks to inflation, deflation, and the frequent replacement of one monetary system by another—now cowry shells, now coins, now Coleman lanterns—it can be pretty hard to figure out your worth. My use of words like "mythopoetic" obviously reflected considerable anxiety about my position. Not that "mythopoetic" isn't a perfectly good word. Not that I wouldn't still use it if I needed it. Just that the nature of that need has changed, and I would no longer risk replicating that earlier, edgy, spurious need in my students.

Not until my preliminary doctoral examination did I begin, by treating literary insight as a variety of personal experience, to hear a voice I might "own," although the emotional din of that occasion threatened to drown out those peepings. The fact that shifting to the Ph.D. program in English literature prolonged my course of study had suited me. I was a happy student, a happy teacher, and, thanks to the chronic progressive nature of my multiple sclerosis, I was almost wholly without professional purpose. The future for which my classmates were preparing themselves diligently, yearningly—freedom from freshmen, publication in *PMLA*, sabbaticals at the Bodleian or in Tuscany, promotion to a full professorship, maybe even an endowed chair—was closing to me. Why hurry toward my own obscurer fate? The university had anticipated hangers-on, however, with a system of regulations designed to purge itself automatically of such indigestible bits if they failed to eliminate themselves voluntarily. My end was in view.

That it couldn't be reached except by examination isn't surprising, given that an academic degree attests to capabilities, one might even say powers, jealously guarded by those who possess them already. The difference between an academic degree and a driver's license, say, or a medical technician's certificate is that at least some academic powers may have no practical consequences, may not even manifest themselves in any quantifiable manner, and so may seem mysterious, elusive, ineffable, transcendent: an awful lot like God's. Testing Godlikeness—as opposed to determining whether a person understands the meaning of an octagonal road sign or can slip a needle neatly into a vein—can be a bit tricky: the results tend to be so mixed. But preliminary doctoral examinations purport to do so.

I did not understand then, and I still do not, what of value this system was believed to reveal. Memory? If a Ph.D. attests to the holder's capacity to retain and retrieve information without resorting to sources, then I oughtn't to have one. I can't even remember how to spell "weird" without looking it up, much less retrace Leopold Bloom's progress through Dublin—or even Clarissa Dalloway's through London, to which I feel far closer—without returning to *Ulysses* or *Mrs. Dalloway*. Or, if not memory, perhaps writing skill? But no matter how substantial, clearly organized, and charmingly expressed a little essay I might whip up in three hours, I would always, always do better in, say, three days, and I suspect everyone else would, too. Grace under pressure? This could indeed be a valuable quality in some circumstances, but not those likely to be encountered by a professor of literature, who can always say, if asked a question he can't answer, "I don't know. Give me a day or so to think about it."

I once heard a professor, challenged by a group of graduate students to defend the examination system, blurt, "Well, I had to go through it, and so should you." There's the real reason, I suspect. Examinations visit the misery of one generation on the next: the scholarly equivalent of hazing. They invite students to exhibit work that, produced under adverse circumstances involving anxiety, lack of resources, limited time, and mental and physical exhaustion, falls short of their best and force them to accept judgments based on that hastily conceived and frantically scribbled or uttered work. Meditation, reflection, revision: The essential elements of solid intellectual production are deliberately debarred.

I remember walking out of my oral prelims to find my husband waiting, a bottle of Drambuie hidden in a paper bag for a toast.

"How did it go?" he asked.

"I passed!" I told him and burst into tears. As a younger woman, I'd believed that opening oneself up to experience—all experience—offered the greatest opportunity for intellectual and spiritual growth. Now, suddenly, I saw that there are some experiences one simply ought never to have, and prelims constituted such an experience for me. Over time, my humiliation—my sense of having been required to present myself in a compromised light I would never have chosen, any more than I'd have chosen to strip my misshapen body to its skin, even less—faded, of course. But a sliver of grief remains lodged near my heart.

I was surprised, then, rereading years later the essays written for the exam, that their tone hardly sounds bleak or distressed. On the contrary, the voice is breathless with excitement, with exertion, with laughter, but not with anxiety. This woman sounds like she's having as good a time as I always do when the world drops away and I am left alone with language. Listening to her, I am carried back to a little room with one high window where I hunch intently at a grey metal desk under fluorescent flicker, sucking at cigarettes and red cans of Coke, pushing my fountain pen across sheet after sheet of yellow legal-size paper . . . and sure enough, I'm having a wonderful time.

"Self. Life. Writing. Self-life-writing. Selflifewriting," the first essay of my prelims began. "Autobiography . . . a particular kind of writing, writing about a real life, one that really (maybe) happened (when?). . . . At once easier and harder to write than biography—easier because the writer doesn't have to do a whole lot of research, except in the archives of memory, which stay open longer hours than many of us would wish, and because she's automatically an authority, whose mistakes (if she's caught) will be forgiven as slips of memory, not excoriated as sloppy research, and because, as at once the writer and the subject, she doesn't risk the confusion of identity biographers sometimes experience; harder because. . . . Well, think of the pain; think of the responsibility."

Out of this half-humorous tumble of words rang my own voice. Not romantic anguish, not guy talk, not muteness or critical bombast masking intellectual cowardice, though I had learned from trying on each of those rejected styles. I would speak plainly out of my own experience, to an audience I liked and trusted, about a woman's life, making it up as I went along. I was on my way to nowhere in particular and in no hurry to get there. I would poke into the byways, much as George and I would later meander through the Cotswolds despite the tuts and stifled groans of my stepfather in the rear seat, for whom getting lost clearly did not constitute a lark. I would take my time. I would sometimes feel pained and burdened by the processes of self-creation/-discovery/-revelation, but I would also laugh out loud more than I could have anticipated, and others, weeping and laughing along with me, would provide consolation. I might *work* alone but I would never *be* alone, not as long as I could call out and muse on a response. "I" would be I.

My reward, such as it might be: my voice's Nancy.

PAUL MARIANI

The Gospel According to Walter

We passed the open Bible round & waited.
Round robin, & it was my brother Walter's turn.
He knucklebrowed the passage, grunted, then began.
"Yeah, here. Right here it says. *Shepherds in the fields*
keeping watch. . . ." He found what it was he wanted.
The angel of the Lord shone round them.
They were terrified, but the angel said, Do not be afraid.
Who the fuck's *he* kidding? Don't you figure
them guys would blow their cookies when they saw that?
I mean, you really ever *see* an angel?
Listen, they got these eleven-foot neon wing spans.
And hook talons on 'em at *least* this big.
With shit like that you do not mess.
Fer chrissake think about it: here it is
the middle of the night & these poor bastards
freezin' their cullyones off when wham! they catch
these mothers hoverin' over 'em like fuckin'
Huey gunships, goin' *whucka whucka whucka.*
Think about it: a buncha roaches like you & me
feeding in the kitchen in the middle of the night
when, whunck! goes the landlord's eyeballin' flashlight
& us there grooling just begging to have ourselves
be stompt & squished when this wingspan croons:
Do not be afraid. You gonna stick around for that?
Whucka whucka whucka & some fuckin' floodlight
saying: Go thou *now* & catch the stable action
in yonder Bethlehem. Who, me? You're lookin'
at one first-class case of heart attack is what."
He stopped to catch his breath, his impromptu exegesis
on the Sacred Text & the Sublime fulfilled,
then wiped his hand across his brow & gave the book
a spin. Eddie popped another beernut in his mouth
& winked as if to say: "OK, numbnuts?
Didn't I tell you so?" The others stared in disbelief
at Walter. Walter leaned forward on his elbows
& stared back hard. He was having

the last word on this one if it killed him.
"You heard me," is what he said. "I said a wingspan
at *least* eleven fuckin' feet."

Fog Warning

Except for a gothic pastel Alfred E.
Newmann of "What, Me Worry?" fame which hung
nailed above my bed as a constant reminder
of my privileged status in Walter's eyes,
the one picture my brother's promise ever
actually "realized," as Cézanne had it,
was a sepia ink & chalk copy of Winslow

Homer's famed *Fog Warning*. This my mother
hung proudly in a five & dime black-
bordered frame in the family's place of honor:
the front hall where Piers & Georgie
& our relatives could view it floating.
Afterward Walter went in for something faster—
girls & motorcycles—& when his first job

fizzled, he did three years for the Army, one
in a quonset hut on the DMZ
trying to read the night chitter of electronic codes
amid the unexpected muffled whumpf of mines
in that "peacetime" no-man's land a mile north.
As for the picture with the fish, that outlasted Walter's
girlfriend, Froggie, & assorted other bimbos, until

the night my mother finally called it quits
& we found a seagreen patch of wall where once
the noble imitation Homer had braved the nightly
household storms. Oh, we all knew it was hers
by right, a son's gift to his mother. But I wonder
if Walter really knew just what he'd caught.
An open boat with the white underbellies

of two huge bottomfeeders lying freshly dead,
a seagreen dizzy keg & two hands gripping oars
suspended between one long heaving wave

& then another, as on the long night comes
with no port anywhere in sight,
the only other boat a distant shadow only,
and a face in shadow staring back into the fog.

The Conning Towers of My Father's War

These the exposed, low-lying inlets,
their unsteady tidewaters disappearing
in the rearview mirror. The riffled
graybrown dunes, the salt grass cowering

before the gale wind's force
and these the bleak gray conning towers
of my father's war, one following the next
with an insane logic all their own,

blank slits staring down the coast
of Delaware, as when U-boats
sent tons of twisting metal pitching
down into the cold Atlantic's ditches.

And now that everything has changed,
now that my mother has been nine months
dead, sunk in those dark waters as deep
as any of us goes, I have come once more,

before the water closes over both of us,
to try again to understand my father.
The winds howl against the mainland
where my father lives and haw & whack

their presence. A tenement on New York's
51st. Long gone, space giving way
to space. Three houses on Long Island
and a handful of out-of-focus images,

exposed at times like this
to the sudden rages of the savaged heart.
A shadow of a woman, starved for love,
starved for words until I hear her

stutter once again, a woman younger
than myself, tucks away a bottle
in a closet. The son averts his gaze,
unwilling to believe. But the father knows.

The father knows & searches with the insane
logic of a drill instructor until
he finds what he is searching for
and the gales of just, unreasoning

anger bellow. The woman cowers until
the spent gales quit, but nothing changes.
The son goes over it again: the galeforce
winds, the exposed, tenacious speargrass,

the pounding surf, the silt, those blind slits
facing out to sea, but nothing changes.
Requiescat in pace, the sick pitch
of a metal coffin lowered. Nothing changes.

Class

A Saturday morning in the early spring of '62. It's not even seven. I've been up late, working the A & P night shift till midnight, then reading for classes till three. I'm tired. I want to sleep. But he's standing at the base of my bed, my father, twisting my big toe. In that half world between oblivion and nightmare I want to lash out and kick him hard for making me go through this fucking Steppin Fetchit routine again, but of course I don't. *Walter*, is all he says. As usual he's in his heavy black workpants and olive drab shirt and boots, the gray hair of his crew cut bristling, his face lined and ruddy, a halfmoon of oily dirt beneath each of his nails. He wants me up and in the truck in fifteen minutes. We're going to pick up Uncle Louie, his older brother, then head down to some bar in Garden City I've never even heard of. I look over at Walter's bed, which hasn't been slept in.

Now we're inside the bar. Outside it's a bright spring morning, but in here everything's the color of fish mud. There's broken glass everywhere: plate glass, broken beer bottles, amber and green. Chairs, some of them smashed, lie on their sides and backs. The glass panels on the front door have been kicked in, the bayglass window facing the parking lot smashed. My father's talking to the owners, the brothers DeNofrio. Walter, up from Georgia on furlough, and two of his friends, Wilbur—whom I know—and a blond kid named Hurley—a linebacker from Post, whom I don't—stand off to the side. They're tired, bruised, and sheepish. Hurley's jaw is gashed; the back of Walter's head is bandaged. A Nassau County cop is trying to talk the brothers DeNofrio out of jailing the three of them.

Here's what's happened. It's one in the morning. Walter and Wilbur have already left the bar and are getting the car. But Hurley, who's had too much to drink, has decided to smash somebody's face as he exits, and suddenly there's a brawl with four guys swarming him. There's a shout, and Wilbur and Walter run back to help. But the door's already locked. Through the glass they can see Hurley flailing as he starts to go under. Wilbur goes right through the glass door, and then two guys are on him. Walter goes in to pull one of them off and someone brings a bottle down hard on his head. Stunned and pissed, he turns like a puma to see a shadow moving backwards across the bar.

In the underwater melee someone shouts that the cops are coming and then suddenly everyone is heading for the exits. Walter and Wilbur and Hurley start up the block towards the car. They're almost there when a cruiser comes up from behind, the spotlight raking their bodies. *You guys*, a voice shouts. *Get over here. How'd you know it was us?* Walter hears himself saying, blood matting the back of his head and soaking his jacket. . . .

I can tell just how pissed my father is by how fast his jaw is working. He's come to assess the damage for himself. He knows what a door and a couple of mirrors cost, and wants to talk turkey with the brothers DeNofrio. He knows that half of what they're saying is a bullshit act to cash in on the fight. It's the way they keep pushing the cops to have the three of them thrown into jail. He knows too the DeNofrios have the law on their side. But he also hates tangling with smartass lawyers and the unfathomable legal system, and now he just wants the thing settled. After all, anyone can see the bar's just a hole in the wall. And what of the others who took off? What about them?

Fifteen minutes, twenty. He pleads, cajoles, waves his hands. And soon it's "goombah" and "kids will be kids," and one of the DeNofrios finally cracks a smile and he's got him, he knows, and then he's taking some bills from his wallet, and collecting what he can from Walter and the others. He makes them apologize to the owners and, though it takes some doing, because they know they've been set up, they do. Each will come up with another one and a quarter. The officer too plays his part. Better, he tells the DeNofrios, in the low voice of authority, better to drop the charges. So at last, having played the grand guignol act out as far as they can, the brothers relent.

But my father's not quite finished, at least not yet. Outside he goes right up to Hurley and grabs his face in his strong right hand. I see Hurley's huge right fist go into a clench. It's clear he's not used to being handled like this. But then he thinks better of it, for it seems my father is only inspecting the fishgape on his jaw. It ain't too bad, my father tells him, but he should get it looked at. For a moment longer than he needs to he holds Hurley's face rigid in that right hand of his, and what looks like a gesture of concern turns out to be his way of letting the kid know this bullshit will not be repeated. At least not with his son.

I'm standing over against the car with my brother, who is hurting and pissed. Fuck if he's going to shell out a month's Army wages, he tells me. "Look," I say, "you don't pay up, you'll have the DeNofrios and their lawyers on your ass for months, maybe longer. And what if the Army finds out? Or down the line some employer? Is it worth a hundred and a quarter to let so many bastards have that kind of power over you?"

"I'll think about it," he says. And I swear for once he does.

The power of money. The power of those in authority. Then as now. No escape. No escape even now from this question of class in this so-called classless society of ours. To stare—at fifty-two—once more into the smoky mirror and count the palimpsest of crosshatched scars. No escape. I think neither my wife nor my sons can understand what this issue of class has cost my parents and siblings and so has cost *them*, except as they've registered the shockwaves of insane anger break through the surface of an otherwise comfortable, middle-class existence over the past quarter century. Class, someone has said, *America's dirty little secret.*

"You know the best things in life is for free," I can hear my brother singing. *"But you can give them to the birds and the bees. I need money."* After all, it's about money, isn't it? Money: that soul-numbing drug. For some there's the early attempt to escape the worst aspects of the "situation" into which one was born. That's where the myth comes from, isn't it? The one about the prince waking up to find himself with two peasant stepparents, one twisting his toe, living in some fucking humble cottage, struggling to make enough to eat.

But where does one escape *to*? Into the philosopher's circle where poets stroll about in puce leggings discussing poetry like something out of *Il Cortegiano*? And yet, we think, what in the world is *not* barbed wired with its own demands? Were Lord Byron and Percy Shelley finally any better off than Keats? Were Lowell and Bishop in the long run any better off than Berryman, drunky Henry? All your life, in spite of whatever you do to alter things, and even if someday according to the "norms" you "make it" as a professional, or as a writer, you will always feel a cut below those with the pedigrees (especially those with the Ivy League pedigrees), those with the gargantuan salaries, the vast pampered country estates, those who serve bons mots which go off in the heart for years after like detonating depth charges, so that some hunchbacked cretin living in the fens of that heart will always want to smash those who make you taste the old bitterness of your first word.

Bill Cosby addressing the assembled faculty at the University of Massachusetts two years ago, reminding us—with our hands out as our patrician governor began dismantling our flagship state university—that he—Cosby—had made and would make more than any of us, and—what was also true—probably as much as most of us put together. No doubt he had the bitter truth on his side. But what, one wonders, could have prompted him to take that particular occasion to remind us of that truth? Race issues at U. Mass? Or the underlying class issue of a Black kid from Philly who had made it to the top, and made it in part by recovering—and capitalizing on—his working-class background?

Bill Clinton: Arkansas boy with his Lincolnesque beginnings, in the photo as a boy shaking hands with mythic Jack Kennedy (the hope of having the mantle passed on to him shining in the young man's eyes), Clinton the Rhodes Scholar, Clinton the Yale and Oxford graduate, spending two hours with the editors of the highbrow *Atlantic Monthly*, even as he avoids the editors of the proletarian *USA Today* and *Reader's Digest*. Clinton, trying to connect with the college crowd, even while his advisors remind him that he shines best working the crowds in shopping malls, interstate truck stops, bowling alleys, in short the people he thought to leave behind with his stepfather long years ago.

Hagiographical exempla? On a more modest scale, you know Cosby's and Clinton's ways out of the morass have been your exit too, their embarrassments and preoccupations your own. The advanced degree become a meal ticket, as you watch yourself half in disbelief becoming "one of them," as Bishop had it, one of the new breed of college professors from the working class who could find breathing space in the magic kingdom of language, surreptitiously pocketing the food others are freely offered at the banquet table.

And yet, against that, the flickering example of not counting costs, of sharing. Learned how? Learned where? From one's mother, who took what she could to give to her kids, as on the marble capital in the Upper Room glimpsed earlier this year, three years after her death, the only image in that whole room spared by the iconoclastic Muslims, a mother pelican feeding its young from her lacerated breast, until she could give no more and sought solace in drinking? Or did it come from that year in the seminary, from the protective walls of those buildings in Beacon, New York, when there was actually time to think and to meditate, to listen to the little German priest reciting Vergil and the amniotic rhythms of the Latin?

> *Dum Argolici reges vastabant bello debita Pergama*
> *que arces casuras inimicis ignibus, non rogavi*
> *illum auxilium miseris, non arma tuae artis que opis,*
> *nec volui exercere te, carissime conjux. . . .*

> While the Greek kings razed those walls, Troy's walls,
> with those wasting fires, I did not ask you to help
> my wretched friends, did not ask your aid, did not
> press you, my dearest husband. . . .

Did the example come from my wife, Eileen, who came from a modest white-collar family but who, like many working-class families, I see now, avoided tearing itself to pieces with money worries and the claylogged succor of sexual fantasies and alcohol and kept away from unbridled anger, anger hot enough for a father, desperate for the failing words, to break his wife's fingers with his fist, even though by accident, because she stood there trying to stop him from smashing his son's—this son's—face with that same right hand?

Ah, here's the rub. No one lives in the magic kingdom of language for long without harking back to the very past which may no longer want either you or your language. And yet: as soon castrate yourself as cut yourself off from that past. To deny those roots, one learns, leads to neurosis, sterility, madness, spiritual death. Is it not better to pay homage to the household gods than to try and seal them off in the basement?

A cousin telling me, with implacable iciness, that he had divorced himself from his brother, that it was bullshit this thing that blood was thicker than water. Then watching him over the next few years as his blood froze in his relations with everyone.

A friend, refusing to acknowledge the effects of a past which held alcoholic parents and messy, working-class beginnings, becoming, as her economic situation climbed skyward beyond her wildest expectations, a chilling, suicidal elitist.

Another friend, so damaged by childhood trauma that for thirty years she managed to block out her past, only to find, as she tried to recover the childhood she'd lost, that her body had locked on her, paralyzed by the frozen river of repression as it began at last to give way and flow once more.

Recover. It's an interesting word which cuts two ways. We recover something by getting it back. But we recover too by covering something up again. So one retrieves something, only to hide it from view. Isn't that what happens when we write? Don't we recover something we thought was gone even as we bury something else?

In spite of an outward show of gregariousness, the men in our family have turned out to be largely reclusive. It is they who have found a hundred ways to be alone and will go to any lengths—legitimate or otherwise—to achieve the drug of solitude. Even at family gatherings, it's not unusual to be joined in the corner of the basement, where one thought to escape with one's ham and potatoes, by one's brother.

Part of the difficulty no doubt is the inevitable claustrophobia that comes with crowding a family of nine (eleven with live-in relatives) into a small Cape Cod, the sense of airless constriction remaining even after thirty years, even when there's no one else about in the three-story Victorian you call home. Which says nothing of the women, who have had to find other, even less satisfactory, ways to cope with the Sisyphean weight of the past. It troubles me that this should be so, that the voices of the women should have been silenced, for their stories are just as important to understanding the wreck of the past. In truth it is as if their tongues had been ripped from them long ago.

Itys. Tereu. The distant trembling notes of the nightingale recalling the violence. The lonely cry of the train slogging through the hills to the east of here at three in the morning. My dead mother.

For each of my brothers the early out was the military. For me—with my hearing disability—it had to be something else. Words. Even the seminary was preoccupied with the word. Words: writing them, reading them, teaching them. I remember how happy—and guilt-ridden—I felt the day Walter told me he was being shipped out to Korea, because it meant our second-story shared bedroom would be mine at last: four slant green and brown walls and a cubbyhole with a lamp and desk at which to read Epictetus and Aeschylus and the Medieval philosophers of light while Presley and Buddy Holly and the unfamiliar, heady music of Bach and Mozart played in the background. My own Skinner box, and it was good. At least for the month it lasted, until my father invited Frankie to move in with me.

Poor Frankie. His father and my father had been cousins, had grown up together in an Italian ghetto in Manhattan in the shadow of the 59th St. Bridge. The cousin had been drafted and sent to fight with the Army in France and there, in late 1944, the chain he was hanging to on the back of the truck had snapped and he'd fallen under the wheels of the oncoming truck in the convoy, its lights out, and then another and another. . . . That left Frankie for my father to watch over. Now Frankie, at eighteen, was through with the New York public school system and trying to find work. I remember giving him something funny to read in the newspapers and Frankie eyeing me before he put the paper down. He looked trapped. What was the matter, I asked him. No sense of humor?

He looked hard at me, and I could tell he was near tears. *I can't read,* he said simply. Like that. *I can't fucking read.* I could feel an inaudible sucking in of air, as if he'd just told me he had cancer or was going to have to do time.

A. The past. The thing we keep trying to make sense of.

B. The present, the moment of relative tranquility. As now, as here. The thing we have been given to make sense of the past.

C. The place the imagination creates when it intersects A with B. The kingdom of language.

It's hard to sit at a desk like this and write. Hard because all sorts of wild things begin stirring again: the demons barely, just barely, appeased by the honey of language. In truth, as I've told my wife, the memories of the past have become more—not less—unbearable with the passage of time, so that it would seem better to leave them alone. Except that the old adage sticks like a thistle: that those who refuse to examine the past, and the class issues snaking through that past, will be doomed to repeat it every waking day of their lives.

Besides, for a writer, out of the tortured descent into the past a difficult beauty can, with luck, sometimes be forged. If I were still living in that first world, working in a gas station, a factory, or a diner—as I sometimes feared I might be stuck—my poems, my preoccupation with words, would have been left to drift off into the thin air, as so much of one's past—thanks to silence and death—seems to have done. On the other hand, if one did not have one's roots in a particular world, say the world of Astoria, Manhattan, Beacon, Levittown, Mineola, Richmond Hill, Flushing, what could one say?

Money, again money. The fear of never having enough. It has pushed me—like so many others—to a succession of stopgap jobs, murderously necessary at the time, in retrospect grist for the writing mill. Working the nightshift at the old Atlantic & Pacific. Pumping gas and cleaning toilets at Scotty's Esso and the Sinclair station across from the Nassau County courthouse in Mineola. Washing dishes in a Garden City diner. Shredding classified government documents with byzantine numerical formulas into the early hours of the morning in a small office room behind the local movie house for an alcoholic boss who paid up weeks late if he paid up at all. Cutting the transparent, sicklysweet knobs from the plastic turtle bowls which the troglodytic machine clanked out at the rate of one every fifty-three seconds. Loading the droppings of two Apaloosas and four Palaminos into the dumptruck come rain come sunshine each summer morning at seven. Painting the bottom of Camp Baumann's Daycamp pool a robin's egg blue, the merciless sun turning one's back a blistering red, while my foreman-father, innured by hard work himself—innured to it by *his* tar-roofing immigrant father—watched over his motley crew.

Seventeen years ago I sent my first manuscript book of poems to a university press for review. They were family poems, mostly, the book itself a pale version of Joyce's *Portrait of the Artist as a Young Man.* Months later the word came back in effect dismissing not only the poems, but—what to me was unforgivable—dismissing the very existence of the world I'd written about. Who, the reviewer had written, could possibly be interested in the world of a working-class American family at mid-century and beyond? Or at least *this* family?

It's one thing for a writer to paint a realistically harsh portrait of the family in which he has invested nothing less than his life. It's quite another for some insensitive outsider to dismiss it. It's good that such university reviews are anonymous, for I still find myself wanting to smash that blank and stupid face. Of the changes which have come over the past few decades, few have been more welcome for me as a writer than the increasing recognition of a plurality of voices, including those from working-class backgrounds, sound *and* dysfunctional.

But then I remember that I left my bluecollar world long ago. Sure, I still mow my lawn, weed the garden, paint the house. But I have my cars fixed, my house cleaned, my kitchen rebuilt by carpenters, my washing machine repaired, my antenna removed, all by members of the working class, all jobs my father and two of my three brothers still do for themselves. Sometimes, on my way to teach classes in Bartlett, wearing a blazer and tie, I note the janitor sweeping the floors or mopping the men's room, jobs I did for a quarter an hour in my father's gas station back in the '50s, and in truth I feel closer to them than I do to most of my colleagues and students.

Many of my poems still take as their subject my first world. The Cape Cod we lived in at 70 Colonial Avenue, across from the old high school football stadium, was long ago sold, the children—married and with kids of their own—scattered over the country, from Vermont to Hawaii, our father remarried, at last retired from all his makeshift jobs, including the last one he had fixing trucks and snowplows for the town of Hempstead, which he took, proud as he was, to earn a small pension, his other pension having been taken from him by the simple twist of a pen. You'll find him on the Maryland seashore now, riding his bicycle by the edge of the Atlantic, up and down the town's streets, still checking the construction on each new building as it goes up. As for my mother, she, having at the end put up a winning struggle with alcoholism and a losing one with lung cancer, died just before she was to retire, her last job a nurse in the V.A. drug counseling center in Syracuse. Instead of working behind the counter of a diner somewhere on Route 17 near the Delaware Water Gap—my father's persistent dream for holding the family together and giving them all jobs—I teach poetry, lecture, give readings. Most of my days—I still can't believe this—are spent writing, for which I get paid. Writing the lives of poets, writing criticism, writing my poems.

And still, class seeps into everything. It enters into the subjects one writes of, it enters the lungs and is expelled in one's language and syntax, in the rhythms one uses. It stains everything. It's behind almost any subject I talk of. Like any coign of vantage, naturally, it limits even as it helps one keep to what is important. Sure, a writer struggles to expand one's subjects and lexical range, to broaden one's view. But always it's home one starts from. So one reads of the worlds of Ashbery and Merrill, who belong like Hecht and Nemerov and Hollander to quite other worlds, though one's deepest instincts are with those who share backgrounds closer to one's own: Wright's Martin's Ferry, Kinnell's New York, Levine's Detroit.

How difficult to speak of what presses one most closely, without overly investing in the I. And yet: "Why even speak of *I*, which interests me not at all," Williams reminds himself in that great, teeming epic of working-class America he called *Paterson*. Yet there it is: Williams' diagnostician's eye trained on the living, fallible, embarrassed autobiographical I.

Consider the peasant staring up at the stained glass windows in the church and reading there the life of Christ, or the lives of the patriarchs and saints in resplendent, hagiographic, soothing blues and greens: exempla for the pilgrim's journey. So too with the poet who follows the narrative thread of other poets' lives, including the roaring boys: Rimbaud, Hart Crane, Dylan Thomas, and Berryman, lives of incredible concentration and love amidst a too-rapid dissolution.

Williams, working the life of the suburban doctor against his great need to be a writer. Berryman, working the life of a gifted teacher, scholar and poet against the oceanic drag of the bottle. Lowell, revising himself and his poems over and over in a lifelong attempt—like some great Dutch realist of the Seventeenth Century—to understand the dark drama of the self against the abysmic drag of history. Or Bishop, like Wordsworth, working the *absence* of both mother and father into nearly every poem she ever wrote.

The writer makes himself or herself out of what he or she translates, in the very act transforming the life of another writer into something personal, something of one's own. Pound—citizen of Idaho and Philadelphia—translating the late Republican love poet Propertius as a way of coming to terms with the mind-numbing insanity of the war. Lowell of Boston transforming Baudelaire's luminous Parisian darkness into poems of his own, or reworking *Benito Cereno* into a personal dialogue on the issue of race. Bishop's preoccupation with a young Brazilian girl's life in the interior as a mirror of her Nova Scotian years. Levine's preoccupation with the impossible dream of the Spanish Republicans, Barcelona his holy city. Berryman's dream of the Zen gardens of Ryoanshi, Kyoto becoming for him a consoling and multi-dimensional touchstone by which to measure the hectic fever of his splendid *Dream Songs*. Again: the omnipresent issue of class in all the choices a writer makes, as well as in the desire to retreat into that magic kingdom each one makes of language for oneself. To move, then, for long moments at a time, beyond the clamant issue of one's origin and stamp.

Biography. Writing the lives of the poets by way of homage. It too is an act of translation by which to continue one's dialogue with the dead, a way of entering a world of riches which would otherwise remain barred. In this the poem differs, for the poem allows one to celebrate one's own world, to re-cover what would otherwise be lost. What does it mean for someone like myself to follow the uneasy Brahmin existence of a Lowell? What does it mean to take the lessons learned, say, from a perusal of *Life Studies* in order to create one's own life study: Boston and New York and London shifting perceptibly to Mineola and Montague, the voice changed, the preoccupations, the expectations, the mode of address: all, all changed in large part by this issue of class.

Berryman in natty tweeds and Oxford tie rubbing Philip Levine's jacket sleeve between the thumb and forefinger of his right hand, the eyebrow slightly raised, the slight grin, as if to say, "Where *do* you get your clothes, Mr. Levine."

And yet one knows one's world can only be recovered by a language equal to its occasion. In this, it seems, we are all equal in our trials: Villon as much as Sir Philip Sidney, Dickinson as much as Mrs. Browning. Part of the difficulty is in deciding on which words to use, the problem here being in having at one's disposal too much language, or language inappropriate to the occasion, revealing a truth other than what one thought one was revealing. As Mailer does in his portrait of Robert Lowell in *Armies of the Night*, in the act of describing Lowell's patrician slouch showing us his own uneasy preoccupation with pedigree and class.

So too—to compare small with great—so too with my own poems, in trying to deal with one's past in mock epic strains, or in a skittery, polysyllabic discourse replete with mythic overtones which quickly— one sees now—crossed over into the Cambodia of the mannerist and the baroque. As when fifteen years ago one tried to deal for the first time with the reality of a mother's attempted suicide. How difficult— then *and* now—to keep the mind on what happened that night. How easy to slide off into the unreal, consolatory dreamworld of language itself. And yet it was a traumatic-enough event that I can still see my sixteen-year-old sister's eyes going blank as a wall of self-protective amnesia descended over her, mercifully re-covering the episode in oblivious silence.

But, as Williams says, you do not get far with silence. Better to learn to trust language, the common language, though to do this is—we learn by slow degree—anything *but* common. It's a learned response, and difficult, this primary attention to truth and clarity. One might even call it, paradoxically, the final, earned, aristocratic use of language. We think this common language belongs to our first world, but it doesn't, for that first world lives now only in the fictive re-creation of a wordless past which nevertheless keeps reminding us that it is what is at the heart of our experience. To re-form the past, we will have first to deform it. I wonder sometimes if the writer is ever really true to his or her past, a past which without a recovering language hardly exists.

It's the fall of 1960. It's late, after eleven. I'm at the kitchen table and again I'm reading. In their bedroom I can hear my parents arguing horribly over the fact of too little money and too many bills. Thinking of what I was thinking then, I'm pretty sure my mother's been drinking. I mean, I *think* she had to be drinking to do what she did. I mean, at this particular moment in 1960 I don't know, and don't want to know.

I look up from whatever book I've been reading to see her slide by me in silence, open the back door and go out. A minute passes, a year, then thirty-five years. Once more I hear the Pontiac start up in the one-car attached garage, and go on reading, for in truth I am afraid to stop. More time passes, fifteen, twenty, thirty minutes. There's not a sound from anywhere inside except the intake and expulsion of breathing. The smell of gas exhaust begins filtering from the bedroom to the kitchen. My sister, four years younger than I, comes down from her bedroom, asks frantically what that smell is, then goes past and outside. Then she's back, saying now she's had it. As she brushes past me, I can see her mouth set, her beautiful brown eyes going blank.

In the cage of the kitchen light, in his longjohns, my father stands, his voice low and cracking. Go out and get her, he tells me, and I go. Outside, it's Mineola. There's fog everywhere, and fumes, and in the shadow of the kitchen light I can see drizzle swirling. There's the eerie Bessemer-like glow from the plastics factories a block away, just beyond the empty stands of the football field.

It's crazy, the whole goddamn thing is crazy, and in truth I am afraid to look through the back door of the garage at what I will find. The garage door's shut tight, but the old Pontiac's in there and it's humming. Through the thickening fumes I can just make out my mother's head. She's upright in there, behind the steering wheel, but she isn't moving. The shock of it all is, I see now, that she's only thirty-seven. Thirty-seven: fifteen years younger than I am now, as I sit here trying to reconstruct this scene. But a hard life with a Master Sergeant and seven kids have made her look older and haggard. I think: she's my mother, for Christ's sake, not a goddamn kid sister or daughter. What's worse is, that in all of this, I cannot make out her face.

I put a handkerchief over my nose and mouth, the metal hook bouncing off the cement floor as I force open the back door, push up the overhead car door, then stare down at the cipher of my mother. I try opening the driver's door but she's locked it. I bang on the window next to her ear, but she's not moving. *Come on, Mom, get out of there*, I am yelling. And still no movement. I can see the glow of the radio lights on the dashboard, but I can't hear the music. Again I bang on the door, the window, ready to smash it. And now I'm pleading at the same time trying to seem as if I were in control. *Please, Mom, for Christ's sake, come out.*

And then my dead mother stirs once again, and turns off the engine and unlocks her door and rises, her bathrobe visible beneath her raincoat, and goes past me and inside the house, past my father, past my sister, who is standing, I think, in the shadow of my father, and goes into the bedroom, and no one says anything, and I turn out the light in the kitchen, and go upstairs to greet the unquestioning oblivion of sleep.

I know they mean well, the people with causes. But I think now that most of them really don't get it. I'm sick of the rhetoric of the liberals as well as the rhetoric of conservatives, of the marxists, the feminists, of my university colleagues, of the shallow irony of the deconstructionists, of most minority spokespersons, of the background noise of *The New York Times*, of those radio and TV talk shows which have eaten up so much of my life with what passes for news.

By the thousands people, especially the little ones, the weak, the powerless, are starving to death in Somalia. You see their skeletal heads and swollen bellies and the look of despair on their faces. In the streets of Sarajevo people are blown up or shot dead as they stand in line for bread or dodge through the streets to get to their jobs. And in households in this so-called classless society of ours, where the question of a wobbly recovery (that word again) remains paramount in the media, hundreds of thousands of people from hurting families—many on welfare or barely ekeing out bluecollar livings—each day are dying, though it often takes years to finish the job.

You do what you can to ease your pain. Rhetoric, the breezy quip, the language of "I know how you feel," when you don't: all less than nothing. Money matters, power matters. Sometimes, you think, they could make all the difference. And yet, part of you knows that, as important as it is, it's not by bread alone that we live. The hard-won truth is there are also the words, the right words, the felt words, the sacred words, the words of felt stories, felt poems, words with blood on them. Sometimes they cut clean through the issues of class and race and gender, through whatever traps us in our balkan states. Sometimes, you learn, they can matter.

ROBERT PACK

South Bronx, 1939

No matter which back route I took
on my way home from P.S. 48,
    the third house on Manida Street,
        a band of Catholic boys
    was waiting there to beat me up.
"Jew boy," they'd taunt, "why don't you tell us who
        nailed Jesus to the cross?
    You answer, and we let you go."
First one would swing at me, and then a bigger one;
        they couldn't make me cry,
    and some unspoken rule we shared
demanded they would have to stop if I
        could hold out long enough.
    Those days were gentler then than now—
        no knives, no guns—just fists;
    I still recall the skinny face
of that one boy who turned to ask his pals
    if he should go on punching me.
One drizzling day, inspired by rage, I sensed
    new power surging in my arms;
I hit a boy, as he was moving in,
    square on the nose. I heard it crack;
I felt his body shudder as his blood
    exploded on his mouth and eyes.
        Surprised, they backed away,
and walking home, I stopped to buy a candy bar.
    It was the most delicious taste
I'd tasted in my life: "Nobody, HA,
    will dare to fight me now."
    The next day they were there again.
    The first boy circled me;
I turned my rage on, charged at him, but when
    he started to retreat
another boy came at me, and together,
    stronger than my doubled rage,
they knocked me to the ground and kicked me

in the belly and the groin.
I realized the rules had changed.
The new rule was: *no rules anymore.*
When I got home, I wept;
my dad enrolled me in another school.
Strange pleasure now
to think back fifty years and know
that suffering, when safely in the past, is good.
For who, in retrospect, would choose
not to have suffered in his life? Yet who
would choose to be in pain right now?
What earthly good can present sorrow be
if you do not survive
to reap its benefits? I have, no doubt
by chance, held on for fifty years
since being beaten in the Bronx, and now
I see my baffled face
in everyone's—and everyone
is circling me and eating candy bars. And now
the sign that said Manida Street
I rename Mars, the blood red star, and I
can hear the howling rings of Jupiter,
and I am laughing HA;
I'm laughing HA, and HA again,
and HA, and HA, and HA!

Clayfeld Prunes His Apple Trees

I might have been a rabbi, Clayfeld thought,
holding the soft tip
of a newly planted apple tree as if
it were a little penis
to be consecrated with a blessing
and a skillful snip.
Just as the Lord made His abiding covenant
with father Abraham and all his seed
by instituting circumcision as a token
of their bond, so, too, would Clayfeld
sanctify his love for what he tended
in the garden of *his* care.

And as God changed old Abram's name
        to Abraham, Clayfeld—
still lording it to entertain himself—
        picked Pentateuchal names
for his adopted family of trees as he
        went snipping down the rows
along his hillside in a tilted flood
        of rising southern light.
"Be fruitful, Shem; be fruitful, Ham; Japheth,
        beget and multiply!"
Clayfeld commanded with his pruning shears,
        pointing at each new tree,
like Adam naming creatures of the field,
        for Adam's name, just like his own,
evoked the very soil from which he came.
        A snip of foreskin
wasn't much, Clayfeld surmised, if it appeased
        a jealously protective God,
though Clayfeld hoped his son, now eight days old,
        would never have to fear
such speechless blame as when his father's stroke
        had locked his tongue,
making his death, at last, unmerciful.
        Distracted, Clayfeld clipped
his left thumb's pulpy end with his dull shears
        and stood there with it
in his mouth as if he could assuage
        whatever pain might come
by savoring the salt taste of his blood.
        A groundhog at the orchard's edge
returned his stare and grimaced, drawing back
        into his hidden hole,
while Clayfeld, furious at his own clumsiness,
        waving his shears, flashed
UP YOURS! at the groundhog's disappearing grin,
        then waited limply, thumb in mouth,
as blunt wind spread his tears about his face,
        hassling the apple trees.
Another wail of wind among the clouds
        above the mountain peaks released
the swirling light to fill a widening expanse
        of the advancing sky—and then,

as if Jehovah heard imploring Abraham
　　　　　call out in Clayfeld's voice
for some assuring sign, a double rainbow
　　　　　arched across the orchard field.
"Not bad for my first miracle!" Clayfeld exclaimed
　　　　　to his adoring apple trees,
his shears bestowing benedictions one by one
　　　　　until the rainbow faded back
into the ordinary dusk. And Clayfeld
　　　　　boasted to his wife that night,
"A rainbow for my apple trees should keep
　　　　　my son's respect!" But Evelyn,
exhausted from her minor miracle, was strolling
　　　　　through the fragrant grove of sleep.

JAY PARINI

Anthracite Country

The culm dump burns all night,
unnaturally blue, and well below heaven.
It smolders like moments almost forgotten,
the time when you said what you meant
too plainly and ruined your chance of love.

Refusing to dwindle, fed from within
like men rejected for nothing specific,
it lingers at the edge of town, unwatched
by anyone living near. The smell now
passes for nature. It would be missed.

Rich earth-wound, glimmering
rubble of an age when men
dug marrow from the land's dark spine,
it resists all healing.
Its luminous hump cries comfortable pain.

Playing in the Mines

Never go down there, fathers told you,
over and over. The hexing cross
nailed onto the door read DANGER, DANGER.
But playing in the mines once every summer,
you ignored the warnings. The door
swung easier than you wished; the sunlight
followed you down the shaft a decent way.
No one behind you, not looking back,
you followed the sooty smell of coal dust,
close damp walls with a thousand facets,
the vaulted ceiling with a crust of bats,
till the tunnel narrowed, and you came
to a point where the playing stopped.
You heard old voices pleading in the rocks;

they were all your fathers, longing to fix you
under their gaze and to go back with you.
But you said to them NEVER, NEVER,
as a chilly bile washed round your ankles.
You stood there wailing your own black fear.

1913

"*Guarda, Ida, la còsta!*"
She imagined, as she had for weeks,
a dun shore breaking through the fog,
a stand of larkspur, houses
on the curling bay.

As wind broke over the gunwales,
a fine low humming.

It was sudden when she came
to rest, the *Santa Vincenta*, thudding
into dock. The tar-faced lackeys
lowered the chains, seals
popped open, and the ship disgorged
its spindly crates, dark trunks
and children with their weepy frowns.
There were goats and chickens,
litters and a score of coffins
on the wharf at once.

Cold, wet, standing by herself
in the lines of custom
under some grey dome, rain falling
through the broken glass above her,
she could think of nothing
but the hills she knew:
the copper grasses, olives
dropping in the dirt, furze
with its yellow tongues of flower.

The Miner's Wake

in memoriam: E.P.

The small ones squirmed in suits and dresses,
wrapped their rosaries round the chair legs,
tapped the walls with squeaky shoes.

But their widowed mother, at thirty-four,
had mastered every pose of mourning,
plodding the sadness like an ox through mud.

Her mind ran well ahead of her heart,
making calculations of the years without him
that stretched before her like a humid summer.

The walnut coffin honeyed in sunlight;
calla lilies bloomed over silk and satin.
Nuns cried heaven into their hands

while I, a nephew with my lesser grief,
sat by a window, watching pigeons
settle onto slag like summer snow.

Coal Train

Three times a night it woke you
in middle summer, the Erie Lackawanna,
running to the north on thin, loud rails.
You could feel it coming a long way off:
at first, a tremble in your belly,
a wire trilling in your veins, then diesel
rising to a froth beneath your skin.
You could see the cowcatcher,
wide as a mouth and eating ties,
the headlight blowing a dust of flies.
There was no way to stop it.
You lay there, fastened to the tracks
and waiting, breathing like a bull,
your fingers lit at the tips like matches.
You waited for the thunder of wheel and bone,

the axles sparking, fire in your spine.
Each passing was a kind of death,
the whistle dwindling to a ghost in air,
the engine losing itself in trees.
In a while, your heart was the loudest thing,
your bed was a pool of night.

LINDA PASTAN

Grudnow

When he spoke of where he came from,
my grandfather could have been
clearing his throat
of that name, that town
sometimes Poland, sometimes Russia,
the borders pencilled in
with a hand as shaky as his.
He left, I heard him say,
because there was nothing there.

I understood what he meant
when I saw the photograph
of his people standing
against a landscape emptied
of crops and trees, scraped raw
by winter. Everything
was in sepia, as if the brown earth
had stained the faces,
stained even the air.

I would have died there, I think
in childhood maybe
of some fever,
my face pressed for warmth
against a cow with flanks
like those of the great aunts
in the picture. Or later
I would have died of history
like the others, who dug

their stubborn heels into that earth,
heels as hard as the heels
of the bread my grandfather tore
from the loaf at supper. He always
sipped his tea through a cube of sugar
clenched in his teeth, the way
he sipped his life here, noisily,

through all he remembered
that might have been sweet in Grudnow.

It Is Raining on the House of Anne Frank

It is raining on the house
of Anne Frank
and on the tourists
herded together under the shadow
of their umbrellas,
on the perfectly silent
tourists who would rather be
somewhere else
but who wait here on stairs
so steep they must rise
to some occasion
high in the empty loft,
in the quaint toilet,
in the skeleton
of a kitchen
or on the map—
each of its arrows
a barb of wire—
with all the dates, the expulsions,
the forbidding shapes
of continents.
And across Amsterdam it is raining
on the Van Gogh Museum
where we will hurry next
to see how someone else
could find the pure
center of light
within the dark circle
of his demons.

A Real Story

Sucking on hard candy
to sweeten the taste
of old age,

grandpa told us stories
about chickens,
city chickens sold
for sabbath soup
but rescued at the end
by some chicken-loving
providence.

Now at ninety-five,
sucked down
to nothing himself,
he says he feels
a coldness;
perhaps the coldness David felt
even with Abishag
in his bed
to warm
his chicken-thin bones.

But when we say
you'll soon get well,
grandpa pulls the sheet
over his face,
raising it between us
the way he used to raise
the Yiddish paper
when we said
enough chickens
tell us a real story.

Rachel (a ewe)

We named you
for the sake
of the syllables
and for the small boat
that followed the Pequod
gathering lost children
of the sea.

We named you
for the dark-eyed girl

who waited at the well
while her lover
worked seven years
and again
seven.

We named you
for the small daughters
of the holocaust
who followed their six-pointed stars
to death
and were all of them
known as Rachel.

A Short History of Judaic Thought
in the Twentieth Century

The rabbis wrote:
although it is forbidden
to touch a dying person,
nevertheless, if the house
catches fire
he must be removed
from the house.

Barbaric!
I say,
and whom may I touch then,
aren't we all
dying?

You smile
your old negotiator's smile
and ask:
but aren't all our houses
burning?

A Secret Place, with View

JANUARY 27, 1932 *"Wed. Busy day. Helped Doc inventory. 2-½ hours. To picture show, 'Dr. Jekyll and Mr. Hyde.' Good. By myself."*

My father wrote that entry in his diary some years before I was born but, even now, I find the words a very accurate portrayal. He worked. He went to movies. He spent time alone. That was the same man I knew during my childhood years in New Orleans, where we lived in a typical neighborhood, not far from Audubon Park. Everything—grocery, dry cleaners, drug store, barber shop, restaurant, bar, hardware store—was within two blocks of our home. And, most importantly, the movie theater, too. Each of those places connects with a vivid memory. My Dad and I ran over to the dry cleaners one night and watched it burn up, the flames making red and orange rivulets in the sky. Our neighborhood restaurant, the air thick with cigarette smoke and the odor of Jax beer and crab gumbo, was the site of the most joyful moment of my childhood. My mother and father were sitting in a booth, deliriously happy, and I was sitting between them. They leaned over to kiss one another, squeezing me from both sides, and I looked up at them, touching lips, and it seemed to me that the universe purred for a moment.

All the places in my neighborhood survive in my memory like souvenirs in a lock box, but the most vivid, and certainly the most important, recollections of my early childhood in New Orleans are of the movie theater and going there often with my father. Sensing that he was more relaxed and happy in that dim haven than anyplace else, I began to feel the same way. Nothing passed between us but the experience; he never said a word about a single movie. We went, we sat, we watched, we walked silently home. He liked it that way, so I thought it was normal. At least I could be with him.

JANUARY 2, 1932. *"Sat. Worked. Hell to be poor. GS and I to picture show 'Frankenstein.' Great Gal. Great time."*

"GS" was my mother and while they must have gone to movies before I was born, they rarely did later. She made another life for herself in New Orleans, one less passive than the movie theater. That my mother understood New Orleans better than anyone was apparent in one of her favorite sayings, "If you can't eat it, drink it, or catch it off a float, it doesn't exist!" The "float" of course was a reference to Mardi Gras, where trinkets are thrown from floats to all the revelers standing along the parade routes. Eat, drink, and make year-round Mardi Gras, that was my mother's philosophy of life and it fit perfectly with the city.

I envied the way she made New Orleans her place, moving about it with grace and assurance. Whatever restaurant we went to she had her own table and a waiter she called by name. At the stores where she shopped there was always a particular salesperson who regularly waited on her. As soon as we walked in that woman would come over and say, "Hello, Mrs. Perry, how are you? What can I help you with today?"

"Helen, I'm just wonderful, darling, thank you. I need some new dress shoes, please."

"I'll be right back. The perfect thing just came in." And Helen always knew exactly what my mother would like.

Unlike my mother, I never conquered New Orleans; it's less a city, even a hometown, and more a place where I went to movies with my father. Strange. Although I grew up in New Orleans, when someone asks me where I'm from, I simply say, "my family is from Mississippi," which is true.

DEC. 8, 1931. *"Tues. Busy Day. Went to show, Greta Garbo 'Fall and Rise of Susan Lennox.' Out to Lake Ponchatrain for house party. Beer and Boiled shrimp. What a spree. Morning found me in bed with shoes on."*

Not too long ago one of my sons and I went to my alleged hometown, New Orleans, for a visit, and, as we got out of the car in a parking lot near the end of Canal Street, close to the Mississippi River, I instantly recognized the heat of the July sun on the back of my neck and the odor of fish that stung my nostrils. That these experiences were familiar seemed obvious, but they were like memories that someone had told me I should have. We walked through the French Quarter for several hours, past the place near Lafitte's Blacksmith Shop on Bourbon St. where I lived for a while as an adult, but each step brought a more recondite sadness. This was my home place yet I felt no pleasure at sharing it with my son. The familiar signposts were there but they had about as much substance as the façade of a movie set. Perhaps that's why I have come to call New Orleans the City of Mystery, a name I first used the day when, as an adult after my parents were dead, I walked out of the Orleans Parish Court House with photocopies of their divorce papers. An aunt of mine had told me that she was fairly certain my parents had been divorced, which was surprising news to me, although given the fact that they only saw each other for two weeks each year after I was nine years old, being divorced would make more sense than their marriage. On the papers I saw my parents' signatures, still so familiar, written when I was eighteen months old. The divorce papers told me nothing except that they had been filed and then resolved with an agreement that my mother would leave town and my father would get custody of me. But no divorce. When did she come back, and why?

JANUARY 12, 1932. *"Tues. Good day. Date with GS. She's a Peach. It's getting serious. To show 'Mata Hari.'"*

The New Orleans that is meaningful to me is not really the city, not the place where the smell of fresh French bread made me salivate, not the town where acorns crunched under my feet, not even the home of the world's greatest dish, Trout Marguery at Galatoire's. The New Orleans that was really important to me was none of these things but rather a dark crawl space under my house. That was my secret place.

Like many residences in New Orleans, our home was built on a pier and beam foundation, fully three feet above ground. To hide this opening, the sides visible from the street were bricked up. When I was nine years old, I crawled under the house from the back, made my way to the front, and then removed a brick after carefully chiseling it out. Through the opening I could watch everything that happened on the street. As each car passed, I would identify it by year and make; people would stop on the sidewalk and carry on conversations, not realizing that I was within earshot. Once I saw a friend, Clotide, who was only nine or ten at the time, secretly pinched by her mother as they were carrying on a conversation with a neighbor. I couldn't tell what Clotide had done wrong, but I saw her mother's fingers pick up a piece of flesh on the child's back and squeeze it painfully until the skin was white. Clotilde didn't move, or even flinch. Her mother never stopped talking. The cruel act was hidden from the neighbor, but I saw everything from my concealed location.

This secret place under the house was pitch-black and damp, and I loved it there. That dark sanctuary with a rectangular window looking out on the world, that was my home place and more than any other site informed my life. Not until years later did I realize how like a darkened movie theater it was. The brick hole was rectangular, like a movie screen, and the events on the sidewalk and in the street were like images on that screen. That dim cave, its rectangular window looking out on the world, was the template that formed much of my sum and substance.

OCTOBER 11, 1931. *"Sun. Up late. Broke with GS. Over nothing. Walked around town. To my own church in eve. Lonesome as hell. To midnite picture show, Marx Bros. in 'Cracked Nuts.'"*

Cracked Nuts is not a Marx Bros. movie; my father must have confused *Animal Crackers*, which is what he probably saw that day, with *Cocoanuts*, an earlier film of theirs. That the title he wrote in his diary seemed strange to me is not surprising; much of my life has been spent not just in going to movies but also in writing, reading, and talking about films. I even made my living for a while by writing and directing documentary films and since then by teaching about films at universities and colleges. It was in a course of mine on voyeurism in cinema that I first realized how much the secret place under my house was so like a movie theater. Halfway through that course, exploring films like Powell's *Peeping Tom*, Lynch's *Blue Velvet*, and especially Hitchcock's *Rear Window*, I realized that these films repeated my experience as a child, a voyeur looking out on the world from a special vantage point.

My attachment to film then is very old and very personal. I've been an avid moviegoer most of my life, and this moviegoing has served me in many different ways. When I am lonely and despondent I go to the movies, and for a while things seem much better. Doesn't everyone? I rub against the screen, get excited, and feel involved; watching the film becomes an autoerotic event. When the world around me is going crazy, I can go to a movie and get relaxed. The emotions there are confined, orderly and measured.

One of my most frequent moviegoing periods was when I lived in Baltimore and attended Johns Hopkins. At first everything was wonderful. A Southern boy, I felt like a young Thomas Wolfe come to the fabled North, walking the streets and uttering prose identical to whole passages in *Of Time and the River*. Movies were the last thing on my mind, and the only problem was the work that I did at Hopkins' School of Public Health. My supervisor was in the middle of a major research project on malaria, so the lab was full of mosquitoes who wanted blood. For several hours each day, I had to stick my arms inside various cages. The *anopheles* and the *culex pipiens* weren't so bad, but one species' radar was broken. Each insect would stick her proboscis in my arm, come up dry, pull out, step over a few paces, then plunge in again, repeating the procedure until she found blood. That annoyed me.

The more blood I gave, the more movies I started going to see. Being broke and feeling inept in my classes didn't help. I needed all the films I could get; yet not a single title or image remains with me today. Passing through my body like an electric current, the movies made me tingle and then disappeared without a trace. For as long as the sensation lasted, I felt potent.

APRIL 1, 1932. *"Fri. Depression is still on. Will it ever end? Made up with GS. First piece of strawberry shortcake. Date to picture show, Geo. Arliss in 'Man Who Played God.' Lost my heart for sure. If I only had a steady job. No more by myself."*

That I created the secret place under my house at a very specific time in my childhood was no accident. I was nine years old when one day my father said to me, "I'm leaving for Africa in a few days. I can make more money overseas, enough to take care of you and your mother. Here, let me show you the route my plane is taking. It's pretty interesting." I watched him spread the map out on the floor and trace a route down to Natal, Brazil, and across the Atlantic to West Africa. It didn't seem interesting to me at all.

And then my father was gone. Within weeks I crawled under my house and fabricated my secret refuge. My film-going dramatically increased, too. My mother didn't seem to mind if I walked to the movie theater by myself, so I went there often. Why? Perhaps I expected to learn from movies something that escaped me otherwise; my father's leaving was such a shock and surprise. Maybe I thought if I looked at movies long enough they would reveal something I hadn't understood about my parents and my home. The movie theater was his place, so if I went there I would find him and answers about him. That might be the reason, although it sounds too abstract. And I don't think I went to the movies for the pleasure of it; most of the time I was terrified in the dark theater by myself. The smell there was a ghastly mixture of popcorn, urine, and old strawberry bubble gum. Every film and every serial I saw seemed to have scenes with quicksand, and my heroes and heroines were always slipping into the dreadful stuff, being sucked down into a horrible, suffocating death. When they fell in, I would quickly put my hands on both sides of my face, so that people on either side could not see that I was closing my eyes. I was too frightened to watch and even more afraid that some schoolmate would see me closing my eyes.

The fear was still with me when I walked out of the movie theater and headed the several blocks home, winding my way carefully among the dark shadows cast by street lights shining through the huge live oaks. I would stop sometimes because the odor of honeysuckle was so thick that I thought some sweet-smelling monster was nearby. And sometimes I would run the entire way home; other times, when I felt really brave, I walked, although in the center of the street, keeping away from the shadows that covered the sidewalk and hid the murderers who were out to get me. Even when I walked in the middle of the street, naturally I whistled. That way the bad people would know how courageous I was; nobody would dare to fool with me.

MARCH 10, 1932. *"Thurs. Out to GS's. On a high horse. Left mad. Seems like we've come to the end of the rope. Shame, too. Nice kid. Late to bed."*

Not only did I go more to movies after my father left, not only did I carve out a secret retreat under my house, I also suddenly began shooting home movies. Shortly after my father arrived in Africa, he sent back to me a small nugget of gold and an ivory tusk. All of nine years old, I got on the streetcar by myself, rode down to Canal Street, walked into the French Quarter, sold the gold and the tusk, then went to Sears and used the money to buy a 16-mm, hand-cranked, Keystone movie camera. Not long ago I looked again at the films I made; they're filled with everything important in my childhood—my best friends, Ralston and Titter Cole; my old green two-story house; my dog, "Tippi"; a scene I staged of my mother picking Crepe Myrtle blossoms; and even a sequence of my father made during one of his later visits. What possessed me in 1946 at age nine, when not a single person I knew made home movies, to get a 16-mm camera and start filming?

SEPTEMBER 26, 1931. *"Sat. Half day. Half crazy. Slept in aft. GS and I to picture show and then Club Forest for dancing. Tried to drink all the beer. Some brawl. Ended in French Market at 6:30 AM."*

Going to the movies, making movies, creating a concealed movie theater under my house—what were all these activities? I knew they had something to do with my father leaving, but what? The answer came to me one day as I was reading a review of *Once Upon a Time*, Gloria Vanderbilt's autobiography, which noted that her way of dealing with meancing and painful childhood events was to make drawings of everything and everybody. From the drawings Gloria made paper dolls: "it all gets very complicated, but with the paper dolls it's easier to sort out. . . . It's *me* who moves everybody around." The drawings and the paper dolls were Gloria's way of subjugating an environment which had too much power over her.

I had done the same thing but with movies. In the dark theater I could have control; I could run the world. Did I wish for the good guys to win and the bad guys to suffer? They did, always. And even when the bad guys threatened, I could handle it. I was strong, so bring on the quicksand. Maybe I didn't always watch everything, but I would endure any terror, absolutely certain that if I could survive the fright inside the movie theater, nothing outside could possibly phase me. I could whistle my way through life.

The movies I made were also instruments of control. People stood still for me to film them, and no matter how many times I projected the images, nothing was different. No surprises, no sudden and painful changes; always the same, predictable actions over and over. Images are magic; they make the world do what you want it to do. Under my house, I may not have been able to dictate what cars drove by, or which people paused to chat, but I knew I was hidden. I watched but nobody watched me. And as long as I could observe, without being observed, I felt very privileged and in control. All my relationships with movies gave me a heightened sense of power and a special sense of myself.

The movies were doing for me what, in the movie *E. T.*, the Extra-Terrestrial does for Elliott. The boy, whose father is also absent, repeatedly proclaims about E. T., "He came to *me!*" If no father is present to declare that Elliott is special, an Extra-Terrestrial will do it. The young boy found an unusual surrogate for his missing father, as did I in embracing the movies. I felt just as unique and powerful when I was making movies, as well as when I was sitting in my movie theaters, and certainly while I hid under my house, and even later when teaching and writing about film. Do the students in my classes know the origins of my desire to watch movies, my film scopophila? I doubt it.

> OCTOBER 20, 1931. *"Tues. Busiest day in the whole week. Tried to stay home all eve. Not safe, being alone. To GS. Sure sweet. Went to see picture show, 'The Squaw Man.'"*

I suppose over the years that all of my moviegoing is some kind of attempt to find my father; I still expect to find him in a movie house. Have I ever found him? Sometimes, sort of. Once when I looked again at David Lean's *Lawrence of Arabia*, some years after it had come out, I recalled that my father's favorite book, the one that seemed to reappear wherever he lived, was Lawrence's autobiography, *Seven Pillars of Wisdom*. I had read it some years before but learned little about my father. This time I decided to read a biography of Lawrence; at a certain point I found myself reading about the famous soldier's masochism, how he liked to be beaten. One of his ruses to get someone to beat him was to say that he had done something quite terrible to an uncle and that the uncle demanded that Lawrence be punished. He would then produce for the acquaintance a letter from this fictitious uncle, a letter that Lawrence himself had written. After beating Lawrence, and being paid, supposedly by the uncle, the person was then to write and give details of the beating. Lawrence would take that letter for posting and then compose an answer from the uncle. As one letter says, "From what you tell me, and from the reports of those who have examined Ted since, it is clear that he had a sound thrashing." The "Ted" surprised me until I realized that Lawrence's middle name was Edward. Ted, a more common diminutive for Edward than it is now, was evidently used as a nickname by his service friends and some family members.

My father had named me "Edward" and called me "Ted." Lawrence died in 1935; I was born in 1937. The connection seemed more than accidental. Suddenly a movie, and a biography, had allowed me to reach back through time and read a message from my father. But what was he saying? That he identified with Lawrence the loner, or the hero, or the masochist? I've answered that question different ways at different times in my life and each time thought that I had the right answer.

> APRIL 23, 1930. *"Weds. Still hunting for work. To P.O. at 5:30 a.m. for job. About 2000 men there. No job. Walked home, only 5 miles. Found two-bits on sidewalk. Saw Buster Keaton 'Free and Easy.'"*

I have met my father in other movie houses, often much to my surprise, as when I went to see an Australian movie, *Careful He Might Hear You*. After I left the screening, I thought back through the film and realized there was a big gap in my memory of what happened. In a few days, interested in what I had forgotten, I went back to the film. As that section approached, I had an overwhelming urge to go to the bathroom. When I returned, the sequence was over. Now really curious, I went back again a day or two later, only to miss the sequence again because I went to get popcorn. Obviously some part of me just didn't want me to see a certain section of that film. I forced myself at last to watch the sequence, only to see on the screen an absent, wandering father, who had abandoned his son, returning briefly and bringing his son a gift—a nugget of gold. Until that moment in that film, I had conveniently forgotten altogether that my father had sent me a fragment of gold from Africa, the one I sold to buy my movie camera, as well as how angry the token gift had made me.

One of my most vivid encounters with my father at the movies involved Antonioni's *Eclipse*. In the scene before the ending of the film, a young couple much in love promises to meet each and every evening forever, *"domani e dopodomani . . . e il giorno dopo e quell'altro ancora,"* at a particular street corner. The last sequence of *Eclipse* then explores that corner and all the activities that occur there and nearby as a day draws to its close. Finally it is apparent that an evening has come when the couple fails to meet. The first time I saw the film I was deeply affected by the ending. "Never ignore the libidinal instinct in your work," one of my graduate school professors told me, so I spent some time writing about *Eclipse*. But only after several years of being stunned by the ending, for reasons that were never clear to me, and after publishing an essay, did I realize that I was gripped by the last moments of the film because they replicated my own experience with my father's departure. One day he was there, loving and attentive, the very center of my life, and the next day, like the lovers in *Eclipse*, he didn't show up anymore.

MAY 16, 1931. *"Sat. Date with GS for show. Saw Lew Ayres in 'Iron Man.' What a swell time we had. Crazy about that girl."*

I'm not sure I always understand the connection between my father and movies, although I am convinced that for a long time much of my moviegoing, movie making, and movie teaching began in my secret movie theater under my New Orleans home and were connected with that father who died 36 years ago, with the rage and mortification I felt when he left, and with my desire to make order and structure in a fatherless world.

JANUARY 31, 1931. *"Tues. Date with GS to show, Charlie Chaplin in 'City Lights.' No good."*

Sometimes now I even feel quite betrayed by films; when I first saw Wim Wenders' *Wings of Desire*, I was deeply inspired by its portrayal of the possibility that human beings could, with enough effort and desire, achieve transcendence. Epiphanies were possible after all. Seeing the film again months later, I was struck by how simplistic it was, just another version of the old romantic myth that if people find the right partner then all of life will be wonderful. I felt humiliated; the film had been so important and now it was patently untrue. I had been lied to.

The more I find falsehoods in film, the less I want to meet my father in a movie theater. And the less I think about my dark cave under my home in New Orleans. I still keep reading his damn diaries though.

I attend movies, of course. After all, I still make my living by teaching about film. In the dark theater, I now watch and listen with a pleasure which is not a substitute for anything else, although given the choice I'd rather have my father there, too. He might point out to me that the hero had just shot eight times without reloading his six-shooter. That's the kind of discovery you expect from a father. Mine never gave me this truth; I observed it myself. But I imagine that such a terrible revelation is a lot easier to handle if your father is there with you. Aren't fathers supposed to teach us what is and is not real?

On second thought, who wants to go to a movie where everything is real? I prefer my transcendences to arrive on the wings of resplendent shadows.

MARCH 1, 1933. *"Wed. More of my bad luck. GS off to Washington D.C. for inauguration of Pres. F. D. Roosevelt. Just when I needed her. Sure miss that gal."*

SAMUEL F. PICKERING, JR.

Gathering

Into the basket on the bicycle I put two cloth book bags, the first distributed as an advertisement for *Riverside Reader*, a textbook for college freshmen, the second given to students at Eliza's school in order to encourage reading. Printed in big blue letters near the top of the bag was "NORTHWEST"; near the bottom appeared "LIBRARY." In between a happy blue whale spouted a fountain of ink while swimming through a sea of letters reading "A WHALE OF A SCHOOL." Later, at the English department I picked up two handfuls of rubber bands and then sixty-eight "Reusable" envelopes, printed for the "State of Connecticut" in order to send "Interdepartmental Mail" from one agency to another. Nine and a half inches long with pink lines dividing the fronts into thirds resembling pages from a small address book, the envelopes were just right for specimens. The day was windy, and a cold rain fell, blowing from drizzle into gray mist then back to drizzle. Weather rarely influences my little expeditions. Earlier in the week I decided to spend Thursday roaming the campus, looking at trees and gathering fruits. Although I could identify all the trees in the woods behind the barns and along the Fenton River, I couldn't name some of the trees growing on the campus, just a quarter mile from my door. After pushing the envelopes into the bottom of the library bag and buckling on my helmet, I pedaled over to the Ratcliffe Hicks building and began my study. Six hours later I finished. I shook in the cold, and my feet were almost numb, but I had a basket wondrously full of warm leaf and fruit.

I am not sure why I brought the fruits home. Gathering, though, is part of my nature, and so long as I can remember I have cluttered house and mind with things. Nowadays as memory stretches thin and becomes pocked with sievelike holes, I gather more, perhaps trying to plug recollection with leaf and bark, or, if not that, then with a grout of stringy words. On the floor of the study between the television and red sofa, I displayed my harvest: the conelike fruit of the tulip tree resembling an ornament carved on an antique newel post, brown spiny balls from sweet gum, from the goldenrain tree small tawny lanterns, the seeds inside dark round bulbs; pods from the honey locust twisting like giant screws; next to them fragile silver pods from the redbud, and from the sweetbay magnolia cones covered with loose red seeds ringing like maracas. Into a low flat box that once held twenty-four cans of beer I put a walnut, a twig bending with the pitted red fruits of kousa dogwood, a hunk of bark from an Amur corktree, green catalpa seeds seven inches long, and then from the osage orange, two hairy fruits, sticky and lumpy, resembling, the children said, "gorilla brains." In a smaller, deeper flat box, one which once contained a quart of peaches from Johnny Appleseed's Farm in Ellington, Connecticut, probably jayhaven or redkist peaches, I dumped twenty-six fruits from the yellow buckeye. Some of the nuts were loose, but most had not broken free from the spongy capsules surrounding them like eiderdowns.

Ripe with berries, instead of bulbs, the floor of the study was bright as a Christmas tree. Near my desk were the green fruits of gallery pear. In front of the television, switches of English and Washington Hawthorne, European mountains ash, and double-file viburnum glowed red with berries. Against a footstool leaned a fan of burning bush, the leaves scarlet and the fruits furiously orange. On the floor lay twigs from fringe trees, the fruits dark blue olives, and then swatches of basswood, the fruits clustered and resembling drops of green tea sloshed from the mug of a careless drinker. I opened the hairy pod of a beech and placed the seed alongside that of the silverbell. Although the beech was only half an inch long in contrast to the silverbell's one and three-quarter inches and had three wings instead of the silverbell's four, the seeds resembled each other, with sharp needles at their tips, helping them, I thought, to dig through grass and into dirt when they fell from branches. Ginkgoes had begun to ripen into fragrance. Eliza and I liked the aroma, thinking it resembled sweet plum jam. Vicki and Edward differed with us, and Vicki ordered me to throw the fruits outside, saying they smelled like "raccoon shit," something she has never sniffed and which I told her was "marvelous," having little odor and often being radiant with the elytra of beetles.

From a tablecloth of fiery red leaves the seeds of sourwood rose in a candelabra. From many trees I did not gather fruit. Instead I brought home impressions of bark: the sharp thorns on castor aralia, spongy redwood, butternut hickory pinstriped and as formal as the dress of a banker, three-flowered maple shredding into scrolls, then lacebark elm, raised dots peppering the surface like small pegs. I picked leaves off all the elms on campus: lacebark, American, slippery, Siberian, camper-down, and Japanese Zelkova. With its leaves cut into sharp greens and yellows and its buds tight bundles along the twigs, a sprig of Siberian elm resembled a cutting of Victorian wallpaper. Twig and fruit often brought things homey to mind, the feathery leaves of dawn redwood and baldycypress reminding me of antimacassars, and, the seeds of box elder musty like old horsecollars hooked and dangling around thick leather twine.

Gathering keeps me vital. If I did not pluck fruit and leaf, I fear I would sag completely out of the present and settle into sentimental memory, into a past as comfortable as a bolster. Happily, the bed on which I doze is often lumpy, even prickly. Last month when I snuggled up to Vicki, she pulled the covers tightly around her shoulders, making her, I thought at the time, resemble the fruit of a yellow buckeye. "Vicki," I started to protest. I got no further. "Sam," she said firmly; "it's enough for me to know that you are here in the bed." "Oh," I answered, then added, "goodnight." "Goodnight," she said, "and sweet dreams." The next morning I drove to Hartford to catch a plane to North Carolina. On the way I stopped at the Enchanted Bakery in Tolland and bought two amaretto truffle brownies. Unlike sugary dreams, desserts leave crumbs behind, something Vicki does not like to find either in a bed or on a car seat. To keep domestic life smooth, I sift carefully through the hours, greasing minutes whenever possible. So that crumbs would not fall onto the seat, I leaned forward over the steering wheel to eat the brownies. In my left hand I held a napkin under my chin. In my right I grasped both brownie and wheel, pinching the brownie between thumb, index, and middle fingers while wrapping my fourth and little fingers around the wheel. By sliding my hand back and forth around the wheel and by dipping my head, I drove the brownie into my mouth while I steered the car along the interstate. And I did so without an accident; not a single crumb drifted beyond the napkin and crashed against the seat. Such care, alas, does not always insure a smooth bed or reception, and when I returned from North Carolina two days later, things at home were almost as bumpy as the bark on a hackberry tree. "Daddy," Eliza shouted when I walked through the garage door, "The brothers are taking my pretend people." "What," I said, putting my suitcase down by the stove. "Edward and Francis won't leave Pillard-Pillard my seagull alone," Eliza said; "I told them that Pillard-Pillard had gone to Illinois to visit his grandmother. Then he went to the state fair and won a stuffed fish for her, but Edward does not believe me. He says Pillard-Pillard went to Florida for a vacation, and Bob-Bob the crocodile ate him." "What," I repeated. "Daddy," Eliza continued, "tell Edward that you'll spank him if he doesn't leave Pillard-Pillard alone. Also tell him to get rid of Bob-Bob. We can't have a crocodile in this house; he frightens all the other pretend people."

After Edward promised to chain Bob-Bob to the desk in his room, Eliza calmed down, and soon her pretend people resumed wandering house and story. At dinner the next day, Pillard-Pillard sent a postcard from Honolulu. At the fair he entered a contest for best bird and won a two-week vacation in Honolulu. I envied Pillard-Pillard. Birds of a feather vacation together, and if I had not been collecting material for the Reverend Slubey Garts, one of the pretend people inhabiting my essays, I would have winged it out to Hawaii and strolled the white sands with old P-P, as I call him, now that I have gotten to know him better. To give my pretend people xylem and cortex, pith, phleom, and cambium, I spend much time gathering words. Minister of the Tabernacle of Love in Carthage, Tennessee, Slubey himself is fond of words. Not long ago he preached a fire and sorghum sermon, urging his flock to prepare themselves for the final shearing. "The fat ain't always going to be on the 'possum. Some cold morning," he declared, "tears as big as taters are going to run down your cheeks. Dr. Sollows won't be able to help you then. Only the Lord can move you from the sickroom to the living room." Spring was in the air, and some of the lambs were a little too frisky, so Slubey urged them to remember the end, that morning when the green pastures would turn sour and the wolf would break into the fold, carving congregations into chop and roast. "Some of you sisters," he said, "think you got the wings of a locust and come Judgment Day believe you can fly right up to the Pearly Gates. Well, I'm here to tell you," he said, rolling his eyes toward the ceiling, "you ain't even going to get as far as Red Boiling Springs. Just as soon as you heist yourselves out of the dirt you are wallowing in, an old peckerwood will see you and flap down out of the woods and gobble you right up. The soul ain't no magic hoe what works by itself. No, sir, you got to pull and chop, pull and chop. You got to fight against sin all the time. The cat don't catch no mice wearing gloves. You've got to seize the devil and shake him. And don't stop. Don't ever sleep. The devil is like that big snapping turtle Deacon Goforth found behind the shed last summer. Our brother chopped that turtle's head off and tossed it into the garden, thinking that would be the end of it. But it warn't. Not by a long shot. You can't kill sin. The next morning the deacon heard a terrible racket in the garden. He rushed out, and what did he see? He seen," Slubey said, raising his hands above his head and wiggling his fingers like serpents, "a sight what would make turtledoves groan. He seen that head trying to swallow a rooster."

Googoo Hooberry rarely left Carthage, and when Loppie Groat met Googoo outside Prunty's store in Little Dover, he was surprised. "Googoo," Loppie exlaimed, "fancy meeting you here. Are you traveling around today, or are you just going somewheres?" Although I travel through books searching for story, I rarely let stories take me anywhere other than Carthage. What I enjoy most is spreading tales across my desk much as I spread leaf and fruit across the study. Occasionally I keep a story, dumping it into an essay as potting soil in which to root pretend people. Loppie Groat was Clevanna Farquarson's first cousin twice removed, and when she applied for the job of cook at the Male and Female Select School, Clevanna listed Loppie as a character reference. After reading Clevanna's application, Judge Rutherford called Loppie to his chambers. "Loppie," he said, "can you vouch for Clevanna's veracity?" For a moment Loppie looked startled. "Judge," he said; "I didn't know such things mattered, leastways for a cook, and to tell you the truth I just don't know her that way. Some say she do, and others say she don't. But why don't you ask her, Judge," Loppie continued; "she'll give you a straight answer. She's as honest as the day is long."

Clevanna got the job, and a week later she cooked a celebratory lunch for Loppie. Although the drive from Little Dover to Carthage prevented Loppie from ploughing, the day was not lost. Early that afternoon, Barlow Warple fell into the hot wax vat at Walduck's Candle Manufactory on Spring Street. "Barlow turned himself into a human wick," Loppie told Clevanna later; "with all that wax on him he was as slick as owl grease and couldn't nobody get him out until Finster Mulrynne come up with the bright idea of using grappling hooks." That morning Mr. Walduck saw Loppie in Carthage with his wagon, and after the accident he hired Loppie to deliver the corpse to Barlow's house in Buffalo Valley. Loppie had not been to Barlow's house before and, for that matter, had not met Mrs. Warple. On arriving at what he thought was the right address, he knocked on the door. When a woman opened the door, he took off his hat and said, "Excuse me. I'm not sure of my directions. But are you the Widow Warple?" "My name is Warple," the woman replied, looking puzzled, "but I'm not a widow." "Ma'am, you just think you ain't," Loppie said gesturing toward the road; "don't say no more until you see the body I've got in that there wagon by the fence."

Every spring the Cumberland River flooded. Often people who lived along the riverbank below Carthage had to leave their homes for three or four days. Although a house was occasionally swept away, the floods were beneficial, depositing silt on the bottomland and providing farmers with an early cash crop. Before abandoning their houses to the water, farmers put out mousetraps baited with doughballs in order to catch catfish. Barrels of fish were caught and sent to Nashville, so many that for a while Carthage advertised itself as "The Catfish Capital of the World." Although I have never pulled a fish from a trap, I have netted a piscatorial tale or two, fishy in its veracity. From the English Midlands I hooked the story of the Fourth Wiseman, Kenelm. A great hero, Kenelm was hurrying to join Gaspar, Melchior, and Balthasar at the manger in Bethlehem when for the good of Britain he turned aside. During the Great

Flood a "hairless dog-headed worm" washed ashore near London. For centuries the worm remained small, causing only minor damage, laying putrid "wind-eggs" in wells and spoiling water. Suddenly, though, the worm grew monstrously large. Not only did its breath cause crops to mildew, but suffering from an unquenchable thirst, it threatened to drink the Thames dry. For six years Kenelm fought the worm unsuccessfully. Whenever he sliced the worm into bits, the pieces rejoined, forming an even larger monster. In the seventh year, though, Kenelm destroyed the creature. Britons constructed a huge bonfire. Once the fire was lit, Kenelm walked into it and remained there until his armor was red hot. Now when he fought the worm and chopped its body into pieces, the hot armor cauterized the wounds, making it impossible for the seperate bits to join together again. A charm protected Kenelm himself from the heat. A thorn had been removed from a white hawthorne and driven deep into his left eye. Although Kenelm lost sight in that eye, he saved his country.

Kenelm carried two presents for the baby Jesus, a cage of doves and an ear of corn. When he saw the worm, he placed the gifts on the ground, and during the long struggle they vanished, at least people with ordinary vision could not find them after the battle ended. The loss of Kenelm's left eye, however, was a blessing, giving him insight and making him farseeing. Not only did the Lord accept the gifts for His Son but he sent Kenelm a sign, showing his pleasure. On the spot where Kenelm set the cage of doves grew a new flower, the columbine, its blossoms resembling doves huddled together in prayer. The actual doves carried the corn to the Holy Land where later it became known as Turkey Wheat. Initially all the kernels on the ear were white. At the crucifixion, however, many kernels changed color, some becoming red to represent the blood of Christ, others going into mourning and turning black, still others turning blue like the firmament itself, making the corn the most beautiful and desirable in the world.

Each fall, I travel around, to use Loppie's words, to several literary gatherings. I make talks, and I like to believe that I am going "somewheres." Not all my friends agree. Recently a novelist sent me a letter. "You should be using more of your time to write," he advised, "instead of running around and giving all these speeches." My friend writes books that have beginnings, middles, and ends. My essays meander, and as I wander through literary gatherings I slip into story. Much as I pedaled across campus cramming bark and twig into envelopes, so I wheel into rooms and pluck phrases from conversations. At a recent conference in Massachusetts, adolescents read poetry. Although the authors were fresh and budding, their poems were a wintry glaze of unhappiness: accounts of suicide, murder, incest, and dismal love. "Does a person have to be middle-aged to laugh," a man muttered. "*Lies* not *lays* on me," a woman said in response to a poem by a cherubic eighth grader. "I don't care if your nipples are swollen red citadels; he lies on you," the woman continued, talking to herself before turning to the man and saying, "What is the world coming to? None of these children know proper English."

A month ago I spent a weekend in Florida. For a fund-raiser a library brought a handful of authors to town. During the day the writers read excerpts from their books while at night local people held dinner parties at their homes. The first evening an Armenian poet and I went to a large house on a riverbank. A string quartet played in the entrance hall. Before a window a silver lazy Susan reached to the ceiling, orchids dangling like water from each shelf. Under a chandelier gleaming like a mall our hosts greeted us, shaking hands with both of us, then pinning a white orchid on the poet's dress. "What did you think of them?" I said to my companion as we strolled into the study. "He was tall and thin. That's good, and she," the poet said, her voice suddenly rising, "she looks like she loves to fuck." "What," I said. "You heard me," the poet said; "now get me a drink, a tall Scotch with no soda or water and only one ice cube." When I handed her the drink, she was studying a painting of two pink-bottomed cherubs hanging above a sofa. "Thanks," she said, taking the glass and gesturing toward the wall; "now it's your turn. What do you think of this?" "It's a little dull," I said. "Right," she exclaimed, her voice once more rising poetically; "it would be better if they were fucking." This last word rushed outward like a wave of sound. Instead, though, of sweeping people away from us it sucked them toward us, and when a crowd began washing around the poet, I drifted off to the dining room. I filled a plate with smoked salmon, crabmeat, and lamb, and sitting at a table began signing posters advertising the conference. All the participants in the conference signed the posters, and friends of the library made donations, receiving the posters as gifts. I had almost finished the stack of posters when the poet appeared. "Let me have some of those things," she said, taking a heavy gold pen out of her purse. Over the *i*'s in my last name, I drew little hearts. "What's this," the poet said, jabbing the pen at one of the hearts. "A heart," I said; "I put hearts over the *i*'s to cheer people up." "Jesus," the poet exclaimed, "that's corny." "Well," I said, the salmon having made me feel bold, "why don't you draw a phallus near your name. That wouldn't be corny." "What," the poet shouted, standing and looking at me; "I will not draw Dicks on these posters." When several people turned and stared at us, she pointed at me and said, "he wants me to draw Dicks all over these posters, but I won't do it." I had only two more posters left to sign. I hurried through them, omitting the hearts, and returned to the dining room. I did not see the poet again until late the next morning. She was a member of a panel which discussed "Women in Literature." One of the participants disliked men, and afterward when I saw the poet, I said, "that woman on the end didn't seem to care much for men." "Care for men," she exclaimed; "that's putting it mildly. She hates to fuck." Again this last word had a whirlpool effect, pulling people toward us. As they circled and began to talk, I slipped away through a eddy in the conversation. Not until that night after the readings and panels ended did I talk to the poet again. In the lounge of the hotel in which they stayed, several writers sat drinking wine and talking about the conference. I was tired, and I dozed on a couch, dreading the long trip back to Connecticut. Suddenly a voice said, "Get me a drink. You know how I like them." Then the poet sat down next to me with a thump. I got the drink. When I returned, people were discussing a foot fetishist who came to the conference. After asking each of the women to sign one of their books, he said he was a shoe salesman. Explaining that he noticed her shoes when she read, the man asked if he could look inside the right shoe to read "the mark," a number, he explained, which revealed the date and place of manufacture. All the women let him examine their shoes. Once he held a shoe in his hands, he complimented the woman's bare foot. "Good Lord," Kaye said; "he told me my foot resembled a lily, and I just smiled and said, 'thank you.'" "He told me my foot looked like a violet," Connie said, "how terrible." During the discussion the poet had been silent. Suddenly she sat bolt upright. "He told me my foot was a daisy," she said, "and I told him to 'fuck off.' Anyway," she continued, "looking at a foot isn't so bad. It's not fucking." "No, it isn't," I said aloud on the plane the next day, unaccountably starting to giggle, the dull flight exploding into brightness; "it certainly isn't." "What are you laughing about," the man next to me asked. "Poetry," I said; "I'm laughing about poetry."

Although the trip home seemed short, traveling tires me. Often I am tempted to stop, not only running around and giving speeches, as my correspondent advised, but also gathering and writing. When Bob Dylan came to Storrs for a concert, I bought tickets for Vicki and myself, telling a friend that during the 1960s when Bob Dylan was really popular, I was too busy studying to notice. By attending a concert now, I explained, I was becoming part of the communal past of my generation. "Get the flowered shirts, the bellbottoms, the Nehru jackets, and the granny dresses out of the attic and go to the concert," I said. On hearing me mention the concert to another friend in the Cup of Sun, a student looked up from his coffee and said, "Dylan? Who would want to hear him? He's as old as you guys." I recorded the student's statement in one of my notebooks. Later I read it and everything I wrote down about the concert to Vicki. "That's fine, Sam," she said; "but can't you ever do anything without thinking about it? Wouldn't it be more natural, and better, if you just lived through days and didn't write about them?" In part I long to take Vicki's advice. I would like to toss pencils and notebooks into the garbage can. Instead of roaming woods sliding from root to root, rock to rock through a sea of damp leaves, I dream of spending damp fall days inside, sitting in a comfortable chair, reading *Time* or watching the National Football League on television. If I stopped writing, life might be more natural. "When you come to the children's soccer games," Mary told me last week in the Cup of Sun, "one of the mothers always says, 'Be careful what you say. Here comes Sam; he'll write it down.'" Because I write I eavesdrop. Often I hear things I wish I had not heard. "When I was small," a man with a blue and green dragon tattooed on his right forearm said on the street last week, "I used to pick gum off the ground and eat it." Even worse, so that I will have sentences to gather, I forever sew the seeds of narrative around me. Last week when I walked into George's for a haircut, a man in the middle chair was giving Sheila directions on trimming his hair. The man was a stranger, but that did not deter me from starting a story. "Don't listen to him, Sheila," I said; "he's dotty and doesn't know what he wants. Just give him a Mohawk and be done with it." Later a retired member of the English department came into the shop. The man spent forty years writing about Edgar Allen Poe. "Charles," I said, before the man sat down, "Am I glad to see you, old buddy. I have been thinking a lot recently about Poe's story, 'The Fall of the House of Usher.' If Usher had hired a good contractor and had a solid foundation laid down, everything would have been hunky-dory. Have you ever thought about that?" When Charles opined that the thought had not crossed his mind, I gave him a five-minute lecture on bricks, listing the grades of building brick: severe weathering, moderate weathering, and nonweathering or SW, MW, and NW as they are known in the trade. I described pointing styles: flush, weathered, struck, concave, vee, and raked. I asked Charles if Usher knew anything about laying bricks on a sand base or with dry mortar, and then suggested that before he wrote anymore about Poe he go to Willard's and talk to Bob about "home improvements." "Sam," Vicki said after I described my morning at the barbershop, "people will think you are moonlighting with Ringling Brothers."

Writing itself distorts life, much as makeup on a clown distorts the human face. Days are infinitely various, and moments do not tumble naturally into sentences. If I bade farewell to gathering, to wandering field and barbershop, to sculpting hours into subject and predicate, if I stopped traveling and talking, making speeches and saying silly things, perhaps my life would appear more natural. "When the ox dies," Slubey Garts said last week at a funeral, "he is carved with a butcher knife. When a man dies, a mouth carves him." I am not waiting for a preacher to shape my life. I'm carving now, and I am not using sterling silver either. My blade is the stainless steel of workaday adjective and adverb, of poetry's low, hard words. Dull in spots, my blade rarely slices cleanly. Instead it rips, tearing complexity and shredding people into hunks of conversation. Yet I am satisfied. Carving makes my days wondrous. If I put my knife away, doves would not huddle amid columbine in the spring; the fragrance of gingkoes would not fill my study in the fall, and paintings of cherubs fat as peaches would not cavort green through the winter. Three weeks ago I introduced the speaker at a dinner celebrating the hundredth anniversary of the *Sewanee Review*. During the introduction I read a poem. That word so popular with my Armenian friend appeared once in the poem. Attending the dinner was an older woman, a friend of my mother, who, I feared, might find the word offensive. Before dinner I spoke to her. "Miss Elizabeth," I said, "in my introduction there is a bad word, of which neither you nor Mother would approve. The word, though, is not one I normally use. It is in a poem, and I hope my reading it won't upset you." "Sammy, don't you worry," Miss Elizabeth said, patting my hand; "I would not want you to say a bad word, but if it's in a poem, then that's all right."

The man who urged me to stop making speeches advised me to put my "pen to use before the ink ran dry." How sad it would be if I did not record Miss Elizabeth's generous remark. If I did not jot such things down, I would forget them. My life would be diminished, and so I will continue to gather, stuffing bits and pieces into envelopes and garish sermons. On Sunday Slubey preached on the evils of drink. The sermon was a rip-snorter. "Throw all your beer into the river," Slubey shouted. "Amen," responded Deacon Goforth. "Toss your wine in the river, too," Slubey continued. "Yes, Lord, amen," echoed the Deacon. "And chuck in your whiskey," Slubey concluded, seeming to follow his own advice, pitching himself against the front of the pulpit then collapsing in a heap. For a moment the congregation was silent, then Brother Goforth rose to the occasion. "Amen," he shouted; "Ride, Salvation, Ride. Praise the Lord. Now," he continued, turning to Mr. Billy Timmons at the organ; "Let us all rise and sing, 'Shall We Gather at the River.'" When the congregation stood to sing, they were not alone. I was there, too, swimming open-mouthed through the crystal tide, praising King Jesus, keeping a weather eye cocked for Bob-Bob, and gathering, yes, Lord, gathering.

Losing the Aristocratic Taint

Class? Hell, when I was a kid, we didn't have any class. Couldn't afford it! Didn't need any! Made our own misery. Why, you'd take a good stick off a tree, whittle one end of it to a point, get a hold of the other end, reach that pointed end out till it was juuust underneath the hem of little Sharon McOwen's dress out there on the sidewalk on Lamb Avenue up the bank from the creek?, then you'd lift up a little, and then you'd yell out "*I see London, I see France, I see Sharon's underpants!*"

What I mean. Sharon McOwen's Daddy didn't make a damn dime more than your old man, or a dime less either, but time she got through screaming and throwing up, you wouldn't have swapped that little moment of arbitrarily imposed hierarchial venality for all the *droit de seigneur* in the Lyon Valley of France.

Class? We didn't have any class when I was a kid. But I guarantee you one thing. We knew the value of our squalor.

All right. I exaggerate a little—a little—for the sake of wising off, which is one trait that distinguished my particular class, the smart-ass class, in Hannibal, Mo., in the late 1940s and 1950s. Of course we had class distinction there. But they weren't the kinds of distinctions people think of when they start with that upper-upper, upper, upper-middle, middle, lower-middle type of mantra. Where I came from, and with the single overmastering exception of race, just about everybody in Hannibal belonged to the same *general* class, which was steerage.

We had a few rich folks in our town. I was best friends with the son of one rich family, and I guess I was pretty pleased with that. We even had a country club. What we lacked was a *culture* of wealth. (Ever watch a chiropractor after he's missed a five-foot putt? Tray *elegante*.) Rich folks were abstractions, comic-book cartoons, as unknowable and as unreal, somehow, as Negroes; they were all snooty monocled people with names like "Mrs. Van Gottrocks." I remember once actually holding my hand up in—uh—class, probably fifth grade, to ask the teacher how it could be that all rich people had names that *sounded* rich. Even my friend had a rich name: Arthur Dulany Winkler III. See?

Rich people were like Margaret DuMont (*see?*) in the Marx Brothers movies or Jiggs and Maggie in the Sunday funnies: harmless creatures who existed only to be deflated, dumped into the fountain spats and all, by people like ourselves, real, normal people. This was still several years before the Laffer Curve.

Within Hannibal's prevailing steerage category the gradations were subtle and interweaving. And stable: Hannibal's social ranks were essentially the same in the 1840s as in the 1940s—and remain, with impressive hunkered-down resilience, in the town's present-day reduced and Wal-Marted state. Mark Twain tweezered the nuances pretty deftly in his *Autobiography*, first published five years after his death in 1917. Although he is silent—in this passage, at least—on the specific matter of racial separation, his fine sorting held true through my boyhood and beyond:

In the small town of Hannibal, Missouri, when I was a boy everybody was poor but didn't know it; and everybody was comfortable and did know it. And there were grades of society—people of good family, people of unclassified family, people of no family. Everybody knew everybody and was affable to everybody and nobody put on any visible airs; yet the class lines were quite clearly drawn and the familiar social life of each class was restricted to that class. It was a little democracy which was full of liberty, equality and Fourth of July, and sincerely so, too; yet you perceived that the aristocratic taint was there. It was there and nobody found fault with the fact or ever stopped to reflect that its presence was an inconsistency.

Not many people I knew bore any strong compulsion to break out of these ranks. (Some of my friends had a strong compulsion to break out of *Hannibal*, but that is a crucially different matter: I noticed that few if any of them ended up in Grosse Pointe, and that most of them ended up in towns named Decatur and Crystal City, similar places that offered the advantages of no major public behavioral catastrophes to live down, at least for a while yet, and a whole different category entirely of road kill. If that is not too grosse a pointe to make here.)

I certainly had no strong compulsion to break out. Not then, not yet. But I did. I broke out from the town and, I reluctantly suppose, from its embracing class as well. More accurately, I was booted out, and into the backseat of a Studebaker that hauled me away from Hannibal alongside my migrating parents, like it or not. It was the year the Postmaster General banned *Lady Chatterly's Lover* from the mails, a class act. I was

17, just out of high school. College lay ahead; I would be the first of my family line since Adam to enroll. Land Grant U.; helluva football team. My father sold Fuller Brushes for a living and made a fool of himself over the St. Louis Cardinals and bowled for fun and, when he was in an expansive mood, he'd pull out a package of spearmint gum, tear a piece in half, wrapper and all, and offer it to you. Gee, thanks. From my new perspective on the campus of Land Grant U., all of that began to seem just a trace—jejune? The aristocratic taint, for the first time, began to smell pretty good.

"Aristocratic taint"—apt phrase, that. Mark Twain played all sides of its rich ambiguities. When a friend once remarked to him that the Rockefeller (SEE?) wealth was tainted, Twain acknowledged that it was sadly true: "Taint yours, and 'taint mine."

I keenly remember the first time I personally encountered the aristocratic taint.

It was my senior year. Based on achievements that now escape me, but that probably had to do with my status as ace cartoonist for the campus weekly newspaper, I had gotten myself invited to join a Supper Club. Till then I'd never heard of Supper Clubs. They sounded like something my father might keep handy at the table in case one of us tried to filch a slab of head cheese off his plate.

Anyway, I was on this Supper Club, and one night we had our first Supper, in some farmhouse a few miles outside town that had been converted into a Country Inn, or a Showcase for Gracious Living, or some damn thing. I wore my new bleeding-madras sport coat; I wasn't nothing, as we Clubbers like to say, but a real cool breeze.

A series of card tables had been lined up for us inside the Country Inn, and covered with white linen cloths, and candles, and dishes that matched. The Supper Clubbers—my fellow distinguished undergraduates and I—lined up on one side of those tables, and some members of the faculty, also Clubbers I guess, lined up on the other. The idea was that each of us was supposed to introduce ourself to the fellow across from us.

When it came my turn (is there a more forlorn and foreboding phrase in the lexicography of hick anecdotes than, "When it came my turn"?) I spoke right up with my name and did what my Mom, no stranger to the soignee, had trained me to assume was the next thing one did on introducing oneself—or "saying one's howdys," as we often put it around the 19th hole. I stuck out my hand. Right one. Stuck it directly across the dinner table. For a shake, don't you see. Directly at this faculty fellow. Fingers splayed. Opposing thumb cocked. If it was a gun it would have blown his brains out. I can see that hand even now, in memory, just as white and hopeful and pathetic as a spaniel pup's grin. And just as lonesome.

It was the only hand out there.

Somehow I had fucked up the whole Supper Club occasion. Maybe even the whole theory of Supper Clubs. In the mysteriously demilitarized zone of digits that was the dinner table, my fingers were violating some Geneva Convention of Supper Club etiquette. Time froze. Nobody moved. I couldn't get my hand down. It hung there in the Missouri gracious-living indoor night air like a stage prop in a vampire movie. In my confusion I think I even imagined that my madras had begun to bleed again, right down on that virginal white linen. Tainting, as it were, the aristocracy.

The worst of it involved the faculty member who was standing across from me, the fellow whose paw I had reached out to pump. I have never been able to recover the likeness of his face in my memory. What I do recall about him with utter clarity is his right shoulder. It is turned toward me at about a 45-degree angle from square-on. I can see the hairs on the edge of the shoulder of his tweed jacket standing out individually, haloed by the glow of the candle on the table. The right arm of the jacket is at his side. He has not reached out to take my hand. He has not reached out to save me, to pull me across whatever black waters of bad breeding I had drifted into. He never will reach out. My hand is suspended always, shy by inches of inclusion within a world above or at least apart from my own. And that is exactly the way it should be.

I can't remember the faculty member's name. I've wondered sometimes whether it sounded rich. But his allegorical name, to me anyway, will always be Class. And I will never stop repaying him for the way he liberated me that night.

He liberated me from liberation from my class. In that Gibraltar of his turned shoulder was contained all the secret protocols I knew I would never know; the keys to all the lodges and brotherhoods; the wine lists; the right pronunciations. In that stony angled stance of his was expressed all the pretense, the plundered authority, the obscene arrogance and the terrifying prerogative of the rich; the cold hard steel behind the cartoon harmlessness.

Armless, this man armed me. He gave me the weapon of hatred, but not hatred for myself (as he might have intended) or of my father or of the yokel town where I'd grown up, and not hatred for people who were even sorrier and dumber and likelier than I to dirty up the linen tablecloth. No. Hatred for the classes of people who made my class of people hate their absence of class.

I have defined my career as a writer, to some extent, by punishing this man. I have replenished my passion (the only impetus to writing I've ever understood, or at least been able to summon; literary *noblesse oblige* sure ain't my style) by conjuring up the shimmering hairs on the turned shoulder of that jacket. There has been a little of him in every tin god of business or showbusiness that I've beaten bloody with words in a newspaper or a magazine column.

Nor have I felt refreshingly "liberated" from all that, since then, as a writer. Quite the opposite, in fact; I've felt disconcertingly shorn. Banished. Exiled. Far from rebelling against those origins and those people and those habits of speech and dress and loyalties and obligations and, god help me, even some of the politics and the orthodoxies and the Shalt-Not taboos (all right, I grant that woofing on Sharon McOwen with the pointed stick was a bad idea, and I heartily repent), I feel that my life as a writer—such as it is—has been constant and largely futile reaching-back toward that lost, likeminded community; a dreamlike effort to restore, redeem, return.

JOHN PRESTON

A New England Chorus

"John! How long ago was it that you lived upstairs?"

"Thirteen years, Bob."

"Thirteen years!" Bob the barber turns to the men who sit on the plastic seats and waves his scissors in the air. "Thirteen years ago, that's when I had the shop up on Fore Street. He lived up there, on the top floor of the building."

The men look at me, say nothing, and nod, almost as one. The message Bob the barber is sending has little to do with my living arrangements. Bob is telling them that I've been around for a while.

I take my seat in one of the chairs and pick up the paper. Bob never has *The Boston Globe*, it's always *The Herald*: this is tabloid territory. Conversation isn't expected, I can choose to read in silence. But there's an open invitation to anyone who wants to join in on Bob's constant commentary on international affairs, local politics, architecture. In this way a barbershop reflects the finest New England institution, the town meeting. Everyone is a citizen in a barbershop. Everyone has the right to his opinion.

Sometimes Bob does want a comment from a specific person. "You see that new library over by the university, John? What's with that?" He's talking about a warehouse on the campus of the University of Southern Maine that's been redone in a slightly modern fashion. Panels of painted metal make up the façade, not very traditional for a New England school.

"Should have been brick," I answer.

Bob sighs, "That's it, John. I knew you'd know what the problem was." I see a couple of heads motion up and down the line of chairs. I am supposed to know this kind of thing. After all I'm the writer in the group. That makes me an expert on art of all kinds. That I am an artist apparently is more important to these men than the fact that I write about gay themes.

I actually moved to Portland to be a writer. That was one of my reasons, anyhow. The big cities I had been living in had become too great a distraction. I needed a slower and more familiar place to live, somewhere I could feel at home and could focus on my work. From the beginning, my writing has presented a problem for people in Portland. For one thing, when I moved here I was best known for a pornographic novel I had written, *Mr. Benson*, which had achieved cult status. I also wrote adamant gay activist essays and a novel, *Franny the Queen of Provincetown*, about homosexual characters who fought back when they were oppressed. These weren't themes that worked well in a small New England city in the early 8os. I sometimes felt like I was out-sized, I was talking about things that no one here wanted to listen to.

But there was a certain pride for many of my new neighbors in the fact that I wrote and that I was quoted in the national press. People certainly wanted to avoid the erotica; we seemed to make believe I didn't really write that. I was once cited in the *New York Times Book Review* about my thoughts on the meaning and function of pornography. Whenever I'd been in the major press like *The Times* before, people were excited about the publicity, even if they weren't sure about what it meant to have me here in Portland, saying those things about gay life here. But when the *Book Review* published that article, no one mentioned it for the longest while, until a lawyer I knew seemed to puff up his chest in preparation for some battle and brought himself to say, "Provocative quote in *The Times*, John." That was about it.

I wonder sometimes if, when I'm not around, other men don't say something like, "He's a queer writer, but he's *our* queer writer."

I finally move up to Bob's chair. He gathers a cloth around me and asks, "You want a trim, John?"

I pat my nearly bald head and ask, as I have a dozen times before, "What's the option, Bob? You going to style it?"

The men who sit in the seats laugh out loud at that. They like a good dose of self-deprecation. But I know that and I work it. I know these men. They are not a fixed set of individuals, their membership changes all the time. They are the men who hang out in barber shops. I could find them in a local bar. They are the men who work behind the counter at the post office. They speak with a certain clarity; I have come to think of them as my chorus.

I like Bob and his shop, but actually I moved out of this neighborhood years ago. Now I live on the West End of town. When I moved I changed barbers, Norm is my man now. I did it the way you might change a parish church. But nostalgia brings me back to Bob's every once in a while and we go through our dance the same way we first did thirteen years ago.

The discussion at both Bob's and Norm's is familiar. It's the conversation among men that I grew up with. I listen to the talk at a New England barbershop today and I instantly remember my father and his father talking about sports. It was not only the way they could be close to one another, it was the way that they, as New England men, had to share a culture.

It's also the smells. I love the odor of the cheap bay rum at Bob's, the talc powder at Norm's. They bring back memories of being a boy, of a time when my life was simple. I was a kid who belonged in my hometown. Generations of my mother's family had lived there. No one questioned whether I was part of the community.

The barbershop in my hometown in Massachusetts was the first place I remember my father taking me, just the two of us. It was a Saturday ritual. The men of the house, both of us, would climb into the car and drive to the center of town. We'd walk in to Alfredo's and we'd be greeted by name, recognized by everyone, and we'd take our place in the chairs that lined the wall to wait our turn. I had the sense, even when I was quite young, that this was the way life went, that fathers and sons went to barbershops together and spent time gossiping and discussing the weather, they argued about Yazstremski's batting average, and got to know one another.

It takes a long time to become a member of a community in New England. Most people who move here from away think it has to do with our cold souls, ice to match the winter weather. It's just that people want to know you're going to be around for a while before they believe you belong. I learned my lessons about New England life from my mother, a small-town Yankee who has always understood how these things work. When I was very young my parents had a small financial windfall. They used the money to fulfill the New England working class dream: They bought a summer cottage. Theirs was on a lake in New Hampshire. My father, who'd grown up in Boston and didn't really know how the rest of New England worked, was furious that the natives kept on referring to the place by the name of the previous owners. My mother, knitting in her rocking chair on the porch, didn't even bother to look up. "It'll take them, oh, about ten years," she said. And it did.

During those ten years my father actually helped things move along. He went fishing with the owner of the local general store. Once that was done, things were easier. A local had called my father his friend, so now he had credentials. I remembered that lesson when I moved to Portland and went out of my way to be friendly with Bob in his barber shop downstairs. I knew I'd made progress when he began to sign for my UPS deliveries when I wasn't home.

You can't force this kind of thing. It has to come naturally. The men at Bob's only warmed up to me when they realized I followed sports well enough to comment on Roger Clemens's ERA and to enter into an argument about Boston College's chances for a bowl bid. I had to *know* those things and withstand a cross-examination about them. To have been caught faking it would have been deadly.

I had learned a lot about faking it. As I was growing up in Medfield, I began to learn something about myself that was so powerful it could cut me off from the community where my roots were so very deep. I discovered that I was homosexual. I looked around and there was no one to tell me how to be that and to be of Medfield.

There were two nurses who lived together in a house down the street who were blunt stereotypes of women who wanted to be men. There was a man in our church who was constantly whispered about because he kept going in and out of the local state hospital, the incarcerations usually occurring after he'd had some drunken encounter with men that got him in trouble with the police. But that was it. Who I was becoming, what I was becoming a part of, was not talked about, certainly not at the barbershop, not even in my school, not in my family. I was becoming something that could not exist in a New England town.

I left. I chose a college as far from home as my family could tolerate, an academically dysfunctional, socially prestigious school in Illinois that was close enough to Chicago that I could find some of the men who were my new peers. I was hiding my sexuality, but I began by hiding my New England background.

My Yankee accent was too rough and uncultured for my college classmates. It spoke of barbershops and the working class. I didn't want to draw attention to myself at all, I wanted to be able to slip into the city without anyone noticing that I had gone. So I spent my freshman year in my room learning how to talk "right." I began to sound like a slightly affected voice on public television, not like a boy who grew up in Medfield. I wanted to merge into the background and just be left to find my new life in bars and clubs on the weekends.

The existence that we gay women and men were living then, in the sixties, was intolerable. There began to be acts of defiance as homosexuals across the country said no. The most famous, which took place on the day of Judy Garland's funeral, were the Stonewall Riots in New York in 1969.

Suddenly, my life as an exile wasn't one that had to be a silent existence. There were bands of people who were marching, talking, yelling, organizing, celebrating. I began to move with the waves of gay men across the country. I moved to Boston, to Minneapolis, to Philadelphia, to New York, to San Francisco, to Los Angeles . . .

Even as I was one of the people creating a new community with a new history, I was always aware of what I had lost. I used to go to Provincetown every summer. I told myself I went there because I enjoyed carousing in the beach resort. But I came to understand I really went there because, no matter how commercial it became, no matter how many people it attracted from around the country, Provincetown was in New England. I went there every year to walk the streets and see the buildings and listen to the language that made me feel at home.

I was not going to be happy living away. I could not be satisfied with the gay life in the cities. I had to find a place where I could live with the new culture and still have a way to be a Yankee.

I was living in New York at the time. I sat down with a pad of paper and wondered where I wanted to go. I made a list of what the place where I would live would have to have. An airport, at least some beginnings of a gay community, the ocean, some cultural infrastructure . . . The list got longer and, as it did, I was startled to discover that I was going to move to Maine. Once I put down on paper what it was that I wanted from a place, the decision became obvious. Portland was it. But would Portland want me? Had the gay life I'd been living been something that I could only have in the fast-paced cities?

Not long after I moved here I got my high school class's twenty-fifth reunion book. I was surprised to see that over half of us had moved to northern New England from Massachusetts. I hadn't realized I was part of any movement, but there was the proof of it in the list of towns where we had moved to in Maine, New Hampshire, and Vermont.

I finally realized that when we had all grown up in Medfield it had been a rural New England village. In the years since our graduation the town became a suburb. It lost whatever was the uniqueness of a Yankee town and became more like something you could find in Arizona or Oklahoma. Some who had graduated from Medfield High School had tried out other regions for new lives and new ideas, just as I had gone to big cities in the midwest and on both coasts after college. Still, most of us had wanted to come back to what we had known in our childhood. When it was obvious that was no longer to be found in Medfield, we moved north.

When I went to buy a car a couple years ago, I had more money than usual and I assumed it was time for me to get a Volvo. Isn't that what cosmopolitan men of a certain aesthetic and accomplishment drive? Volvos were cars I associated with literary types in Cambridge. They were the cars the wealthy suburbanites brought with them to Medfield when they transformed it. They were ugly, boxy things, but they spoke of wealth and a kind of supposed good taste that would never talk about it. I went and picked one out. I even had the colors down—forest green exterior with a tan leather interior. I couldn't write the check. To this day I doubt the salesman understands what happened, but how could I buy a Volvo and then go to the barbershop, drive to the smoke shop for my papers, be seen by my post office clerks? I went across the street and bought a black, four door Buick Century. ("It'll save the family some money," my father said, approvingly. "One less limo we'll have to rent for the next funeral.")

"I'm a Ford man, myself," someone said at Norm's when I first parked the car out front, "but that Buick is a damn good car."

The chorus motioned their heads with emphatic approval and added its support with specific comments.

"Front wheel drive."

"Solid construction."

"Buy American."

I had never admitted to any of them that I'd wanted a Volvo, but they seemed to understand it had been a possibility and immediately moved to bolster me up.

"Damn Volvos are no good in winter."

"Hell no."

"Rear wheel drive."

"Do you know what they have to do to get those things through snow?" That brings a whole new chorus of examples of the extremes that yuppies have to go to give a Volvo traction in a Maine winter.

"Parcels of sand."

"Bags of cement."

"I heard of one man put those big concrete bricks in the trunk and then couldn't get to his spare tire when he got a flat until he unloaded every damn one of them."

"You can't trust those people with Volvos, either," one voice insists. "They don't know how to drive worth shit."

When the first serious snow fell that year I got the Buick, I was greeted by a wild whoop of laughter when I went into Norm's. "John! Saw your Buick going up the State Street hill the other day. You should have seen 'im," the voice said to the rest of the chorus, "that damned Buick just went right up the hill with no problem, all those little foreign cars were sliding and slipping and there was this new Volvo, couldn't make the grade, just in a little snow storm. John just zipped right by them all."

"That Buick's a decent car," a voice said and the chorus nodded. I had made the right choice. My other friends, the artists and writers, were aghast at the Buick. "It's so bourgeois!" they complained (as though a Volvo wouldn't have been). But they don't have the same power over me as this chorus.

Sometimes the identities I strive for can speak together. When I went to buy a dog, I got a Vizsla, a short-haired, rust-colored pointer that was rare enough that it impressed my neighbors in the West End, the trendy part of town. They could tell it was pedigree right away and seemed to enjoy the fact that they had to ask just what breed he was. I took my time to explain that Vizslas had been the hunting dogs of the Magyar nobility and had for centuries been native to the Hungarian steppe.

The noble ancestry didn't impress the men's chorus in my life, but they were impressed by the dog. One beautiful summer day I was walking him up to Longfellow Square. Most of the chorus from Norm's had moved outside and was on a bench, taking in the warm air. "Good looking dog you got there," one of the voices said.

At that moment, as if on cue, a pigeon flew down in front of the dog, who immediately went on point. A Vizsla *is* a good looking dog in any event, but on point . . .

The chorus gasped. It was the first time I'd ever heard that come from them, a collective loosening of the will. A voice had to explain, "That's a *fine* looking dog." Their heads gestured assertively.

At that moment I knew I had made a perfect decision.

No matter how many books I might publish on what subjects, I am becoming one of the men in the barbershop here in Portland. They can smell me, they can see me coming. This chorus of New England men narrate an important part of my identity and their collective voice is so strong that I have stopped fighting it. I sink into it. This is the beginning for me. I start here.

The Portland chorus's acceptance of me still can be grudging. I don't make the mistake of thinking that my sexuality is unconditionally embraced. (A joke heard at Norm's: "That one's two dollars shy of a five dollar bill." [Translation: "He's as queer as a three dollar bill."])

I know I make it all the more difficult by being so public about my sexual identity, mentioning it whenever I'm interviewed in the media and often acting as a spokesperson at rallies or press conferences. I insist I'm making a political statement; many people in Portland have let me know they think I'm flaunting intimate details of my life which they would rather not know about.

I have friends who've been so offended by gay jokes or comments spoken at Joe's, the local smoke shop, that they've refused to go back, instead driving extra blocks to buy their papers. I've never heard those taunts, but there was tension when I first began going to Joe's. It used to be that when the topic of gay rights came up in front of me, the men who work at Joe's wouldn't even look me in the eye. Whenever there was a gay rights story in the local paper—an increasingly common event as the years passed—the men at Joe's would act as though I personally wounded them.

But there are other times when the chorus does come to the defense of the local citizen. If there's someone at Norm's who doesn't know me and he starts to say something that might offend me, the chorus shuts him up. "Don't talk like that in front of John," Norm has said on more than one occasion.

Even at Norm's, I'm sometimes blamed for all the actions of all homosexuals. One day a wildly stereotypical gay man wearing outlandishly tight capri pants and a shirt cut to expose his midriff sauntered down Congress Street outside the barbershop. Norm looked at me with dismay and said, "Jesus, John!" as though I had picked out the guy's wardrobe myself.

In 1984 a young man named Charlie Howard was murdered in Bangor, Maine. A trio of toughs threw him off a bridge into the Kenduseag Stream where he drowned. They did it because he looked too gay to them. I was enraged. It wasn't just that a brutal act had occurred. Of course I was offended that the civil society that is Maine was violated by the bullies' ruthless attack. Of course I was horrified that a young man was murdered. I was also furious that my own right to be in this place, Maine, was challenged. I took the murder personally. They would have killed me if I had been walking down that street that night.

I moved through the streets of Portland daring someone to hassle me. I wasn't going to let anyone take me out so casually. There was going to be a fight. There was going to be some vengeance if I was attacked the way that Charlie Howard had been. I spoke with fury to any audience who would listen. I declared at a press conference that no matter what one thought about homosexuality, sexual identity didn't deserve a death sentence. That hit home to a lot of people. Violence is something that offends the truly democratic society; the town meeting only works when there are rules of conduct that everyone follows and when freedom of speech is protected. Why have a town meeting if the right to open debate is threatened with violence? The whole point is for every citizen to speak his piece and that citizen cannot be expected to speak if there's a danger of physical retaliation.

At Joe's, the clerk—one of Joe's many sons, grandsons, or nephews, I can never tell which is which—stared at me when I walked in the next day. I took my papers and walked to the counter to pay for them. "Heard you last night," he told me. Then he put out his hand to shake mine. "Some things have to be said, and you said them well."

My HIV diagnosis came years later. I kept it a secret for a long time. I wasn't sure how it would be handled by the chorus. I wasn't sure how it would be handled by *anyone*. I froze. At first, I thought this was only my personal crisis. It was, I thought sometimes, a disease that I had brought with me to Maine from away. It had nothing to do with this place. I thought about leaving, wondering if I would be better off near the medical centers of the big cities I had left.

In a short time—a very short time—I learned that there were more men in Portland who had been diagnosed. I discovered that we all felt isolated. Many of them were much younger than I, and their illnesses— soon their deaths—crushed me with grief. I had somehow kept my own disease as something I could deal with, I would face it, the stoic Yankee would get through. But the sight of young men dying drove me to the limits of what I could endure. I cried. I cried often. I found myself un- able to perform the most simple tasks, because I would break into tears thinking about a nineteen year old I had seen that day, who I knew wouldn't live out the year. Or I would remember my friend who, on the last day he was alive, burst out that it was so unfair that he was going to die, he had finally gotten a job that had earned him more than five dollars an hour and now he was going to lose it all.

Being isolated with these experiences and these emotions inside my- self became intolerable. I worked with community organizations to set up care for those of us who had the virus. I sat with men who were dying without any family to comfort them. I talked endlessly with others who had the disease. I discovered that we were a new chorus. There was strength in finding one another and in just talking, even about some- thing as seemingly inconsequential as the Red Sox.

I eventually edited a book of essays about AIDS called *Personal Dis- patches*. When it was published I did a local radio talk show and dis- cussed the book and my own health status. The next day I went to the post office to pick up my mail. The men moved to the side and waved me over. One of them asked, "Is it true, what we heard on the radio?" Yes, I told him. There was a minute's silence and I wondered what was going to come next. "Shit, we all gotta die, John, but it must be hell to be standing on the tracks, watching the locomotive coming with your name on it."

That was all. It was enough. I sincerely thanked them for their con- cern and moved on.

I actually thought that Norm's would be the place where I'd have the most trouble. There were all those razors and the possibility of blood, my contaminated blood that terrified so many other people.

"Got something to ask you," Norm said as soon as I walked in to his shop after the word was out about my infection. He left his current customer in the chair and took some papers out of a cabinet. "The state says I got to take a correspondence course on that HIV-stuff. Look through this, will you, and tell me which one you recommend."

The chorus approved.

It's spring as I write this. The baseball season is only a few weeks old. Clemens has won two games already and the Red Sox are in first place, just having won back to back shut outs against the Chicago White Sox. The sap's rising, and not just in the trees.

"Do you think they'll win the pennant?" some neophyte asks.

The rest of us in the chorus glare at him. It is the role of the New England man to be seduced and abandoned by the Red Sox. No matter how good they look today, it's far too early to think of such things as playoffs, let alone the World Series. The man slinks back into his chair, realizing the stupidity of what he's said.

We'll all be going through that soon enough, we all know it. The Red Sox will rise up in glory and break our hearts, they always do. It's their fate, and it's our fate to watch them do it. You can change so many things, but there are some that don't ever change. The chorus of New England men knows that, it always has.

WILLIAM H. PRITCHARD

Ear Training

The critic William Empson once said that he did not know how much of his mind T.S. Eliot had invented. In setting out to write about myself as a teacher in Amherst classrooms, the only proper place to begin is with an earlier self in those same classrooms, forty or so years ago, when my mind—such as it is—was invented. The inventors were essentially three in number—Theodore Baird and G. Armour Craig, both professors of English at the college, and their colleague Reuben Brower who had an effect on me at Amherst but even more when he became a teacher and I a graduate student at Harvard. I encountered Armour Craig in the fall of freshman year when I took the required Composition course, conceived by Theodore Baird some years previously and, by 1949, having come fully into its own as a brilliantly original approach to writing as an activity. That activity, performed by us three times each week—in short responses to difficult, sometimes impossible questions about thinking, meaning, knowing, and other essential human pastimes—was my introduction to serious inquiry. Having graduated from high school, I had already become an expert in solemnity, but the Amherst English inquiry, as it was conducted in the questions asked us and in the professor's response to our papers, was invariably playful, therefore puzzling to us. By the end of term if not earlier, we began to suspect that language was something other than the mirror of reality; that—in a phrase of Joseph Conrad's I would come to later on—words are, among other things, "the great foes of reality"; and that the way we went about marshaling our words into sentences, "composing" reality, could be both a matter for despair and for hopefulness, but was nothing less than central to what we did every day.

Freshman Composition was valuable to me partly as a deterrent to flatulence. Since among other things the course was an elementary education in irony, it was salutary for a young achiever whose high-school valedictory address three months previously was titled "Health" and stressed the importance of all of us staying healthy. In the extended activity of writing as practiced in English 1 (thirty-three times the first term), we—teacher and students—looked at what we had written, at what could or couldn't be said in a sentence. The course took no notice of literature; that noticing occurred the following year in the sophomore "Introduction to Literature," another staff course, this one mainly the creation of Reuben Brower. English 21–22 had the effect, whether intended or not, of helping us regain some of the confidence we might have lost the previous year, since Brower and his staffmates had what looked to be a useful vocabulary for talking about what went on in poems and stories and novels. That vocabulary—which featured such terms as tone, attitude, dramatic situation—was derived from Brower's study with I. A. Richards, author of the extraordinarily influential *Practical Criticism*. In Sophomore English, and in the Humanities 6 course Brower subsequently introduced at Harvard (in which I did my first teaching), we engaged in collaborative reading carried on in both a leisurely and a sharply focused manner. Just as Freshman Composition consisted in examining the particular essays, paragraphs, and sentences we students had produced, so the literature course never wandered for long from its intent consideration of the words on the page—of the individual poem or stanza or line or word that momentarily engaged us.

The words on the page—well, yes; but what I remember most about my Amherst English teachers is the way they took words off the page and brought them to life through the speaking voice. Baird reading aloud a soliloquy from *Hamlet* in a rather self-consciously loud, deliberately un-actorish way, yet one that was scrupulously observant of the syntax and sense of the lines; Craig beginning his consideration of Milton's poetry with an extended reading out of "Lycidas" ("Yet once more, O ye laurels, and once more / Ye myrtles brown, with ivy never sere"); Brower imitating the finicky, weary cadences of the lady in T.S. Eliot's "Portrait of a Lady":

> So intimate, this Chopin, that I think his Soul
> Should be resurrected only among friends
> Some two or three, who will not touch the bloom
> That is rubbed and questioned in the concert room.

Behind such performances—the insistence that in the beginning, first of all, the poem needed to be *heard*, realized in the manner through which it was read aloud—was the example of Frost ("Now I'm gonna *say* a few poems for ya"). It was the same Frost who remembered hearing Brower, when he was a student at Amherst, read aloud in class a sixteenth-century poem by an otherwise forgotten poet, Richard Edwards, which began "In going to my naked bed as one that would have slept." "Goodness sake, the way his voice fell into those lines, the natural way he did that very difficult poem," said Frost years after the event.

This primacy of the speaking voice, this insistence on getting the tone right—on (in Frost's own words) seizing the special "posture" needed to deliver it correctly—informed, in ways I surely wasn't conscious of at the time, my "approach" to literature and eventually my dealings with it in the classroom. Nor was I conscious that Frost's discovery, so he truly thought it, of the primacy of voice in poetry was the cornerstone of what theorizing he did about the act and the art of reading. He put these thoughts powerfully and succinctly in a letter written home from England in February of 1914:

The ear does it. The ear is the only true writer and the only true reader. I have known people who could read without hearing the sentence sounds and they were the fastest readers. Eye readers we call them. They can get the meaning by glances. But they are bad readers because they miss the best part of what a good writer puts into his work.

My education at Amherst—that part of it conducted within the English department, both in the composition and the literature course, and in their successors—was essentially a training in ear reading, whether the bit of writing under scrutiny was (as it often was) a lyric of Frost's, or the opening of Henry James's *Portrait of a Lady* ("Under certain circumstances there are few hours in life more agreeable than the hour dedicated to the ceremony known as afternoon tea"), or one of the unwittingly fatuous sentences I turned out in my papers. Do you want to sound like *that*? was the direct or implied question we were invited to put to our own prose; while practice in listening to Frost and James brought the awareness that other designs, other ways of sounding, were possible, at least within reach of our ears.

Despite my introduction to ear reading, I graduated from Amherst a philosophy major, with the intention of becoming a teacher of that discipline. Accordingly, I spent a year listening to some very good eye readers in the Columbia University Department of Philosophy. Unlike Frost's eye readers, who speedily picked up the meaning by glances, these professors were hard-nosed teasers-out of the sense of passages in Locke or Kant or Whitehead. But outside of class I was reading Kenneth Burke's *A Grammar of Motives*, in which Burke performed "dramatistic" readings of and listenings to the philosophers, showing how their sentences talked to each other and made for a "life" in their words analogous to that found in poetry or fiction. Burke's subversive demonstrations of how philosophic meaning was as much a creation of language, of voice even, as was "literary" meaning, pushed me out of the formal study of philosophy and into literature. Subsequent work quickly showed me, however, that the academic study of literature could be every bit as "eye"-oriented as traditional academic philosophy. With the important exception of Brower, by then teaching at Harvard (the institution to which I transferred), professors of literature were either scholars or historians of ideas, English literature being conceived of as a matter of sources and influences, traditions and literary movements. Reading, it was assumed, was something people did on their own time and presumably were perfectly capable of doing. Were we not, after all, in graduate school and at Fair Harvard to boot?

Whether or not Harvard English was right or wrong in its procedures and assumptions, we—the Amherst people studying literature there, a substantial number—were up to something rather different. Insofar as we conceived of our purpose in criticizing and teaching literature, it was something very different from the way Harvard laid out the map of literature and placed individual figures and groups on that map. Most of us in the "Amherst contingent" (we were sometimes referred to as such) didn't think of ourselves as scholars, or even as potential writers of books. There was rather—and I think in contrast to many of our peers from other institutions—an eagerness to get into the classroom and instruct others about the kinds of literary discoveries we were making. While our peers were busily contriving to get a first article published (so it seemed to us, perhaps paranoically), we contrived to ignore the whole matter of publication, even though it might be necessary to move our professional careers into orbit.

If my own career didn't exactly get into orbit, it began to assume a direction when, suddenly and unforgettably, a call came in December of 1957 from the then chairman of the Amherst English department, Benjamin DeMott, asking me how I'd like to come down for an interview with the president and the department, with the likely outcome of an appointment at the college. For someone who had carried around with him since undergraduate days the notion of teaching at a small college like Amherst, this was a heady and risky invitation—for now it was to be not just "like" Amherst but the very thing itself. How fitting it was that, in preparation for my interview with President Charles W. Cole, the only piece of advice I received was a simple, memorable injunction from Theodore Baird: "Speak up!" I was, in other words, to announce myself at the outset as a young man with a voice, someone who was going to be heard. I must have spoken up at least enough to convince the department and president of my adequacy; later, when it came time for the tenure decision to be made, I was again smiled upon and became—in one colleague's phrase—a "keeper." Except for terms spent on sabbatical leave, I've been teaching at this college since the fall of 1958.

So much, then, for autobiography: there follows an attempt to say what I've been doing in the classroom during the past three decades. Along with describing one or two pedagogical clarities or discoveries, I need also to name what I'm "against"—approaches to teaching, to literature, to students that seem to me markedly unhelpful toward, sometimes destructive of, good reading and writing. My examples are taken from courses I've taught over the past few years: period ones in Romantic and Modern British poetry; seminars in literary criticism and in seventeenth-century poetry; larger lecture courses in Reading Fiction and Modern Satiric Fiction; and the introductory course, Writing about Reading, which I teach every fall.

Recently a secondary schoolteacher of English asked me what I expected or hoped my students would "know" about poetry, about literature, when they came to college as first-year students. My response was, after thinking about it for a while, that students need not necessarily know anything in particular—need own nothing except, in Yeats's phrase, their blind stupefied hearts. Less melodramatically, let them own an ear open to the soundings of words; let them also own feelings not wholly dedicated to immediate suppression in favor of preparing for law or medical school exams. What then do they need, to read with some success the following lines from Shakespeare's *Antony and Cleopatra* in which Cleopatra eulogizes her dead lover:

> For his bounty
> There was no winter in't: an autumn 'twas
> That grew the more by reaping; his delights
> Were dolphin-like, they show'd his back above
> The elements they lived in: in his livery
> Walk'd crown and crownets: realms and islands were
> As plates dropp'd from his pocket.

In asking a class of first-year students what's going on in this sequence I don't expect they will immediately begin talking about the difference it makes that the lines are enjambed; that the sentence units run over the lines and create an impassioned—and vividly metaphorical—utterance quite different from, say, a speech in *Romeo and Juliet*. My main concern has rather to do with the quality of feeling these lines about Antony project or express through the extraordinary language Shakespeare gives Cleopatra. But of course that quality of feeling can be approached only by readers who listen to the pace and cadence of the verse instead of merely moving their eyes across the lines.

For a moment, suppose we forget that poetry is written in feet and lines, thereby presenting special challenges to the reader who is attempting to tune in. One of the hoariest prejudices or assumptions among my students is that it takes a special talent or faculty to read poetry well, whereas everybody is pretty much equal before prose. (My fiction courses are much more heavily enrolled in than the poetry ones.) In fact, as I try to show them, such is not the case. Consider the ending of one of Hemingway's early stories, "Indian Camp," in which the young Nick Adams witnesses his father-doctor's makeshift cesarean operation on an Indian woman, the operation undertaken with "a jacknife and nine-foot, tapered gut leaders." During this operation the woman's husband slits his throat, and as Nick and his father return home in their boat the following dialogue between them concludes the story:

"Why did he kill himself, Daddy?"
"I don't know, Nick. He couldn't stand things, I guess."
"Do many men kill themselves, Daddy?"
"Not very many, Nick . . ."
"Is dying hard, Daddy?"
"No, I think it's pretty easy, Nick. It all depends."
They were seated in the boat, Nick in the stern, his father rowing. The sun was coming up over the hills. A bass jumped, making a circle in the water. Nick trailed his hand in the water. It felt warm in the sharp chill of the morning.
In the early morning on the lake sitting in the stern of the boat with his father rowing he felt quite sure that he would never die.

This lovely moment in Hemingway's work is especially vulnerable, in its delicate poise, to unlovely attempts by interpreters of the story concerned to tell us what it Really Means: one of them has called "Indian Camp" the "story of a boy coming into contact with violence and evil"; another has informed us that, at the story's end, Nick has "rejected his father and retreated from reality."

With Shakespeare's figurative and tonal richness everywhere evident ("For his bounty / There was no winter in't"), it would be a travesty to say that in praising Antony lavishly Cleopatra has "retreated from reality" or has exaggerated his virtues through the enlargements of metaphor. These would be unfortunate attempts to "understand" Shakespeare's language by reducing it to formula and pretending that the characters made up their own speeches. With Hemingway, who—unlike Shakespeare—leaves out rather than puts in, aggressive and all-too-confident ways of understanding (such as are offered by the critics above) get in the way of good reading. They do so by providing crude and hasty ways for us to avoid what we should be engaged in; namely, with *listening* to the rhythms and manner of presentation, the "feel" of the scene. "A bass jumped, making a circle in the water. . . . It felt warm in the sharp chill of the morning": How could anyone who really listens to those sentences want to go on and talk about rejection of the father or retreating from

reality? Why would they not want instead to talk about the beautiful sequence Hemingway has created here, from the father rowing, to the sun
coming up over the hills, to the jumping bass, to Nick trailing his hand
in the water and feeling it "warm in the sharp chill of the morning."
Why would they not want to engage with what Frost says all poetry is
about—"Performance and prowess and feats of association." "Why don't
critics talk about those things?" Frost went on to ask. "What a feat it
was to turn that that way, and what a feat it was to remember that, to be
reminded of that by this. Why don't they talk about that?"

"They" don't—and here I mean by "they" many secondary school and
college teachers of literature, as well as professional critics—because
they are looking for literature to provide kinds of stabilities, the moral
and psychological certainties writers like Shakespeare and Hemingway
are concerned to undermine, or at least to ignore. When students of mine
begin sentences telling me that in such a poem Keats or Emily Dickinson says that . . . , or how, in "Sunday Morning," Wallace Stevens believes
that . . . , or how Shakespeare thinks that . . . —such sentences are tip-
offs to a conception of literature as the repository of messages, opinions,
and beliefs about life held by the writer and conveyed (doubtless in excellent language) to readers ready to be instructed. And if the teacher
or critic has a strong agenda, the poem or story may be enlisted as an
ally in furthering the cause. Or perhaps it is simply that teachers con-
fronting a class and critics trying to get their essay written are reluctant
to live with the instabilities and fluidities that imaginative writing like
Shakespeare's or Hemingway's presents us with. "Did Shakespeare think
anything at all?" T.S. Eliot once asked somewhat mischievously. "He
was preoccupied with turning human actions into poetry," added Eliot.
And it was Eliot also who remarked that Henry James had a mind so fine
"no idea could violate it." Such challenges were aimed at disconcerting
readers eager to extract ideas or beliefs from the work of notable artists;
Eliot reminds us that these artists will not be reduced to the pedagogical
or analytical needs of those who talk and write about their art.

One of our best critics and teachers of poetry, Helen Vendler, wrote recently of her teacher at Harvard, I. A. Richards (who, years previously,
had been Brower's teacher at Cambridge), that he was the only professor
she encountered there who—as she put it to herself at the time—"taught
poetry":

My other teachers rarely talked in detail about poems they had assigned: they
talked about history, or politics, or theology, or literary movements, or arche-
types—but not about those radiant and annihilating complexes of words that
seemed to me to be crying out for attention, so inexplicable was their power and
so compelling their effect.

My experience at Harvard tallies with Vendler's, though with Brower's and other Amherst voices in my head I didn't feel the need, as she did, to seek out Richards. But Vendler's speaking of poetry's "complexes of words" as both "radiant and annihilating" should give us interesting pause. Annihilating of what? Perhaps Richards's own writing provides a clue, if we remember what he once said about the final moment from *Antony and Cleopatra* when Octavius Caesar gazes down at the dead Cleopatra and observes that

> She looks like sleep,
> As she would catch another Antony
> In her strong toil of grace.

After quoting once more the final line—"In her strong toil of grace"—Richards asked, "Where in terms of what entries in what possible dictionary, do the meanings here of *toil* and *grace* come to rest?" This is a question not to be answered by neat measurement, and one provoked, I think, by the way a particular complex of words, used by a master of language, can be "annihilating" of boundaries and limits as defined by the dictionary, or by the teacher intent on fixing a character or the play within some "meaningful" scheme of his own.

Most Amherst students who elect to take a poetry course with me expect that we will be centrally concerned with "complexes of words" as they are laid into lines and stanzas. But when fiction rather than poetry is the subject, such an assumption about focus is less common. In Modern Satiric Fiction we read many books during the semester—about one a week—so that there isn't time to pay the kind of respectful and detailed attention to language one can afford a lyric by Hardy or Yeats. Does that mean that attention must, initially or ultimately, be turned somewhere else than toward language? There are different ways to view this issue, and one critic (Marvin Mudrick), whose major interest was in fiction rather than poetry, has warned us that in "the beginning of poetry is the word; in the beginning of fiction is the event." Mudrick argues that the words of a work of fiction needn't be so precise and special as the words of a poem, and that fiction's words should not arrogate to themselves too much precision or "radiance" (Vendler's word). Perhaps so; yet the characters and events in a novel are perceived—are constructed by the reader—only through language. If some novelists, Dreiser, say, or Dostoyevsky, ask to be considered in terms other than their "precise and special use of words," there are other ones, James or Proust or John Updike, who as far as I can see stake everything on their "verbal complexes," on their styles.

In any case, I find that students in my fiction class are often puzzled as to what, in their papers, they should be writing about. I remember vividly how one member of the class who had done poorly on his first essay came to talk to me about this matter: What did I, in the famous word, "want"? I may have been somewhat evasive, but finally he asked, point blank, "You mean you want us to write about the language?" Remaining calm, I said that this didn't seem a bad idea to me; sure, why not try writing about the writing, rather than about the truth, or American society, or male-female relationships. No doubt the student left my office figuring that he'd pegged me as one of those aesthetes interested in technique rather than substance. What he didn't know, and what I couldn't tell him at that point, was that "technique" is more mysterious and even "annihilating" of clearly marked boundaries and dictionary definitions than he might have thought. Once more Eliot provides the useful formulation: "We cannot say at what point technique begins or where it ends."

Writing well about writing—whether that writing is poetry, drama, or fiction—means that the student must be helped to listen well; so, in a recent term of Reading Fiction, I invited the class (which had just completed works by Dickens, Trollope, and George Eliot—the latter two items were fairly short, and I assigned only half of Dickens's *Pickwick Papers*) to see what would happen if they practiced some of Frost's "ear reading" with respect to a particular sequence from one of these writers. They were to select a passage, quote it at least in part (such focus localizes attention to individual sentences) and then—in a deliberately vague question I often resort to—try to describe their "interest" in the sequence or passage. One student quoted some sentences from Eliot's short novel *Amos Barton*, in which the clergyman's wife Milly is introduced: "[A] lovely woman—Mrs. Amos Barton: a large, fair, gentle Madonna, with thick, close chestnut curls beside her well-rounded cheeks, and with large, tender, short-sighted eyes." The student felt, rightly, that such language contrasted rather sharply with Eliot's comic and satirical presentations of other characters—most notably, the Rev. Amos Barton himself—in previous chapters. Where on earth, asked the student, did "this gentle Madonna" with her "placid elegance and sense of distinction" come from?

Is she perhaps instead a divine being descended directly from the heavens? Somehow it is too much to swallow without choking a bit. Are we to believe that the sly wit so skillfully exhibited on the preceding pages can perform such an abrupt about-face?

He went on to quote more of Eliot's picture of Milly as possessing the "[s]oothing, unspeakable charm of gentle womanhood! which supersedes all acquisitions, all accomplishments. . . . You would even perhaps have been rather scandalized if she had descended from the serene dignity of *being* to the assiduous unrest of *doing*."

All this, the student felt, was too much. Was it possible, he wondered, that Eliot, "a highly intelligent and sensitive woman in a society dominated by the male sex," felt contempt for the "regard" in which women were held? Could indeed the description of Milly be understood as "a parody of the skewed, romantic, Christian notion of the 'ideal woman' current at the time"? Could Eliot, in going so far as to write the following sentence—"Happy the man, you would have thought, whose eye will rest on her in the pauses of his fireside reading"—be deliberately mocking the conception of woman as pure and sacrosanct, a conception given much currency by male poets and novelists?

Whether his speculations and inferences are wholly correct or need to be adjusted and qualified needn't concern us here, though they were of concern when we discussed his paper in class. The point is that the student gave us something to argue about, and did so by beginning with George Eliot's "technique": with matters of voice, diction, and intonation—words on the page brought off the page and brought to life in an imagined utterance. We can't say where technique begins or where it ends, proof of which statement is there in the student's move from small, local matters of hearing and noticing, to speculations about male and female in nineteenth-century England—large matters indeed. But the respect paid to Eliot's art is both evident and admirable. This is an "English" paper, a piece of literary criticism rather than a sociological or political argument.

One further example of how practice in listening to, in constructing and describing the "sound" of a particular novelistic moment may lead to results that couldn't otherwise have been achieved. The climactic chapter of Jane Austen's *Persuasion* is one in which the heroine, Anne Elliott, and her lover-husband-to-be, Captain Wentworth, become fully aware of their love for one another. Anne is engaged in conversation with a mutual friend of hers and Wentworth's, Captain Harville, while Wentworth sits nearby, writing a letter, but in fact eavesdropping on the conversation. Anne and Harville get into a friendly argument about the differences between men and women, and which sex has the stronger capacity for feeling, for "loving longest" especially "when existence or when hope has gone." (Anne and Wentworth, through her decision, were separated years previously and she has never ceased to grieve for him.) Anne claims the privilege for women, but Harville somewhat teasingly reminds her that "all histories are against you, all stories, prose and verse." He tells her that

"I do not think I ever opened a book in my life which had not something to say upon woman's inconstancy. Songs and proverbs, all talk of woman's fickleness. But perhaps you will say, these were all written by men."

"Perhaps I shall.—Yes, yes, if you please no reference to examples in books.

Men have had every advantage in telling their own story. . . . I will not allow books to prove any thing."

Since throughout this particular book Anne has been characterized as a very serious reader, exceptionally responsive to fiction and poetry, her forbidding any reference to books has a sharp ring to it. The discussion continues with her own voice gradually becoming firmer and more poignant as, without ever mentioning his name, she indirectly confesses to the ever-more-attentive Wentworth the faithfulness and durability of her love for him.

In the exercise I gave my students I said that this passage in *Persuasion* could be studied for what it might reveal about Jane Austen's attitude toward the sexes. But, I suggested, it might be studied—at least *read*—for something else, and I asked them to try to describe that something. I had in mind the way, as Anne assumes the ascendancy and moves toward a quite glowing affirmation of her love, she responds to Harville's polite admission that, since the evidence he alludes to comes from books which were all written by men, she is justified in denying their authority as foolproof indication of female inconstancy: "But perhaps you will say, these were all written by men." Then, with no narrative indication of how Anne says them (vigorously, teasingly, scornfully, determinedly?), we are given her three words back at Harville: "Perhaps I shall—." My point was that in this wonderful moment Austen is inviting, indeed compelling individual readers to do something, to "hear" these three words in a particular way—or at least to entertain some different ways in which they might be spoken. Whether the reader opts for calm certainty on Anne's part or a sudden seizing of the reins as the opportunity presents itself; whether she makes a humorous, eye-twinkling riposte to Harville or settles into a righteous affirmation of her claim's virtue—the three words need to be heard as rendered other than in a monotone. It is a moment in a dramatic sequence, in a conversation that has a before and after; it is progressive; it issues in something beyond itself. Returning to Frost once more: "The ear does it; the ear is the only true writer and the only true reader." My mildly polemical point in the exercise was that a reader interested only in what Jane Austen "thinks" about the sexes (in fact she thinks lots of things, contradictory ones even) is engaged in eye reading merely, and is losing the best part of the experience of art.

> I'd no more set out in pursuit of the truth than I
> would in pursuit of a living unless mounted on
> my prejudices. —Robert Frost

Kingsley Amis, one of the most entertaining novelists currently at work, once said with regard to a question of English usage: "I sometimes feel I have shifted a good way to the right in this matter over the years, but I feel no less often that (as in other matters) I have stayed more or less where I was while nearly everybody else has shifted to the left." There are a number of matters involving teaching, colleagues, students, and curriculum where Amis's observation strikes home to me. Some are trivial; others perhaps less so. For instance: I still call students by their last names (Miss Jones, Mr. Smith) in class; still give a two-hour final examination in my courses. I dislike catalog descriptions by colleagues that go on for too long, or use "critique" as a verb ("students will critique each others' papers"), or show an overfondness for words like "problematizing." I look with a wary eye on courses that appear to have a political agenda with a view to replacing presumably unexamined student prejudices with "correct" left-liberal ones—though sometimes I think the left-liberal ones are correct. (It will of course be pointed out to me that the claim to have no political agenda is but another sort of political agenda. My withers are unwrung.) Although my department offers serious courses in film, I would prefer that students choose to study Shakespeare or Romantic poetry first; just as I want them to read and study literature before they take a course in literary theory, if they ever do. And at a time when the cry is for "opening up" what is termed the literary "canon" so as to include within it (or substitute for it) works by recently discovered or rediscovered female and minority, non-Western, non-white-male writers, my interest is in going deeper into the canon as currently perceived: or rather, in exposing students to the canonical works few of them are even acquainted with.

Some years back I had occasion, in a required course for English majors, to ask the class what it thought of this notion of opening up the canon; to a man and woman they replied that it seemed like a fine idea. I then threw out some names of well-known works and authors from the unopened canon—Marvell's "Horatian Ode," Wordsworth's "Resolution and Independence," Samuel Johnson, John Henry Newman, Anthony Trollope, Bernard Shaw. Not just the majority but virtually the entire class of intelligent and articulate Amherst College students had no sense at all of these writers and their work. Admittedly this fact isn't about to impress teachers dedicated to opening things up. But it brought home to me that, in these days of "pluralistic" (to use the dignified word for it) approaches to the teaching of English—days in which, more or less, anything goes—that it might be adventurous to teach the canon. Accordingly over the past few years I have offered old-fashioned "period" courses in English poetry from Spenser to Pope, or Wordsworth to Tennyson, and I plan to offer further ones involving eighteenth- and nineteenth-century British novelists and prose writers. In an important sense this is a selfish act on my part, since I'm serving my own need to explore further an already established list of writers and to share my discoveries with an audience. (It is easy, by the way, to forget how important students are in providing ears—sometimes responsive ones—for talk about writers, Marvell or Wordsworth or Samuel Johnson, on whom you'd have trouble focusing the conversation at a dinner or cocktail party.)

How much does my resistance to some of today's going concerns have to do with being one of the tiny number of Amherst graduates who currently teach on its faculty? (There are four extant, three of us in our late fifties.) I do know that I'm strongly prejudiced against the notion that education at Amherst has improved over the past few decades as a result of gradual liberation from a required curriculum—The New Curriculum. Those who delight in Amherst's current pluralism have been known to characterize the learning atmosphere of that old New Curriculum as an "intellectual boot camp." On the other hand, nobody has suggested that the U.S. Marines were not well trained, and there is a case to be made for the kind of learning that, sometimes, went on in Amherst between 1946 and 1966. Still, the teacher-alumnus must also distrust his own affection for an undergraduate experience he may well be idealizing. The last two lines of Randall Jarrell's "In Those Days" put the case with proper ambiguousness—"And yet after so long, one thinks / In those days everything was better." "One thinks" that everything was better back then, when in fact things were, perhaps not worse, but certainly different. And to a nostalgic eye like my own, the very fact of difference, of something that was once and is now retrievable only in memory and imagination, imperceptibly elides itself from "different" into "better."

An unskeptical eye may also view the profession of English studies in rather more glamorous colors than are appropriate to the case. A useful critic of such glamorizing, Richard Poirier, has written of what he calls the "illusions" under which many academics labor:

... the illusion, first, of the necessity, and second of the enormous importance of literary studies. These illusions, shared in some degree by anyone occupationally involved, are difficult but necessary to resist. They intrude themselves because the study is confused with the subject, and teaching confused with the thing taught, the teacher, very often, with the author, whom he is "making available" to the young and to himself. It's a heady experience, after all, to have a direct line to Shakespeare, especially when it's assumed there's only one.

The warning is worth heeding, and yet—as Poirier himself admits—anyone who teaches English has to share such illusions "in some degree." Who knows when a line of poetry, read aloud in the classroom or to oneself in one's dormitory room, may come home to roost? More than once I've received testimony from a student about how—fifteen, twenty years after the fact—something Yeats wrote in a poem (a poem read sophomore year at Amherst) suddenly made sense. There is a poignant moment in Saul Bellow's *Seize the Day* when its hapless protagonist,

Tommy Wilhelm, on the edge of failure and disaster, recalls involuntarily some words from a Shakespeare sonnet—"love that well which thou must leave ere long." Wilhelm begins to think about his college days and "the one course that now made sense"—"Literature I":

The textbook was Lieder and Lovett's *British Poetry and Prose,* a black heavy book with thin pages. Did I read that? he asked himself. Yes, he had read it and there was one accomplishment at least he could recall with pleasure. He had read "Yet once more O ye laurels." How pure this was to say! It was beautiful.

> Sunk though he be beneath the wat'ry floor . . .

For all his clunkishness, Wilhelm has got it right, and the rightness involves his listening to a voice—Shakespeare's or Milton's or his own buried one—that suddenly surfaces with something momentous. Here, it seems to me, "the enormous importance of literary studies" (Poirier's words) becomes not illusory, but real and inescapable.

This account of teaching may well sound too simple and schematic in its dwelling rather exclusively on matters of voice and listening as my focus in the classroom and in the papers I ask students to write. I might have gone on at some length about the mutually enhancing relationship I feel between the teaching I do in class and the writing I do outside of it. Or, if it were not an impossibly self-regarding occupation, I could have written about my teaching style as a humorous one. "If it isn't any fun, don't do it," D. H. Lawrence once advised; as I grow older I grow less interested in classes where there's no laughter. "Humor is the most engaging form of cowardice," was Frost's inventive definition, and it's clear to me that, with the exception of one or two transcendent geniuses like Milton or Wordsworth, few poets and novelists live without engaging us in humorous ways (in fact the poetic behavior of both Milton and Wordsworth can be the occasion for a good deal of fun in the classroom). So the teacher—and the student as well—needs to speak back to the work in a comparably fresh and enlivening manner. The most awkward moment in any class term is that first meeting, in which any pronouncement, no matter how outrageous, is likely to be met with total, if not totally respectful, silence. To make that silence come to life is part of the fun and point of any academic term. One of my best recent students wrote me a note at the end of a semester, saying that her sister was planning to take a course of mine in the fall, and that she had advised her sister to read the books carefully, write honestly on the papers, and listen hard for my jokes. If it's true that "the ear really does it," then her final bit of advice to her sister was a particularly good one.

LEV RAPHAEL

History (with Dreams)

> History is as light as individual life, unbearably
> light, light as a feather, as dust swirling in the
> air, as whatever will no longer exist tomorrow.
> —Milan Kundera

One Sunday in the Metropolitan Museum of Art near the top of the wide main staircase, my best friend Sandy gasped at the Canova Perseus: "That's *him*."

I knew he meant my brother Paul. It was more than the rich cold marble body, it was the cool contempt with which Perseus, on his pedestal, twice, three times our size, held Medusa's head away from himself: that was all of us, thrust at arm's length, hanging.

Paul was four years older than me, tall, grey-eyed, large and strong, far handsomer than me or our parents. The three of us were small and kind of squat. Paul seemed the son of old-fashioned TV parents, the kind he wanted: those chirpy couples drifting in their large houses, worried about their children's parking tickets and bake sales. Paul was ashamed of Mom and Dad, of the way they could suddenly fling Yiddish curses at each other in a department store when they disagreed about a toaster or a rug; ashamed of how they criticized what we wore, fussing, tugging, yanking. They were triumphantly foreign. Dad with his one after-dinner cigarette, slicing an apple for his dessert, Mom with her quick little laugh that sounded learned from a language tape.

Paul was also ashamed of the past they couldn't share. There was so little—reminiscences of their school days, summer vacations, family dinners almost always brought them to the War, to their bitter losses. They wanted to forget.

My father loved nothing more than lying in the hammock in our little overplanted back yard in Forest Hills, with the high wooden fence between him and the world. He lay in the shade, eyes closed, singing to himself in Russian, a gypsy song, one of those on the fat 78's he occasionally removed from their brown paper sleeves and dusted with amused reverence before playing. But somehow Dad's relaxation annoyed Paul, as if he expected Dad to be busy around the house when not at work—sanding, staining, hammering, nails projected from his lips, as if Dad had no right to such indolence, because he was only a jeweler in another man's store.

One Saturday afternoon while I sat out on a lawn chair breathing in the chaotic mix of scents produced by our scrap of garden, Dad had said, "I just wanted, in the mud, something green, something mine. A tree."

In the silence I felt as if all the cars, lawnmowers, bikes, air conditioners for miles around were frozen, expectant.

"Where?" I asked. "Where?"

"Stalingrad."

And what I knew of that murderous seige and battle in which three of my cousins had died, choked me.

But Paul wouldn't listen. It wasn't France, Italy, or the Pacific, it was another, uglier, less acceptable war to him. And my father hadn't been a hero, just a Jewish slave laborer for the Hungarians.

And Mom, with her unsteady little eyes, quick jumpy walk like a sparrow snatching at a worm, Mom was not acceptable to Paul either. She wasn't slim and silent enough, but could sometimes talk as if she were a slot machine spilling noisy bright coins. She even talked to herself when cooking, or back to the radio announcer or as she read. Mom loved to shop for food, to eye and handle and sort and squeeze. It took her hours, from which she'd emerge red-faced, ecstatic.

I think the neon-lit plenty was a dream for her after the flight from Poland deep into the Soviet Union, the years of near-starvation, the cities in flame.

Mom and Dad's history of madness was so different from the waves of death back home—ghettos, concentration camps—but no easier to understand. They were survivors, and so were all of their friends, as if relating to someone without a similar past were inconceivable to them. They had a minimal social life. They took walks with their friends, played cards sometimes, the passive pursuits of inmates at a rest home, as if these moments together were merely episodes in a convalescence that would never end. Survivors. It had always seemed an ugly jagged term to me—people ripped from a larger, richer life, isolated, drowning in their loss.

I could not, as Paul did, loathe Mom and Dad, even when they drove me crazy. Dad would pass me on the phone in the kitchen, and drop, "Hang up—someone might call." Mom would lurk at the door of my room and wonder, "How many shirts do you need on the floor?" or "What did that book do to you, you treat it like garbage?" These quirks usually made me laugh—at least when I'd tell Sandy afterwards.

I couldn't feel Paul's contempt for them, but I *could* see them as Paul did. Mom lost in coupons, labels, sales, Dad selling watches and clocks, chains and rings. Dad was too harsh to Paul, suddenly cornering him and shouting, "You treat us like dirt!" when Paul was younger and refused to do his homework or his chores. Paul simply looked off to one side, blank, lifeless, even when Dad would lunge at him, force him down into a corner, grabbing at his shoulders, striking, kicking. Paul could have fought back, could have hurt Dad or at least kept him off, but he did nothing.

Later Dad would drag himself around the house, mournful, heavy-eyed, his silence a naked castigation I hated as much as his rage. Paul said nothing when he was beaten, but I yelped and begged so much Dad would laugh at me and stop: "Coward!" I'd nod eagerly, smiling, anything was fine for me.

"Just say you're sorry," I told Paul when we were both little. "Say sorry, it's just a *word*." But he wouldn't.

Mom often recalled overhearing me give Paul that advice, the story sounding like some ancient legend whose figures were metaphors of experience, not her living sons. She made so much of Dad's "sick stomach" after the beatings, proudly telling us how bad he felt, how awful, especially with what he'd been through.

In the War, I added to myself.

The lesson of it all? We shouldn't hurt them.

There were many mysteries in our home, not least of which was wondering who Mom and Dad had been before the War. They spoke so little about their families, how could we tell what in them had changed, what been intensified, what crushed? Reading memoirs of the Holocaust and histories, as I did endlessly, didn't offer a clue. But the War was everywhere, and leaked out especially when something unexpected and terrible happened. Mom would usually just go quiet and grim, seeming to disappear into grief so large it robbed her not only of words but of her very self. And Dad raged around the house, throwing things, cursing in Polish or Russian, *Sook in sin, pja krev*—curses that seemed so much tamer in English: sonofabith, dog's blood—but sounded grisly dropped from a face all red and dark with rage. Disasters, even small ones, triggered the darkness of their past, which seemed as large and unknowable as a howling sea in which we were just a tiny craft struggling to keep on course.

Sandy and I stepped closer to the Perseus now. "Amazing," he said. I nodded.

Sandy and I circled the statue, a little breathless. Sandy grinned and murmured so that only I could hear, "Even his *buns*. Nice and tight."

I had to agree. I'd been getting a good look lately. Paul had been working out much more heavily than usual, and had taken to drifting around nude from his room to the bathroom and back (when our parents weren't around), as if after the months of crippling bench presses at the Y and all the rest of it he had recreated himself as Arnold Schwarzenegger. I had seen him at the gym performing each repetition in a set with grunting violent heroism, like Samson bringing down the temple.

Sandy and I moved on, but I couldn't help turning back to glance at the Perseus, which was more beautiful now that I had to leave it behind. We were only fifteen, but I hoped that while staring at it before, we might have been mistaken for those art students with sketch pads who appeared never to see a work itself, but rather the problem it represented or solved. I did not want us to look hungry or exposed.

Once I asked Paul if he thought our parents' experiences in the War had influenced us.

He said no and didn't even bother changing the subject, just stared at me until I left the room.

Paul did not look *inside*. He looked ahead, wildly, spouting visions to me of wealth, of yachts and summer homes, travel around the world. He was going to be rich, he claimed, and for many years I listened with the credulity of a child whose friend asserts, "I saw a ghost." He was so blind, so sure—how could he be wrong?

For someone so relentlessly macho, I was a little surprised that Paul's vision of freedom and wealth was fired by late-night Thirties reruns. Over and over he watched TV movies on Channel 2 like "Midnight," "Holiday," "Bringing up Baby," movies of wit and style, the elegance sharpened by the grey, black and white screen. I'm sure he saw himself smoking a cigarette in a Rolls, or crossing a lavishly statued marble hall, or sipping brandy in a barn-wide library, flirting on a veranda under a private moon. I couldn't enjoy the movies he had memorized. The world of villas and repartee seemed too cold and unreal; the Thirties were ugly years, the glamor Paul clutched at, a lie.

Even the girls he dated seemed plucked from those movies, but not the stars, the minor actresses sitting at nightclub tables or getting into limos, sleek and blonde, alien, remote. His girlfriends looked alike and had some of the vacant intensity of those young dancers surging in pigeon-toed waves around Lincoln Center, those blank silent girls with anchored-back hair and gleaming foreheads.

"They don't seem Jewish," Mom said once in our small wall-papered kitchen nook where she, Sandy and I feasted on fresh marble cake and coffee. I'd watched before with greed as she had poured the two batters together, anxiously licking the corner of her mouth as if she were handling plutonium. Sandy was always over at my house, and Mom liked him so much she hardly spoke to him.

"I mean the Jewish ones," my mother explained.

"Well, they're American," I said.

"American Jews just don't make it," Sandy said seriously, as he had to me many times before. "They don't know things."

"Like what?"

"We have too much—we're too lucky."

"Am I American?"

While my mother's back was turned, Sandy mouthed to me: "You're cute."

Sometimes, when Sandy tickled my chest or the hair coming in on my toes and called me "Hobbit," I felt cute. He, on the other hand, was indisputably much more than cute, always sought after by the girls for his looks and his attentive respectful silence, admired by the boys for his skill at baseball. We'd been schoolmates since kindergarten, and Sandy's popularity had been a constant.

My mother nodded and said to Sandy, "You're right about Americans." She had said this before, that because Americans had been spared centuries of murder and lunatic pride as national boundaries sliced across Europe like a strangler's wire, they did not, could not, know how lucky they were, how free.

Now she burst out, "Okay, your father's a boy in Ohio. Did he have to run away to Michigan because bandits from Pennsylvania burned his village and chopped up his family? There were armies ready to crush his people? What did his family die from? Sickness, drowning, accidents, tornadoes. In Poland—hah!—we had human tornadoes. Russians, Ukrainians, Poles, *zol zey brennen in fire*, they should burn up!"

Sandy and I nodded, a little scared by her intensity.

Later, over at Sandy's apartment a few blocks away in Rego Park, he said, "Your parents are so real. I think about that a lot."

I looked around the living room, a lavishly curtained little box with bowls of grinning fake fruit and lamps all in the form of buxom gold goddesses lost in swirling robes. Crystal pendants gleamed from unexpected corners.

"For us being Jewish is like someone else's buffet—a little this, a little that." Sandy leaned back on the streaky gold tufted velvet sofa and spoke as if to history: "It's not that important."

"What d'you mean?"

He shrugged and I reached to stroke his neck. He stopped my hand, gripped now by what he was thinking and trying to say.

"Why's it bother you?" I asked.

"When I'm with your parents, it's like, they know so much I'll never know."

Well that was true for both of us, but we couldn't talk about it then because Sandy's parents would be back from Alexander's, and we only had an hour in his room. We left the door open, and a Monopoly game set up, so that we wouldn't be surprised when they returned, and they would surely think we were flushed with the excitement of the game.

Walking back home later, I thought about what he'd said. Sandy's family was fitfully Jewish, some years deciding to keep kosher and kashering the kitchen, some years ignoring all the holidays, and dropping or changing Jewish magazine subscriptions, changing congregations, flailing for some consistent way to make a Jewish life. Both Sandy's parents taught at Queens College, and so they had a lot to say. Their Jewish discussions were long and exhausting. My father privately dismissed both Sandy's parents as yentahs.

But Dad liked Sandy very much, because he was so respectful, because he was an ardent Zionist. Dad and Sandy would talk politics and agree with delight on most issues. It could be very peaceful, the four of us sitting out in the back yard on a late spring or summer weekend, eating seedless grapes very slowly, savoring each cool little globe before crunching it open, drinking iced tea, with Mom idling through a newspaper, occasionally reading aloud to us in a comic high-pitched lecturing voice. She'd read fragments of articles without introduction or explanation and those darts of news would whiz from her chair.

Sometimes I'd think: They may have suffered, but they have *this*, and I'd feel grateful that I was not, had never been a disappointment. I made few waves, had no rowdy friends, did consistently above average at school (Paul was the real brain) and had discovered great talent in French, which entered me like a magic potion the first year of junior high. I'd won our school's French award and my teachers pressed me to consider taking a summer study program in France when I got to high school, or even a year abroad. My parents were very proud and agreed it would be good for me.

Paul *was* a disappointment. He was inaccessible, sneering, more aloof as he became a remarkably handsome man. Girls were always leaving messages for him and after Mom took them she told Dad it wasn't dignified, though what she said in Yiddish was *nisht shayn*, not nice or decent.

Sandy didn't like my brother, but the most he'd say against him was that the two of them were "very different." Sandy tried not to malign people; he was on guard against *lashan harah*—Hebrew for evil talk. "It's so easy for things to just pop out, and then you're stuck."

"What if it's true?"

"Doesn't matter."

Sandy seemed to watch Paul as if waiting for trouble, and he was right. The time when Paul and I were friendly, when we enjoyed each other's company, when he tied my little shoes and taught me games seemed prehistoric to me in Junior High. What followed was years of snarling and insults, as we drifted further apart. Paul's flood of girlfriends made him insolent, as did his weightlifting. I would find him constantly posing in front of the bathroom mirror, body oiled and shiny, wearing a tiny swim suit, making his muscles bulge and dance. His strong hairless body was like a holy relic borne in a procession in some huge dark canvas, shining its own light. I'm sure he wanted me to admire his strength, his masculinity, but I couldn't, because it seemed inhuman.

So did Angela, when I first met her. I thought, "Yes, she's the one." Not a girlfriend for Paul so much as a consort.

Angela went to Fordham at Lincoln Center, the Catholic college Paul had chosen, I think, not for its small size or midtown location, but because he'd encounter few Jews there, unlike City College, NYU, or Columbia, which had all accepted him.

Paul brought Angela by one afternoon of his sophomore year. She was tall, bleary-eyed, blonde, with the slack-shouldered elegance of someone like Jean Harlow. Despite myself, I saw her trailing one of those silky Thirties gowns with feeble straps, diamonds bragging in her hair. I was alone at home and Angela just sat in our plant-crazy living room as if she wished she were a hovercraft and could float her designer jeans above the couch that suddenly looked a little shabby to me.

They pretended an interest in me for a bit before I left for Sandy's and had dinner there, trying not to feel angry. Paul and Angela were both so disdainful and aloof I wondered at first how they could converse or even touch each other. They seemed like two exquisite parallel lines, drawn on to their glorious and separate futures.

Angela lived in Queens too, but in Kew Gardens, in a Tudor frenzy surrounded by reverential big trees with a low stone wall cutting along the edge of a half-block plot. I didn't like the house when Sandy and I walked by it a week after Angela's first visit. People who don't know New York are often surprised there can be these lovely-tree-swathed neighborhoods with magazine houses, but I felt embarrassed to see Paul was dating that house and that street.

"It's so corny," I told Sandy. He didn't ask what I meant.

"Angela," Dad said. "Italian?"

"I don't think so. Her last name's White."

"And what else?"

I hesitated. Dad looked up from his basement worktable seething with bits of metal and tiny nonsense stones. Around us were drills, buffers, a small kiln and piles that would eventually give birth to jewelry or junk. He looked up, but not at me.

Mom had more to say. "Why doesn't he bring her to meet us?" she wondered at dinner. "He's ashamed she's a goy? I won't like her because of that? Believe me, I can find something else if I have to!"

But Angela was not a goy, not exactly. Her mother was the daughter of Russian Jews who'd fled after a pogrom. They had slipped their Jewishness like an anonymous corpse over the rails of their ship into the hungry Atlantic and raised Angela's mother American—that is, dreaming ready-made dreams, yearning for what she might never have. She died when Angela was three, before her husband's real estate career brought him the Tudor home, the Caribbean condo, the BMW's. Angela's father was a Unitarian, from Maine.

"What is that?" Mom asked me. "Unitarian."

"They believe in units."

She laughed, "America!" In their international shorthand in which Germans were killers, Poles thugs, the English anti-Semitic snobs, Americans were crazy. And even after thirty years that craziness was to Mom and Dad a perpetual delight—the way parents marvel at their infant's eyelashes, smiles. And a source of sorrow. The infant will grow into something unpredictable.

Paul's stream of girlfriends, his perplexing (and goyish) fascination with his own beautiful body, made some sense to them, fit into their larger understanding of America. But their steady reference to the broadest context sometimes struck me as restricted, draining away the day into history. I remember a wave of grave desecrations in Jewish cemeteries on Long Island and how I fantasized forcing the black spray paint cans down the mouth of whoever thought swastikas were funny. Dad reminded me, calmly, that anti-Semitism sparked in bad times.

"Yes," Mom nodded, oddly secure. "It's the recession."

And I, I felt cheated of my rage. Likewise with Watergate. They had long predicted that Nixon was dishonest and so couldn't raise their voices about the scandal. Sometimes, though, the historical perspective was funny. Like when in fifth grade Paul was rude to his teacher before Parents' Night and she demanded Mom and Dad punish him as *she* had done. Mom said that—as she understood it—the Constitution barred being punished twice for the same crime. This became a minor family legend, told with ceremony as if it grounded us in the past and explained our present.

I don't think they were threatened by Angela. They seemed to pass her off as the vision of escape many Jews yearn for, the soft-haired Lorelei, seductive on her rock.

And I was glad Paul spent so much more of his time away from home, at parties, movies, whatever.

The first time Angela came over for dinner, Paul told a news story of some honeymoon wife falling naked from a Midtown hotel window to a fatal street. Angela grinned and topped him with someone burning to death sliding down a plastic emergency shoot off an airplane that didn't explode. They were united in contempt for the unfortunate.

That first dinner was alternately very noisy and painfully quiet, and I drank five glasses of wine despite Dad's heavy glances. Sandy tapped my foot under the table now and then, but whether to slow my drinking or just connect, I don't know.

Overdressed and wearing too much perfume, Angela had loudly proclaimed how cozy our dinette was, as if she were a media-conscious monarch posing gracefully in a hovel. She signaled Mom's garnet ring for her attention, admiring it so loudly I felt a billboard had smashed into the dining room, smearing us with letters too large to read.

But Mom beamed. "My husband made it."

Angela nodded, eyes sweeping the dish-heavy table. "How long have you been a jeweler, Mr. Levy?"

"Since before the War."

Angela frowned away the ugliness of that reference and turned to me.

"What does your father do?" Mom asked warmly as if eager to discover hidden qualities in Angela.

"He owns things."

That's when I poured my fifth glass.

All through dinner, Angela took such mingy portions of salad, roast, potatoes and corn you would've thought her determined to make a show of delicacy. When I found myself silently counting the kernels on her plate, I knew I was drunk.

"She didn't like our food," Dad muttered in the kitchen when Paul took her home.

"How could she tell?" Mom shot. "She had, what, three bites?" Then they switched to Yiddish and moved to Russian. Sandy and I listened to the heavy cadences of the language that always sounded dark and sad to me, even in marching songs. From the kitchen, I heard a snarled *Amerikanski* a few times.

Sandy and I sat in the living room for a while before he went home.

"She's a lot like Paul," he finally said, with my parents' conversation drifting out to us, tantalizing, unknowable.

Oh yes, I thought, she was like Paul: cold, beautiful, critical. She'd glanced around our home as if every picture were crooked, cheap and vile, all the furniture needed dusting but she would overlook it. Watching Angela, I'd thought of the Greek and Roman sculpture galleries of the Metropolitan—those high rooms of tender light and silence. I never understood the raving about "classical beauty." Those private faces perched above tunics, cloaks, vague draperies seemed too removed from life to be beautiful. Now Sandy, *he* was beautiful, dark and romantic-looking.

"God, I'm lucky," I said to Sandy, who flushed with pleasure, understanding I meant him.

In bed, later, reading *Paris Match*, the room around me blurred, tenuous, I found myself wishing for things. Wishing I'd learned Russian as a child and taken Yiddish more seriously so that I could know my parents in a deeper way, think with them in languages they had not learned so much as lived. Paul was not alone in hungering for another life.

I longed for escape in my own way—what else was my dream of France, of barges on the Loire? Of wandering through Vaux-le-Vicomte and Chambord? Of exploring the bastide towns in the Dordogne? It was all a delightful patchwork for me: vermouth cassis, de Maupassant, Monet. My France was untouched by Dreyfus, Vichy, transit camps or De Gaulle's anti-Zionism, it was *La Belle France*, Europe's jewel, civilizing the world, the fantasy land that had infused each ringing high *"Bonjour!"* of my first French teacher. I imagined myself biking home with my baguette, writing letters in a Boul' Mich' cafe, smoking a Gitane on a train snaking down to the Mediterranean. It was a strange sort of return across the Atlantic, a retreat in time, wiping out history and death.

I adored my name pronounced in French; Robert became Row-bear with that wonderful rolled "R." But I shared these fantasies and visions with no one, especially at school where I covered my facility at translations, my mastery of the subjunctive with adolescent *je m'en fichisme*. Sandy disliked the French, so I couldn't imagine him my *copin*: "Everyone says they're nasty. My folks went there and hated it."

Sandy's dream was Israel, but not as a tourist (which he'd done) matching life to film scenes or photographs, not as a pretend kibbutznik for a few months. Sandy wanted to live there, work, travel, study Torah in Jerusalem.

"When I'm ready," he said, which meant after college. "Life is important there, you know why. You have to—it's a choice."

Maybe all dreams are a choice, a way of plunging reality, like a piece of sizzling, forge-worked metal into a barrel of water to cool its form.

Sandy was always bringing back loads of books from the library, reading Buber, Wiesel, collections of Yiddish stories in translation, essays on religion, the Sabbath, anything, everything, as if preparing himself for a long and hazardous voyage. He talked about his Jewish reading, and I listened in admiration, with a little distance.

Like Paul, I had lost my interest in being visibly Jewish after an undistinguished bar mitzvah, so Sandy's appeals for me to join him at synagogue, sometimes, *any* synagogue, were annoying. I could still follow a service but it led nowhere, the words heaped around me with each turned page until I felt stifled, trapped. Luckily our Seders at home were brief and every other holiday, including Rosh Hashanah and Yom Kippur, was less celebrated than talked about, passed around in conversation like a trange carving that gathers speculation with the heat of each hand. If I'd lived outside of New York I might have done more—but who needed to be Jewish in Queens when someone else could do it for you? I wanted to be French, to feel the dusty red medieval walls of Carcassonne as mine. I had no desire to grow old in Queens or Israel.

"You think because you're not like Paul," Sandy snapped one evening, "that anything's all right."

"What did I do?"

"Nothing—that's the point." Sandy wanted me to join a Jewish youth group, march for Soviet Jews, sign petitions, to do something more than dream of going abroad. He claimed I'd never really come back from France, or wouldn't want to. "It's the same thing. You'd forget about me! And Paul's going to marry Angela!"

I knew Paul wanted to, after graduating. He'd been strutting around nude a week before, scratching at his heavy rich chest and bragging about how Angela was his "slave," how she'd do "anything" for him.

"And she loves this." He flicked at his crotch.

"You're gross."

"That's right. Big." He gave it a shake.

After a pause, I said, "You want her money."

He smiled. "I'm not gonna be like Dad and his lousy little yard. Look at him, he's nothing."

"What about the War?"

"Plenty of people made it after the War."

Bastard, I thought in English, then in French: *espece de salaud.*

"And I sure won't be like you," Paul went on, leaning on his door frame. "You'll never get to France, that's bullshit. You'll stay here jerking off with your little Golda Meir."

I froze.

He laughed. "You think I couldn't figure it out? What a little homo!" He turned and slammed his door.

I fled to the bathroom, ripped off my clothes and stood under the violent shower while I heard Mom come upstairs from the basement to ask about the noise.

They knew Paul and I didn't get along, but Mom kept trying. There was the abstract approach: "It's nice for children to get along." The apocalyptic approach: "He's all you'll have when we're gone." And even the ethnic approach: "It's a shame for the goyim to see brothers not friendly." To which I'd reply, respectively, "Yes it is"—"I hope not"—"They don't have to look."

Right about that time, Paul was bragging about an MG he'd bought from a friend at school with money saved from summer jobs. I, who spent all my earnings on movies and books and hanging out places with Sandy, had jealous visions of Paul in an accident or arrested for drunk driving, with Angela running from the scene or just sobbing her shame and fear in a greasy station house. I couldn't believe how jealous I was!

One May afternoon of my senior year of high school, and Paul's at Fordham, I came home with Sandy and heard Mom weeping in the kitchen. I had never heard her cry like this, with hysterical heavy gasping sobs that seemed wounded, alive. We stood inside the front door as if trying to fight the energy of that grief, but it pulled us through the house to the kitchen, where she sat in a chair pushed against the wall, head back, legs together, arms and hands dead on her thighs like one of those serene Egyptian tomb effigies.

"Your brother," she moaned. "Your brother and his *dripkeh* are junkies!"

I dragged a chair to her, sat close.

"Junkies!"

I didn't understand. Wouldn't I have seen the tracks?

Dad, she said, was upstairs. The doctor had been to give him a sedative. I made tea for her, brought a dishtowel soaked in cold water for her abused eyes and Sandy and I sat at the empty table while Mom told the story.

A professor at Fordham had discovered Paul in a basement bathroom handing an envelope to another student who tried to duck out the door. It was cocaine. Angela and Paul apparently had a little business going (the money for his car, I thought). But no one was arrested, they were just expelled. The school wanted to protect its good Catholic name and the Chancellor made calls to keep the story out of the news. I knew that was possible; the same thing had happened with a suicide at Fordham the year before.

"A junkie!" Mom said again. "And don't defend him!"

I didn't try.

Angela's father, a large handsome man with glamorous white teeth and hair, came over that night, but there were no voices raised. Together, they sat hushed and defeated by their own ignorance, drinking vodka in the living room, like the victims of a flash flood marveling at their enormous unexpected loss.

Paul moved out. Angela was shipped to relatives in California. Dad abandoned his workroom, and even in his hammock strung from two big trees that were his vision of security and peace, he looked miserable. Mom took to chain reading mysteries, walling herself in with shiny paperbacks.

"We lived so long like dogs," she said to me and Sandy. "I only wanted for my sons to be happy."

I knew then that I could never tell her who I was.

Distant Cousins

I am a native of the South, and it was not until last April that I began to understand how native I am. It's quite possible that I am a twenty-plus generation southerner.

Among my ancestors are those who roamed the mountains of Tennessee for thousands of years, Irish people who left the Irish frontier in the late 1880s, and at least one Danish woman from Stonewall, Tennessee, who for now remains a mystery. (When I discovered that, I began to realize why I had such an affinity for Kierkegaard in my late teenage years.) And that's what searching for the details of one's background is similar to: a whodunit. But every time I've found a new fact, a new lead, I've discovered that my fiction has been ahead of me.

The made-up moments in my creative work arising from another murky part of consciousness seem to have a had a better take on my origin than I. For example, in the early 1970s I read of a state called Franklin that was almost admitted to the Union. All I knew about it was that its population was black, Indian, and white and that it was led by an idealistic governor named Sevier. I wrote a poem called "The Lost State of Franklin." This work was the basis for a performance created by Carla Blank and her Japanese collaborator, Susuhi Hanayagi.

When I visited my father's sisters and brother for the first time, last year, I discovered that their homestead was located not too far from the site of Governor Sevier's home and that the street before the one they lived on was named Franklin.

I found that others knew details about me that were lost to me. Native Americans in the Southwest, Pacific Northwest, and Alaska knew about my ancestry before I was able to locate it. Leslie Silko, after hearing me read from my work, told me that I was an Indian. A group of Native Americans with whom we were joshing around in Ellensburg, Washington, removed a headdress from a white man who claims Native American ancestry and placed it on my head. That's more like it, they said.

After learning of my Cherokee great-grandmother, I phoned my friend Andy Hope and asked, in jest, why, given the fact that I had a Native American heritage, I wasn't invited to the Returning-of-the-Gift-Festival held in Oklahoma City. Andy said he hoped I wouldn't be bitten by a mosquito so that my Native American blood would be drained. Some of the comments of these Indian writers came back to me in April as, en route to Alcoa from Knoxville, we passed through a section of land called the Old Cherokee Trail, and while discussing my ancestry, the lost part, with aunts I'd never seen, I was told that my grandfather's mother was a Cherokee who was spared the trip west, the Trail of Tears, during which thousands of Cherokee Indians were uprooted from their traditional homelands in Tennessee. I was informed that my grandfather attended Cherokee school.

The Afrocentric exploration of the black past only scratches the surface. A full examination of the ancestry of those who are referred to in the newspapers as blacks and African Americans must include Europe and Native America. The pursuit of this journey requires the sort of intellectual courage that's missing in contemporary, politically correct America, where certain words cannot be spoken and certain secrets cannot be unearthed and certain investigations are frowned upon.

Black Americans who desire to uncover their past face problems. They must encounter not only the intellectual timidity of some black Americans, but red racisim (Native American novelist and critic Gerald Vizenor surprised me with his comments about the racist views some Native Americans hold toward blacks). Yet probably the thorniest impediement to the discovery of the black past is southern denial. The inability of some southerners, not only laymen but academicians, to face the fact of miscegenation is such an explosive issue that this word simply means "mix" has taken on a sinister meaning. The denial that generations of southern white men have lived in polygamous arrangements is a hypocrisy that exists to this day. As someone whose fiction plays with the hypocrisy, I was delighted to point out in my latest novel, *Japanese by Spring*, that among the recent candidates for president who were running or about to run on the "immorality in the inner city" ticket, two were fathers of out-of-wedlock children, two were accused by a blond lobbyist of having engaged in assignations with her, and one was accused by a beauty queen of giving him more than a massage when he visited her in a New York hotel. In fact, a Civil War writer named Martha Higgens wrote that plantation owners still thought of themselves as good husbands and fathers. Maybe this is why an exploration of the African American past can become so dangerous: an exploration hat would reduce the newspaper, bureaucrat, and think-tank idea of a Black America, a place inhabited with people of an uninterrupted African genealogy, to speciousness.

Black people growing up in the 1940s and 1950s were told by their education that if they behaved like Anglos and assumed an Anglo identity, opportunities would appear. In order to become this other identity, one had to reject one's past. I think this is why there appears, frequently, a scene in the novel of assimilation, by those not only of black but of white ethnic background, in which the narrator invites college friends home and is ashamed of his or her parents speaking English with a German, Italian, Irish, or Yoruban syntax. Our parents were viewed by our education as dumb and backward, and the sooner we abandoned their attitudes and style, it was proposed, the better our chances for success. It took me many years to understand that my parents' style was in some ways hipper and more sophisticated than mine. In the 1950s, they were listening to the blues, Charles Brown, and others, while I was listening to West Coast jazz.

An exploration of those ancestors who lay behind their generation was considered unthinkable. You'd find yourself in some cotton field, and if you went back further than that, you might find yourself in a jungle surrounded by these teeth-gnashing natives. My education told me that I was an uncivilized infidel and that I could be redeemed only by cutting all ties to my background.

Travel, world events, and my contact with black intellectuals would change my outlook. At the age of fifteen, I traveled to Paris as part of a YMCA delegation, and while there, met with Africans for whom my education had not prepared me: students who were studying at the Sorbonne, articulate and intellectual.

The type of colonialism that today's students could only imagine began to fade in the 1960s. New and dynamic leaders arose in Africa—Patrice Lumumba and Kwame Nkurmah. I remember watching a shaken Adlai Stevenson being interrupted by black demonstrators as he sought to defend some backward American African policy. I excitedly turned to my mother and shouted at her that some black people were interrupting Stevenson's speech. Adlai Stevenson had been my hero.

In high school, when the teacher asked students to select countries to represent during United Nations Day assembly, we black students were too embarrassed to choose Africa. We preferred to represent someplace like Norway.

At the beginning of the 1960s, African Americans were claiming Africa. I met Malcolm X, who put it plain. In what was to be the beginning of a number of exchanges I had with him in both Buffalo and New York City, he said that black history was cotton-patch history as it was being taught. He was right. In the textbooks we read, the blacks seemed to be having a great time. Real party animals. So what was the fuss? We hadn't read W. E. B. Du Bois's *Black Reconstruction*, and so the Reconstruction period became another source of embarrassment, since our view of the Reconstruction period was framed by D. W. Griffith.

During the early 1960s, African Americans changed their style. Many stopped straightening their hair in favor of an Afro fashion. I went to New York and joined a black writers' workshop called Umbra, and we wrote poetry about the greatness of African civilization. I began to name my style after that of nonacademic folklore based upon the secret allusions to the Hoodoo culture I'd heard the old black people whisper about. If folklore was a despised culture, then I would embrace it. I would base my literary style upon a culture that embarrassed middle-class blacks and of which the white literary culture knew little, at least the northern white literary culture. I would wave this lost aesthetic in their faces. My use of what I called Neo-Hoodooism was an act of literary defiance. Little did I know that I was embarking on an aesthetic journey that would ultimately take me to the Yoruban people of West Africa.

Black Pride did wonders for the emotions. It was a great intellectual high. It made you feel good. It's significant, I think, that after the collapse of the Black Power movement, some of its leaders turned to physical drugs. But however exhilarating Black Power was, it could not put out of one's mind those rumors: family stories of ancestors who "could have been white," or who were white.

I was in my late thirties when one day, sitting at a table with my eighty-year-old grandmother, I asked her the identity of her father. (To this day, I wonder why it took me so long.)

She said he was an Irishman who had to leave Chattanooga for his role in organizing the pipe workers. It all came back to me—the early years, 1940, 1942, when I lived with my grandmother's brother on 1019 Elm Street in Chattanooga, before my mother returned to take me to Buffalo, New York. There was a pipe manufacturing plant located at the bottom of a hill from the house. Across the street from my uncle's house sat a huge mansion that dominated the neighborhood. It must have been about twenty acres. Built in the Spanish hacienda style, it was owned by the eccentric owner of the pipeworks. His name was pronounced Montegue, and my grandmother's brother remembered him as a man who, despite his wealth, walked down the hill toward his factory wearing overalls and a dirty rag around his neck. I remember staring for hours at the mansion, wondering what lay behind those walls. There were rumors that the mansion was haunted, but not, I was beginning to discover, as haunted as my genealogy. Nobody had ever told me that there was a connection between this man and an ancestor of mine.

When I hired a professional genealogist to trace my ancestry on my mother's side, I discovered that the name of the man whom my grandmother identified as an Irishman was Marion Shaw Coleman, who was born in December of 1869 in either Alabama or Georgia. The surprises wouldn't end with this discovery of an Irish American on my grandmother's side. In an interview I conducted with my mother and her cousin, I uncovered another ancestor of Irish American background, on my grandfather's side. My mother's cousin, whom we call "Sister," said that her grandfather, my mother's father's father, was a mean Irishman. My genealogical chart identified this man as Ezekiel Hopson or Hopkins, born in Alabama between 1854 and 1859. His father, Pleasant Hopson, was born in about 1830.

These European ghosts in the African American past have been shoveled under by the passionate claims made by the "pure race" theorists, black and white, who hold so much sway over our political and cultural life. These relatives would prove that racial supremacy is, as you say down here in Little Rock, a dog that won't hunt.

The late humanitarian John Mohare introduced me at a meeting of the Celtic Foundation as an Irish American poet. His reasoning was that if a drop of black blood made me black, why didn't a drop of Irish blood make me Irish? The people at my table—Irish American celebrities—seemed stunned. Pete Hamill, however, shook my hand. Feminist Deidre English stunned both me and the audience by announcing that I was an Irish American, all right, because I was a "liar and a thief." I then understood why her last name was English. Ms. English is ignorant of the fact that blacks and whites have been sneaking back and forth across the racial fences since they came in contact with each other in the early seventeenth century. Later I wasn't surprised to read her comments—printed in the New York Times—about the African slave trade, comments that must be the most ignorant on record.

I asked the late Sarah Fabio, a poet who was called the mother of black studies and whose features betrayed a European heritage, how one would reconcile the obvious European strain in the blood of an African American with the African American's identification with Africa, and she said that she was black because it was the black people who nurtured her. She had a point. Marion Shaw Coleman left his African American wife, whose maiden name was Mary E. Hardy, with a number of children whom she had to support by operating a restaurant in Chattanooga for more than twenty years. White American males may be the original runaway fathers of the African American experience.

In the census report of about 1870, Ezekiel Hopson's/Hopkins's children's names are listed. Under "Racial Classification," some children are listed "Black." Other children are listed "White." On the document,

White has been crossed out and the letter *M* for *mulatto* is substituted. According to family oral history, the children who looked white or near white were beneficiaries of the family's assets and eventually abandoned their darker relatives. Don't look for a story in the *Atlantic Monthly*, *Harper's*, or the *New York Times Magazine* about how darker relatives were cheated out of millions of dollars in assets by white and near-white relatives. There are millions missing from the American black family. These millions have long since passed over into whiteness.

In 1983, I came in contact with family members whom I'd never seen. Children of a father I'd never met. And this is how I found that there were Europeans and Native Americans on this side of the family tree.

The complex racial background of those who are referred to as black Americans has seldom been submitted to serious scrutiny. One could understand why the Identity Crisis nonfiction is a popular genre among assimilated intellectuals, but the fact that I could obtain as much information as I did for only $100 indicates that Identity Crisis intellectuals aren't seriously interested in discovering their roots, or are afraid of what they might find. Besides, millions of dollars are involved in continuing the black-white polarization. Think of all of the journalists and oped writers, along with a profit-feeding media, that would be out of business were there a fresh and revised look at race in America. If one allows the Native American ancestry of blacks, then W. E. B. Du Bois's theory of double consciousness, which has thrilled black intellectuals for decades, would fold.

I still haven't pieced together all the strains of my identity, but I'm much closer than I was before that day when I decided to ask my grandmother about her father, and his father. I know now why it took me so long to ask her the question. I also know that there's no such thing as Black America or White America, two nations, with two separate bloodlines. America is a land of distant cousins.

RICHARD RODRIGUEZ

Family Values

I am sitting alone in my car, in front of my parents' house—a middle-aged man with a boy's secret to tell.

What words will I use to tell them? I hate the word *gay*, find its little affirming sparkle more pathetic than assertive. I am happier with the less polite *queer*. But to my parents I would say *homosexual*, avoiding the Mexican slang *joto* (I had always heard it said in our house with hints of condescension), though *joto* is less mocking than the sissy-boy *maricon*.

The buzz on everyone's lips now: Family values. The other night on TV, the vice president of the United States, his arm around his wife, smiled into the camera and described homosexuality as "mostly a choice." But how would he know? Homosexuality never felt like a choice to me.

A few minutes ago Rush Limbaugh, the radio guy with a voice that reminds me, for some reason, of a butcher's arms, was banging his console and booming a near-reasonable polemic about family values. Limbaugh was not very clear about which values exactly he considers to be family values. A divorced man who lives alone in New York?

My parents live on a gray, treeless street in San Francisco not far from the ocean. Probably more than half of the neighborhood is immigrant. India lives next door to Greece, who lives next door to Russia. I wonder what the Chinese lady next door to my parents makes of the politicians' phrase *family values*.

What immigrants know, what my parents certainly know, is that when you come to this country, you risk losing your children. The assurance of family—continuity, inevitability—is precisely what America encourages its children to overturn. *Become your own man.* We who are native to this country know this too, of course, though we are likely to deny it. Only a society so guilty about its betrayal of family would tolerate the pictics of politicians regarding family values.

On the same summer day that Republicans were swarming in Houston (buzzing about family values), a friend of mine who escaped family values awhile back and who now wears earrings resembling intrauterine devices, was complaining to me over coffee about the Chinese. The Chinese will never take over San Francisco, my friend said, because the Chinese do not want to take over San Francisco. The Chinese do not even *see* San Francisco! All they care about is their damn families. All they care about is double-parking smack in front of the restaurant on Clement Street and pulling granny out of the car—and damn anyone who happens to be in the car behind them or the next or the next.

Politicians would be horrified by such an American opinion, of course. But then, what do politicians, Republicans or Democrats, really know of our family life? Or what are they willing to admit? Even in that area where they could reasonably be expected to have something to say— regarding the relationship of family life to our economic system—the politicians say nothing. Republicans celebrate American economic freedom, but Republicans don't seem to connect that economic freedom to the social breakdown they find appalling. Democrats, on the other hand, if more tolerant of the drift from familial tradition, are suspicious of the very capitalism that creates social freedom.

How you become free in America: Consider the immigrant. He gets a job. Soon he is earning more money than his father ever made (his father's authority is thereby subtly undermined). The immigrant begins living a life his father never knew. The immigrant moves from one job to another, changes houses. His economic choices determine his home address—not the other way around. The immigrant is on his way to becoming his own man.

When I was broke a few years ago and trying to finish a book, I lived with my parents. What a thing to do! A major theme of America is leaving home. We trust the child who forsakes family connections to make it on his own. We call that the making of a man.

Let's talk about this man stuff for a minute. America's ethos is anti-domestic. We may be intrigued by blood that runs through wealth—the Kennedys or the Rockefellers—but they seem European to us. Which is to say, they are movies. They are Corleones. Our real pledge of allegiance: We say in America that nothing about your family—your class, your race, your pedigree—should be as important as what you yourself achieve. We end up in 1992 introducing ourselves by first names.

What authority can Papa have in a country that formed its identity in an act of Oedipal rebellion against a mad British king? Papa is a joke in America, a stock sitcom figure—Archie Bunker or Homer Simpson.

But my Mexican father went to work every morning, and he stood in a white smock, making false teeth, oblivious of the shelves of grinning false teeth mocking his devotion.

The nuns in grammar school—my wonderful Irish nuns—used to push Mark Twain on me. I distrusted Huck Finn, he seemed like a gringo kid I would steer clear of in the schoolyard. (He was too confident.) I realize now, of course, that Huck is the closest we have to a national hero. We trust the story of a boy who has no home and is restless for the river. (Huck's Pap is drunk.) Americans are more forgiving of Huck's wildness than of the sweetness of the Chinese boy who walks to school with his mama or grandma. (There is no worse thing in America than to be a mama's boy, nothing better than to be a real boy—all boy—like Huck, who eludes Aunt Sally, and is eager for the world of men.)

There's a bent old woman coming up the street. She glances nervously as she passes my car. What would you tell us, old lady, of family values in America?

America is an immigrant country, we say. Motherhood—parenthood —is less our point than adoption. If I had to assign gender to America, I would note the consensus of the rest of the world. When America is burned in effigy, a male is burned. Americans themselves speak of Uncle Sam.

Like the Goddess of Liberty, Uncle Sam has no children of his own. He steals children to make men of them, mocks all reticence, all modesty, all memory. Uncle Sam is a hectoring Yankee, a skinflint uncle, gaunt, uncouth, unloved. He is the American Savonarola—hater of moonshine, destroyer of stills, burner of cocaine. Sam has no patience with mamas' boys.

You betray Uncle Sam by favoring private over public life, by seeking to exempt yourself, by cheating on your income taxes, by avoiding jury duty, by trying to keep your boy on the farm.

Mothers are traditionally the guardians of the family—against America—though even Mom may side with America against queers and deserters, at least when the Old Man is around. Premature gray hair. Arthritis in her shoulders. Bowlegged with time, red hands. In their fiercely flowered housedresses, mothers are always smarter than fathers in America. But in reality they are betrayed by their children who leave. In a thousand ways. They end up alone.

We kind of like the daughter who was a tomboy. Remember her? It was always easier to be a tomboy in America than a sissy. Americans admired Annie Oakley more than they admired Liberace (who, nevertheless, always remembered his mother). But today we do not admire Annie Oakley when we see Mom becoming Annie Oakley.

The American household now needs two incomes, everyone says.

Meaning: Mom is *forced* to leave home out of economic necessity. But lots of us know lots of moms who are sick and tired of being mom, or only mom. It's like the nuns getting fed up, teaching kids for all those years and having those kids grow up telling stories of how awful Catholic school was! Not every woman in America wants her life's work to be forgiveness. Today there are moms who don't want their husbands' names. And the most disturbing possibility: What happens when Mom doesn't want to be Mom at all? Refuses pregnancy?

Mom is only becoming an American like the rest of us. Certainly, people all over the world are going to describe the influence of feminism on women (all over the world) as their "Americanization." And rightly so.

Nothing of this, of course, will the politician's wife tell you. The politician's wife is careful to follow her husband's sentimental reassurances that nothing has changed about America except perhaps for the sinister influence of deviants. Like myself.

I contain within myself an anomaly at least as interesting as the Republican Party's version of family values. I am a homosexual Catholic, a communicant in a tradition that rejects even as it upholds me.

I do not count myself among those Christians who proclaim themselves protectors of family values. They regard me as no less an enemy of the family than the "radical feminists." But the joke about families that all homosexuals know is that we are the ones who stick around and make families possible. Call on us. I can think of 20 or 30 examples. A gay son or daughter is the only one who is "free" (married brothers and sisters are too busy). And, indeed, because we have admitted the inadmissible about ourselves (that we are queer)—we are adepts at imagination—we can even imagine those who refuse to imagine us. We can imagine Mom's loneliness, for example. If Mom needs to be taken to church or to the doctor or ferried between Christmas dinners, depend on the gay son or lesbian daughter.

I won't deny that the so-called gay liberation movement, along with feminism, undermined the heterosexual household, if that's what politicians mean when they say family values. Against churchly reminders that sex was for procreation, the gay bar as much as the birth-control pill taught Americans not to fear sexual pleasure. In the past two decades—and, not coincidentally, parallel to the feminist movement—the gay liberation movement moved a generation of Americans toward the idea of a childless adulthood. If the women's movement was ultimately more concerned about getting out of the house and into the workplace, the gay movement was in its way more subversive to Puritan America because it stressed the importance of play.

Several months ago, the society editor of the morning paper in San

Francisco suggested (on a list of "must haves") that every society dame must have at least one gay male friend. A ballet companion. A lunch date. The remark was glib and incorrect enough to beg complaints from homosexual readers, but there was a truth about it as well. Homosexual men have provided women with an alternate model of masculinity. And the truth: The Old Man, God bless him, is a bore. Thus are we seen as preserving marriages? Even Republican marriages?

For myself, homosexuality is a deep brotherhood but does not involve domestic life. Which is why, my married sisters will tell you, I can afford the time to be a writer. And why are so many homosexuals such wonderful teachers and priests and favorite aunts, if not because we are freed from the house? On the other hand, I know lots of homosexual couples (male and female) who model their lives on the traditional heterosexual version of domesticity and marriage. Republican politicians mock the notion of a homosexual marriage, but ironically such marriages honor the heterosexual marriage by imitating it.

"The only loving couples I know," a friend of mine recently remarked, "are all gay couples."

This woman was not saying that she does not love her children or that she is planning a divorce. But she was saying something about the sadness of American domestic life: the fact that there is so little joy in family intimacy. Which is perhaps why gossip (public intrusion into the private) has become a national industry. All day long, in forlorn houses, the television lights up a freakish parade of husbands and mothers-in-law and children upon the stage of Sally or Oprah or Phil. They tell on each other. The audience ooohhhs. Then a psychiatrist-shaman appears at the end to dispense prescriptions—the importance of family members granting one another more "space."

The question I desperately need to ask you is whether we Americans have ever truly valued the family. We are famous, or our immigrant ancestors were famous, for the willingness to leave home. And it is ironic that a crusade under the banner of family values has been taken up by those who would otherwise pass themselves off as patriots. For they seem not to understand America, nor do I think they love the freedoms America grants. Do they understand why, in a country that prizes individuality and is suspicious of authority, children are disinclined to submit to their parents? You cannot celebrate American values in the public realm without expecting them to touch our private lives. As Barbara Bush remarked recently, family values are also neighborhood values. It may be harmless enough for Barbara Bush to recall a sweeter America— Midland, Texas, in the 1950s. But the question left begging is why we chose to leave Midland, Texas. Americans like to say that we can't go home again. The truth is that we don't want to go home again, don't want to be known, recognized. Don't want to respond in the same old ways. (And you know you will if you go back there.)

Little 10-year-old girls know that there are reasons for getting away from the family. They learn to keep their secrets—under lock and key— addressed to Dear Diary. Growing up queer, you learn to keep secrets as well. In no place are those secrets more firmly held than within the family house. You learn to live in closets. I know a Chinese man who arrived in America about 10 years ago. He got a job and made some money. And during that time he came to confront his homosexuality. And then his family arrived. I do not yet know the end of this story.

The genius of America is that it permits children to leave home, it permits us to become different from our parents. But the sadness, the loneliness of America, is clear too.

Listen to the way Americans talk about immigrants. If, on the one hand, there is impatience when today's immigrants do not seem to give up their family, there is also a fascination with this reluctance. In Los Angeles, Hispanics are considered people of family. Hispanic women are hired to be at the center of the American family—to baby-sit and diaper, to cook and to clean and to ease the dying. Hispanic attachment to family is seen by many Americans, I think, as the reason why Hispanics don't get ahead. But if Asians privately annoy us for being so family oriented, they are also stereotypically celebrated as the new "whiz kids" in school. Don't Asians go to college, after all, to honor their parents?

More important still is the technological and economic ascendancy of Asia, particularly Japan, on the American imagination. Americans are starting to wonder whether perhaps the family values of Asia put the United States at a disadvantage. The old platitude had it that ours is a vibrant, robust society for being a society of individuals. Now we look to Asia and see team effort paying off.

In this time of national homesickness, of nostalgia, for how we imagine America used to be, there are obvious dangers. We are going to start blaming each other for the loss. Since we are inclined, as Americans, to think of ourselves individually, we are disinclined to think of ourselves as creating one another or influencing one another.

But it is not the politician or any political debate about family values that has brought me here on a gray morning to my parents' house. It is some payment I owe to my youth and to my parents' youth. I imagine us sitting in the living room, amid my mother's sentimental doilies and the family photographs, trying to take the measure of the people we have turned out to be in America.

A San Francisco poet, when he was in the hospital and dying, called a priest to his bedside. The old poet wanted to make his peace with Mother Church. He wanted baptism. The priest asked why. "Because the Catholic Church has to accept me," said the poet. "Because I am a sinner."

Isn't willy-nilly inclusiveness the point, the only possible point to be derived from the concept of family? Curiously, both President Bush and Vice President Quayle got in trouble with their constituents recently for expressing a real family value. Both men said that they would try to dissuade a daughter or granddaughter from having an abortion. But, finally, they said they would support her decision, continue to love her, never abandon her.

There are families that do not accept. There are children who are forced to leave home because of abortions or homosexuality. There are family secrets that Papa never hears. Which is to say there are families that never learn the point of families.

But there she is at the window. My mother has seen me and she waves me in. Her face asks: Why am I sitting outside? (Have they, after all, known my secret for years and kept it, out of embarrassment, not knowing what to say?) Families accept, often by silence. My father opens the door to welcome me in.

Chrysanthemums

Miss Yamada knew if a girl was tall and thin, or short and plump, by the sound of her voice, and she also knew if a girl was hiding a piece of candy in her mouth. This is what oka-san said. I worried that Miss Yamada was some kind of oni, a devil, with eyeballs peering out from inside her ears and nostrils, blinking on her fingertips. She lived with her mother and never left the house. My sisters and I were all frightened of Miss Yamada's mother—balding and stopped, she did all of her shopping and errands in dark, old-fashioned kimonos, and geta shoes that made a hollow clop-clop sound as she walked. But Miss Yamada turned out to be delicate and quiet, with milky-white skin and cool fingers like weeping willow leaves. As she leaned over the koto, the back of her neck, in between wisps of black hair and the curving lip of her pale blue kimono, gave off a sweet, powdery scent from the rice talcum she used. She was like the women in woodblock prints—except for her eyes, which were cloudy like old tea that has been left in the pot for too long. Her voice held no sharp edges, but it had the same effect on me as listening to a shakuhachi flute—a kind of music that makes you feel sad inside. I fell in love with her. Sometimes I imagined Miss Yamada unpinning her hair at night, heavy black folds unfurling down to her waist. I longed to stand behind her and brush her hair, one hundred strokes, the way my mother sometimes let me do. I wished that I were a boy, so I could grow up and marry Miss Yamada.

I used to wait in her garden until it was time for my koto lesson. One day I kept waiting for a long time, and I began to have a hot, ugly feeling inside—like a dragon blowing smoke inside my stomach. Miss Yamada was inside her house with Natsu Matsumoru. Was she feeding Natsu the rice candies she sometimes gave to me at the end of a lesson? Had she forgotten all about me? The garden was filled with chrysanthemums—explosions of color and petals that reminded me of the fireworks

236   LEE ANN RORIPAUGH

over Sumida River during the Star Festival. And while I sat there with this bad feeling inside, they kept watching me, nodding at me on their stems, laughing at me until I couldn't stand it anymore and began to pick them—carelessly tearing them off, the ragged stems oozing single, clear drops.

I kept a red one to wear in my hair, and the rest I dismembered over by the pond, pulling off the petals one by one, chanting She Loves Me, She Loves Me Not. It was filled with giant, fan-tailed goldfish—mottled orange, red, and white, colored like the marbles my brothers sometimes played with. Some of them had puffy, exploded heads. I was afraid of these kind of goldfish because my mother had told me this was what happened to girls with tonkachi heads who didn't listen to their mothers. Soon the pond was filled with chrysanthemum petals, swirling in gentle whirlwinds around the shining bodies and dancing fan-tails of the agitated goldfish. Miss Yamada is blind, I kept saying to myself. She will not know that I have picked her chrysanthemums. But then I heard the shoji screen to the garden slide open, heard her call for me. I walked into the house with my heart loud as taiko drums. *I see that you are wearing a chrysanthemum corsage today.* This is what she said to me.

But this was years ago—before the war, before my koto was wrapped in silk and put in storage, before my father moved us up to the mountain house to protect us from the bombs. The day after the B-29 bombers flew over Ota City my brothers and sisters and I rode down from the mountain on our bicycles to see if our house was still standing. It was, but on the way there, we saw many others that were not—people searching rubble for belongings, relatives. This is when I rode my bicycle as fast as I could to Miss Yamada—pedaling, pedaling, out of breath. Her house was gone. The garden gone. And in front of where the house used to be, Miss Yamada's mother was screaming. The neighbors were trying to take something away from her. And even though it was burnt, blackened, the long fingers crushed, I saw whose hand it was before my eldest brother found me and dragged me away.

Today the American man with the gentle eyes, the big nose that he is always putting inside a book, has left chrysanthemums on my typewriter at the American occupation camp where I work. He is not like the others—he tosses rubber bands into my hair instead of trying to put his hand around my waist, and he shows me how to spell the long American words that I have to type all day without understanding what they mean. I hold the chrysanthemums up to my face and breathe in their tangy, pungent scent. Suddenly, I can see everything. Petals raining down to the bottom of Miss Yamada's goldfish pond. He Loves Me, He Loves Me Not. The smell so strong it makes my eyes sting. These chrysanthemums stolen, crossing an ocean to return them.

Ningyo

She took me everywhere
in my crocheted
lace dresses,
embroidered initials.
It pleased her
I could say
hippopotamus
so I said it
in the supermarket.
After hot baths,
laid out on the counter,
my hair floating
in the sink
like seaweed,
she would hand me
a mirror. *See?*
Tako-chan, the octopus
has left his ink.
I had a Japanese doll,
a snow queen
in a glass case
I couldn't touch.
I named her Yoshiko,
my mother's name.
Sometimes
when she was sleeping,
I pried
her eyelids open,
to make sure
she wasn't dead.

I was angry we ate
Ramen every night.
She wouldn't let me
shave my legs,
and my grandparents
were stern pictures
wrapped in rice paper.
She said I gave her
high blood pressure,
and I felt

she was cold
as Yoshiko.
My father bought me
an orange hat,
vest, earplugs,
a cheesecloth
for the carcass.
She packed up obento,
a coolerful
of Tab and beer.
We got to Shirley Basin
before dawn, gutting
my antelope by noon.
Some drunk men
drove by in a pickup
and yelled, *Goddamn,
it's a girl.* Circling
the prairie he told me,
*There are things
you don't understand.*

That night we cooked
over a kerosene stove
and drank Coors.
As I lay awake,
I could see a woman
who married an enemy
soldier. The frost
began to glisten
on my sleeping bag.
Stars, an eyelid
opening the sky.

SARAH SCHULMAN

Rat Bohemia

The world's largest rats are the capybaras, the web-footed denizens of the Amazon. Their hair bristles when they get angry and they are extremely hostile to humans, even ones they know over a long period of time. There was a special series on capybaras in the Kuala Lumpur newspaper. My friend David sent it to me when he was on vacation because he knows how much I care about rats. The article basically discussed the pros and cons of raising the animals for food. Bandicoots, which is what giant rats are called in India, are not eaten. Originally they lived in the country but got too fat to climb the stalks of wheat. So, they traded places with the smaller city brand which migrated to the country and wiped out the crops that the fat ones couldn't reach. David is HIV+ but he still had 600 t-cells when he went to China so we didn't have to worry that much. Once over there he went to Guangzhou and wrote me about a rat-control campaign where the city published special recipes trying to get the residents to eat those rodents up. He said he saw red lacquered ones, basted with honey and soy, hanging by their tails in the market. But, like their American counterparts, all Chinese rats are not equal. So, people generally complained about eating sewer rats which was considered only one step removed from eating sewage.

Last summer the mayor of New York decided to cut back on rat extermination. He also cut back on street lights. As a result, night increasingly meant these dark outlines of buildings surrounded by the scampering of 18 inch varmints. Ten million of them at least. My best friend Killer and I spent a lot of nights that summer just walking around because we didn't have any money. I was saving up to move out of New York and Killer hadn't had a job in two years. She came over every night to eat and then we'd take a walk. She'd forgotten how to even look for a job. She'd forgotten how to sound employable on the telephone. One day I glanced over her shoulder at the Help Wanted pages of the *New York Times*, only it wasn't what you'd call *pages*. It was more like half a column. One Saturday we saw a kid get shot in front of The Unique Clothing Store Going Out Of Business Sale and the next day we watched a guy go crazy and throw glass bottles at people for twenty minutes. I've always wanted to shoot rats.

Killer and I are hard-core New Yorkers. But when we were kids the only homeless person you'd ever see would be a wino on The Bowery or an occasional bag lady. You never saw anyone sleeping on a subway car unless they were coming home from the night shift. The streets were not covered with urine then. That was considered impolite. There have always been rats, though. I remember as a teenager watching them run around on the subway tracks waiting for the Seven train to get me out of Jackson Heights. But mostly, when I was a kid, rats were something that bit babies in a mythical far-away ghetto. You never saw them hanging out in the middle-class sections of Queens.

An average rat litter is twenty-two little ones and they can reproduce at the rate of six litters a year. Some time in the nineteen eighties I started to see them scampering regularly in the playgrounds of Central Park. Reagan had just become president and I held him directly responsible. Rat infestation felt like something the U.S. government should really have been able to handle. That's when I started thinking about getting a gun and shooting each one of them on sight. Picking them off the way hillbillies shoot squirrels.

That guy, last Sunday, who was throwing glass bottles? All he cared about was himself. His personal expression was more important to him than other people's eyes. That's the kind of attitude that makes this town a dangerous place to live. You never know when it can hit. The shooting in front of The Unique was more reasonable. It was just a bunch of friends killing each other. Don't have friends like that and it will never happen to you.

Every morning I go over to the old Veteran's Administration building on West 25th Street and wait on line to go through the metal detectors. Then I have to ride up in the elevators with all the whacked out veterans scratching and getting into fights. Then I get off at the seventeenth floor where there is The Food and Hunger Hotline office and walk through them. Their walls are covered with these old World War Two murals of soldiers getting fitted for artificial legs by nurses in starched caps. The women lift up the veterans' new legs and demonstrate how to use them. Then I sign in at Pest Control and waste about half the day unless I get sent out on a job.

When I'm sitting in the Pest Control office hanging out waiting, I pay close attention to the goings on at Food and Hunger. I want to see everything I can. Everything. I want to be a witness to my own time because I have a sneaking suspicion that I'm gonna live a lot longer than most of the people I meet. If I'm gonna be the only one still around to say what happened, I'd better pay close attention now.

Killer usually stops by the office at ten for coffee and peanut butter sandwiches. Then she checks in at a couple of restaurants to see if they need any prep cooks. I know for a fact that they're only hiring Mexicans and Israelis. Everybody knows Americans can't work. They want to talk on the phone in between high salaries and free meals. In the meantime she's living on forty dollars a week from watering plants for a couple of offices and boutiques. The rest gets paid by the Bed and Breakfast guests she hustles at those four dollar cappucino places. Mostly Swiss people or Germans. They think it's quaint. She gives them a bed and then tells them to make their own breakfast. Then she comes to the office to eat some of mine. We've been living this schedule for a long time already. It is one big fat habit. You know one thing I don't like about homeless people? They ask you for a light and then hold on to your lighter for forty-five minutes blabbing on and on about some misfortune. The whole thing is designed to make it seem that they don't realize that they've got your lighter. But the fact is, they know they've got it.

Killer was brought up to be a racist. One night I went over to her place to watch TV and her parents brought over some food. Next thing you know the news came on and it was all "Nigger" this and "Nigger" that. Her parents had these sharp teeth whenever they said that word. They scrunched up the skin around their eyes. It wasn't said calmly. Killer knows better but when she gets emotional, that's what she falls back on. Like one time some Puerto Rican guy was beating up his kid in the hallway and Killer said, "Look at that low-rent over there."

"Shut-up," I said. "You haven't had a job in two years. If you had enough patience to stand in line you'd be on Welfare yourself."

"I'd be on Welfare if it wasn't for the strength of the Euro-Dollar," she said as some blonde couple rolled over in the bed. That was the way she looked at things.

God that summer was hot. There's that way that Puerto Rican girls sit close together on the stoops. They have skinny arms and those ten dollar pink dresses. They smile and wear their hair long with a headband.

Every day homeless people come into Food and Hunger looking for food but they only get Contact Cards. I gave Killer one of those cards but she said the food they advertised wasn't nutritious.

One time, before breakfast, Killer walked me to work but she wanted to stop off at the xerox store on Tenth Street that was run by some Moonies. They were clean-cut peculiar and wore polyester pants up to their necks.

"They give away free bread and free Chinese buns," she said.

When we walked in it was kind of slow and real hot. It stunk of xerox fluid. The polyesters had a few day-olds sitting on the counter and a bag of day-old buns.

"Don't eat it," I said. "It's old pork."

"Hi Killer," they said handing her two loaves. Then they turned to me. "What about you?"

"I don't need free food," I said.

"Look," Killer whispered. "Take it. I need it. I'll give you a fresh one later for your birthday."

"OK. No, wait. I don't want bread for my birthday. I want a colander."

"Do you think I need a professional portfolio?" she asked.

Killer was still thinking about jobs.

"How is everything going?" Killer asked the Moonies, remembering to be gracious.

"We're having problems with rats," they said.

That woke me up.

"Do you have big ones?" I asked. "One pounders?"

"Yep," they said.

"Did you put out poison?" Killer asked.

"Poison doesn't work," they said. "They're too strong. Besides, if you kill one that way it's just gonna stink up your place and bring maggots."

"Did you try traps?" Killer asked, trying to cut me off because she knew what I was about to recommend.

"Traps don't work," I said ignoring her. "The rats are too smart. They spring the traps and get the bait."

"What about walk-in traps?" one of the Moonies asked.

"Too expensive," I said. "Doesn't work on a massive scale."

"Well, what do you suggest?" he asked.

"You gotta shoot 'em," I said. "You gotta get 'em one by one."

The reason that all of this background information had been on my mind was because I spent most of last summer thinking about the fact that, frankly, I have not made as much of my life as I would have liked. I have never learned how to achieve. That's why I've been saving up to move out of New York. Florida might be nice. Learn how to drive. Go swimming.

Working this job is a real downer except when we go out for the kill. That's the best. But in the meantime, I have to sit here with the crew from Food and Hunger and listen to them make small talk. Especially that Mrs. Sabrina Santiago. She almost always has a city worker attitude and therefore kicks my butt psychologically and regularly. Everything is about her territory and her ability to lord it over me. But she has nothing to brag about since she moves real slow and wouldn't say "How are you?" if it was worth a million dollars in food stamps. These types of relationships and social encounters are what has made me question my life.

Killer and I talk about this all of the time, about how we are going to better ourselves. The problem with Killer is that she's a pretender. She pretends that something is going to happen when nothing is ever going to happen. Then, when it's over, she pretends that something did happen when actually it was nothing. I love Killer. I don't mean to judge her but I have to.

Mrs. Santiago called me from across the hall and asked if I would messenger something over to the computer store on Forty-Third Street. Now, I knew that she was supposed to bring that over herself because Food and Hunger doesn't have the kind of money to buy a messenger service. I also know that Mrs. Santiago lives in Bushwick Brooklyn which is in the opposite direction from Forty-Third Street. So, out of the kindness of my heart I said *yes*. Then she made me stand there, freezing my butt off in that central air conditioning while she chats away on the phone for forty-five minutes. City worker.

Of course I'm eavesdropping because I've got nothing else to do and the whole conversation seems to be about these storerooms filled with flour that the City got a hold of. But, all of this flour doesn't do hungry people any good because most of them don't know how to bake bread. Or, if they do know, they've got no place to make it. Especially if you are a person with a substance abuse problem. You will never find the time to make bread. Therefore, all this potential food was sitting there going to waste. Mrs. Santiago was suggesting on the phone that they could get all the new prisoners in all the new jails to learn how to bake bread and they could bake up all this flour and distribute it already made. She was suggesting that, in the future, when they build prisons, they could include bread baking facilities and kill two birds with one stone.

By the time she actually handed me the package and I got downstairs, I found out that Killer had been waiting around in the lobby because both detectors broke down and everyone was being searched by hand.

"Fuck that," I said and we both set off for the computer store.

Unfortunately we decided to take the subway which promptly got stopped between stations.

"Fuck that," I said.

After about ten minutes the conductor's voice came on over the PA system.

"Attention passengers. Due to a police shooting at the next station we have been temporarily delayed. But we will now proceed with caution."

"Proceed with caution?" Killer said. "What is this, *Stagecoach*?"

"What are we going to do?" I asked.

"Look," she said. "When we pull into the next station, duck behind the seats. You gotta get lower than the bench in case the bullets come through the window."

So, when the train eased into the next stop we ducked. But, we both kept sticking our heads up to peek because we wanted to see what was going on. Sure enough the place was swarming with cops and a bunch of medical personnel, all looking very tired and overworked. Then the guy across the aisle from us started to have a psychotic episode. He started meowing. At the next stop, Killer and I got off the train.

"Killer," I said as we walked uptown. "Tell me something. What the fuck are we doing? What are we doing with our lives? I think about this all the time now and I can't figure out what category I'm in."

"Category?"

"Yeah, I mean, I don't have any money but I'm not *poor*. I have aspirations but they're spiritual ones, not careers. I look around at how people are really living and I can't identify. But, when I turn on the TV I don't understand that either. What the hell is going on, Killer?" I asked. "Who the hell do we think we are?"

"We're bohemians," she said.

"What?"

"We're bohemians. We don't have those dominant culture values."

"We're bohemians?" I meekly asked.

"Yeah," she answered. "Ever heard of it?"

"Of course," I answered indignantly. "It's people who go to foreign movies."

I was identifying already.

"In the past there were decade specific names," Killer said. "Like hippies, beatniks, New Age, punks or Communists."

"What do we call them now?"

"That's the whole thing," Killer said, her black hair flapping carelessly against her green skin. "Nowadays it's not generational. Bohemians aren't grouped by clothes or sex or age. Nowadays, it's just a state of mind. Anyone with a different idea is in."

We were standing by the front door of the computer store and Killer obviously wasn't planning to enter. So, we stayed out on the sidewalk and discussed existence like any New Yorker would do in our place. We were outside in that inside kind of way. There's weather and a sky at the top of the corridor. The walls were made of buildings, and streets ran on like cracks in the plaster.

"But what about turn on, tune in, drop out, Socialism and other social outcast stuff?"

"Listen," Killer said. "In the fifties, the Beats, those guys were so all-American. They could sit around and ponder aesthetic questions but a cup of coffee cost a nickel. Nowadays, with the economy the way it is, you can't drop out or you'll be homeless. You gotta function to be a boho. You have to meet the system head on at least once in a while and that meeting, Rita, is very brutal. Nowadays you have to pay a very high price to become a bohemian."

Being There

Eighty-year-old Diana Angel Stamoulis remembers that there were Greek men working on the roof of her Manhattan apartment building on March 2, 1983. At about eleven in the morning, they banged on her door to tell her, speaking in Greek, that they saw smoke. "Stop making fun," she said, and closed her door. They banged again. This time she went out into the hall and opened the window. She saw smoke coming up from the fourth floor below. She climbed the stairs to the sixth floor, where she saw smoke coming from under the door of apartment 6D.

Mrs. Angel phoned her daughter Adrienne, an actress who lived in the building next door, and told her there was a fire. Adrienne also didn't believe it at first, but a short time later she arrived and the two women left the building, walking down the five flights of stairs. Once outside, where fire engines were already gathering in front of 547 Riverside Drive, Mrs. Angel decided to go back to save some of her possessions. There were thousands of dollars' worth of stamp collections, knick-knacks, jewelry, a trunk full of fabrics—she had been a dressmaker like her mother before her—as well as valuable papers and correspondence with Mayor John Lindsay, Governor Nelson Rockefeller, and President Lyndon Johnson. Apparently no one saw her re-enter the building and climb the five flights.

In her seven-room apartment again, Mrs. Angel felt intense heat coming from 5D, next door. She heard the loud crashing of windows exploding from the heat, and when she looked out her kitchen window she saw flames. She sat down on her living room sofa and spoke to God in Greek. She said, "You're not going to let this building burn. But if it's time for me to go, I'll go with this building." At that moment the large mirror behind her, above the sofa, crashed and splintered, the glass flying right over her without hurting her. Mrs. Angel knew then that God felt it wasn't time for her to go.

Hot water coming from the ceiling fell on her left shoulder. She thought the building's boiler must have burst, and wondered how water from the boiler in the basement could have gotten so high up. She soon realized it was water that had been hosed into the floor above and heated by the flames. Mrs. Angel walked to her front window, facing Riverside Park and the Hudson River, thinking the falling water couldn't reach her there. Up on the hill across from the building, a small crowd of people who had gathered to watch the fire noticed her and waved at her to come down, but she shook her head. She was not afraid. She was "in a sort of trance," watching the beauty and the colors of the flames, hearing the loud crashing of windows. She stayed there, listening, and gazing at the gorgeous black and gray smoke, at the reds and blues and greens. "People don't realize how beautiful fire is."

When the fire broke out, Coula Lurier, Diana Angel's younger sister, who lived in 1B, was at her senior citizens center. She had recently returned from her daughter's home in Washington, D.C., where she was recuperating from a series of radiation treatments. "Just in time for the fire," her son Harold later commented. Harold Lurier, a dapper, white-haired professor of medieval history at New York's Pace University, is the only man left from the original Dalianis family that came from Greece in 1904. He had rented the seven-room apartment in 1957, then moved into his own place farther uptown a year later, while his mother remained.

"My cousin Adrienne called me," he recalls, "and said, 'Sit down, the building's burning.' I went over and there it was, water was pouring in. My mother came and we ran into the house. There were no lights. We grabbed what we could and out we were. My mother went to Adrienne's apartment next door. I went in and out about three times, taking the TV, some silver, some jewelry. Did my Aunt Dina tell you how she could have died in the fire? No? She went back up after she had been persuaded to come out. She went into a closet, looking for a coat, and something fell against the closet door, jamming it and shutting her in. It just happened that James Kyrimes, from Columbia's Housing Office, was looking through the building and heard her calling. Otherwise she would have been killed there. Maybe she forgot."

As Mrs. Angel remembers it, a fireman noticed her standing at the front window looking out at the beauty of the flames. Very soon two firemen, along with Adrienne, came up the steps to get her. Mrs. Angel didn't want to go, but Adrienne took her by the hand and said, "Mother, these are only *things*. I need you." Together they led her out of the building. About a half hour later the roof of the apartment above collapsed and fell through to Mrs. Angel's apartment.

In 1964 I returned from a year in Rome, where my husband, Harry, had a Fulbright grant to study urban history and planning. We had no money, no jobs, no place to live, and I was pregnant. We camped at my parents' house in Rockland County, and Harry would go into the city every day to look for an apartment. One day he came back pleased: six rooms in a nice old building on Riverside Drive, near Columbia, where we had both been students. I went with him to have a look. I saw mostly that it was big, and that its wide front windows overlooked the green of Riverside Park and the Hudson River. Soon after, Harry got a job at the New York City Planning Commission. It wouldn't make any sense for me to get a job, we agreed, since I would be having the baby in November, and it was almost September.

The day we officially moved in I took a good look around. The ceilings were very high, the walls all brown, and in the long hall, especially, they pressed in with a feeling of hushed desolation. I felt suddenly desolate too, and I cried. We began painting; my family came to help. My brother and my nephews painted the hall; my brother, who is very tall, could paint all the way up to the ceiling, past the molding, without a ladder. As he moved smoothly along the hall with his roller, turning it from brown to white, I stopped crying. It would be a place to live, for a while at least. We were nomadic. Before Rome we had lived in one apartment in New York, three in Philadelphia, and two in Boston, in the space of six years, so I expected we would keep moving. Because I was quite pregnant, I painted that segment of wall which could be reached without much bending or stretching. Every day I left a border on top for Harry to finish when he came home from work. Sometimes I would sit on the floor and creep around the perimeter of a room to do the lower moldings.

Among his many endeavors, my father, by profession a tax lawyer and CPA, had a furniture store in Chinatown. Since we had no furniture, it seemed natural to him that we should go to the store and pick out what we needed. Others like us, young people brought up in provincial sections of Brooklyn, would buy furniture when they set up house: bedroom suites, living room suites, and carpeting to match. But we wanted never to "set up house." We wanted to be the opposite of the way our families were, and to play house. Wherever we went, we made bookcases out of shelves and bricks and had big pillows in the living room. Our bed was a mattress on a frame. To placate my parents we did go to the store and pick out a few things—a round white kitchen table and four red chairs, a kitchen cabinet, and a couple of simple lamps. I remember my father looking with some contempt at one simple red lamp and saying, "That's all you want?" What we lacked in furniture we made up for on the walls—countless posters, prints, and odd hangings; over the years to follow we added works of art done by our children and some real works of art loaned by friends who were painters. Harry also cultivated eighty-two plants, so the place was green and not desolate.

Towards the end of the pregnancy I would sit at night in a red and white flowered wing chair we had gotten at some thrift shop and look out over the river at the bright lights of Palisades Amusement Park over on the New Jersey shore. I could see the outline of the roller coaster, all its snaking figure eights, and the cars swooping around them. I watched the moving letters on the park's huge marquee, advertising products I no longer remember, till I had memorized all the slogans in a trance of lethargy and muted panic over having a baby. The baby was late. Thanksgiving came and I called my mother to say I hadn't the strength to come to Rockland County for her big dinner. She had a solution. Hours later my mother and father and brother, my sister and brother-in-law and their two sons, marched in carrying the Thanksgiving dinner and set it up on paper plates, the first of many parties in our apartment. When they left I sat in the dark and watched the lights of Palisades Park, wondering when I would ever have this baby.

When Rachel was a few months old my mother began coming over once a week to stay with her so I could, in her words, "get out of the house." Soon I hired a woman from around the corner to come in one and a half days a week so I could get out some more. I found a part-time job writing publicity material for an open housing program in Harlem, which was close enough to walk to, and my mother remarked, "I always thought a woman should stay home with a baby, but in your case I see you can't. Go."

During six years of marriage, I had gone to work, and we had done the housework infrequently and together. Suddenly I found myself in a spacious, solid apartment with a baby it was universally assumed I should take care of, and wondered how on earth it had come about. I suppose both my parents were relieved I had married at all, since I had always threatened to do bizarre things with my life, and relieved that I had gone so far as to have a baby and do the conventional things for it like buy a crib and a playpen, dress it and feed it and take it to the park in a carriage with a hood and a row of plastic balls strung across the front. My mother told me things I ought to do for the baby; one was to give her a lamb chop for lunch when she got old enough to hold a bone. My mother believed in lamb chops the way later on people came to believe in yogurt and, more recently, in tofu. And once a week she arrived at around nine-thirty in the morning (my father dropped her off on his way to work) and I would fly out of the house to my job in Harlem.

When we took the apartment, the real-estate agent told us another couple just back from Rome had moved in on the third floor, both artists. Coming out of the elevator one day, I saw a young man who looked like he might be an artist, and who looked as new to the place as I did. I inquired and he said yes, he was the one, Bob Birmelin. We invited him and his wife, Blair, over for coffee. I tried to heat a frozen Sara Lee banana cake in the oven and ruined it—the frosting melted and dripped and I was embarrassed serving it. Nevertheless we became very good friends, especially Blair and I. I discovered she read Proust and Henry James and liked to sit and talk about books just as I did. Amidst our marathon talks, periodically there would be a new baby. First I had a girl, and a year and a half later she had a boy. I visited her in the hospital, bringing books, and when she came home with her baby we talked about childbirth and about the books. Two years later I had another girl, and a year and a half later Blair had another boy. We went to the park together, Riverside Park across the street, and in the course of an afternoon shifted our equipment from the benches near the slide to the benches near the jungle gym to the benches near the sandbox, along with other local mothers, women whose husbands were studying at Columbia or at Union Theological Seminary or Jewish Theological Seminary. I have a photo of Blair and me in heavy wool sweaters and jeans, playing hopscotch in the park. We look intent and defiant, as the children stand by and watch.

In our early years the park had a sprinkler for hot days, but one year it disappeared. Too much vandalism, the park man said. And the kids took water into the sandbox. I never understood what was wrong with taking water into the sandbox, but the park man, a jovial short dark man who liked to flirt with the mothers, was adamantly against it. He would sit and talk to any women alone, as if part of his job for the Parks Department was to keep young mothers company, and it was in fact pleasant to be flirted with at a time when babies and sandboxes constituted so much of the once variegated world. When he hurt his leg and disappeared soon after the sprinkler, I missed him equally.

After the park, Blair and I would take the children back to one of our apartments and have drinks while they played and fought. We would be talking about Proust or Henry James or the like, drinking and smoking, feeling like grown women, when one of the children would rush in insulted or injured, and we would have to mediate. I tried to settle disputes by reason and fairness, but in her house, I remember, she always gave the children apples. Blair seemed to have an unlimited supply of McIntosh apples, which seemed to soothe all injuries better than sweet reason.

The children, especially as they all got older, made so much noise that it was a wonder we could manage to talk about Proust and James and such, but manage we did, and like my mother she helped rescue me; perhaps I did the same for her.

At night the four of us grownups would get together to eat and drink and play games like pick-up-sticks; it seemed all right to leave the children alone on the sixth floor or on the third, and dash out from time to time to check on them. We were all very competitive, and so the games of pick-up-sticks were tense. Especially we women were competitive, for the men were out working at their chosen professions while we had little outlet for our competitiveness. Probably we would have been competitive in any case. On and off we played with a Ouija board, which predicted the date of the birth of Blair's and Bob's first baby, the results of the 1968 presidential election, and later on spelled out the name of Rachel's nursery school teacher.

After a few years of babies and, for me, graduate school, we began to write fiction, Blair downstairs and I upstairs. She started first, after her second child was born. She had always been the painter and I the writer, at least in my mind. But there she was, writing. If a painter could write, I thought, surely I, a writer, could write too. When I had no private place to work she let me use a room in her apartment, so that sometimes we were both writing there, in different rooms. Now what we were both writing is in books and in bookstores, which seems miraculous.

Meanwhile, once a week for maybe seven years, my mother kept coming over to take care of the children while I got out. When I returned home I would find she had done some laundry and ironing too. She bathed the first baby, but with the second she said she couldn't anymore—she was older and this baby was heavier; her arm ached. But she took both out to the park, for she believed in fresh air as in lamb chops, and sometimes on her return she would rest for a few moments in the lobby on one of the old high-backed velvet-cushioned chairs that flanked a large oak breakfront. One day these pieces of furniture vanished. Stolen, our building superintendent, Mrs. Flanagan, said in amazement. The mystery of how and when these massive items could have been stolen was never solved. After that there was no furniture in the lobby.

My father would come by after work to pick my mother up, and we would sit and talk for a while, my mother enumerating what wondrous things the baby, and then babies, had done and said that day. During one of these talks the lights suddenly went out. First we thought it was our building alone, but out the window, up and down our side of the river as far as we could see, was blackness. Across the river New Jersey's lights were bright. We sat in the dark bemused. I unearthed a few candles. A neighbor from across the hall rang the bell to offer us a huge Christmas candle, and she sat with us for a while. She said she kept a lot of candles around for emergencies. She had the reputation of being eccentric, and indeed she had a touch of the Ancient Mariner about her, stopping us in the hall occasionally when some far-fetched topic seemed to weigh on her mind. She didn't have a glittering eye, but she did have a pale, waxy-looking face, as if she never went outdoors, and her hair was done in two long braids wound about her head like an Edwardian heroine's. She wore strange dun-colored shabby clothes that also seemed never to have seen the light of day—there was an overall mustiness to her—and those who had been in the building longer than we had told fantastic tales about primeval chaos in her apartment; and she had some strange habits as well, like reading late at night on the hall steps, to save electricity, she explained when we jumped back, startled, at the elevator door. She was often seen carrying shopping bags in and out, and she drove a repainted mail truck, which took up more than its share of precious street parking space. But with all that she could be pleasant to talk to, and she was intelligent. She was a public school teacher. And so we sat there bemused by the blackout—none of us could remember this happening in New York City before.

Soon my parents groped their way down the stairs. When they got home my mother called to describe to me how strange New York had looked from across the river, black and empty like an abandoned city. All evening, people in our building roamed the stairs and halls with flashlights, seeing if everyone was all right, if everyone had candles. It felt like a great adventure. But later on I was frightened, alone in the dark with a year-old baby. Even when the lights were on I was often afraid that something terrible would befall the baby and that I would not know the right thing to do. How much worse in the dark. It must have been from my mother that I had the notion that for every eventuality—particularly in the case of children—there was a right thing to do, as opposed to any number of wrong things, and that the acquiring of wisdom was learning all those right things in advance. Harry got home around midnight. He had walked all the way from the Lower East Side in stages, stopping off at friends' houses along the way, resting and gathering strength in the various darknesses. He brought news of the outside, like a courier in the Dark Ages.

Around this time Harry's family—mother, sister, cousins, and all—decided to have a surprise party for Harry's father's seventieth birthday in our apartment. Well, fine, except we hardly had suitable furniture. We felt we should dignify the occasion with a couch, at the very least. We did have a couch of sorts, but it was ragged and falling apart, having traveled to Philadelphia and to Boston and languished in storage for a year. Harry went to an auction in Brooklyn on the day of the party and found an elegant, old-fashioned tufted couch for eleven dollars, plus twenty-five to have it delivered the same day. The couch was white, which I thought beautiful. I was very proud of it when all the family arrived. Later my mother informed me that, beautiful or not, the white was merely the muslin that belonged under a covering. I didn't doubt this; she knew all about such things. She said we ought to have it covered. "Slipcovers," like "bedroom suite" and "carpeting," was a word connoting things Harry and I did not want any connection with. We kept it white for a long time. At last—perhaps our principles began to lapse or perhaps it was simply the dirt—we had it covered (though not with slipcovers) in blue velvet, which, even with my father's upholstery liaisons, cost many times more than the couch itself and the delivery. Blue velvet was beautiful too; that became the couch our children and our friends' boys from downstairs jumped on and off for many years. It was destroyed in the fire. Not burned: the living room window frame collapsed on it, doing more damage in one instant than four children over twelve years.

The feeling of having one's things desecrated was not new to us, though. Twice, while the babies were small, I came home to find the apartment had been burglarized. Drawers emptied onto the floor, a typewriter my father had given me when I was in high school gone, a watch, cufflinks, jars of pennies, gone. Both times I rang our next-door neighbors' bell and they came over to commiserate. George and Nena O'Neill, with their sons Michael and Brian, had moved in the same week we did, and we had become friendly comparing notes about painting those fine high-ceilinged rooms with their interminable moldings. George said if I was ever home alone and burglarized, I must bang on his door and he would come with his machete. As anthropologists, he and Nena had traversed jungles in Mexico and South America, and besides the machete had brought back Latin American rugs, wall hangings, and masks that decorated their apartment. Late one afternoon as I was stirring sweet and sour chicken in an electric frying pan, I heard footsteps in the hall. Harry was at work, Rachel with a friend down the street, and Miranda in her crib. The sweet and sour chicken was for a Barnard College freshman for whom I was a Big Sister, and her visiting parents from Cleveland. I advanced into the hall armed with my vegetable spoon and saw a skinny boy in a porkpie hat coming towards me. My face froze, a prefiguring, for I recognized my end. We both stopped moving at the same time, as in *High Noon*. After an eon I asked what he wanted, though I thought I knew. I was wearing a striped minidress. Too much of me was exposed, I felt; certainly he would want to rape me and then possibly kill me. He said he came to tell me the house was on fire and the hall was full of smoke. I walked past him to open the door and see. The hall was not full of smoke—he had climbed through a bedroom window. He walked past me and out, turned back to jeer, then went up the steps to the roof. I banged on George's door. Wearing a bathrobe, he ran for his machete and chased the boy. Buddy Maggart, an actor who lived on the fifth floor, joined in, but they never caught him. The police arrived to do their everlasting paperwork, and I finished cooking the chicken—it seemed pointless not to—and everyone came and ate it. For a year I was nervous about being in the apartment alone, then it passed.

The O'Neills' best-selling book on contemporary mores, *Open Marriage*, was reviewed in *The Village Voice* in 1972 by a critic who fantasized about the authors' holding group orgies on Mexican rugs with their next-door neighbors. We all had a laugh over this, since all we ever did with the O'Neills was talk lengthily in the hall, and visit now and then for drinks; also we went to their Christmas parties and George came gallantly to my aid with his machete. We were both couples who argued a lot, in loud voices, near our front doors. We never took each other's arguments very seriously, but we were well aware, tacitly, of their styles and contents, and that knowledge established an intimacy very different from the kind that would have existed had we had group orgies on Mexican rugs. The uncanny thing about the *Voice* reviewer's fantasy was that the O'Neills did in fact have Mexican rugs.

For sixteen years we watched their sons and they watched our daughters grow up. I admired Nena's elegance. She had left Akron, Ohio, years earlier to attend Barnard College and loved New York so much that she stayed. She became one of those warmly earthy kinds of women who manage to look glamorous even when their spirits are frazzled: dark hair streaked with gray, olive complexion, and soft, pensive features, tinted glasses and flowing, colorful clothes. She had a distinctively low voice which seldom veered from its mellow composure. A reasonable, tolerant, yet dashing middle-aged woman—everything I had no hopes then of ever becoming. Assiduous, too. Early one morning, when I opened the door to investigate the rapid rhythmic sounds coming from the hall, I found her jumping rope. She seemed faintly abashed to be discovered, but kept on jumping. After that, whenever I heard the morning sound of her rope slapping against the linoleum, I felt the sense of security that rituals—even those of other people—afford.

Then one September evening I met Nena coming into the lobby. I hadn't seen her all summer and so we fell into each other's arms. She started to cry and said George was dying. He had septicemia and was in St. Vincent's Hospital in Greenwich Village. I tried to encourage her, but people are usually right about such things, and George died in October of 1980. At the funeral, Jerry Silverstein, an actor and broadcaster who lived just across the hall, spoke long and eloquently about his friendship with George, their late-night talks, their seeing each other through hard times. Jerry and his wife, Selma, had been closer to the O'Neills than we had—though neither had they had orgies on the Mexican rugs. Only long friendship.

This was not our first loss. Bob Hedges on the second floor, widowed, genial, lonely, always helping out in the community, had died. Many of us attended a memorial service in The Riverside Church up the street. Bob's children (once our baby-sitters), grown now but still recognizable, returned from their homes out of town to sit with the neighbors in the church. Rebecca Rikleen's husband, Alexander, an architect, had died, leaving her with four children: Sander, the oldest son, in law school, Daniel and Annie in college, and Ethan, who was then seven. Rebecca, a tall woman with a mane of long brown hair and an air of competence, had been in the building almost longer than anyone—since 1951, when she moved into a first-floor apartment with her parents and two younger brothers. After Rebecca married, her parents and brothers moved elsewhere, leaving the couple the apartment, where they remained and raised the four children.

Ben Irving, an assistant executive secretary of Actors Equity and unofficial mayor of our building, had also died. Ben used to take care of everyone's problems, large and small. Particularly if you were having trouble with the landlord, you called Ben. He was universally available and loved for his warmth and wit and generous spirit—a big robust man with a ruddy face, a booming voice, and thinning honey-colored hair. Jerry Silverstein, who had gone to college with Ben in the 1940s and known his first wife, who died leaving two small children, said he had always been that way. Ben moved into 547 in 1956 with Debby and Jonathan, and in 1957 Inge, an actress, moved in with him. They were married the following year, and Victor was born in 1960. For a while Inge continued to work in the theater, but finally going to auditions became too difficult with three young children, and she became a travel agent, together with her sister, Eva.

Inge and Ben used to give large parties, stretching over afternoons into the late evenings, where food overflowed and neighbors and friends, many of them theater people, drifted in and out with children of all ages. And then one day in 1968, when the Irvings were returning from a vacation, Ben had a heart attack in the lobby of 547. Inge called for help and did mouth-to-mouth resuscitation until the ambulance from St. Luke's Hospital arrived, too late. He was forty-eight. At his funeral, so crowded that people had to stand at the back, the actor and folk singer Theodore Bikel said the Kaddish. Bikel said that though Ben may not have wanted a religious service, he himself wanted Kaddish said for his friend and so he was going to say it. The poet Eve Merriam, a next-door neighbor and friend of the family, wrote and recited a memorial poem which began:

> In a world where friend and neighbor
> are old-fashioned words,
> he was an old-fashioned man.
>
> In a world where honor and kindness
> have not yet found a place,
> he was a man of the future. . . .
>
> All who knew him claim kinship. . . .

I went down to Inge's the morning after Ben died to offer to buy some groceries. She was sitting in a chair looking weak, surrounded by family, not only her three children but her sister Eva and Ben's sister Esther. Inge was always a forceful, highly assertive person—it was unsettling to see her weakened. Assertive she still was: she said I could not only get the groceries—Esther would give me a list—but also over the weekend perhaps Harry and I could take Victor out somewhere for a change of scene. In the evening Harry and I went down to visit. Jonathan, who was thirteen and always a wise child, said that if it had to be, it was better that it was his father who died—he couldn't have borne losing another mother. Over the weekend we took Victor, who was seven, on a boat ride to the Statue of Liberty, along with Rachel. It started to rain on the ferry, a chill, stinging rain; Rachel cried and we had to take turns carrying her; I was pregnant again and the climb up to the torch was arduous. Later I thought we might have come up with something better. To this day I sometimes think, why, of all places, the Statue of Liberty, which Harry and I had seen before and Rachel was too young to appreciate and Victor, in his state of grief, probably didn't care about?

A year or so after the Statue of Liberty, Rachel began attending a free nursery school run by the Parks Department in Morningside Park, ten blocks away. Lots of kids from the neighborhood went. On Riverside Drive, Tiemann Place, and Claremont Avenue flourished the oldest estabilshed permanent floating cooperative walking pool: each parent made only two trips a week but they were epic—half a mile with six four-year-olds. I took Rachel and Julienne Maggart from the fifth floor, and pushed Miranda in a stroller. Picking up the third and fourth kids was tolerable, but the fifth and sixth stops were harrowing, what with heavy front doors, timed buzzers, stairs, stroller, elevators, traffic, and the nature of children. There existed two imperfect strategies for getting the children safely across wide and heavily traveled Broadway and Amsterdam Avenue—in one mighty swoop or in shifts. I chose the swoop, never daring to let them get behind me. One of the mothers, an experienced one with four children, took a shortcut on snowy days through Cherry Park up on the Drive. Its attraction was an enormous flight of stone steps completely obliterated by snow. She let the kids slide down one by one, then slid down herself.

Julienne's father, Brandon, or Buddy, as we called him then, did the nursery school trek with the nonchalance of a father of five, and at first my children, each in turn, were thrilled since they saw him daily in the Buddy and Jim comedy skit on *Sesame Street*. Also, any time Buddy appeared in a television commercial—touting the softness of a baby's diaper or twirling pizza dough—they would call us to come and watch. But very quickly they grasped that Buddy, however nonchalant, made them hold hands like the rest of us, and not run in the street, and the experience became far less thrilling. Soon they would even stop calling us to the TV screen but lackadaisically, hours later, let fall the news that Buddy was now doing wine or chocolate.

Accidental gatherings in the halls, the lobby, or at the elevator door propelled the life of the building like the conjunctions that take place at nerve endings. With the Silversteins, we held long and rather grandiose conversations at the elevator door, all about our lives and aspirations. The Silversteins were two of the most energetic and bouncy people I had ever met. They were always jogging or playing tennis, and would turn up at the elevator in their various sporting costumes, with their reverberating actors' voices and beaming faces, and sometimes they would scold me because, with my babies trailing after me and my vague dreams of being a writer in abeyance, I wasn't lively enough for their high standards of *joie de vivre*. They were a wonderfully matched pair, Jerry dark and earnest and cheerful, Selma fair and wry and practical—even their squabbles were entertaining, like a performance. They had married way back in 1947 and spent their early summers acting in summer theater. During those years Jerry worked as a teacher, while Selma acted: she was in the Greenwich Village Circle in the Square's first production, *Dark of the Moon*, in *A Majority of One* on Broadway, and in many off-Broadway plays and radio and TV commercials.

But at the time I knew them, Selma was already bouncing on to something new; she was studying for a master's degree in social work and planned to become a therapist, and naturally she recommended therapy for everyone, in her energetic, wry way. And Jerry was now on TV every week, doing a news program for children, which won countless awards; at the elevator he would stop to tell me the topic of the week— the death of Nasser, or New York City's water shortage. If I had time I would watch and marvel at the way he conducted panel discussions with kids, inquiring into their opinions with the greatest respect and attention. And always, at the elevator, one of us would finally say, How silly to stand here at the door, let's get together for an evening. The evening would arrive: We would eat and drink; Jerry would tell jokes with Yiddish punch lines that he translated for Harry, and Selma would tell anecdotes about Jerry's large and forthright family, especially his brother the rabbi, whose pithy pronouncements she rendered so vividly that when I finally met him at one of the Silversteins' family Chanukah parties I felt I already knew him. And so these evenings would laugh themselves by, with little said about our grander aspirations. Soon we would meet at the elevator again. . . .

The Silversteins' son Kenny was our baby-sitter, and the O'Neills' son Brian, and Inge's three children, Debby, Jonathan, and Victor in turn, and Rebecca Rikleen's daughter Annie from the third floor, and Yvonne Uehling from the first floor. To this day, our children can rate them all, now in their twenties and thirties, on the various aspects of baby-sitting. We know which ones slept on the job and which foraged for food and which talked on the phone all evening, as well as their varying degrees of patience and imagination. Jonathan Irving was a favorite because he would let the kids stand on his big shoes, facing him and gripping his hands, then walk them around with giant steps; this they found irresistible. Jonathan wrote a story for Rachel about the adventures of an umbrella, and bound it and presented it to her with a flourish; she still has it. Years later Rachel baby-sat for Joan Regelin's three children, on the second floor, and doubtless they can rate her too.

Joan was my unemployment companion. When New York City underwent its fiscal collapse in 1975, I lost my job teaching English at Hunter College, and would take the subway to Washington Heights every Monday to claim unemployment insurance. I stood in line in an enormous dingy green room that made everyone in it look dingy. There were about twelve lines stretching the length of the room, and about seventy or eighty people on each. Naturally I looked for the shortest line, but in the end it never made much difference. Joan, then a sporadically employed singer, sometimes collected unemployment at the same hour—three o'clock—and she offered to drive me up. She was a large, dark-haired, dramatic-looking woman perhaps around thirty then, with, like many singers, a rich, sensuous, persuasive speaking voice. While she zoomed a tortuous path up the West Side Highway, we had talks about our parents and our children. She told me about growing up the oldest in a family of five children in North Carolina. She told me, too, how her grandparents used to live on our block, three buildings down, in the building that was taken over by Union Theological Seminary and became a dormitory for married students—her grandmother was the last holdout tenant. And she told me some of the adventures and idiosyncrasies of her car, which she spoke of as a member of the family. The car, a plucky, mustard-colored 1971 Volvo which for many years had borne North Carolina plates, was something of a local legend, its adventures with crime and bureaucracy making it seem almost human. It had been stolen and retrieved, it had been towed away, it had weathered near-terminal illnesses. On weekends, Christian would often be in front of the house, washing it or applying first aid. (Little did we know then that in 1982 the car would suffer the ultimate indignity of being stolen for good.)

Joan took me to claim unemployment and I gave her outgrown toys and down jackets, and we sent the kids back and forth endlessly for cups of sugar and milk. After a year of standing in line I got my job back, and then the following year lost it again. But this time my unemployment depot was changed to Fifty-fourth Street. I missed the rides with Joan, not least the skill and verve of her driving, the energy with which she hauled that stick shift through its paces.

There were no longer as many children around when Joan's three were small. Columbia had bought the building in 1966 and from then on rented mostly to graduate students and junior faculty. But in the early years our daughters were part of a troop, the Maggarts' five, Blair's and Bob's two boys downstairs, a girl named Carla on the first floor, and Yvonne's younger brother, Gregory. Traipsing about on Halloween, they could never comprehend how Mrs. Lurier on the first floor, who gave the best treats—individually wrapped packages of homemade cookies— could be the same Mrs. Lurier who the rest of the year yelled to scare them off when they played in the lobby or in the courtyard right under her window.

Mrs. Lurier's sister, Mrs. Angel, on the fifth floor, was reputed to be strange as well, since, as she let everyone know, she was writing to President Lyndon Johnson, among other leaders, about the disability case connected with a portion of ceiling having fallen on her arm in 1963, aggravating an injury sustained at work two years earlier and making it difficult for her to continue as a dressmaker. She would talk about the evils of bureaucracy to whoever would listen. But I liked her and shared her feelings about the evils of bureaucracy, and given my verbal and vociferous and large family of Russian Jewish immigrants, I saw nothing strange about people expressing themselves in forceful and extreme ways; indeed, it made me nostalgic for my childhood, when stately people like Mrs. Angel—aunts and uncles—sat around oilcloth-covered tables dotted with glasses of amber tea and shouted at each other warmly. I also liked her because she admired my children and said so whenever we met. Since I had long ago given up broiling lamb chops for lunch, her pronouncements were reassuring. And I liked the way she looked, big and squarishly built, a square unlined face, high cheekbones and clear eyes, dark brown hair close to auburn pulled away from her forehead to show a widow's peak and done in a knot. Stern and formidable, she used to walk erectly down Riverside Drive with the gait of one who has business abroad in the world. I often imagined her up on an outdoor podium, exhorting crowds to justice and righteousness, and in fact she once told me she might have gone into politics like her father, had she been a man, and thought she would have done well, but that now, after three turbulent marriages—one arranged when she was sixteen, one "the love of her life," and one to an excitable Greek naval officer—and a lifetime crowded with incident, it was too late.

As a matter of fact it was politics that brought her to this country. In 1904 her father, George Dalianis, ran for office in his home town of Amalias, population 26,000, and lost. "In America," she said, "when they lose they shake hands and make up, but in Greece they could shoot themselves." To help Mr. Dalianis get over the pain of losing, the family set off on a trip to America, leaving Diana, only three months old, with her grandmother, who, as it turned out, brought her up till she was nine. Then in 1912 the Turkish war started, and her parents, who were prospering in the restaurant business, decided to bring her to America. When she arrived in Worcester, Massachusetts, she discovered, along with her older brother Peter, three more children born since the move—Coula, Joan, and Charles.

And when she spoke of these things, alternately laughing and scowling, her voice would traverse the scales, penetrating the air. She might well have been addressing a group rather than just a woman less than half her age, wide-eyed—her narration had that sweep and force of one born for public oratory. But when she laughed she became suddenly girlish and I could see she must have been a beauty. Eventually I even found out what the correspondence with Lyndon Johnson was all about. Because Mrs. Johnson's private secretary was a girlhood friend of Diana's daughter Adrienne, the President had actually responded to the pleas about the disability claim as well as sent Diana New Year's and other greetings, plus a book containing the laws he drew up while in Congress, plus a flag.

One Sunday afternoon Diana got stuck in the elevator of 547. Getting stuck was not unusual; ours was a highly capricious elevator. Among its whims was a periodic refusal to sort out the numbers above 4. During those spells, if your destination was 5 you pressed 6, and if it was 6 you pressed 7, which was the roof. People who got stuck pushed the alarm button, setting loose a loud and terrible clanging which those of us on the top floor had learned to distinguish from the loud and terrible clanging set off when the roof door was illicitly opened. At the sound of the elevator alarm we would stream out in the halls to shout encouragement to the prisoner until Mrs. Flanagan or her brother, Tom Kelly, either fixed it or called the elevator men.

Diana Angel was not a patient victim; invisible, she shouted furiously about her nerves and her stress—everyone of course understood she had been tried to the limit by the ceiling falling. Finally Tom Kelly induced the elevator to come within a foot of our floor, and, even more difficult, induced Diana to climb out, shaken, trembling, and vociferous. She came to our apartment for a cup of tea. Calm at last, her stalwart self emergent, she pronounced as usual that my children were very well brought up.

Tom Kelly lived in the basement apartment with his sister, Anna Flanagan, and helped her out with chores in the building. I was put off by him at first because when he drank he was silent and sullen. He would answer the door looking irritated beyond measure and quickly get his sister to deal with the complaint. But when he wasn't drinking—and for long periods he would stop, till he stopped altogether—he was wry and witty, with a fund of mordant comments on life in its most grand or petty manifestations. During his dry spells he would often get jobs in other buildings around town as a doorman or elevator operator, and set off for work very well dressed and very brisk. But these jobs never lasted long.

From May to October, Tom and his sister, and the super from next door and her daughter, would sit out on the ledge in front of our building every evening, taking the air. We never had a doorman like more elegant buildings farther south: the party of supers, sharp-eyed and vigilant, was for a long time the closest we got to any sort of guardianship. Comings and goings provided the raw material for their criticism of life. Boyfriends and girlfriends of our teenagers were duly assessed, and reports to the parents submitted promptly, though unsought. Passing by, I would stop to catch up on local news delivered in Tom's trenchantly satirical style. He liked children and would tease mine, when they were small, asking them to take him along to school or to camp—perhaps he had fantasies of escape from the basement into a life of youthful capers— and at first they were leery because he was gruff, with a low, snarling voice that sounded like it had snaked its way through a wringer, besides which he had an ailment that made his head lean permanently to one side. But once they got past these traits they grew fond of him too. When Tom brought plumbers or plasterers to our apartment, he would hang around diverting me with his snarling opinions on everyone in the building, and also cadge cigarettes, since he had to have a cigarette dangling from his lips at all times. He was a thin, white-haired man with a caved-in chest and a squarish face: rheumy blue eyes, pinkish cheeks, full lips, and a dangling cigarette. While plumbers probed, we would discuss the atrocious state of the sixth-floor apartment across the hall, to which the tenant refused to give Mrs. Flanagan a key, and to which she admitted no repairmen. Yes, Tom would grunt bitterly, it was a terrible hazard.

Tom knew I was a writer; in the fall of 1981 he asked if I would write a letter for him to a CBS News commentator who had broadcast a segment about a chewing gum that supposedly helped people stop smoking. He snarled that it was only fair I should do this since I had rung his bell with a complaint while he was watching the TV news, and because of my interruption he hadn't caught the name of the gum. I wrote to CBS News a few times and finally telephoned. The name of the gum was Nicorette, I reported back to Tom, but it wasn't yet available in the United States, only in Europe. He accepted this news ruefully, his cigarette drooping. A few months later I was in Italy, where I'd promised him I'd look for the gum, but I didn't find it. Tom developed lung cancer and would go for what his sister called X-ray treatments. He was glum and resigned about his disease, and when we all tried to encourage him with visions of recovery, he would nod sarcastically and snarl. He grew weak. His chest caved in even more. He kept smoking. He said he might as well, now. Before I left for Iowa in the summer of 1982, where I had a temporary teaching job, he asked me to ring his bell and say hello when I came home for vacations, which I did. He never asked me in—that was not part of our friendship—but at the door he brought me up to date on which elderly neighbors were growing eccentric and exactly how, who was moving out to greener pastures, whose children were getting married or going away to school, and the observable love life of the recently divorced; also how his disease was progressing, and how hard it was to stop smoking. After the fire, Columbia moved Tom and his sister to a tiny apartment ten blocks south on 113th Street, which they hated. He died about a month later, in the spring of 1983. I was still away and was sorry I could not go to his funeral as a final tribute, but even more sorry that I never got to hear what he would have snarled about the fire. Soon after he died, the gum was approved for sale in the United States.

Our apartment had a big living room and dining room joined by an archway, both rooms facing west, graced by large windows overlooking the park and the river with its boats going by. We painted that windowed wall red, and it framed the outdoors. North, we could see all the way up to the George Washington Bridge. In spring and summer the trees in the park were so lushly leaved we could barely see the water through them, but in winter and fall the view was broad and clear. On windy days there were whitecaps all along the river so that it looked like a printed fabric billowing about, or the wet fur of a large beast with the shivers. Often in winter ice would clog it for weeks at a time, huge chunks of jagged ice like cold driftwood, and for those weeks no ships could pass. Sometimes a ship got stuck and stayed there for days at a time, till the ice melted. Most of the ships we saw were barges or small cargo ships or the Circle Line taking tourists on a pleasure cruise around Manhattan Island, but now and then a good-sized ship would float by, and when the children were small I would call them to watch. Even when they were older, I still sometimes called them for a truly spectacular ship.

Also out the living room windows, across in Riverside Park, was the big hill all the neighborhood kids and their parents used for sledding. Early on, Harry and I would go out sledding with the kids; in later years we could keep an eye on them from the window, as they skimmed down and trudged up, dragging the sleds behind them. But the finest things we watched from the window were the sunsets, especially the late ones, June through October. We abandoned cooking, eating, or homework to rush to the window, for once it began, each instant's configuration of clouds and color above the Palisades, of light and shadow on the surface of the water, could vanish in a trice. Irreverent, we even rated them— better than yesterday's, not so fine as last Sunday's—and sometimes on summer evenings we were lured out to walk along the Drive, to get closer up. We grew to be connoisseurs, knowing from the way each sinking began whether it would be drawn out or abrupt, magnificent or humble, whether it would start out splendid and dissipate, or start out nondescript and turn splendid, whether the best part would be just before or just after the sun went down. We could tell from the formations of the clouds and the color of the air, pink, or violet, or amber, and sometimes even a pale weird lime green.

Off the once-desolate long hall were three bedrooms, medium-sized, small, and very small. The advantage of the very small one was its own private bathroom—it must have been a maid's room in the days when the building housed the rich. Harry and I always had the small back bedroom as our own, but the other two rooms went through countless changes of role over nineteen years, mostly depending on the phases of our children. When they could live and sleep peaceably together we used the tiny room as a study, two desks crowded in. When they couldn't we moved elsewhere: in the end, I wrote three books under our loft bed. But way back in the sixties, I don't remember what I expected to do at a desk—I don't remember any plans except a vague notion that somehow I would become a writer, as if it happened to a person like puberty or gray hair. I did some translations in the medium-sized room during Rachel's first year, as well as a few free-lance proofreading and editing jobs. Eventually, in the seventies, I dropped out of graduate school to write, because being a writer showed no signs of happening to me like puberty or gray hair. In the tiny bedroom I wrote my first published article, a Watergate satire, in June of 1974. When it was published Harry made a big party with all our friends to celebrate: there was a feeling of buoyancy abroad over the climax of Watergate, with its satisfying cast of heroes and villains.

That party took its place in the annals of parties held in the apartment, parties like the snows of yesteryear. Sometimes now we recall and compare them—the New Year's Day party thrown together that morning, where Rachel at a mere twelve years old concocted a triumphant eggnog; and the surprise party for Harry's father which occasioned our getting the white couch; and then the party for Harry's fortieth birthday, when he got piles of presents like a child; and the July 4 party in the Bicentennial year, when friends gathered on our tarred roof to watch the glorious procession of tall-masted and bannered ships parade up the Hudson all that long sunny summer afternoon. Parties the children cannot remember, Halloween parties where guests masqueraded as their secret selves, a frog, a toad, Lolita and Superman and Al Capone. Not to mention the two children's birthday parties a year with the requisite balloons and whistles, parties I smiled through because I poured Scotch—which can pass for apple juice—into my paper cup.

Like a person, the apartment had a few chronic ailments. The bedroom doors never closed completely. The closet in the largest bedroom had no door. We never got around to asking the landlord for one, and hung up a curtain instead. The shower didn't drain properly—one stood ankle-deep in water. The plumbers who came to remedy this once and for all were a merry troop who stayed for days, creating chaos out of order, but in the end nothing much was changed. In the tiny bathroom in the erstwhile maid's room, a leak in the pipes in the wall would spring mysteriously every New Year's holiday. We had no evidence of it, but the Launays in 5A or Inge in 4A would call to report that water was pouring down from the ceiling. Eventually Inge had only to call on New Year's, say hello in a certain wry tone, and we would know. After a few years the plumbers didn't bother to plaster up the wall when they were finished, but simply put in a wooden panel that could be easily removed the following New Year's.

I knew every person in every one of those twenty-four apartments until the last few years, when Columbia began putting students in and the students, just passing through, were not interested in knowing their neighbors. But for most of the nineteen years I knew the feel of people's apartments, the furnishings and the quality of the light on the different floors, people's relatives—Jerry's brother the rabbi, Inge's sister Eva and Ben's sister Esther—and their children, what schools they went to and how they turned out. I watched as Yvonne Uehling, our babysitter, a slender, shy, soft-spoken girl, became a beauty at fifteen or sixteen; for a year or so we all endured crowds of boys mooning outside on the front step waiting for an appearance, a word, a glance. Together we also endured the summer Columbia replaced our ever-ailing boiler, when those of us with no vacation plans learned how to take cold showers, which is not so hard once you get used to it. Worse to endure was the collapse of the wall separating our back courtyard from the opposite building, on Claremont Avenue—a mighty and prolonged roar on a still Saturday afternoon. We were in the papers, notorious. For weeks our gigantic heap of rubble was a place of interest for the locals, less historically evocative than Riverside Church or Grant's Tomb, where tourists went, but more dramatic for those in the know. Apparently Columbia had been aware of the tremulous wall for some time, but had been haggling with the Claremont Avenue landlord over whose responsibility it was to fix it. At last workmen arrived with cement trucks and sacks of sand and gravel. They began their dragging and drilling at six in the morning, which incensed Buddy Maggart most of all since he worked nights and slept mornings. When the wall was rebuilt months later, Mrs. Flanagan and Tom complained bitterly, since the courtyard they had used to hang out wash and grow plants and cool off in on hot nights was a third of its original size.

I knew when Mrs. Flanagan's son had a heart attack and exactly how overweight he was. I could even remember the days when Mrs. Flanagan, a talkative kind of super, complained that her son and his wife had no children; then, overnight it seemed, there were four, and her talk switched to proud anecdotes of the grandchildren. When they visited she even brought them up to display them. I knew when Joan's son hurt his head and she feared there might be serious damage but there wasn't, and when Jerry Silverstein suffered from tennis elbow; and when Ethan Rikleen was hit by a car and stayed in Roosevelt Hospital for weeks with a leg injury. Likewise everyone knew when Rachel tumbled off the back of Yvonne's bike in the park and I rushed her, holding the torn ball of the bleeding finger in place with a towel, to the emergency room at St. Luke's Hospital in the back of a passing police car. Police don't like to take passengers, but they didn't refuse. Everyone knew that if you called an ambulance you'd go to Sydenham Hospital, farther away, and it was better all around to get to St. Luke's if you could. Everyone knew, too, when a man in the building next door was killed by a speeding car at the corner, and then finally the city put up the traffic light we had long been asking for, with a pedestrian button as a bonus.

I had been inside Grant's Tomb and climbed to the top of Riverside Church during the ringing of the carillon bells, and ridden my bike in Riverside Park; I knew who played tennis there and who ran, and who, like us, had picnics. Where people walked their dogs, who cleaned up after them and who didn't. Who walked around late at night and who was afraid to. Who was mugged, when and where and how. Mrs. Lurier of the Halloween cookies, beaten up in her apartment and no one heard her scream—an empty Saturday afternoon in spring. Inge, coming home from work, by a boy with a knife. Joan, bringing home groceries. Nena, on the subway steps. We organized a tenants' association on the block. Harry was the chairman. With money from those willing to pay, we hired a uniformed guard to patrol at night: genteel Mr. Crawford, who reported for duty in a shiny black Cadillac. The supers taking the air resented his presence, as if it impugned their ability to keep the street safe, but that did not stop them from including him in their nightly conferences on the ledge.

It was hardly possible to get down that street without stopping to talk. Over the years we came to know people all up and down the block, and when the old ones stopped appearing we knew they had died. I didn't like everyone equally, but it was scarcely a question of liking. They came with the territory, and when they moved or died I missed them. It is possible to miss even people you don't like.

I never liked the apartment that much either, or never thought I did. I found it cramped. Despite its six rooms there never seemed to be enough privacy, though perhaps it was the way we lived, with no clear boundaries and turfs, that inhibited privacy. And the neighborhood wasn't safe, especially at night, even during the years Mr. Crawford patrolled with his reassuring black Cadillac. I also never quite forgot the three dreadful spells when we had mice, and how Jonathan Irving of the big shoes came up and baited our traps with chocolate—he claimed mice preferred chocolate to cheese and judging from the results he was right. Yet now it strikes me that I lived in that apartment longer than any other place in my life, and the placement of the furniture and the pots and pans and the pictures on the walls seems fixed and preordained, the only way we could have lived.

There are times, opening my eyes in the morning, when I am astonished to find myself in alien surroundings; I close my eyes, not yet fully awake, and imagine taking my old route through the morning, first to the front windows to look out at the park and river and see what kind of day it might be. Only lately, more than a year after the fire, do I allow myself to remember in detail how it was to move through those rooms in patterns developed over the years; how, when it rained, I whisked from room to room in a well-worn path closing windows, then stood in the front watching it pour into the abundant river; how we put speakers in the kitchen so I could hear records while I cooked; how I was lulled to sleep watching old movies on TV up in the loft bed; and how, as I talked on the kitchen wall phone, my eyes panned every plane of the room, so every square foot is now forever printed on my retina—yellow walls, dark green cabinets, striped curtain, the arrangement of pots and pans on a dark red pegboard; the plastic magnetic letters on the refrigerator that our grown children still fooled with, messages like Happy Anniversary or Good Luck on SAT's, or messages from their friends—Julie Was Here; and the round white table which, to my father's gratification, we bought at his store, and the orange chairs. For after my father's red plastic chairs gave out we replaced them with wooden ones bought for a dollar each from a local synagogue that was clearing out old furniture. I made covers out of bright printed corduroy for their ugly plastic seats, covers that looked like shower caps, and the children, aware of my limitations in the domestic arts, laughed at them, but lo, when stretched out they fit perfectly.

I remember most of all being pregnant with my first baby in that apartment, and towards the end, when it was an effort even to move, sitting in the old wing chair looking out over the river, and watching the moving lights over Palisades Amusement Park advertising things I cannot remember now but which twenty years ago I knew by heart. I would watch the letters slide by again and again, wondering what it would be like to be a family in that apartment, wanting the pregnancy over but fearing the birth, and falling into a trance induced by the glitter of the faraway roller coaster. Maybe I might live in that static condition, pregnant forever, a permanent trance. Years later they tore down Palisades Amusement Park to replace it with two high-rise apartment buildings which were nothing at all to look at. But on clear nights we could still lean out the window and see the strand of lights that was the George Washington Bridge looping the water.

We were ignorant then, our lives full of vast and unformed possibilities that narrowed and congealed to specifics. In that apartment we raised two children, and I made myself into a writer instead of dreaming it, and I learned that the getting of wisdom is something other and more fruitful than finding out the right things to do on every occasion. By the end, the family forced out was four grown people, two of whom had never known any other home.

One Last Time

Yesterday I saw the movie *Gandhi* and recognized a few of the people —not in the theater but in the film. I saw my relatives, dusty and thin as sparrows, returning from the fields with hoes balanced on their shoulders. The workers were squinting, eyes small and veined, and were using their hands to say what there was to say to those in the audience with popcorn and Cokes. I didn't have anything, though. I sat thinking of my family and their years in the fields, beginning with Grandmother who came to the United States after the Mexican revolution to settle in Fresno where she met her husband and bore children, many of them. She worked in the fields around Fresno, picking grapes, oranges, plums, peaches, and cotton, dragging a large white sack like a sled. She worked in the packing houses, Bonner and Sun-Maid Raisin, where she stood at a conveyor belt passing her hand over streams of raisins to pluck out leaves and pebbles. For over twenty years she worked at a machine that boxed raisins until she retired at sixty-five.

Grandfather worked in the fields, as did his children. Mother also found herself out there when she separated from Father for three weeks. I remember her coming home, dusty and so tired that she had to rest on the porch before she trudged inside to wash and start dinner. I didn't understand the complaints about her ankles or the small of her back, even though I had been in the grape fields watching her work. With my brother and sister I ran in and out of the rows; we enjoyed ourselves and pretended not to hear Mother scolding us to sit down and behave ourselves. A few years later, however, I caught on when I went to pick grapes rather than play in the rows.

Mother and I got up before dawn and ate quick bowls of cereal. She drove in silence while I rambled on how everything was now solved, how I was going to make enough money to end our misery and even buy her a beautiful copper tea pot, the one I had shown her in Long's Drugs. When we arrived I was frisky and ready to go, self-consciously aware of my grape knife dangling at my wrist. I almost ran to the row the foreman had pointed out, but I returned to help Mother with the grape pans and jug of water. She told me to settle down and reminded me not to lose my knife. I walked at her side and listened to her explain how to cut grapes; bent down, hands on knees, I watched her demonstrate by cutting a few bunches into my pan. She stood over me as I tried it myself, tugging at a bunch of grapes that pulled loose like beads from a necklace. "Cut the stem all the way," she told me as last advice before she walked away, her shoes sinking in the loose dirt, to begin work on her own row.

I cut another bunch, then another, fighting the snap and whip of vines. After ten minutes of groping for grapes, my first pan brimmed with bunches. I poured them on the paper tray, which was bordered by a wooden frame that kept the grapes from rolling off, and they spilled like jewels from a pirate's chest. The tray was only half filled, so I hurried to jump under the vines and begin groping, cutting, and tugging at the grapes again. I emptied the pan, raked the grapes with my hands to make them look like they filled the tray, and jumped back under the vine on my knees. I tried to cut faster because Mother, in the next row, was slowly moving ahead. I peeked into her row and saw five trays gleaming in the early morning. I cut, pulled hard, and stopped to gather the grapes that missed the pan; already bored, I spat on a few to wash them before tossing them like popcorn into my mouth.

So it went. Two pans equaled one tray—or six cents. By lunchtime I had a trail of thirty-seven trays behind me while Mother had sixty or more. We met about halfway from our last trays, and I sat down with a grunt, knees wet from kneeling on dropped grapes. I washed my hands with the water from the jug, drying them on the inside of my shirt sleeve before I opened the paper bag for the first sandwich, which I gave to Mother. I dipped my hand in again to unwrap a sandwich without looking at it. I took a first bite and chewed it slowly for the tang of mustard. Eating in silence I looked straight ahead at the vines, and only when we were finished with cookies did we talk.

"Are you tired?" she asked.

"No, but I got a sliver from the frame," I told her. I showed her the web of skin between my thumb and index finger. She wrinkled her forehead but said it was nothing.

"How many trays did you do?"

I looked straight ahead, not answering at first. I recounted in my mind the whole morning of bend, cut, pour again and again, before answering a feeble "thirty-seven." No elaboration, no detail. Without looking at me she told me how she had done field work in Texas and Michigan as a child. But I had a difficult time listening to her stories. I played with my grape knife, stabbing it into the ground, but stopped when Mother reminded me that I had better not lose it. I left the knife sticking up like a small, leafless plant. She then talked about school, the junior high I would be going to that fall, and then about Rick and Debra, how sorry they would be that they hadn't come out to pick grapes because they'd have no new clothes for the school year. She stopped talking when she peeked at her watch, a bandless one she kept in her pocket. She got up with an "*Ay, Dios,*" and told me that we'd work until three, leaving me cutting figures in the sand with my knife and dreading the return to work.

Finally I rose and walked slowly back to where I had left off, again kneeling under the vine and fixing the pan under bunches of grapes. By that time, 11:30, the sun was over my shoulder and made me squint and think of the pool at the Y.M.C.A. where I was a summer member. I saw myself diving face first into the water and loving it. I saw myself gleaming like something new, at the edge of the pool. I had to daydream and keep my mind busy because boredom was a terror almost as awful as the work itself. My mind went dumb with stupid things, and I had to keep it moving with dreams of baseball and would-be girlfriends. I even sang, however softly, to keep my mind moving, my hands moving.

I worked less hurriedly and with less vision. I no longer saw that copper pot sitting squat on our stove or Mother waiting for it to whistle. The wardrobe that I imagined, crisp and bright in the closet, numbered only one pair of jeans and two shirts because, in half a day, six cents times thirty-seven trays was two dollars and twenty-two cents. It became clear to me. If I worked eight hours, I might make four dollars. I'd take this, even gladly, and walk downtown to look into store windows on the mall and long for the bright madras shirts from Walter Smith or Coffee's, but settling for two imitation ones from Penney's.

That first day I laid down seventy-three trays while Mother had a hundred and twenty behind her. On the back of an old envelope, she wrote out our numbers and hours. We washed at the pump behind the farm house and walked slowly to our car for the drive back to town in the afternoon heat. That evening after dinner I sat in a lawn chair listening to music from a transistor radio while Rick and David King played catch. I joined them in a game of pickle, but there was little joy in trying to avoid their tags because I couldn't get the fields out of my mind: I saw myself dropping on my knees under a vine to tug at a branch that wouldn't come off. In bed, when I closed my eyes, I saw the fields, yellow with kicked up dust, and a crooked trail of trays rotting behind me.

The next day I woke tired and started picking tired. The grapes rained into the pan, slowly filling like a belly, until I had my first tray and started my second. So it went all day, and the next, and all through the following week, so that by the end of thirteen days the foreman counted out, in tens mostly, my pay of fifty-three dollars. Mother earned one hundred and forty-eight dollars. She wrote this on her envelope, with a message I didn't bother to ask her about.

The next day I walked with my friend Scott to the downtown mall where we drooled over the clothes behind fancy windows, bought popcorn, and sat at a tier of outdoor fountains to talk about girls. Finally we went into Penney's for more popcorn, which we ate walking around, before we returned home without buying anything. It wasn't until a few days before school that I let my fifty-three dollars slip quietly from my hands, buying a pair of pants, two shirts, and a maroon T-shirt, the kind that was in style. At home I tried them on while Rick looked on enviously; later, the day before school started, I tried them on again wondering not so much if they were worth it as who would see me first in those clothes.

Along with my brother and sister I picked grapes until I was fifteen, before giving up and saying that I'd rather wear old clothes than stoop like a Mexican. Mother thought I was being stuck-up, even stupid, because there would be no clothes for me in the fall. I told her I didn't care, but when Rick and Debra rose at five in the morning, I lay awake in bed feeling that perhaps I had made a mistake but unwilling to change my mind. That fall Mother bought me two pairs of socks, a packet of colored T-shirts, and underwear. The T-shirts would help, I thought, but who would see that I had new underwear and socks? I wore a new T-shirt on the first day of school, then an old shirt on Tuesday, than another T-shirt on Wednesday, and on Thursday an old Nehru shirt that was embarrassingly out of style. On Friday I changed into the corduroy pants my brother had handed down to me and slipped into my last new T-shirt. I worked like a magician, blinding my classmates, who were all clothes conscious and small-time social climbers, by arranging my wardrobe to make it seem larger than it really was. But by spring I had to do something—my blue jeans were almost silver and my shoes had lost their form, puddling like black ice around my feet. That spring of my sixteenth year, Rick and I decided to take a labor bus to chop cotton. In his old Volkswagen, which was more noise than power, we drove on a Saturday morning to West Fresno—or Chinatown as some call it—parked, walked slowly toward a bus, and stood gawking at the winos, toothy blacks, Okies, *Tejanos* with gold teeth, whores, Mexican families, and labor contractors shouting "Cotton" or "Beets," the work of spring.

We boarded the "Cotton" bus without looking at the contractor who stood almost blocking the entrance because he didn't want winos. We boarded scared and then were more scared because two blacks in the rear were drunk and arguing loudly about what was better, a two-barrel or four-barrel Ford carburetor. We sat far from them, looking straight ahead, and only glanced briefly at the others who boarded, almost all of them broken and poorly dressed in loudly mismatched clothes. Finally when the contractor banged his palm against the side of the bus, the young man at the wheel, smiling and talking in Spanish, started the engine, idled it for a moment while he adjusted the mirrors, and started off in slow chugs. Except for the windshield there was no glass in the windows, so as soon as we were on the rural roads outside Fresno, the dust and sand began to be sucked into the bus, whipping about like irate wasps as the gravel ticked about us. We closed our eyes, clotted up our mouths that wanted to open with embarrassed laughter because we couldn't believe we were on that bus with those people and the dust attacking us for no reason.

When we arrived at a field we followed the others to a pickup where we each took a hoe and marched to stand before a row. Rick and I, self-conscious and unsure, looked around at the others who leaned on their hoes or squatted in front of the rows, almost all talking in Spanish, joking, lighting cigarettes—all waiting for the foreman's whistle to begin work. Mother had explained how to chop cotton by showing us with a broom in the backyard.

"Like this," she said, her broom swishing down weeds. "Leave one plant and cut four—and cut them! Don't leave them standing or the foreman will get mad."

The foreman whistled and we started up the row stealing glances at other workers to see if we were doing it right. But after awhile we worked like we knew what we were doing, neither of us hurrying or falling behind. But slowly the clot of men, women, and kids began to spread and loosen. Even Rick pulled away. I didn't hurry, though. I cut smoothly and cleanly as I walked at a slow pace, in a sort of funeral march. My eyes measured each space of cotton plants before I cut. If I missed the plants, I swished again. I worked intently, seldom looking up, so when I did I was amazed to see the sun, like a broken orange coin, in the east. It looked blurry, unbelievable, like something not of this world. I looked around in amazement, scanning the eastern horizon that was a taut line jutted with an occasional mountain. The horizon was beautiful, like a snapshot of the moon, in the early light of morning, in the quiet of no cars and few people.

The foreman trudged in boots in my direction, stepping awkwardly over the plants, to inspect the work. No one around me looked up. We all worked steadily while we waited for him to leave. When he did leave, with a feeble complaint addressed to no one in particular, we looked up smiling under straw hats and bandanas.

By 11:00, our lunch time, my ankles were hurting from walking clods the size of hardballs. My arms ached and my face was dusted by a wind that was perpetual, always busy whipping about. But the work was not bad, I thought. It was better, so much better, than picking grapes, especially with the hourly wage of a dollar twenty-five instead of piece work. Rick and I walked sorely toward the bus where we washed and drank water. Instead of eating in the bus or in the shade of the bus, we kept to ourselves by walking down to the irrigation canal that ran the length of the field, to open our lunch of sandwiches and crackers. We laughed at the crackers, which seemed like a cruel joke from our mother, because we were working under the sun and the last thing we wanted was a salty dessert. We ate them anyway and drank more water before we returned to the field, both of us limping in exaggeration. Working side by side, we talked and laughed at our predicament because our Mother had warned us year after year that if we didn't get on track in school we'd have to work in the fields and then we would see. We mimicked Mother's whining voice and smirked at her smoky view of the future in which we'd be trapped by marriage and screaming kids. We'd eat beans and then we'd see.

Rick pulled slowly away to the rhythm of his hoe falling faster and smoother. It was better that way, to work alone. I could hum made-up songs or songs from the radio and think to myself about school and friends. At the time I was doing badly in my classes, mainly because of a difficult stepfather, but also because I didn't care anymore. All through junior high and into my first year of high school there were those who said I would never do anything, be anyone. They said I'd work like a donkey and marry the first Mexican girl that came along. I was reminded so often, verbally and in the way I was treated at home, that I began to believe that chopping cotton might be a lifetime job for me. If not chopping cotton, then I might get lucky and find myself in a car wash or restaurant or junkyard. But it was clear; I'd work, and work hard.

I cleared my mind by humming and looking about. The sun was directly above with a few soft blades of clouds against a sky that seemed bluer and more beautiful than our sky in the city. Occasionally the breeze flurried and picked up dust so that I had to cover my eyes and screw up my face. The workers were hunched, brown as the clods under our feet, and spread across the field that ran without end—fields that were owned by corporations, not families.

I hoed trying to keep my mind busy with scenes from school and pretend girlfriends until finally my brain turned off and my thinking went fuzzy with boredom. I looked about, no longer mesmerized by the beauty of the landscape, no longer wondering if the winos in the fields could hold out for eight hours, no longer dreaming of the clothes I'd buy with my pay. My eyes followed my chopping as the plants, thin as their shadows, fell with each strike. I worked slowly with ankles and arms hurting, neck stiff, and eyes stinging from the dust and the sun that glanced off the field like a mirror.

By quitting time, 3:00, there was such an excruciating pain in my ankles that I walked as if I were wearing snowshoes. Rick laughed at me and I laughed too, embarrassed that most of the men were walking normally and I was among the first timers who had to get used to this work. "And what about you, wino," I came back at Rick. His eyes were meshed red and his long hippie hair was flecked with dust and gnats and bits of leaves. We placed our hoes in the back of a pickup and stood in line for our pay, which was twelve fifty. I was amazed at the pay, which was the most I had ever earned in one day, and thought that I'd come back the next day, Sunday. This was too good.

Instead of joining the others in the labor bus, we jumped in the back of a pickup when the driver said we'd get to town sooner and were welcome to join him. We scrambled into the truck bed to be joined by a heavy-set and laughing *Tejano* whose head was shaped like an egg, particularly so because the bandana he wore ended in a point on the top of his head. He laughed almost demonically as the pickup roared up the dirt path, a gray cape of dust rising behind us. On the highway, with the wind in our faces, we squinted at the fields as if we were looking for someone. The *Tejano* had quit laughing but was smiling broadly, occasionally chortling tunes he never finished. I was scared of him, though Rick, two years older and five inches taller, wasn't. If the *Tejano* looked at him, Rick stared back for a second or two before he looked away to the fields.

I felt like a soldier coming home from war when we rattled into Chinatown. People leaning against car hoods stared, their necks following us, owl-like; prostitutes chewed gum more ferociously and showed us their teeth; Chinese grocers stopped brooming their storefronts to raise their cadaverous faces at us. We stopped in front of the Chi Chi Club where Mexican music blared from the juke box and cue balls cracked like dull ice. The *Tejano*, who was dirty as we were, stepped awkwardly over the side rail, dusted himself off with his bandana, and sauntered into the club.

Rick and I jumped from the back, thanked the driver who said *de nada* and popped his clutch, so that the pickup jerked and coughed blue smoke. We returned smiling to our car, happy with the money we had made and pleased that we had, in a small way, proved ourselves to be tough; that we worked as well as other men and earned the same pay.

We returned the next day and the next week until the season was over and there was nothing to do. I told myself that I wouldn't pick grapes that summer, saying all through June and July that it was for Mexicans, not me. When August came around and I still had not found a summer job, I ate my words, sharpened my knife, and joined Mother, Rick, and Debra for one last time.

ROBERT B. STEPTO

Idlewild

I t is summer again, and time to dream again of summers past. Lately, my mind keeps wandering back to the many boyhood summers I spent in Idlewild, Michigan, on the edge of the Manistee National Forest. Idlewild was in some ways a typical retreat. There was a lake of some size, a small commercial patch, and a few amusements—a roller rink, a supper club, a place to go horseback riding. But in one respect, Idlewild was and remains decidedly untypical. It is an all-black town of roughly three hundred people that swells to three thousand or more residents in the summer months—or so it did in the 1940s and 1950s. Most of us arrived at our families' cottages from Detroit and Chicago. But I remember summer friends from other cities such as Cleveland and Cincinnati, and you could always spy license plates informing you that there were black folks in town from just about anywhere within a two-day drive.

At this point in my life, Idlewild is but a dot on a good map, a dot beside the slightly larger dot of Baldwin, Michigan, which may be on the map only because it is the county seat of Lake County. My parents sold their lakefront house, incredibly a shade of pink with white shutters, matching my mother's pink and white DeSoto, in 1959 or 1960. My grandparents held on to their place—"Deerpath" (lots of cottages had names)—a little longer, no doubt because they had had it longer (since 1941), had transformed it from a flimsy structure to a sturdy home, and had dreams of retiring there. But when certain realities set in—the harshness of the winters, worse than Chicago; the need for older people to be near medical care *and* their children—"Deerpath" went up on the block as well. In my immediate family, reasons for selling were abundant: you kids don't want to go to the country any more ("Well, yes, I did hate leaving my baseball team right in the thick of the season"); with the money, we can install central air-conditioning in the Chicago house ("ok"); endlessly entertaining family and friends is *no* vacation ("I guess it wasn't, but I didn't know that then . . ."). My grandparents, on the other hand, didn't talk about this change in their lives at all; selling "Deerpath," like selling soon thereafter the Chicago house they'd owned since the 1920s, was after all a wrenching concession to the mounting pressures of age. They didn't speak of that much, least of all to me, and it was only my grandmother who said things which led me later to think how devastating it was for them to face squarely that neither her dream of returning to Atlanta (she was Spelman College, class of 1907) nor her husband's dream of retiring to Idlewild was going to happen. They were stuck in Chicago, without central air conditioning, at least until they moved into my parents' house, in the spring of 1966. It jolts me to recall that they both were eighty years old at the time.

But let me return to Idlewild, as I did the other day when my finger followed the line of route 37 on a map, north from Grand Rapids, past Newaygo, past White Cloud (onion fields and a golf course), into Baldwin, with the lumberyard and dry goods store on the left of Main St., the movie theatre, bank, and ice cream parlor on the right, the courthouse and jail straight ahead. To get to Idlewild, you turn right, roughly a block before the courthouse, drive past the fish hatcheries, and then slow down terrifically for the sharp right turn around the huge oak (yes, the oak that George Young's father ran into, losing his life). After the rodeo grounds, you can ease into a forty-mile-an-hour spin, the road isn't challenging, and that's good, because if you are interested, there is much of a subtle nature increasingly on view. If you want to know something about how black people live, year round, in northern Michigan, well, look to the left and right. Idlewild of the Lake and the summer and of the summer folk is still a few miles ahead.

I sometimes review my thoughts about how Idlewild came to be in the first place. There is a story, somewhat self-disparaging in a way black stories about blacks can be, contending that Idlewild was founded by runaway slaves who, after traveling north for agonizing weeks on end, were convinced that they had reached Canada. And so they settled, and dug out a life, prosperity being out of the question for them and whites, too, until ironically, blacks with *some* money started to summer there, and needed the goods and services which the "natives" could supply. It wasn't Canada, but it wasn't America either: Idlewild had a black postmaster and an all-black fire department; Baldwin was lily white but, surprisingly for the 1950s, free of prejudice and racial tension. Perhaps I am forgetting something, or perhaps, as a youth, I was shielded from situations and confrontations. But I do not recall any lectures about how to behave in Baldwin (lectures of the sort drilled into me when I was about to go into certain parts of Chicago or its suburbs), and I do not recall any incidents in the stores, the movie theatre, etc. One could say that the small businessmen of the area were simply too pragmatic to discourage the fat summer trade, albeit brought to them by blackfolk flush with coin from the Great Lakes cities. As a child, however, my simple view was that prejudice was a matter of geography, and that we were too far north for trouble.

But of course prejudice had played a role of a kind in the creation of Idlewild and black summer resorts like it. While blacks of some means did plan and take summer vacations, there was always the question of where to go, or where you could go, and the quality of the welcome once there. Simple matters—where to stay? where to eat?—never were really that simple, unless you stopped with relatives, as people still do. I remember an occasion in the 1950s when the whole family had to sleep in the car because the motels we had tried all were mysteriously full. The next morning, the insult continued when the first place we entered for breakfast wouldn't serve us. These things happened not in the Deep South, but in supposedly less treacherous places, Ohio and Pennsylvania. In the 1960s, when we were making the last of our family motor trips, I vividly recall how my father would stop at a gas station, just before we arrived at our destination, just so he could "clean up," and maybe put on a fresh shirt *and* a tie. The idea was that such "precautions" would minimize "incidents" at the hotel's check-in counter. And yes, it was a hotel, always a hotel; motels were too iffy, too problematic, probably because they were too often owner-operated.

If these were the perils of summer travel at mid-century, we should not marvel at all at how serious and determined early-century blacks were about founding their own summer enclaves, notably Oak Bluffs on Martha's Vineyard and in the Midwest, Idlewild. Above and beyond the pleasures of fresh air and clear skies, of water sports and sylvan walks, these places offered the prospect of safe harbor for one's family, removed from the heat and dangers of urban life, and protected as well from random acts of racism in other vacation settings. But gratification for the "patriarchs" was not limited to what came from providing summers to family or owning additional property: some genuinely relaxed, had fun, and in many ways restored themselves. Charles W. Chesnutt, for example, the black novelist and lawyer from Cleveland, summered in Idlewild in the 1920s, and evidently found there much release from the affairs of business. His daughter, Helen, remembers her father's pleasurable unwinding this way: "At Idlewild Chesnutt relaxed in the clear, pine-scented, health-giving air. He spent his days fishing, sitting in an old willow chair at the end of his little pier, absorbing the golden sunshine and catching a bluegill now and then with a bamboo fishing pole. Or, feeling more energetic, he would row out into the lake in his flat-bottomed boat (Susan [his wife] had insisted on this type of boat) to cast for bass with rod and reel. . . . If the weather was rainy or too cold for fishing, he would sit before the log fire in the living room and read, or play solitaire, or do crossword puzzles, which he enjoyed immensely, calling in all the members of the family for assistance which he never needed at all."

Chesnutt's schedule of simple diversions was, my memory tells me, less sought and less available by the 1950s. But what Chesnutt desired and apparently got from summer life in the Idlewild of the mid-1920s was largely what my grandparents and their generation of summer folk were seeking when they bought or erected their cottages in the thirties and early forties. My grandfather, for example, never to my knowledge fished, but he and my grandmother did go deer watching at dawn and both loved boardgames at dusk; and the constant cottage improvement projects that occupied the hours in between gave my grandfather, a man otherwise cooped up in either a laboratory or a post office in Chicago, immense pleasure. My grandparents, like the Chesnutts, went to Idlewild not for bouts of parties and nightclubbing, but for the pleasures of rustic life. But by the late fifties, the resorters far outnumbered the rustics—or so it seemed. And I distinctly remember concluding, youth though I was, that everything I had heard about the perils of having your city neighborhood "change" apparently could apply as well to the village of your country cottage.

In another passage from her book about her father, one that startled me upon first reading since my memories of Idlewild are of another, later time, Helen Chesnutt writes: "Nature was lavish at Idlewild. Brilliant blue skies reflected in the lake; the most gorgeous sunsets imaginable, fading away gradually to let the night come on, its sky studded thickly with brilliant stars and constellations that a city-dweller could never dream of. The sunrise was equally beautiful if one rose early enough. Nothing could surpass the thrill of seeing at that hour a crane stepping daintily along the shore of the lake, stopping now and then to dip its bill into the water in search of breakfast." Some of this rings true for me. What I know—and everything I have forgotten—about the stars and their constellations I learned in Idlewild at night, at the end of a pier or in the middle of a field or just outside the door of a cottage. The books that guided my seeing were from Chicago, but what I saw and printed on my brain I saw as a youth in the Idlewild of my summers. The touch about the breakfasting crane, however, stretches my credulity, though I guess such sights were possible before my time at the lake. The birds I saw which I never glimpsed in the city were usually woodland birds, high in the branches of some oak or birch, or ducks flying in formation across the sky, just above the pines on the point across the lake. In other words, the birds I recall were never quite as extraordinary as Helen Chesnutt's crane, and I don't recall that they were ever quite as at home on the Lake as was her crane. However, what is most befuddling for me about Ms. Chesnutt's description is that it is so unqualified in its praise, so untainted by the onslaught of countermemories of, say, a couple of beer cans, bobbing in the lake in uncanny rhythm with the dipping motions of the crane. This is not to say that Chesnutt's memories are suspect, for I can imagine a time when Idlewild was pristine. But in my day, I would have seen the beer cans and *maybe* the crane, and that in itself places me in another time, another Idlewild.

By the 1950s, Idlewild was noisy. The part known as the island, which had been a focal point since the 1920s primarily because The Clubhouse (a place for business meetings among lot owners, but also a place for dances and boardinghouse-style meals, especially in the early years) was there, was by then a strip of bars, nightclubs, and cafes, anchored on one end by a hotel and on the other by a roller rink, which I believe was occupying the original Clubhouse building. If the genteel Charles Chesnutt had still been alive, I'm sure he would have been apoplectic about the blaring rock and roll music from the roller rink, which didn't so much drift as charge across the lake, invading cottages a mile away. I think, too, given the religiously sedate man that he was, Chesnutt would have been astonished to hear daily through the trees and across the waters the evening broadcast of "Ave Maria," emanating from the PA system in the belfry of the evangelical church near the post office.

But there was more, for in addition to the cacophony of "Ave Maria" competing with the roller rink's "Why Do Fools Fall in Love"—truly an instance of dueling sound systems, as both sides must have admitted in secret—there was the nerve-rattling scream of the huge horn atop the volunteer fire department everyday at six, not counting, of course, the times it went off when there was actually a fire. Beyond that, there was the constant din, from the island specifically, of honky-tonk-cabaret street life. While we might have been in the country, there was clearly as much gaiety—loud, raucous, and sometimes dangerous gaiety—as there was along any strip of bars and pubs in urban Negro America. Indeed, there is a certain irony about me and other youths being protected from all of that "adult behavior" in Chicago, Detroit et al., only to be exposed to it while on "fresh air holiday" in the woods. Later in life, when I found myself taking everything in at night on, say, Chicago's 47th St. or Harlem's 125th, I could say to myself, "This reminds me of the country, of being in Idlewild."

Another form of what we would now call noise pollution (and environmental pollution, too) was the motorboat. I report this with mixed emotions, for I then loved motorboats, and constantly designed and redesigned all sorts of powercraft in the leaves of the sketchbooks received as presents, especially after I forsook piano lessons on the South Side for drawing (and painting and sculpture) lessons downtown in Chicago's Loop. So ardent was my interest, fueled by afternoons along the shores of Lake Idlewild, and Lake Michigan, too, that occasionally I would take the money that would have purchased several comic books and buy a copy of *Motorboating* instead. These purchases invariably occurred on Saturdays, after art school, in the Van Buren St. Station of the Illinois Central Electric (the "IC"), while I was on my way home. *Motorboating*, along with a few captivating issues of *Yachting*, provided a cornucopia of aquamarine fantasies, whether by critiquing a particular boat, analyzing some new lethal Chrysler inboard engine, or describing an incredible race or excursion—on ocean or fresh waters, I didn't care.

It must have been out of some number of *Motorboating* that I got an accurate address for the Chris-Craft Corporation, for soon thereafter, with what can only be called a youth's innocence and impetuosity, I sent to Chris-Craft several of my designs. As I remember them, they were for rakish powercraft of the thirty-to-forty-foot class. What distinguished them from what Chris-Craft and their competitors were producing was more power (of course), and wrap-around windscreens, identical to the wrap-around windshields that were then appearing on Detroit automobiles, including my father's new Oldsmobile. Much to my pleasure and astonishment, I received a reply from Chris-Craft. It said in effect—and I wish to hell I knew where I put that letter—that the designs were promising and that I should contact Chris-Craft when I finished college. (Apparently, I must have put in my letter something like, "I hope you like my boats—I am only ten years old"). A decade later, in the last months of college, I found myself choosing between seminary, law school, and graduate study in English—naval architecture was no longer a part of my dreams or options. But I thank the man at Chris-Craft for taking five minutes to write a kind note to a dreaming boy; it was a decent thing to do.

Given all this, you can imagine my rapture when an uncle, the only family member to serve in the Navy, arrived one summer with a handsome Thompson clinker in tow behind his Studebaker. Rolling back the tarp for the first time was like opening a huge Christmas present, for stowed inside, cradled by the ribs of gleaming wood, were all sorts of marine paraphernalia—cushions, lifejackets, a gas tank, and yes, a Johnson outboard motor of reasonable power. With the arrival of Uncle Rog and the Thompson, my days *on* the lake began, as did my education about boat safety, boat maintenance, about how to read the water for shallows and submerged objects (I nevertheless sheared at least two propeller pins), and about how "half of the Negroes on this lake don't know squat about how to run or care for the boats they keep buying." With all the lessons and all the cautions, I was like a pup on a leash. But it didn't matter, for as far as *this* pup was concerned, it was more important to be out of the kennel and on a walk.

Sometimes we didn't dare go out on the lake: it was too treacherous—not because of the weather, but because of the near gridlock of boats whizzing the waters. There were a lot of daredevil maneuvers (some people freely do things in a boat they'd never do in a car), often bringing fast boats perilously close to swimmers, piers, and to each other. And there was a lot of slow-speed styling: people who knew how to drive a turquoise Cadillac at twenty miles an hour down an urban avenue also knew a lot about how to purr a Chris-Craft inboard along the edges of the lake, at just the speed that would allow onlookers to check out the driver's resort clothes and process, and to agree that the fine sister on the back cushion was indeed last month's centerfold in *Jet* magazine. Memories such as these make it hard for me to imagine Charles Chesnutt out on the lake in his flat-bottom rowboat—rowboaters often were nearly swamped by the buffeting wakes of the fast boats—or sitting at the end of his pier in a willow chair, trying to catch bluegill. That might have been possible in the twenties, but by the fifties, during the season at least, a pier was not a site for fishing but rather a seat for the show—the parade of bloods in boats, doing anything and everything as long as they didn't get their hair wet.

Accounts of Idlewild's early years mention mostly either the elderly cottagers, pursuing their version of life on Golden Pond, or the entrepreneurs who built the nightclubs which in time made Idlewild a desired booking for many black entertainers who appeared in big-city clubs and also in theatres, including Chicago's Regal and Harlem's Apollo. The accounts also remind us of the distinguished Negroes who were variously involved in Idlewild's development and destiny. Dr. Daniel Hale Williams, for example, the noted pioneer heart surgeon from Chicago, owned a magnificent home on the lake called Oakmere, and bought many lots which he eventually sold for a tidy profit. Dr. W. E. B. Du Bois, the extraordinary historian, sociologist, political economist, and editor of the NAACP's *Crisis* magazine, bought Idlewild lots for investment purposes, and even put in writing his praise of the white capitalists (Erastus Branch, Adelbert Branch, Wilbert Lemon, Mamye Lemon, Alvin Wright, and Madolin Wright) who had formed the Idlewild Resort Company in 1912 in order to purchase the black resort's original 2,700 acres, plus the lake. Du Bois was no great friend of American capitalism, but perhaps his endorsement of the Idlewild Resort Company can be explained by noting that the company sold the resort, rather soon as these things go, in 1921 to the all-black Idlewild Lot Owners Association, to which Du Bois belonged as long as he owned his lots. Celebrities, including athletes and stars of the stage and music world, made investments as well, though to my knowledge, they rarely built summer or retirement homes on their land, even when they owned coveted lakefront properties. This often vexed the people owning adjoining land who had cottages, and who naturally were anxious about whether another cottage suddenly was going to go up, sometimes just a stone's throw away. My parents, for example, after buying a house of their own in Idlewild, near my grandparents and on the lake, tried repeatedly to protect their privacy by purchasing the lot just north of them, owned by Lil Armstrong, Louis Armstrong's former wife. She refused their offers, and they had to settle into the hope that she would neither sell to someone else nor crowd a cottage in between us and the elderly woman presently next door.

Perhaps there were some truly distinguished summer residents in the Idlewild of my days, but I wasn't aware of them. Daniel Hale Williams and Charles Chesnutt were of course long gone, but what surprises me is that people that famous left so few traces of themselves. I do not remember, for example, overhearing adults saying things like, "that used to be Dr. Williams's place," or "did you know Miss So-and-So is one of Chesnutt's granddaughters?" When I ask my parents where Dr. Williams's Oakmere was located, thinking they might know because of the Chicago connection and because of my father's affiliation with the hospital Williams helped to found, they say, "I don't know." When I push the matter and ask, "Well, can you at least tell me what side of the lake he was on?" my mother says, "our side, I think," while my father replies, "that was before my time." Of course, there is somebody out there who can tell me, and there are property records, too, but that is not the point: the point is that Idlewild's elite pioneers had a way of not just dying but vanishing. And yet, consider this as well: the 1950s were not a time when black Americans put much effort into preserving or recovering their history, and probably doubted that the history of a black resort was history at all. Perhaps, too, the *carpe diem* mentality of being on vacation or seeking retirement stifled any sort of communal historical awareness. At any rate, in my youthful days on the lake, the collective focus was on the present and there were no ghosts from the past. Moreover, for me at least, the people who stood out were neither the respectable black professionals from the cities nor the flamboyant entertainers from what used to be called the "chittlin' circuit." I was fascinated instead by the handful of mystery men, the black Jay Gatsbys who sprang, as Fitzgerald's character did, from Platonic conceptions of themselves, apparently to serve as Gatsby did obsessively, "a vast, vulgar, and meretricious beauty." One such Gatsby lived just two piers away from us, and it was all I could do not to stop and stare when he appeared.

Milton Winfield—Mister Winfield—was a quiet, private man who nonetheless had subtle ways of calling attention to himself. There were plenty of Cadillacs in Idlewild, but Mr. Winfield's was one of the few of a somber color, and one of the few that seemed to be simply about its owner's need for proper transportation. Of course, the fact that Mr. Winfield sometimes had a driver at the wheel, a man built like a prizefighter who probably was a bodyguard, put him and his motorcar in a class of their own.

Mr. Winfield also had an imposing house, a real house in comparison to the summer cottages. There could be no doubt that it was weatherized, furnaced, and provisioned for sojourns in the country in any season, including trips of an urgen spontaneous sort. The house was white with blue trim; there were plantings and a lawn (I cannot remember another lawn in town, groomed and well cared for). It may have possessed a second story—unheard of in a resort village where some folks still didn't have indoor plumbing. While I'm not sure of the second story, with its suggestion of airy bedrooms with lake views, I am certain about the fence surrounding the property. Fences weren't entirely unusual; my grandfather, for example, had put up a wooden rail fence which did nothing more than please the eye and define a few boundaries. It was a horse country fence. In contrast, Mr. Winfield's was a formidable chainlink fence, as high as what you see around a tennis court, only the fence was not for confining sports activities to the grounds, but clearly for keeping people out. I doubt that the fence was supplemented by an intruder alarm system, but if any resident of Idlewild had such a system in the 1950s, Milton Winfield did.

Given the armatures and public style of the man, I was always pleased when Mr. Winfield gave me a little nod or wave. I felt I had a little arrangement, a small piece of business going, with the local padrone. But my place in his world was always clear, for the nods and waves never led to conversations, let alone to avuncular kindnesses such as outings in his sleek boat. I was surprised to learn much later on, from my father, that Mr. Winfield had a son, for I had never seen a son, and I don't even remember a Mrs. Winfield—a wife. I had always assumed that Mr. Winfield had no family, and didn't want any. That, too, was what the chain link fence was about.

The first time the police came was early on a sunny morning. I was up and dressed because it was fun to trot over to my grandparents' cottage, before my mother rose, for a biscuit or a plate of fried apples. They came in three or four cars, stealthily yet swiftly, decelerating from forty miles an hour to zero and stopping, at strategic points around the perimeter of Mr. Winfield's property, with the quiet of cats finding themselves just yards away from prey. As I recall, one or two cops ran through our neighbor's lot—or maybe it was *our* lot—to cover the rear, which was Mr. Winfield's door and cascading steps to the lake. The rest marched to the front door, and, for all I know, rang the bell.

I anticipated a shoot-out. I thought that if I could hide behind a pine tree, or behind my mother's pink and white DeSoto, I could watch while a dozen erstwhile black prizefighters thrust rifles or machine guns out of Mr. Winfield's windows and fired on a bunch of white Chicago cops while they took cover behind their big Fords and drew their weapons. It would be a whole lot to check out before going horseback riding at ten, and a monstrous story to tell once back on the block in Chicago.

But nothing happened—Mr. Winfield wasn't there, and the cops packed up and left. When they came again, and again, he wasn't there either. But I am certain that at least one time, maybe more, after the cops departed, Mr. Winfield soon thereafter came down the steps to the lake with one of his burly men. After unlocking the gate in the fence, he went out on his concrete pier, where his inboard launch lay, wrapped up and hulking. After firing up the boat and donning a yachtsman's cap, he assumed the wheel and took what might be called a victory lap around the lake.

Perhaps it is odd to associate boyhood summers with reading and learning, but this is much the case for me. Every morning, after the chores, I was free to head out for wherever on my bicycle, the sole condition being that I return home at a designated hour for a proper lunch and an hour's worth of reading in my bunk. After the reading hour, I could again jump upon my bicycle and adventure around until the fire-house whistle blew at six. Then it was my solemn duty to tear myself away from whatever boardgame, ballgame, or nightclub rehearsal was enthralling me, and to pedal home briskly. Later in the evening, perhaps after a twilight spin in the boat, or after giving up on finding something good on the radio, I would return to my book, more curious about the next chapter than I ever wanted all the schoolteachers in the family to know. I seem to remember my mother coming into my room and exclaiming with unconcealed delight, "Oh, you're reading," and my wanting to growl back, "Yeah, well, don't get the wrong impression—I'm just passing the time."

The whole summer reading project—the parent's insistence, the child's complaints and footdragging, and then the child's seduction—began in June in Chicago, during the days after school ended, when preparations for going to Idlewild began in earnest. The Chicago public library system had in those days a summer book loan plan which allowed kids (and maybe adults, too) to check out twenty or thirty books for the entire summer. My mother, a public school reading teacher, considered this to be the best uplift scheme since Tuskegee, and so there was no question as to whether I would appear on one of the check-out days at the Kimbark branch library with my library card, and a duffel bag to be filled to the zipper.

One such trip stands out in my mind because it was a sunny, hot day, and I had to walk both legs of the trip. Walking to the library probably was a delight. I imagine I veritably skipped along, taking in all I liked to observe along the route: the Wedgewood Towers Hotel (a kind of flatiron building wedged in the vee created at 64th St. where Minerva Avenue veered off Woodlawn), where Minnie Minoso and a few other black baseball players lived—sometimes you could see them up close or admire Minoso's pink Cadillac; the music store on 63rd St., which still had a ceramic RCA Victor dog outside its entrance; the marquee of the Kimbark Theatre (cartoons and cowboy movies had not yet given way to the all-Spanish programs run in our last years in the neighborhood). However, the walk *back* was another matter: the duffel bag brimmed with books (given the kind of kid I was, it never occurred to me that I could undo this whole project by returning with only a book or two) and I was truly struggling with the bulk and weight. The heat didn't help, and matters became worse when a handle broke off the bag.

And so there I was toiling home, carrying a huge bag of books in my arms in the manner of a child struggling with heavy groceries or firewood, or with an infant brother or sister, burdens we all remember because when the hefting becomes *work*, we say things like: "I don't eat any of this stuff," or "Who needs a fire anyway?" or "I never wanted a kid brother/sister." Right at the point the books were becoming a true chore, some kids I vaguely knew from the library caught up with me. One or two of them had books in hand, but none was as stupid as me to be laboring along with a whole satchel full. And so while I toted my bale, they pranced like long-legged puppies, circling like pups do when they want a walker or a postman to drop everything and play.

One such pup I remember to be a saucy girl; she perused me several times while I was struggling, sweating, and then said: "Hey, you sure have hairy arms." That set off a titter in the group, mortifying me. If the temperature had been ninety degrees moments before, it was now ninety-five. My arms were not especially hairy, and now I know, after having been out in the world a bit, my arms aren't especially hairy at all. But being at the time ten years old or so, and black, and of a black community, I was terribly sensitive not just about the hair on my arms but about the fact that the summer sun always quickly bleached them a dusty blond. That was some unexplainable, inexplicable stuff; and what could I do right then and there, my arms were exposed for all to see, since they enfolded the treasure of library books, burdening me then as they promised to do later once I was up North in the woods.

But the saucy girl wasn't through. She circled again, and then let loose with, "Hey, with hairy arms like those, I'd sure like to see your *balls*." Even now, I still cringe at the memory of how the banterers guffawed, how the books in my arms tripled in weight, of how I said next to nothing while melting like butter on the hot sidewalk. Just a few years later, when, say, thirteen or fourteen, I think I could have managed, even with the books in tow, an appropriate, even withering retort—a reply comparably sexual. But I wasn't ready then, and I was the one withered. We all indulge in the fantasy exercise of "what I should have said"; to this day, I fashion replies to that girl, wondering still what her name was.

And then there was Eddie Gray. Eddie is now a Chicago lawyer, living in the same townhouse complex where my Uncle Herman lives; he's a buddy I don't mind seeing when I'm back home. In the fifties, however, Eddie was more acquaintance than friend, perhaps because we went to different schools. We were aware of each other because we were acolytes at St. Edmund's, and because the network of black middle-class youth clubs, with its interminable schedule of holiday parties and wholesome events, had us forever bumping into each other. Yes, I knew Eddie, but having him up to our house in Idlewild and sharing my room for a fortnight was not my idea. It was the sort of thing parents cook up, and, indeed, Lil Gray and my mother were close enough friends to think such a visit a "great idea."

And so it came to pass that Lil and Eddie arrived one day in Idlewild, and I had to be couth enough to greet him cheerfully while showing him to what had suddenly become *our* room. As the days went by, I was less and less the good host. In fact, I was a raging ass. Eddie was not athletic, and so there was no chance that a game of catch with a baseball could turn into something splendid and rousing, complete with fly balls to be snared and ground balls to be deftly turned into double plays. Playing catch with Eddie was enormously about hoping that if you threw him the ball you might see it again, soon, and not after searching through the weeds with a stick. I got impatient, and started giving him a lot of crap whenever our mothers were out of earshot. For good measure, I started in on him about his weight—he was pudgy—and kept that up until one day tears welled in his eyes. Eventually, my mother grabbed me, took me outside as I recall, and gave me the talking-to I deserved. I agreed to behave—or to behave better—but I didn't change my mind about Eddie and the whole miserable visit: I wanted it to end, I wanted my room back, I was willing to suffer a whipping if that was the price I had to pay to hear the sound of Lil and Eddie packing to go.

But one afternoon, I did change my mind about Eddie, unexpectedly, during the reading hour. Eddie apparently was on the same uplift schedule I was, or found it no problem to be on my schedule; at any rate, he had some books with him. I was curious about what he was reading, and was dumbstruck, after glancing at the pages of his book, to realize that he was reading poetry. I asked him who the poet was; he replied, "Paul Laurence Dunbar." I confessed I'd never heard of him. Eddie then told me what seemed like a great deal about Dunbar. What I remember best is that he spoke not like a young student into whom some facts have been poured, but absolutely like someone who knew Dunbar because he had *read* Dunbar, and had entered into some sort of company with him. What I recall, too, is that Eddie rose from his chair, and, while strolling the room, recited from memory Dunbar's "Little Brown Baby With the Sparklin' Eyes."

This is a memory that returns to me most every summer, and certainly every fall, for it is in the fall that I teach my Modern African American Poets course, and Dunbar is the first poet encountered. A year ago, a student I rather like came up to me after the Dunbar classes and said, "I enjoyed the Dunbar but must ask you why you didn't assign 'Little Brown Baby With the Sparklin' Eyes'? It's my favorite Dunbar poem." I replied, "It's one of my favorites, too." But of course I hadn't answered her question, and I knew that as soon as I thought about our conversation while walking back to my office. Why *don't* I teach that poem? Is it because it doesn't fit into what I want to say about Dunbar? Or is the reason less pedagogical, less professional?

The poem seems to be for me Eddie Gray's poem. And while I could doubtlessly say more about the poem today than he did when we were ten or eleven, I seem to be willing to leave it alone, so that what Eddie taught me about it and himself may remain intact.

Summer reading also brought me and a boy named Mike together. But maybe I should say that reading brought Mike to me, since he was always coming over to our cottage and poring over everything on the bookshelves and in the magazine racks. I liked Mike—he was a good fellow to know for bike rides, fishing, and for ways to sneak in afternoon nightclub rehearsals. But his nose-in-a-book routine, in full view of elders, was very annoying; I didn't need any behavior from friends that called into question my own commitments. Indeed, it was right about the time I felt I had succeeded in convincing everyone that no normal boy on summer vacation read more than an hour a day, that Mike started coming over to scan the shelves, hardly knowing what grand act of sabotage he was committing.

Like Eddie, Mike was from Chicago. But our buddyship was strictly one of summertimes up north in the woods. Once, in Chicago, we ran into each other in the lobby of a movie theatre, and were stunned to discover that outside Idlewild we barely knew how to speak to each other—conversation was forced and virtually impossible. I recall once trying to bridge this gulf by inviting Mike over to my house one wintry Saturday—or maybe the invitation was for us to go to the movies together, perhaps (although I couldn't have put it this way then) to repair the awkward moments we'd had in a theatre before. But Mike couldn't come—he wasn't allowed out that day. He seemed, in our few, brief telephone conversations in Chicago, more confined to his house and more shackled by chores than he ever was in Idlewild, if that was possible. His anxious, almost whispered, replies to my cheery hailings told me that.

Mike's circumstance was that both parents were dead, or might as well have been, and he was living with a grandmother who was clearly angry about having to raise him. I am certain she wanted the best for him, and saw that the best might come from a thorough grounding in regimen, routine, and responsibility. But anger was mixed in the schedule as well; there were too few kind words from her to think otherwise. Mike's grandmother was obviously a woman of property—houses both in Chicago and in Idlewild—and evidently had the income, albeit probably a retirement income, to maintain the houses, herself, and Mike. But money was always an issue, or was *made* an issue. I soon became careful in Idlewild about suggesting that we swing over to Ti-Jon's (the ice cream parlor) or to the general store for something cold on a hot day, for I knew that Mike probably had only 25 cents in his pocket and that that had to last him a week. Sometimes Mike bravely asked his grandmother for another quarter, and sometimes he got it. But having heard the sorts of interrogations he had to suffer for 25 cents, I decided that I would just as soon avoid playing a part in putting Mike in that position. Instead of going to the general store, we might as well repair back to my house. Perhaps this is how Mike first ended up at our cottage in the late afternoon, the seduction of a cold drink leading to his eager study of the books.

On one such afternoon, Mike picked up my copy of Bertha Morris Parker's *Natural History of the United States.* The book was hardbound and heavy, and while I often saw it to be one of my summer ball and chains, I had to admit grudgingly that it had taught me all I knew about flora and fauna of the upper Midwest, and about birds and small animals, too. If I could walk as a youth along a country road in Idlewild, casually identifying every tree and most every bird, it was because Bertha Morris Parker's book was my trot, though I was damned if I was going to admit that in a manner approaching gratitude. After all, Ms. Parker was not just a renowned author but a science teacher at my school—the Laboratory School of the University of Chicago—and I was determined to keep my Chicago schoolteachers in place, bracketed outside of my Idlewild summers.

But Mike pored on through the Parker, and for my part, no profferred boardgame, no provocative conversation about, say, the young ladies in the neighborhood, could tear him away. I can see it all now, Mike bent over the book, his knees awkwardly crimped to keep it in place in his lap. Meanwhile, my relatives are glancing up from their bridge hands, to adore Mike and to frown at me, and then to nod approvingly to themselves, as if to say that despite Bobby's proclivities, they could play on with the bridge game, since thanks to Mike the race's fate was in good hands.

Around five, Mike had to leave. A gloom descended, for rather than accepting the explanation that Mike had to be home for dinner, we all believed that he had chores to perform with the chickens and other barnyard creatures. We fantasized furthermore that Mike might even have to patch a roof or pour a concrete walk before sundown. Perhaps it was this which charged somebody to step forward and say, "Mike, take the book with you. Bring it back in a few days, but take it with you."

Mike left, and an evening rain came. We had dinner and began to settle into what amused each on a rainy evening. I think I was noodling with the radio on the porch when, at twilight's last moment, Mike knocked at the door. I was surprised to see him, and he was mortified to be knocking. When I opened the screen door, he handed me back the Bertha Morris Parker book, now carefully wrapped to protect it against the steady rain. A relative burst out from the shadows and asked, "Why, Mike? I said you could borrow the book." "My grandmother says this is a fine book," he told us, when he finally spoke, "too fine to be in her house, too fine for me to read." With that, Mike walked away, having done what his grandmother wanted him to do, what he could do in response. My relatives stared at each other; I simply went to bed.

I don't think I read quite as much in the last year or two at Idlewild, though there were singular achievements such as working through all of Mark Twain and Sherlock Holmes. One distraction was the little portable television, now out on the porch: while my grandparents continued to ban all such modern appurtenances from their country life, my parents relented, and even installed a telephone as well. The TV picked up only one channel, the broadcast from Cadillac, Michigan, and that in itself monitored just how much television became a part of an evening's activity. However, the Cadillac station offered plenty of Detroit Tiger baseball games, and I must have watched at least three a week.

Then, too, there was "the girl next door"—actually, the ravishing cousin of the girl next door. Sometimes in the evening, we would meet down by the lake and talk about everything and nothing while sitting on the end of the pier. After the sun went down, the few motorboats still on the lake would turn on their running lights and purr back to their docks, and we would sit a little closer. Of course, we could have done that while the boats were still on the lake, but we weren't going to risk that—we could be *seen*, and our "love" was supposed to be some Big Secret. Parents couldn't know about us, her boyfriend and my girlfriend (whoever they were) couldn't know, the entire cities of Chicago and Detroit (she was from there) had to be kept in the dark for sure, since after all we had to *return* to those places. On the other hand, the cousin—the real "girl next door"—*had* to know, because somebody had to know and be sworn to secrecy.

When it really was nighttime, we had to get cracking at whatever we were going to do to each other, since it would be only a matter of minutes before some parent would step out of a house, wondering where the children were. It was like petting with the kitchen timer going, only in this case the timer could not only beckon, but walk up and ask questions. But those were still sweet moments, moments filled with slow dancing on the beach to the tunes on the jukebox at the roller rink, moments that were all they could be—given the fact that the other girl from next door was there too, and, being twelve, we didn't know what to do about that.

My secret love of that summer turned out to be the first girl not from Chicago whose address I took and carefully memorized. I wrote her several times—long distance calls were never considered, as I have told my son when I see his phone bills to Barcelona—and she wrote back, on perfumed stationery no less. This kept up until maybe Thanksgiving, at which point we both decided, I guess, that the summer was over. But more than that was over, for it would be that winter that the Idlewild cottage would be sold. Thereafter, summer reading, writing, and dancing on the beach would occur in other territories, other climes.

When I talk with my mother about closing up the Idlewild house at summer's end, she says, "Oh yes, we used to go up and do that over Columbus Day weekend. There was no school on Monday." This puzzles me, mainly because since I attended private school, I never had Columbus Day off, as the public schoolers did. But maybe we did go up that weekend to put things in storage and to board up the windows: I certainly remember the change the fall brought to the air and to the lake, and perhaps those are October days I recall, not September ones. But September, too, was a time when the other summer people had gone, when the air had a nip in it, and we were in Idlewild. This was usually so because my school had not yet started (as part of the University it was on the University's quarter system schedule), and because, for a few years at least, my parents chose to stay up to the country through their anniversary, September 13th.

We never saw much of my father in August; I don't know what the statistics are for other parts of the country, but in August in Chicago, obstetricians are monstrously busy, delivering every baby created when the first winds of the last winter blew and folks naturally had to snuggle. He made up for this, sort of, by arriving during Labor Day weekend and staying on through the thirteenth. Having my father around was always a bit of an experiment, one which reminded me far too much of when I was four or five, and we moved out of my grandparents' house to a home of our own, the two-flat on Minerva Avenue. Suddenly, then, we were a nuclear family under one roof, not an extended family in the same house, and I didn't know what to think about it. Good thoughts were expected and possibly *de rigueur* (after all, we're talking about the fifties), but bad thoughts, negative assessments, were oh so tempting. I recall sitting in the midst of the construction of the new kitchen of the new home, sipping the worst glass of orange juice I had ever had (it was my first glass of frozen orange juice), and thinking, this isn't going to work. Where are Grandma and Grandpa?

Another version of this was soon played out in Idlewild. To be in Idlewild was to be back with my grandparents, to repair the rupture created when we moved out of their house and into our own. But when my parents bought their own home in Idlewild, three or four years after buying their own home in the city, I had to adjust once again to the concept, the bounding imperative, that a boy should live within the bordered place that gave his parents identity and ease. The realities of that were starkly evident in September, after summer playmates had left; after Uncle Rog departed with his boat; after Mr. Jones, who each year carted to Idlewild our various boxes and bicycles, came to retrieve the same; after Grandma and Grandpa were no longer just around the corner from the firehouse.

How did I pass the time, the interminable days of summer's end? I know I read, and in the last year or two at Idlewild watched baseball on the little television as the pennant races heated up. I felt lost without a bicycle, and doubted that a walk, or a hike offered the same gratification as a fast spin along the blacktop road to the center of the village. But I learned how to take walks and how to find pleasure in them, even though I was sometimes astonished, stopped in my tracks even, to discover that I was walking and alone, and not biking with Mike and Eugene, cavorting and claiming the road as much as we dared, until a car honked us to the side.

Truly the most exciting thing I did in September was to ride in Sarge Johnson's horse round-up. Sarge was an Idlewild institution—a wizened old black man—a blind veteran of the Spanish-American War—who ran a stable from which you could go on horseback rides around the lake. You couldn't go anywhere else—or at least kids couldn't—and Mrs. Johnson, a brusque woman half Sarge's age, made sure you didn't by driving slowly along behind you in her Oldsmobile. Two honks from her and the horses commenced to trot; one honk later and they fell back into a walk, much to the relief of the tourist folk who didn't know how to post and usually got jostled up pretty bad. I remember some of them moaning, as people do in the midst of a rollercoaster ride, and my being secretly amused by that, especially when the moaners were adults.

I rode the horses at Sarge's every summer of the 1950s, and reveled in advancing from the tottering, ancient mounts to the friskier horses requiring some skill to ride. In the last years, I had a "job" at Sarge's, leading strings of riders and horses on the route around the lake. My pay was that I rode for free, and I rode enough to have saddle sores, which I would vividly remember in the winter whenever a cowboy in a movie would creakingly climb out of a saddle. I felt I knew what that was all about.

There were two of us boys who led horses around for Sarge, and when Mrs. Johnson found out that we would still be in Idlewild after Labor Day, we were asked to help with the round-up. Why it was called a round-up was even then something of a mystery, for we obviously didn't have to ride out into the sagebrush, as the movie cowboys did, to round up wild ponies for breaking or branding. And certainly there was no mythic black stallion holed up in some canyon that nobody had ever been able to put a rope on. Our task was to saddle up two horses and to herd the rest down ten miles or so of dirt roads I'd never been on, to a field simply known as The Pasture. In this, we were assisted, or rather overseen, by the ever-present Mrs. Johnson, who was never too far behind us in the Oldsmobile. What made this shadowing different, however, was that Sarge always came along with her for the round-up, as did their daughter, an adopted white girl of five or six, who was wild and boisterous, and whose presence in, say, Sarge's lap never failed to raise an eyebrow or two.

The boy riding with me was older, a teenager, and had ridden plenty of round-ups before I first came along, or so he convinced me. He took me aside and explained that late in the day, when we got closer to the pasture, the horses would realize that they weren't going for yet another trudge around the lake—they were going to horse heaven, The Pasture, the reward for putting up with a summer's worth of giddy kids and roaring adults, with daily saddlings and harnessings. At that point, he said, they would break into a canter, and some would run, and if we got far enough ahead of Mrs. Johnson, or around some big bend in the road, we could run our horses, too—just to catch up to the horses bolting ahead, of course—and that would be fun, more fun than I could imagine.

Things happened mostly that way. The round-up began with us squiring the dozen or so horses down familiar roads, and then around bends and up and down grades where I'd never been. At that point, we were just escorting the band, and I had plenty of opportunity to scan the landscape, taking in the scrub pine, white oak, birch, the wildflowers, the occasional rough house set back from the road; to wonder where I was and how far from Idlewild. But it was no time before the horses became frisky, agitated in fact. They would snort and prance; they would stroll up to some former stablemate and nip him or her, and maybe add a swift kick for good measure. With the kicking, the band became unruly, and I cautiously attempted to assume authority and impose order, as I had seen movie cowboys magically do with hundreds of cattle or scores of horses. But nothing worked. For one thing, I could see in the eyes of every horse that they thought I was a chump from the city who didn't know his ass from a stirrup and they weren't about to let me interfere with their pleasure. And for another thing, my horse, the liveliest horse I had graduated to riding, wasn't cooperating. I knew that when he suddenly veered in a direction quite opposite from that in which I thought I was reining him, and kicked the business out of a horse I couldn't imagine deserving such treatment. I just barely stayed in the saddle. My buddy, the teenager, just winked and chuckled, while riding and *controlling* Sarge's most majestic horse, riding handsomely, like John Wayne.

Soon thereafter, the dangerous cavorting stopped and the horses, sensing that they were near the pasture, raised their ears like antennae, and got serious about moving down the road. There were a few surprises: some horses that had been absolute dogs during the summer season, sullen about giving any rider the smallest thrill, took off almost like thoroughbreds. Other horses, the most sprightly and cantankerous, predictably were the first to run and indeed to stretch out in running; it was truly something to see them in their drive to leave summer and Idlewild behind. "Now's the time," my buddy said, and sprinted ahead like a jockey in a money race. I glanced behind to see how close Mrs. Johnson was in the car, and seeing that she wasn't close at all, slapped the reins, leaned into the mane of the roan I was riding, and just let things happen.

We were going fast; I was actually on a horse that was running full tilt. We weren't herding in the other running horses, we were passing them, breaking out for fresh territory. After maybe ten minutes of pure thrill and exhilaration, it occurred to me that I needed to rein in my horse. Otherwise, we weren't squiring the other horses to pasture, and I would catch hell from the Johnsons. But reining in was another thing that didn't work for me that day. When I pulled on the reins, and then really pulled, my horse began to buck and swerve. I was convinced it wanted to ditch me. And so I said, "All right, let's go," and leaned into the mane again, while the horse ran and ran and lathered.

I remember riding, at breathtaking speed, not knowing where in the world I was going. At one point, my buddy caught up and yelled, "Hey, cool it, the Johnsons are going crazy, you're running that horse too hard." Then the Oldsmobile pulled alongside of me, and Sarge leaned out. "Rein that horse in or I'm going to kick your ass." Profanity from adults always had great effect on me, but I feared more being thrown by an angry horse into a patch of poison ivy. That forced me to say to myself, "I'm riding this one out."

Then came a fork in the road. I didn't know which way to go, and my buddy and the Oldsmobile had drifted back behind me, perhaps to keep watch on the other horses. As the fork approached, I simply gave the horse its head; it knew where it was going, and went left. After a quarter mile or so, we swung into the pasture, and the lathered horse found enough energy to buck me off. I was still half-lying on the ground when the rest of the horses thundered in with the Oldsmobile right behind them.

The car ride back to Idlewild was excruciating. Sarge cursed me every minute of the way, and everyone else, including the buddy (now suddenly innocent of running *his* horse), had their own way of joining in. After I was dropped off at home, the Oldsmobile left with a roar and spewing of gravel. When I approached the kitchen door, tired and forlorn, my father asked, "What was *that* all about?"

Staying in Idlewild after Labor Day was dedicated to my parents' finally having some summertime together, and my walks and round-ups helped that happen. But there were family moments as well. I recall trips to Ludington and traipsings on the beaches and dunes there, and visits to the Dairy Queen for hot fudge sundaes. Then, too, there were the longer drives to Traverse City—about as far as we ever ventured from Idlewild— where there was a kind of North Country zoo, full of moose and elk and caribou. There was a sign on the fence boundarying the moose area that warned, "Don't Stand Close." One day I did, as curious kids will do, and got the scare of my life when a moose crashed into the fence, almost opening a hole in the chain link.

But what I remember best was the chilly September day my father and I went down the hill to our Idlewild beach and built a fire. I was delighted by the special lunacy of it: it was cold and windy and the lake almost had whitecaps; everything pointed to retreating back to the house, building a fire *there*, and maybe having a cup of cocoa. But we stayed down on the beach and got a driftwood fire going and huddled around it as if shelter was nowhere in sight. Then my father suggested that we cook something. I scampered up the hill and found a kielbasa in the refrigerator.

Eventually, the makings for a grand lunch were assembled, put in a sack, and carted out into the chilly day and down to the beach. My father had cooked for us, for me, only once before, during a harrowing time when my mother was sick. This time was better; it was as good as it would ever be.

Between Silence and Sanction

A crazed wind swept through the desert, turning the quiet after-noon upside down. Red lightning splintered the sky like an incandescent spider's web hung over the mountains. Massive thunderheads swallowed Rincon Peak, their underbellies swollen with rage and rain. Tumbling over itself, the wind swirled into unruly cones of dust and grit, snapping at mesquite trees, distorting saguaros and ocotillos, rattling our win-dows, taunting me. I had to get out of the house, untangle my thoughts and figure out what to do with the chapayeka masks my brother had given me.

Chapayekas are distinctly dangerous. They represent the extremes of malevolence as they are made, but once a mask is worn, fitting over the entire head, it becomes an incarnation of evil, so it must be ritually burned toward the end of the ceremony. But these were like no masks I had ever seen. They stood only four inches high. Eight of them. Very old, very powerful.

No one ever knew Louís possessed the chapayekas. We were at my mother's home, when he gave me the masks. "You know," he said quietly, almost gently, "Dad was Yaqui." The room became extremely quiet. I looked out the window and watched the sun disappear behind brooding storm clouds; it was the middle of the monsoon season, and thunder-heads were rapidly gathering over the Santa Catalina Mountains. Such a simple sentence, "Dad was Yaqui," but for us the ordinary had never been simple. I thought of my father and his difficult battle with can-cer, and I was surprised that my brother would resurrect his memory as he gave me the chapayekas. Louís had always avoided talking about our ancestry. His was a silence born of solitude, sustained by a tentative autonomy. I understood his reluctance.

Miscegination. An unusual word, Latin in its roots. A word we had to contend with. It means "the interbreeding of what are presumed to be distinct human races, especially marriage or cohabitation between white and non-white persons," according to *The American Heritage Dictionary*. Until 1962, laws prohibiting Indians from marrying non-Indians ruled Arizona with an indelible grip, and we were caught in its vice like crazed coyotes who gnaw raw wounds to escape iron teeth. We were the forbidden and that fact dictated and dominated our actions. Disguise was our medium. Shame dogged our steps.

Yet it is curious that the idea of miscegenation rests upon a presumption which assumes distance and the necessity for maintaining hierarchy. It is an aggressive presumption, desperate in its desire to obtain purity and insure domination. Cultures clashed at the dingy fringes of fear, and laws were conceived to keep people at odds: Blacks were not allowed to marry Whites, Whites could not marry Indians, Indians could not marry Italians, and on it went in a grotesque kaleidoscope of legal strictures distorted by presumption. Levels of superiority bred by legislation, enforced by incarceration. Autonomy denied. To presume is to displace any questioning of the superior.

But doubts gather at the margins of rules regulated by privilege. To believe that one is inherently superior to another is to be guided by sharp fears, nurtured by delusions, fed by greed. By dissecting according to difference, purists clung to an illusion of preservation, unwittingly promoting deception and duplicity, creating dangerous zones. Marriage prevented by law created a bounded territory, a legally sanctioned space where arrogance thrived, and non-whites participated as aliens, subordinates identified, tagged, subdued, conquered, tamed.

However, there were those who sought to transform their oppression, and they learned to be at ease with the liminal. By necessity, they mastered the intricacies of illusion. Comfortable with chaos, they became artists of dissemblance. Not with malice, not confidence men, they became superb manipulators of fictions, constructing identities like puzzles made from pieces pierced by prejudice, their faces momentary mosaics rearranged in the silence of a second. They became incomparable performers in a macabre twentieth century masquerade for survival. Boundaries, legal or otherwise, were permeated carefully, cautiously, or suddenly. Contingency ruled. Metamorphosis was their essence, and narratives become surreptitious blueprints for continuance.

To exist as a family, we had to continually construct who we were. We learned how not to be ourselves. Around strangers, words were spoken carefully or not at all. Silence became a strategy for survival. But we had to comprehend its subtle complexity, recognize its disguises. We came to understand silence as a powerful rhetorical tool which cuts and gives shape to sound and meaning—not to confuse it with the inarticulate and illiterate, or the inchoate place of nonbeing, the silence of suppression, a void which lends itself to shame and insecurity. Rather, in the inscrutable solitude of silence, we learned that there is such a thing as the unspeakable, something we might call the silence of the sacred, which signals that this is an inappropriate time to speak. That some things ought not to be articulated, in fact, cannot be. We discovered that silence is the beat and pulse, the rhythm-keeper of the oral tradition, and storytellers who are not afraid of silence can tame the unknown. They are survivors.

But survival through storytelling is a protean process which shifts and changes, metamorphosizing as the voice of the teller responds to the dictates of time, the needs of the listeners, the contours of the landscape, and the fluctuating pressures and tension of the rhetorical situation. Stories eased our pain, kept us together, protected us from prejudice. It was easy for words to slip past hatreds, create momentary utopias, make tangible intangible histories, and beckon sturdy futures. In the labyrinth between silence and sanction, listening to the lines of a story, I came to understand the legacies of my heritage, its beauty and inconsolable solitude. Like renegades, we lived in the cracks between hierarchy and law, on the fringes of the familiar, and there my affiliation with the Pascua Yaqui Indians was affirmed.

At the turn of the century, the Yaqui were a people bound by secrecy and separation, held together by their sheer will to survive. Their history is marked by domination and conquest, rebellion and subterfuge. Yaquis recognize life as no easy existence, and they share an acute religious sense of the tragic as a metaphysic of conflict and renewal. Permeating Yaqui consciousness is a sense of loss and displacement. Yaquis say we live on *inim buin bwia*, this earth of weeping, this world of mourning, of suffering.

In the 1820s, Mexico's war for independence sparked rebellion in the Yaqui territory of southern Sonora where the sacred *Wohnaiki Pweplum*, *Los Ocho Pueblos*, or the Eight Sacred Towns, had been established in the *Batnaataka*, the timeless past of all origins, on the Yaqui River, which is about three hundred miles to the south of the Arizona-Sonora border.

Since at least 1533, Yaquis had fought decisively and victoriously for their homeland and had managed to attain a degree of autonomy from the Spaniards. When Spanish conquistador and slave trader Diego de Guzmán reached Yaqui territory, he was met by warriors who warned him not to travel farther. In the earth, they cut a sharp edge, marking their boundary. Guzmán defied their warning and stepped across. A fierce battle ensued, and the Spaniards were forced to withdraw. A Spanish soldier later reported that these "Indians showed the greatest fighting ability of any natives of New Spain." Not until 1540 when Coronado pushed beyond to "Cibola" did the frontier open to the Spaniards.

The Jesuit priests Andrés Pérez de Ribas and young Thomás Basilio entered Yaqui land in 1617 by invitation of the Yaqui people or Yoeme, as they called themselves. Almost 30,000 Yoeme met and molded Jesuit thought and practice, giving it a distinctly chameleon character.

Throughout Spain's domination, the Yaqui managed to maintain a strong collective identity and tight hold over their homeland, so the idea of an independent Indian nation inspired by Yaqui leader Juan Bandera in 1820 was enthusiastically received not only by the Yoeme but also by the Mayos, the Opata, and the Lower Pimas. Bandera, inspired by a vision of the Virgin of Guadalupe, effectively formed a strong Indian military organization, which held its own against Mexican forces and was very close to gaining independence when the Indian units were defeated in 1832. However, the Yaquis, determined and rebellious, continued sporadic fighting with the Mexicans for the next sixty years until the early 1890s, when they were soundly defeated.

By 1900, under the tyranny of Porfirio Díaz, the Mexican government instituted a policy of deportation and extermination which was ruthlessly carried out. Throughout Sonora, Yaquis were rounded up and sent as slaves to the henequen plantations of Yucatan and the sugar cane fields of Oaxaca. It was one of the darkest times in Yaqui history. The Eight Sacred Pueblos were abandoned as Mexican military occupation took control, and Yaquis again fled to the Bacatete Mountains to carry on a guerrilla warfare while others, pretending to be Mexicans, escaped to the north across the border.

In their flight, Yaqui identity, linked with their land and their language, began to splinter. Survival meant subterfuge. Freedom was attained in the perfection of masks. Yaqui names were masked by Spanish names. Displacement became a mask for endurement; to be displaced meant to be alive. The liminal became their center. Nowhere were they in command of anything they would have been willing to call their own. But the Yaqui, like chameleons, learned to shift with the land, whether it was surviving as guerrilla fighters in the sacred Bacatete Mountains, gandy dancing for the Southern Pacific Railroad, or dancing deer down at Pascua in Tucson, Arizona. They were tenacious survivors.

But by 1910, Yaqui numbers had been decimated; perhaps there were 15,000 yaquis in existence, but they were haunted by the fear of deportation, enslavement, and genocide. They became a people on the edge, living in the periphery and interstices of the dominant culture, where they were, at every turn, keenly aware of their marginality and vulnerability.

It was during this time of profound upheaval that my grandparents fled their rancheria in Altar, Sonora. They followed deer trails through thick chapparal, traveling under the protection of the night sky and the evanescent moonlight, guided by the patterns in the stars. Hiding in dense thickets and caves, they were hunted like prey. By listening to any unusual sound carried on the wind and to the sudden flight of frightened quail, they learned to track their enemy and discovered how to blend into the desert, becoming as obvious and invisible as mesquite trees and prickly pear cactus. The desert fed and sustained them, but food was not often abundant, and the path was arduous, the rigors deadly. But the wilderness was their sanctuary. Its tough terrain and unyielding summer sun, its sudden thunderstorms and poisonous creatures were their challenges and shields. As the fervent dust storms overtook them, it blinded their hunters, and the torrential downpours washed clear their trail, befuddling their trackers. Fransisco, my grandfather, used to contend that he would rather face the fair heart of a diamondback rattlesnake than the capricious cruelty of Díaz' cutthroats. Their stalkers were sadistic, mercenary men with a license to kill, but they had limited stamina for the treacherous terrain of the Sonoran desert.

My grandfather explained that an unusual and deadly, almost exquisite, intimacy existed between the hunted and the hunters. And he always maintained that he survived only because he treaded the way as a traditional Yaqui hunter, continually aware of this intimate bond. He said that no matter how terrified you were, you had to remain calm. Even if you had been caught and someone had a pistol to your temple, then it was ok to be frightened, but never could you panic. That was your sole advantage. You might be vanquished but you never surrendered. And he always laughed at the harsh irony and uncanny twists that made him the hunted.

When they reached the foothills of the Baboquivari Mountains, the palo verde and mesquite trees were in full bloom, covering the hills with a thick, green tapestry. They came upon a canyon who sides were steep but gently tapered into sandy terraces along an arroyo which flowed strongly from the heavy monsoon rains. The river ran swiftly, zigzagging through the canyon like a silver sidewinder. At one bend, a line of the river disappeared under a tremendous boulder only to reappear suddenly, creating a solid, steady beat like a sacred water drum. When he heard the sound, my grandfather searched the rocks for metates made by the ancient ones. He found them and knew that they had reached a sanctuary. They rested there, feeling safe for the first time since the beginning of their dangerous journey north. To keep their spirits high, they told stories about the old ones, the Surem, enchanted, powerful ancestors who lived in sacred mountains. Though they traveled surreptitiously, disguised as Mexicans, speaking Spanish, they carried carefully their songs and stories. Memory and voice bound together the past and present in a tenacious presence. Under the layers of deception, they held an internal core concealing tradition.

After a few days, they came upon Tohono O'odham hunters who were hunting for deer rather than Yaquis. Fransisco spoke O'odham fluently and learned about old friends who lived by San Xavier Mission. There, my grandparents found refuge and shelter. When they were strong again, Fransisco and his wife, Jesusita, with only one young son who survived the journey, walked the final miles to a small pueblo in Arizona, which in 1912 had just become a state.

For my grandmother, Jesusita, the journey north was a desperate flight from oblivion. Survival was never insured, only a tentative gamble governed as much by chance and luck as wit and fortitude. Forces that she could only construe as malevolent destroyed her homeland. Evil was too real for her, a palpable presence combated with constant prayers and offerings. "Evil," she insisted, "must be respected and resisted with a good heart, *tu'i hiapsimak*, no matter how hopeless the situation." Holding her rosary, Jesusita made the sign of the cross when she talked about their desperate journey north, shaking her head at the lunacy of the world.

Though she was very kind, there was a remoteness about her, as if she was wandering in the weight of her years, remembering something or someone who was far away or almost within reach, and her eyes moved with a vague sadness and a bewilderment, as if she couldn't quite believe all that she had seen. She always wore black and never stopped grieving, even her laughter was laced with sorrow. She was intimate with death, having seen too much of it in Mexico. "Death, my child, has many faces—as many as all the chapayekas that have ever been or ever will be. Like a chapayeka, death can be cruel and capricious, or a bumbling fool who tricks you into dying, who can even make you laugh at his treachery. Listen to death, child, and you will learn many secrets." On long hot afternoons, she would sit under the ramada by an ancient mesquite tree, sipping strong black coffee, "chatting," she said, "with death."

Not so long ago, child, there was a man who lived out at Pascua. His name was Miguel, like your father's. Well, Miguel had a problem, ay, did he have a problem! Miguel's poor wife had just given birth to their thirteenth son. Oh, can you imagine, thirteenth son! Well, he was a very good father, and he went all over the pueblo searching for a godfather for his son, but there was no one left. Miguel was very worried, so he went walking north toward the Santa Catalina Mountains, the mother mountains. He walked and worried, worried and walked, wondering who would be his new son's godfather. Suddenly, the sky darkened and a wind swept up, swirling in great circles. Miguel looked up, startled. Out of the whirlwind stepped a man who was very elegantly dressed, muy suave. He walked with a confidence and a fancy cane. "Hello, Miguel," said the mysterious stranger. "Do not worry, hombre, I will be your son's godfather." Well, you can imagine that Miguel was stunned. "H-How do you know my name? H-How do you know about my son? W-Who are you?" stammered Miguel, as he eyed the stranger. "Ah, well, Señor, I know many things, and I can help you," he replied. "But who are you?" insisted Miguel. "Oh," the stranger paused, "some call me the devil, but you know how people are." "Ay chingaso, vete!" swore Miguel, "out of here! You are for the rich." The devil disappeared in a swirl of wind. Miguel sighed and decided to turn east toward the Rincon Mountains. He walked slowly, pondering his fate. Again, the sky darkened with clouds and dust. Miguel looked up and spotted a man in the distance. He, too, was elegantly dressed, but moved silently as if his feet didn't touch the ground. "Dios mio, my god," mumbled Miguel as he prepared himself to meet this man. "Hello, Miguel," the man said solemnly, nodding his head. "Do not worry. I will be your son's godfather." "But who are you, Señor?" Miguel asked cautiously. "I am death," answered the dark stranger. "Ah, well, since you take from both the poor and the rich . . . ah, yes, you will be my son's godfather," said Miguel. "I will make your son a great healer, a curandero. The best in the territory. On his thirteenth birthday, I will come for him so that he can begin his training. Is that understood?" "Yes, of course, as you wish," replied Miguel. Death disappeared. Miguel turned for home. His heart was glad.

His little son grew into a fine young man. On his thirteenth birthday, his godfather, Death, appeared and took the boy in a swirl of wind off to the yo añia, the enchanted desert beneath the dawn. There, Death taught the boy, Miguelito, all about the different plants and herbs, explaining their benefits. Taking a special herb, he said, "Miguelito, use this plant with care. It has great power. When you enter the sickroom and I am at the head of the bed, then that person may be cured and you may give him the herb. No one else will be able to see me. If I am at the foot of the bed, then apply no medicine for that person must die. Do you understand? Do you agree to do as I ask?" said Death, his godfather. "Oh yes, godfather. I will do as you say," agreed the boy. So Death flew them back home. Miguelito became a great healer. He always knew who was to die and who was to live. Miguelito grew rich as well as famous.

One day a beautiful young woman came to see Miguelito. Her name was Socorro. Miguelito took one look at the beautiful woman and fell hopelessly in love. Of course, it happened that her father was very ill. Socorro begged the curandero to help her. Her father was a very rich man, and the healer was taken to a fine hacienda. There, the old man's servant directed Miguelito to the dying man's room. Before they entered the man said, "Señor, if you cure my patron, he will give you his daughter, Socorro, for your wife." Ah, Miguelito could barely breath he was so excited by this news. He entered the sick man's room, and where, my child, do you think his godfather was standing? Yes, that's right. At the foot of the bed. Miguelito paused only a moment. Thinking of Socorro, he looked at his godfather, and at the old man, then he quickly turned the bed around. His godfather said not a word, nothing, not a sound. Silently, he watched Miguelito give the old man the herb. "Well, what can he do to me? I am his godson, am I not," boasted Miguelito as he glanced up at his godfather, who remained silent.

Surely, in time, the old man recovered, and a big wedding was planned at the Cathedral. There was to be lots of food and drink, even Pascola dancers. Finally, the wedding took place. It was a grand affair. But just as the couple was leaving the church, Death appeared to his godson. Quietly, he grabbed Miguelito by the arm, whirling him away, back to the enchanted wilderness. This time, Death took him into a large cave. What a sight they saw! There were rows upon rows of candles. Each candle represented a person's life. Some candles were tall, burning brightly. Some were small, almost a puddle of wax, barely flickering. Others were only half-way burned down. Miguelito could hardly believe his eyes. "Oh, godfather," he begged, "please show me my candle." "Why certainly, godson." Death led the way through rows of burning candles, moving deep into the heart of the cave. Finally, they came upon a large candle, not even half-way burned down, its flame burning brightly. "Godson, here is your candle," said Death as he pointed to a beautiful, thick candle. Slowly, Death turned, looked at his godson, leaned over and blew out the candle.

Jesusita ended her story, yet I quickly protested, "But, grandmother, what about Socorro?" "Sometimes, child, death is a disciplinarian. The boy gave his word. That can never be changed," she answered sternly. "Oh," my voice was small. I felt hot with shame, but I wasn't sure why. Her words stayed with me. "Do you know what a *manda* is, child?" I nodded my head and she explained, "Never make a *manda*, a vow, unless you can fulfill it. If you fail, it will be terrible for you. If you love someone who is in trouble with all your heart, then you make a *manda*. That is the only way. If you have no love in your heart, your promise is no good. Your words are empty. You will be punished for it. Keep your words and your heart strong, child. That is the only way. Remember what we tell you, *'No hay mal que por bein no venga*, there is nothing so bad that something good doesn't come from it.' " Such was the conviction of my grandparents.

For them, it was a tenuous time ruled by chance and uncertainty. They lived in and around Tucson, following my grandfather as he traveled with the Southern Pacific Railroad as a blacksmith. They grieved as much for the land they lost as for friends and relatives who were deported or killed. It was a constant refrain, like a steady dull ache. When I was a child, talk of deportation still clung to the air, feeding their fears. "It was the work of evil," they'd simply say, quite pragmatically yet passionately. They lived on the edge of their memories, trying to survive.

They had no respect for English, refused to speak it. My father grew up fluent in Yaqui, Spanish, and O'odham or Papago as it was then called. The Chinese cook on the Southern Pacific taught him a little Chinese, so when I was a child, my father would change languages like they were hats, speaking Yaqui with his relatives, Spanish and O'odham with family friends, and Chinese with the little storekeeper on Meyer Street where he had learned to cut meat for a living. His family's desperate situation left him no opportunity to attend high school. Consequently, English eluded him. For years, he was tormented by a language that seemed inaccessible and incomprehensible. English was cold, hard, and foreign, unrelenting in rules that seemed to have no rhyme or reason, and I came to understand that men articulate and dynamic in Spanish or Yaqui appeared ignorant when they spoke in bits and pieces of broken English. I saw them scorned and mocked. Too many of my father's friends and relatives were shamed by their circumstances, confounded by a language that had no tolerance for Pascola stories, singing trees, or dancing deer.

By the early 1940s, when my parents married, the *Arizona Daily Star* characterized the Yaquis as "men without a country"; the director of alien registration emphasized this fact in his indictment of aliens, which appeared in the daily newspapers: "At least two classes of aliens must register who have no opportunity to become citizens, one, Chinese, and the other Yaqui Indians who are in this country as political refugees from Mexico. Many of the latter have lived in this country for years after fleeing from Mexico, and are actually a people without a country, no longer being citizens of Mexico, and unable to become citizens of the United States."

Undeniably, Yaquis were trapped in a legal limbo. However, those born in the United States did have rights to American citizenship, but, unfortunately, language and cultural barriers collided in confusion, and the Yoeme came to understand that *all* Yaquis were "men without a country." In this interminable frontier of indeterminacy, many Yaquis were cast by the community as Mexicans or Mexican Americans. Most spoke Spanish fluently, so when this mask was convenient or necessary, it was used. However, the danger was that the mask had the power to imprint itself so strongly that it took over, becoming permanent. Given the tenuous times, it was not only dangerous to be Yaqui but also a burden. The scorn and resentment they faced is best expressed by an Arizona state senator who declared his worry concerning Yaqui infiltration by exclaiming, "I have watched the Yaqui problem for a number of years with terror. . . . We have made efforts to send them back to their wild hill-life in Mexico, but without success." Against such odds, the Yaqui foothold in America seemed tentative, a precarious position that took almost forty more years to stabilize.

In the 1970s, with the sponsorship of Representative Morris Udall, Arizona Yaquis argued their case for identity as American Indians. Their efforts culminated on September 27, 1978, when they presented their case before the U.S. Senate Select Committee on Indian Affairs. Yaqui leader Anselmo Valencia successfully argued that Yaquis had lived on the land now called the United States long before international boundaries divided the continent; many people of the Pascua Yaqui community were born in the United States, and many Yaquis had served in different sections of the Armed Forces, risking their lives for the United States. Anselmo Valencia emphasized the traditions of his people: "The Yaquis are Indians in every sense of the word. We have our own language, our own culture, such as the Pascola dancing, the deer dancing, and the coyote dancing. These dances are Indian in origin. In the deer dance, we sing to honor the great mountains, the springs, the lakes. We sing of our father the Sun, and of creatures living and dead. We sing of trees and leaves and twigs. We sing of the birds in the sky and of the fish in the ocean. Our drummers play their music in their drums and flutes. All the songs sung and played are to the olden times—ancient Yaqui Indian stories. . . . The Catholic faith and the various governments under which the Yaquis have had to suffer have tried for centuries to undermine our 'Yaquiness,' but after 400 years they have not succeeded. We have retained our language, our culture, and our Indianness."

Consequently, in 1978, President Carter signed into law S. 1633, providing trust status for the Pascua Yaqui Indians of Arizona. After years of suffering, living in an oppressive limbo, the Pascua Yaqui Indians had gained legal recognition as American Indians. No longer were they "men without a country."

Through disintegration, war, and deprivation, the Yaquis have endured and continue to flourish. Even during the darkest times, Yaqui elders continued and sustained their traditions. It is in the telling and retelling of "ancient Yaqui Indian stories" that a collective identity is forged. It is a dynamic, protean process with smooth starts and abrupt endings, moments of victory and sure defeats. Yet sharing these collective narratives invites endurance. Theirs is an oral tradition filled with the tragedy of war and deportation, resistance and survival, of love and betrayal, evil, cruelty, faith and ceremony. Ancestors are evoked as their adventures are recounted. The eight sacred towns, *Ume Wohnaiki Pweplum*, are transported, through stories, from the Rio Yaqui in Sonora, Mexico, to the barrios and villages of southern Arizona, and a link is maintained between ancient origins and new beginnings. The history of the Yaqui is preserved, continued, and reinvented through stories.

The wind had disappeared. It was almost too quiet. A pair of red-tailed hawks glided slowly over the cliffs above Coyote Canyon where the sky was clearing. The thunderheads moved north toward Mica Mountain, their shadows falling unevenly along the land. In the deceptive light, the chapayeka masks looked unearthly, inscrutable. Clearly, they were not a legacy detailing luxury and ease. I headed out of the house, hiked up the canyon, thinking about chapayekas. As ambiguous creatures, they invoke extremes and contradictions. They move in the shadowy realm of ritual, between the mundane and the extraordinary where the inconceivable becomes possible.

When I was a child, the chapayekas terrified me. For forty days, beginning with lent, their configurement of evil reigned over the ordinary. They would torment all living creatures. To be caught by one seemed the epitome of terror. Nothing was concealed from their satire or scrutiny. Sacred foundations crumbled before their sardonic pantomines and burlesques. At times, their comic contortions helped us transcend the tragic.

As they grew in number over lent, their irreverent play slid into the sinister. Their evil would build until all seemed intolerable, hopeless, and then on the *looria*, the holy Saturday before Easter, they would storm the church at Old Pascua, the village where we celebrated our ceremonies.

When I was very young, I was part of the angel guard who opposed the chapayekas. I was an *angelita*, a little angel. For protection, Jesusita embroidered slender, fine crosses and intricate flowers, *sewam*, around the hem of my dress. White satin and silk. Before sunrise, on holy Saturday, as I got ready to face the chapayekas, my mother braided delicate white rosebuds through my hair, while Jesusita told us stories about Sea Hamut, a brave, young woman of wisdom and beauty, who lived in the enchanted wilderness beneath the dawn.

Everyone gathered out at Old Pascua. The deer and pascola dancers, all the angelitas, the coyote and matachin dancers. Together, we defended the church, throwing flowers, *sewam*, at the evil chapayekas, ending their reign of terror. It was like being in a maelstrom. Later the masks and their talking sticks, the swords and daggers, would be burned. Their demise was celebrated with a nightlong fiesta, a *panko*.

My reveries were interrupted by the muffled roar of thunder coming over the ridge. The storm clouds had circled back over the peak and were descending upon the canyon. I was sitting at the base of a dry, sheer waterfall in a slender crescent carved into the rock face by searing winds and cascading waters. It was no place to be in a summer thunderstorm. As I turned to go, I noticed a strange coloration in the boulders on the north face of the canyon wall a few yards away. I walked across the dry riverbed and looked over a slick rock jutting out of the cliff face. Stretched out long and lean was a diamondback rattlesnake, but she was like no rattler I had ever seen. Her back was a deep brown vermillion, the lines of her diamonds blood red. Her body looked beaded, and she moved easily over the outlines of the boulder, gracefully molding her body to its crevices. She glided over the rocks, fluid like red water. When she came upon the sand, she lifted the end of her tail. I could see the black and white stripes tapering into the grey of her rattle. If she noticed me, it didn't seem to bother her at all.

I felt vacuous, stunned into silence. There is some primal force that rattlesnakes beckon. They live intimately with the earth and sun, moving swiftly or dreaming deeply in conjunction with the turning seasons and shifting light. They remind us of ancient beginnings and ineluctable endings. Though bound to the earth, their fluidity and motion are precise and incredibly lovely. As creatures of transformation and purveyors of death, they elicit our deepest fears.

Like the chapayekas of my nightmares, snakes have always frightened me. My father and I often came upon diamondbacks on our journeys into the desert. I always panicked, especially when they coiled, hissing, tails rattling, a small explosion erupting suddenly on the desert floor. As I looked at the red diamondback, I remembered my father warning me, "Your fear will always haunt you, unless you learn to face the snake and the chapayekas with a steady heart. Chapayekas and rattlesnakes only appear evil because of your fears. On the *looria*, you must fight the chapayekas without ill will. You know, chapayekas perform all their despicable and destructive duties without malice. Many of the men— Mosco, Memo, Chato, and Milo—carry rosaries in their mouths under their masks. It is a physical burden and test of endurance to be a chapayeka. On the outside, they are evil. Inside, they are peerless men of virtue. Only those with the highest integrity can withstand and control the domination and sinister influence of the mask. It takes great courage to be a chapayeka or face the rattlesnake. The diamondback is the spirit guide into the enchanted realm, the *yo aña*. There, the wilderness and the snake will test you, challenging your heart, your faith, your fortitude. The only way to survive is to remain calm. No matter what you see, hear, or feel, stay calm. To panic is to fail, and you will either go insane or die in the wilderness; your spirit will roam aimlessly, lost in an endless, tedious enchantment. If you contain your fear, calmly face the diamondback and the wrath of the wilderness, you will be rewarded with a precious power, an exquisite art that will aid you throughout life. The snake will confront you in the desert or in your dreams, so you must stay calm whenever you see him—even in your dreams."

Dense clouds now hid the cliffs of the canyon. A steady mist covered the mountains in grey iridescence. The wind was a low moan among the boulders, and a treacherous green fog crept down the ridges, shrouding the foothills in a mantel of gloom, saguaros transformed into solitary, stoic sentinels. It took a great deal of courage for Louís to give me the chapayekas. For him, it was an act of defiance, even deliverance, and it brought a quiet peace between us. I had always listened to the stories, believed in them, participated in the ceremonies, while Louís, terrified, believed they would betray us. For him, disapproval and secrecy eliminated our dangerous lineage. For years, he refused the past, ignored it, buried memories. Solitude imprisoned him.

A simple act, a gift, eight old masks eased his isolation. Within worn hides and fraying colors was hidden our history. Whether we liked it or not, together we were inscribed in those masks. To acknowledge them was to defy years of ridicule, regret, and shame, to affirm, finally, a shared identity carved from devotion, disgrace and deceit, endurance and desert winds. Eight old masks, a simple act, a gift eased old animosities. Without guilt or recrimination, we embraced the most recondite recesses of our deceptions.

My father died before we heard that the Yaquis had finally been recognized as American Indians. During his life, he endured despair and displacement, survived the solitude of suppression, and gently, relentlessly challenged me not to lose my way in the labyrinth between silence and sanction. Calmly, I hiked out of Coyote Canyon, leaving my fear, the fog, and the diamondback behind. Perhaps the chapayekas are simply a legacy of love.*

*Warm thanks to my parents for teaching me the stories, and to Bob Pack for his continued encouragement and generosity of spirit.—M.T.

GAY TALESE

The Italian-American Voice: Where Is It?

In the winter of 1955 I began writing a novel about my father, describing his childhood in a highly superstitious post-Medieval mountain village in Southern Italy, a village that had been warped by earthquakes and the sadistic rule of foreign kings and that had been altered spiritually by the ministrations of a levitating 15th-century monk. Before the novel was half done, however, I decided to abandon it. I was concerned that a book focusing on my father's past would bring him unwanted attention and perhaps even ridicule from his American friends and neighbors in the conservative Anglo-Saxon community along the New Jersey shoreline, where, after thirty years of residence, he was accepted as an assimilated citizen of the United States.

The instinct to protect my father should come as no surprise to Italian-American writers of my generation. Not to protect the privacy of your family from the potential exploitation of your prose would have been considered unpardonable within our ethnic group, which was overwhelmingly of Southern Italian origin and which was still influenced, even a generation or two after our parents' or grandparents' arrival in America, by that Mediterranean region's ancient exhortations regarding prudence, family honor, and the safeguarding of secrets. A region that for 2,000 years had been conquered and reconquered by despots of every imaginable variety and vice is a region with an implicit history of caution and a people united in the fear of being found out.

Although the conquest of Southern Italy by Northern Italian forces in the 19th century unified the country for the first time since the fall of the Roman Empire, it parenthetically destroyed a once-autonomous Southern Kingdom centered in Naples and further undermined the latter's fragile economy—encouraging a massive turn-of-the-century departure of Southerners heading for America with new hopes and old fears. My grandparents were on those boats, along with the forebears of many future Americans who would fulfill the greatest of immigrant expectations and add to the front pages of newspapers such headline names as LaGuardia and DiMaggio, Sinatra, Iacocca, and Cuomo. And yet as an American-born youth growing up during World War II (a war in which two of my father's brothers fought in Mussolini's army against the invading Allies), and as a young writer in the postwar years coming to terms with my insecurities as an American. I began to sense broadly within my ethnicity, and narrowly within myself, lingering ties to the old fears of the turn-of-the-century boat people—a fear of being pulled down, or pulled back, by currents having nothing to do with the ocean and everything to do with the Italian peninsula from which I was socially estranged and linguistically ignorant. I began to see myself not as a hyphenated American but as a hybrid American, a maverick struggling to break loose from the huddled masses that I saw as an obstacle to my singular identity and freedom.

But how free could I be when I was caught between the gravitational pull of two worlds? How American can one feel when growing up in a home headed by a proud and assertive father who spoke English with an accent, who restricted our family record-player to Italian operas, and who, failing to get our town's Methodist school board to include Ovid and Dante in our classroom studies, nearly convinced me that I should retaliate by not reading the works of Shakespeare? "Italy was giving art to the world when those English were living in caves and painting their faces blue!" my furious and defensive father often declared to me during the war years. It was a time when most Americans saw Italians as ditch-diggers or gangsters or Fascists, and when my pubescent paranoia, augmented by my father's Anglophobia, persuaded me that Shakespeare was indeed partly to blame for the lowly status of Italians in America.

With anguish and confusion I left home in 1949 to attend the University of Alabama, which had accepted me after I had been rejected by the half-dozen Eastern colleges to which I had applied earlier. My entrance into Alabama should in no way demean an institution to which I remain grateful; rather let me suggest that as a Southern school not yet ready to admit blacks, but neither wanting its campuses overcrowded just with people whistling Dixie, it was most generous in welcoming out-of-state students that the Klan saw as borderline whites—students who were Italian or Jewish, Greek, Lebanese, or Syrian.

At Alabama, a literature faculty with exclusively Anglo-Saxon surnames assigned us to read writers with exclusively Anglo-Saxon surnames. For me this meant more Shakespeare and Marlowe, and also Donne, Pope and Fielding, Blake, Wordsworth and Tennyson, and countless others, as well as their literary cousins and offspring in New England. I read them all begrudgingly, critically, almost hating myself when I loved them (as I did Byron and Browning), while always reminding myself that they were not my literary ancestors and that they had nothing to do with my world—if indeed, as a fractional American, I had a world.

Unable to find contemporary novels by Italian-American authors in the university bookshop or the library, I was drawn to writers who were Irish-American or Jewish, my reading passion then being modern fiction. Among the Jewish writers my favorite was Irwin Shaw, whose smooth style I devoured as delectably as the chocolate candy bars that nourished my acne; among the Irish, it was John O'Hara, in whose outsider's voice I heard echoes of my own.

Although I sometimes thought of becoming a writer, and served on the staff of my college newspaper, I never tried out for the campus literary magazine, nor applied to Professor Hudson Strode's writing class; in fact I never felt compelled to write about anything in depth until, after college, while I was in the army and stationed in Germany, I went on furlough to my father's village in Italy. It was a furlough into the Middle Ages. It was there among crumbling Norman walls, and veiled women balancing clay pots on their heads, and bloody-kneed penitents crawling up rocky paths, and my kinfolk tilling the soil of the family farm with antique hoes, that I saw the opening chapter of a novel about my father's escape to America—an escape with feelings of desertion and guilt that I also believe accompanied his quest for a better life.

But when I began describing this in the book, together with my own boyhood conflicts with my father during World War II (my memories of him smashing my model airplanes of Allied bombers and fighters as the U.S. Air Force was raiding Southern Italy), I began to feel that I was violating the tradition of family confidentiality that was fundamental to my father—an assimilated man on the surface, but with interior ties to the ancient Southern Italian code of *omerta* (silence) that guided not only the Mafia but also their countrymen who had traveled with them to the New World. And so I, too, became protective of my past, and distanced myself from myself, eventually entering a profession that encouraged this—journalism, which would provide me with a career-cover for the better part of a decade.

Journalists specialize in revealing *other* people's lives and families, their achievements and shortcomings; and in this profession, from the late 1950s into the mid-'60s, I proved to be more than capable. But denied the emotional involvement that writers fully feel only when writing from the "inside," I identified strongly with the works of other writers— not the writers of current events, or history, or biography, or other categories of nonfiction or "realism" in which we journalists were the foot soldiers of fact-gathering—but rather with those seemingly uninhibited autobiographical novelists, short-story writers, and playwrights who, unlike myself, were not adverse to exposing themselves and their loved ones under the guise of "fiction."

Whether it was a protagonist on a Broadway stage that a Tennessee Williams or a Eugene O'Neill had clearly drawn from a family closet, or the alter ego in a novel by John Cheever or Philip Roth who drank or lusted his way through life, I was no less in awe of these writers' candor than of their literary talents. It was more than awe; it was an envy of their freedom, and an awareness as well that these and similar writers had gained wide public acclaim through the exploitation of intimacy. And, of course, I was conscious of the fact that, among the nation's most famous novelists and dramatists, there was a conspicuous absence of Americans with Italian surnames.

Why was this? How was it possible that of the estimated 20 million Americans with Italian roots—a group that among my generation produced such heralded Americans as the painter Frank Stella, the architect Robert Venturi, and hosts of film directors, educators, financiers, and scientists—that this group was so *under*-represented in the ranks of well-known creative American writers? Were there no Italian-American Arthur Millers and Saul Bellows, James Baldwins and Toni Morrisons, Mary McCarthys and Mary Gordons, writing about their ethnic experiences?

When seeking answers to such questions from my acquaintances in Italian-American cultural and academic circles, I often received lists of worthy plays and books by writers I was accused of ignoring. But my inquiry had less to do with literary worth than with why this presumed worth had not been nationally recognized with Pulitzer Prizes or at least commercial successes comparable to those achieved by Italian-Americans in the film business or record industry and other creative endeavors. The mass movement of Italians to America began more than a century ago, and thus their offspring certainly had adequate time since then to rise above whatever illiteracy prevailed in their homes and to develop writing skills and interesting dramas drawn from their backgrounds to emulate the great success, for example, of many Jewish-American novelists and playwrights (some of whom also came from marginally literate working class families), and the many renowned Black American writers who overcame even worse economic and social handicaps than other minority writers.

Would national recognition come only to those Italian-American writers who mocked their ethnic backgrounds in the manner of the old radio show *Life with Luigi*, or who presented it in a context conforming to the American media's most notorious stereotyping of Italian males—

as *mafiosi*? The best-known contemporary Italian-American novelist, Mario Puzo, owes his fame not to such fine but uncommercial novels as *A Fortunate Pilgrim* but rather to *The Godfather*; while at the same time there exists no widely recognized body of work in American literature that deals typically with the Italian-American experience. The critically acclaimed Don DeLillo has written ten novels—and not one about Italians. For a best-selling literary novel about representative Italian-American life it is necessary to go back more than a half-century and cite the success of *Christ in Concrete.*

It was written by Pietro di Donato, a grade school dropout who was born in 1911 in Hoboken, New Jersey, and became a bricklayer like his immigrant father. In 1937 he wrote a story for *Esquire* that recounted his father's death in a construction accident, and in 1939 he expanded it into his bestseller—a novel that also became the Book-of-the-Month Club's main selection over John Steinbeck's *The Grapes of Wrath*. But while Steinbeck's subsequent work continued to attract a large readership and win literary prizes, di Donato's later efforts failed to maintain his popularity in the American mainstream—a level unequaled by other Italian-Americans until Mario Puzo arrived in 1969 with *The Godfather*. Between the careers of these two men, however, there did emerge a prodigiously successful Italian-American mystery writer who in 1953 discarded his Italian surname and subsequently wrote several bestsellers under the names of "Ed McBain" and "Evan Hunter."

Born sixty-five years ago in Manhattan's Italian Harlem on the Upper East Side, and a graduate of Hunter College on the G.I. bill following his discharge from the Navy in 1946, the aspiring writer had grown weary of hearing his family name mispronounced after he had left the familiarity of his neighborhood. Ultimately, he also became convinced that his surname was detrimental to his acceptance as a writer with America's reading public. He concluded this while working in 1952 at a New York literary agency, from where he occasionally mailed out manuscripts to publishers that he himself had written under various pseudonymns. One day in 1953 he received a call from an editor eager to meet "Evan Hunter" and publish his novel. During the meeting, after the author had revealed his true identity and was relieved that this disclosure would not hinder the book's publication, he contemplated using his real name on the cover. But the editor discouraged him. "I know it's your book," the editor said, "but I can tell you this: 'Evan Hunter' is going to sell more tickets." That week the author went to court to initiate the process of changing his name legally to "Evan Hunter," which is the only name he would thereafter answer to.

I also failed to see my own name on the first freelance work I sold after coming to New York in the 1950s. The magazine company's editor-in-chief, who had an Anglo-Saxon name, rejected my byline and used instead the name "Hyman Goldberg." I learned of this only after the editor had mailed me an advance copy of the magazine, along with my promised fee and a note explaining that he had decided not to use my name because it struck him as too attention-getting, and also somehow inappropriate for the subject of the article, which was about twin actresses then appearing in a Broadway musical. I was baffled by his reasoning then, as I am to this day; and while my fury prevented me from ever again communicating with him, I have since remained anything but dismissive of those Italian-American writers and academics who become emotional while offering explanations, theories, and excuses concerning the limited number of Italian-American names on bookshelves.

"The book business is made up of editors and publishers whose backgrounds are mostly Anglo-Saxon and Jewish," said Fred L. Gardaphe, an Italian-American writer and professor of English at Columbia College in Chicago, who made no secret of his chagrin at having his anthology of Italian-American literature turned down three years ago by every main commercial publisher he sent it to, after which he placed it with a small academic press. "The acceptance or rejection of manuscripts is influenced by editors' personal tastes and commercial judgements," he continued "and with so few Italian-American editors in the mainstream, it's not surprising that there are so few widely circulated books on Italian themes—except, of course, those dealing with gangsters. There are not only few Italian-American editors, but just as few book columnists and critics. In the print media as a whole, at least half the well-known Italian bylines you see belong to reporters writing about organized crime. The Italians are so metaphorically linked to organized crime that even Mario Cuomo was identified in a Mafia context by Bill Clinton during the Presidential campaign. And what chance did Geraldine Ferraro have against the so-called 'ethics' charges in her Democratic race for the Senate?" he said. "My God, what chance did *Christopher Columbus* have this past year in not being smeared as a villain? And what chance could *my* anthology featuring Italian male writers have in this climate? But if I'd submitted an anthology on African-American writing, or Native-American writing, or Hispanic writing, or Ethnic Women's writing, or Lesbian or Gay men's writing, I'm confident I'd have found a commercial publisher. But we Italian-Americans as a whole get little support from the mainstream.

"There's no Affirmative Action to push Italian-Americans up the corporate ladder, or to get their kids into Harvard and Princeton. And the big news organizations and networks, which again are run by people who are mostly Anglo-Saxon and Jewish, aren't recruiting young Italian-

Americans as they're recruiting other minorities—most often to avoid bias charges. Turn on your local TV news at night, and what you mostly see are anchormen and women who are Black, Hispanic, and Oriental. While the anchors on the three major networks remain, of course, white Anglo-Saxon males."

If I am overindulgent in the space I have allotted to the views of Mr. Gardaphe, it is because in a freewheeling way he encapsulates the frustrations and rationalizations that I have heard piecemeal from several other Italian-American writers and teachers, although these sources sometimes concede that Italian-Americans themselves play a role in the situation they complain about. In an article published last year in *The South Atlantic Quarterly*, Anthony DeCurtis—a writer and editor who earned a Ph.D. in English literature, who once taught English in college, and who now works for *Rolling Stone*—characterized the Italian-Americans, generally speaking, as "too isolated, untrusting, and proud to make demands of the government," and at the same time "too unpolished and prole for the right wing" and "too independent and unfashionable for the left." Their "instinctive clannishness," Mr. DeCurtis suggested, has slowed their assimilation into the literary mainstream, although other factors were influential as well.

One factor mentioned by several people—including Mr. DeCurtis, whom I spoke to after reading his article—is the Italian-Americans' lack of zeal in educating themselves in areas that might further their opportunities in publishing. Too many Italian-Americans, they said, are nonreaders, and thus fail to form a book-buying market that publishers cater to. Even those Italian-Americans whose parents were born in the United States grew up most often in homes without books, or very few books; and those books available tended not to be ones that inspired a literary imagination, but instead were those of a practical nature, such as books on business, or cooking, or gardening or personal health. The popular classics in children's literature were rarely found in Italian-American homes. Few of the Italian-Americans I spoke with—including those who overcame the odds to become editors, English professors, and writers— had enjoyed a childhood familiarity with Winnie the Pooh.

The 41-year-old Mr. DeCurtis, reared in an Italian neighborhood in Greenwich Village, remembers his mother—"an affectionate woman with a sweet voice"—trying to read to him as a child; "but she'd hesitate, she was not a comfortable reader." Neither of his American-born parents had completed high school. And while scholarships would transport him from his neighborhood and help to qualify him for positions at campuses and in editorial offices, he said he remained conscious of the fact that, among a majority of his colleagues in both places, there existed "a climate of shared experiences that I'd never had." And such experiences, he believes, often originate in a pre-adolescent bonding with the wondrous figures described in children's books.

A similar sense of youthful exclusion was acknowledged by 44-year-old Jay Parini, a novelist, poet, and professor of English at Middlebury College in Vermont. Born and reared in a nonliterary home to American-born parents in a coal-mining region of Pennsylvania, Mr. Parini first became aware as a young college teacher that nearly all of his students had cultivated a fondness for books much earlier in life than he. And if Parini has compensated for this in subsequent years, he apprehends it perhaps in the passion with which he presents to his classes those literary classics that changed his life after discovering them as a teenager in his high school library—the novels of Dickens, the poetry of Frost, and the works of other masters that inspired his devotion to literature and learning. But such a devotion is unfortunately not typical of Italian-Americans, concedes Mr. Parini, who explained that during his teaching career—which began at Dartmouth, where he taught English literature for seven years before moving to Middlebury in 1982—he encountered very few Italian-American students who had elected to take advanced courses in literature.

This point was echoed by Frank Lentricchia, a 52-year-old writer and professor of English at Duke, and a onetime scholarship student from Utica, New York, who has also taught at Rice University in Houston and at the University of California campuses in Irvine and in Los Angeles. In pondering the scarcity of Italian-Americans registered in advanced literature courses, Mr. Lentricchia wonders if the brightest and most ambitious of the young Italo-Americans are not just too pragmatic to be lured by the uncertain or meager financial rewards that too often accompany careers as writers and teachers of literature. He pointed out that many of these students are products of an ethnic past not long removed from hard labor and a hunger for job security, and that their traditions also stress a personal responsibility for the well-being of their families and friends—a responsibility that their Italian-born ancestors learned from experience should not be entrusted to characteristically inefficient, if not corrupt, government bureaucrats. As a result these brighter students, he suggested, gravitated toward such careers as medicine and the law, where, in addition to making money, they might cater personally to the needs of those kinsmen who become their patients and clients. Or they might prefer business schools, from which they could emerge as entrepreneurs and provide their relatives and friends with employment. Or they might aspire to becoming Hollywood film directors, where, in addition to the glamour and possibility of becoming rich and at the same time being considered an "artist" (an unlikely prospect for a highly commercial writer), they might also hire family members and friends as extras.

In any case, Mr. Lentricchia went on, only wayward souls like Parini and DeCurtis and himself have ventured into careers for which their personal backgrounds seemingly provided so little foundation—those backgrounds being marked for the most part by growing up in homes without books.

Not only without books but without even *bookcases*, added Gerald Marzorati, a 39-year-old deputy editor at *Harper's* magazine, who recalls that in his Italian-American neighborhood in Paterson, New Jersey, he never saw bookshelves in his working-class home nor in the homes of his friends and classmates. Most of his male classmates regarded reading as "effeminate," Marzorati explained, and whenever a teacher read aloud from Shakespeare or another poet, Marzorati remembers trying to conceal his interest, not wanting to be perceived as different—more studious—than his macho contemporaries. Desiring to get ahead in class was, in a sense, leaving others behind, and therefore could be interpreted as a form of desertion and disloyalty.

Inspired by the revolutionary spirit of the Youth Movement that extended into the 1970s, Marzorati escaped the commonplace aspirations of the neighborhood and went on to college and a staff job on the *Soho News* before joining *Harper's*. But few of the neighborhood women pursued higher goals than the men, Marzorati came to realize, because both sexes were influenced by the neighborhood's prevailing old-fashioned Italian patriarchial system that (differing from the more matriarchal homes of Jewish and Black Americans) saw education and book-reading as a "threat" to the superiority of modestly educated fathers. It was a threat that I myself connect historically to an ancient proverb I once saw quoted in a sociological study of Italian peasant families: "Never Educate Your Children Beyond Yourself."

That proverb reflects the thinking of impoverished families struggling to survive in the feudal system of class-stratified Italy, a system that existed in the South well into the 19th century. It warns against exposing young family members to alienating ideas that might be communicated by teachers or by the written word—ideas that could undermine the solidarity of the family, which was the patriarch's main source of comfort and strength in a land controlled by foreign oppressors. When such families immigrated to the United States, the "foreign oppressors" often took the form of American school boards and teachers. There were numerous reported incidents in New York City and elsewhere in which immigrant parents fought to keep their children from attending school, thus presenting a dilemma of divided loyalty to those children who determinedly rose above their backgrounds. An educator named Leonard Covello lamented that the process toward assimilating into the American mainstream often began "by learning to be ashamed of our parents."

Still, there were countless parents who unselfishly assisted in the higher education of their children, doing so at times when the educators themselves advised against it. This was true in my family. After I had completed high school in the lower half of my class, the principal told my father I was intellectually unfit for advanced learning and refused to write letters of recommendation in my behalf to any college in New Jersey, New York, or Pennsylvania. When my father insisted on financing my entrance into the University of Alabama, being encouraged by an alumnus who was his customer and fellow Rotarian, the principal chided my father and assured him he was wasting his money.

My Brooklyn-born cousin, Nicholas Pileggi, who had earned top grades in grammar school, discovered on entering high school that based entirely on his surname he was separated from his friends who were enrolled in college-preparatory courses and was grouped instead with those students who would presumably enter the job market after graduation. His complaints, accompanied by those of his parents, rectified the situation; and after matriculating at Long Island University, and receiving a degree in English literature, he would become a journalist, an author of nonfiction books, and a screenwriter. With Martin Scorsese, Pileggi would write the screenplay of *Goodfellas* which was based on his book, *Wiseguy*: it would win an Academy Award nomination.

Martin Scorsese's own upbringing on the Lower East Side was more representative of the nonacademic home life shared by Marzorati, Parini, and DeCurtis; and in DeCurtis' interview with Scorsese in *The South Atlantic Quarterly* the director recalled that during his student days at New York University he had shocked his parents one day by walking into their home carrying a book! "There were discussions about whether or not I should bring the book into the house," Scorsese told DeCurtis. Scorsese's American-born parents, who worked in the garment center, had failed to complete grammar school. The only reading matter in their home was tabloid newspapers, and Scorsese said he grew up "cowed a little by the tyranny of art" and particularly "the tyranny of the word over the image."

It was perhaps natural, he suggested, that he would initially shy away from words and seek to express himself in pictures. In fact, the critic and academician Camille Paglia thinks of film as a truer, more traditional outlet for artistic Italian-Americans than books. She sees the great internationally known modern filmmakers like Scorsese and Francis Ford Coppola and others as kinsmen of the Renaissance artists who pleased the popes and ennobled the museums of the world. I could add reasons of my own to explain why the art of the written word has less appeal than film-making to Italian-Americans.

The writer's life is a solitary one, and I believe solitude is a most unnatural condition for the village-dwelling people that the Italians essentially are, and the crowd-pleasing performers they strive to become whenever the least bit of attention is paid to them. Whether their piazza is occupied by film crews offering them parts in movies, or invading armies offering them preferential treatment as collaborators, the ordinary Italian is adept at playing many roles, as indeed has been his entire country through its centuries of taking directions from many masters.

Such a history has made it wise to put nothing in writing of a personal nature, nothing that might expose one's family and friends to the scrutiny of authoritarian forces—be they foreign despots, domestic dictators, or the pious censors of the Holy See. The word is dangerous. It is traceable to a single source. And I also believe that these ancient concerns were transferred to America—we reluctant Italian-American writers are extending the reticence of our forebears, evading scrutiny as they had for centuries in the harsh extremities of their homeland that is justly renowned for its saints and sinners, its Holy Fathers and Godfathers, its unstable governments, its stable families, its arias, its silences, and its legacy of laying low.

West Point

O n the table at which I write is a small silver mug with a square handle; it is inscribed to *Eugene L. Vidal, Jr., October 3, 1925*—a gift from the West Point football team to its mascot, which that year was not a mule but me. I drank milk from the cup for a good many years and from the look of the rim did a bit of teething on it, too.

I have no early memory of West Point. Apparently I was born in the cadet hospital on a Saturday morning because my mother had decided to stay on the post and go to a football game. I was delivered not by an obstetrician but by one Major Howard Snyder who happened to be officer of the day at the cadet hospital. Later, as surgeon general of the army, he looked after President Eisenhower ("Just indigestion, Mamie," he was reported to have said when she rang him in the middle of the night with news of the Great Golfer's first tussle with the Reaper. "Give him some bicarbonate"). More than thirty years later I visited General Snyder at his office in the basement of the White House. He recalled my birth; was still angry at my mother for not having gone to a civilian hospital; was most protective of his old friend the President. "Tough South German peasant. There's nothing at all wrong with him, you know, except this really nasty temper. That's what'll kill him." Then the inevitable question, "Why didn't *you* go to the Point?" A member of a West Point family had chosen *not* to join the Long Gray Line. Something wrong there.

At the time of my birth Eugene L. Vidal, Sr., was known as Gene Vidal to the world of jocks—and to just about everybody else in the country for in those days college athletes were like rock stars (Scott Fitzgerald's apostrophe to Princeton's Hobe Baker is plainly tribute to a god). Class of 1918 at West Point, G.V. was an All-American quarterback; he is still regarded as the best all-around athlete in the history of the Academy, moving with equal ease from track to basketball to football to rugby (learned in one afternoon); a master of every sport except the one invented by Abner Doubleday (West Point 1842). "Baseball is the favorite American sport because it's so slow," G.V. used to say. "Any idiot can follow it. And just about any idiot can play it." After graduation, he came back to the Point as football coach; he was also the first instructor in aeronautics.

Shortly after I was born, G.V. resigned from the army (he found it boring) and went into civil aviation. But, as with most West Pointers of his generation, the links between him and the Academy proved to be unbreakable. Although his disposition was ironic, his style deflationary, his eye for the idiocies of the military sharp, he took some pride in being not only a part of the history of the Point but also a sort of icon for those graduates who came to prominence in the Second War.

The Eisenhowers, Groveses, Stratemeyers, Ridgways, and Taylors created the American world empire; they also gave us the peacetime draft, a garrison state, and the current military debacle in Southeast Asia. With the best will in the world (and with the blessing of their civilian masters to whom the cold war was good business), these paladins have in the quarter century since Hiroshima wasted lives and money while treating with contempt the institutions of the republic. Now the game is changing—the army, too. Currently the West Pointers are fighting for a permanent draft. Otherwise, they tell us, we will have an "unrepresentative" (i.e., black) military establishment. But these same officers never objected to the prewar army, which was redneck and every bit as dumb as the coming black army because nobody smart (black or white) is going to be an enlisted man in the American army if he can help it.

I was less than a year old when my parents moved into the Washington house of my mother's father, Senator T. P. Gore (where I was put to bed in a bureau drawer). Like a number of high-powered cadets Gene Vidal was hypergamous. Yet, as a boy growing up in Madison, South Dakota, he was not particularly ambitious, as far as one can tell—which is not much: he had no memory for the past, his own or that of the family. He was so vague, in fact, that he was not certain if his middle initial "L" stood for Louis, as he put on my birth certificate, or for Luther. It was Luther. At fourteen I settled the confusion by taking my grandfather's name Gore.

As it turned out, the congressman from South Dakota was ambitious enough for two. After watching G.V. play football at the University of South Dakota, the congressman said, "How would you like an appointment to West Point?" "And where," answered my father with his usual charm and inability to dissemble, "is West Point? And what is there?" He was promptly appointed; thus ended his dream of becoming a barber because barbers seemed to have a lot of free time. Apparently in a town like Madison there was no one very interesting to emulate. Certainly G.V.'s father Felix was no model. Felix had been an engineer on whatever railroad it is that goes through South Dakota; for reasons unknown, he got off at Madison one day and went into the coal business.

Felix's father had been born in Feldkirch, Austria, of Romanic stock (descendants of the Roman legionnaires who settled Rhaetia in the first century).* A hypergamous adventurer and phony MD, Eugen Fidel Vidal married Emma de Traxler Hartmann of Lucerne, Switzerland—an heiress until she married him and got herself disinherited. "A *real* countess," my aunt used to say with wonder. In 1848 the unhappy couple came to Wisconsin where the Gräfin was promptly deserted by her husband. She brought up five children by translating American news stories for German, French, and Italian newspapers. She had every reason to be bitter; and was bitter. I go into all this family history because it has a good deal to do with the kind of men who went to West Point in those days.

Athlete. Lapsed Roman Catholic. The meager prairie background, somewhat confused by a family tradition of exciting wars (the Traxlers and Hartmanns had been professional soldiers for several hundred years). Then West Point and the companionship of men like himself. In the class three years ahead of G.V. were Bradley and Eisenhower (Ike was known as the "Swedish Jew"—my father as "Tony the Wop"); while in the class of 1918 were Mark Clark, Leslie Groves, and Lucius Clay (who once persuaded me to write a speech for his friend President Eisenhower on the virtues—if any—of integration: the speech was not delivered). Among those my father taught was the grand architect of our empire's Syracusan adventure in Southeast Asia, the Alcibades of counterinsurgency, Maxwell Taylor.

These men had a good deal in common even before they were put into the pressure cooker on the Hudson. Most came from rural backgrounds; from lower-middle-class families; certainly they were not representative of the country's ruling class. In this century our nobles have not encouraged their sons to go to West Point. There were also no blacks at the Academy and few, if any, Jews or Roman Catholics. West Point was a very special sort of place.

According to K. Bruce Galloway and Robert Bowie Johnson, Jr. (*West Point: America's Power Fraternity*),[†] "The Military Academy offers an ideology, not an education, and because of this and the uniform, the graduates find themselves anointed with access to America's ruling

---

*A certain venerable vendor of American book-chat thought it preposterous that I should claim descent from the Romans. But the Romanic Vidals were originally called Vitalis and from Trieste north to Friuli to Vorarlberg, Roman monuments bear witness to our ubiquitousness.

†Simon and Schuster, 1973.

elite." The authors take a dark view of the Academy and its graduates, and they tend to see conspiracy where there is often only coincidence. For instance:

By 1933 President Roosevelt had created the position of Director of Aeronautics . . . and appointed Eugene L. Vidal (W.P. 1918) as first director. Vidal had to deal immediately with the controversy over the place of aviation in—where else?—military affairs. He survived that problem, only to be faced with the airmail scandals of 1933 and 1934. . . . In the years following, West Point control of civil aeronautics lapsed only temporarily.

Actually, it was civil not military aviation that pushed for my father's appointment, while the decision for the army to fly the mail was Roosevelt's. After a series of aerial disasters, Roosevelt turned to my father one evening and said, "Well, brother Vidal, *we* seemed to've made a mistake." Ever a good (if sardonic) soldier, G.V. took the rap for the President. "I liked that 'we' he used."

Galloway and Johnson would be more nearly right if they simply said that all West Pointers tend to look out for one another. In 1943 (aged seventeen) I enlisted as a private in the army and was assigned to a much publicized Training Program, which promptly collapsed. Aware that I was about to be shunted off to an infantry outfit that was soon to contribute a number of half-trained eighteen-year-olds to be butchered on the Rhine, I signaled to the nonexistent but very real West Point Protective Association. I was promptly transferred to the Air Force. I do not in the least regret this use of privilege and would do it again; but privilege comes from the Latin words meaning "private law," and even in a would-be canting democracy like ours there ought to be only public laws.

Duty, Honor, Country. That is the motto of West Point. It is curious that no one until recently seems to have made much of an ominous precedence that makes the nation the third loyalty of our military elite. Duty comes first. But duty to what? Galloway and Johnson are plain: the officer class. Or as a veteran instructor at the Point puts it, "In my system of values West Point comes first, the Army second, and the country comes third."

Honor. Galloway and Johnson are particularly interesting on the origins of West Point's honor system. The Academy's true founding father, Sylvanus Thayer, was a passionate admirer of Bonaparte; he also found good things in the Prussian system. Although the United States did not seem to have much need for an officer caste when he took charge of the Academy in 1817 (of course the British had burned down Washington a few years earlier but that sort of thing doesn't happen very often), Thayer set about creating a four-year hell for the young men sent to him from all over the country. They were kept constantly busy; treated like robots; given an honor system which, simply put, required them to spy on one another.

This sort of system is always diabolic and usually effective, particularly in an environment like West Point where, according to Colonel L.C. West of the Judge Advocate General Corps, "at a tender age, the West Point Cadet learns that military rules are sacred and in time readily accepts them as a substitute for integrity. As he progresses through his military career, the rules remain uppermost in his code of honor. In fact, his 'honor' is entwined with the rules and so long as he obeys the rules, whatever their content, or whatever manner of man or fool may have written them, his honor is sound." This explains the ease with which these self-regarding young men whose honor is, officially, not to lie, cheat, or steal (or go to the bars in Highland Falls) can with such ease cover up a massacre like My Lai or, like General Lavelle, falsify bombing reports, invent military victories in order to help one another get decorations and promotions—not to mention take bribes from those large corporations whose manufacture of expensive weaponry absorbs so much of the military budget.

Country. To the West Pointer loyalty to the United States comes after loyalty to the Academy and to himself. Over the years this lack of patriotism has not gone entirely unnoticed. In fact, ever since the Academy was founded there have been critics of Thayer's military elite and its separateness from the rest of the country. According to the third superintendent, Alden Partridge (W.P. 1806), the Academy was "monarchial, corrupt and corrupting . . . a palpable violation of the constitution and laws of the country, and its direct tendency to introduce and build up a privileged order of the very worst class—a military aristocracy—in the United States."

In 1830 Tennessee's show-biz congressman Davy Crockett introduced a bill to shut down the Academy, while in 1863 another bill in Congress also proposed abolition. Speaking for the later measure, the radical Republican Senator B. F. Wade of Ohio declared: "I do not believe that there can be found on the whole face of the earth . . . any institution that has turned out as many false, ungrateful men as have emanated from this institution."

For more than a century West Pointers have returned the compliment. They do not like civilians, while their contempt for politicians is as nearly perfect as their ignorance of the institutions of the country that they are required to serve—after duty, that is; after honor. Specifically, my father's generation—the empire-makers—disliked Jews, regarded blacks as low comedy relief, politicians as corrupt, Filipinos as sly . . . still fresh in everyone's memory was the slaughter by the American army of some three million Filipinos at the beginning of the century:

the largest experiment in genocide the world was to know until Hitler. The West Pointers regard only one another with true reverence.

The authors of *West Point* are particularly interesting when they discuss what goes on nowadays in the classrooms at the Academy. One of the authors graduated in 1965 and no doubt writes from personal experience. Since the teachers tend to be graduates, they often have no special knowledge of the subject they teach—nor do they need to have because each day's lesson is already prepared for them in "blocs." But then, according to General George A. Lincoln, the Academy's academic guru (and Nixon adviser): "West Point is an under-graduate scholarship school without many scholars or any great motivation for learning as far as a material proportion of each class is concerned." He seems rather pleased by this. Galloway and Johnson are not. They believe that the cadets are taught "the ability to think and reason without really being able to do so."

Boys who go to West Point today do so for a variety of reasons, none having much to do with learning. There is the romantic appeal of the Long Gray Line. There is the cozy appeal of a life in which all important decisions will be made by others. There is the attractive lure of retirement at an early age—not to mention translation to the upper echelons of those corporations which do business with the Pentagon. Simply by stepping on an escalator, the West Pointer can have the sense of duty done, of honor upheld, of country served—and self, too. It is an irresistible package. Yet an instructor at the Academy recently commented (anonymously), "The cadets at West Point are fifth rate." To which the answer must be: they are fifth-rate because that is what the system requires of them. Since they are not different from other American boys their age, their intellectual torpor is due to a system that requires loyalty and obedience above all else—two qualities that flourish most luxuriantly in the ignorant; most dangerously in the fanatic.

It is no surprise that the military elite was delighted by the anti-communist line of their civilian masters. The Truman-Acheson, Eisenhower-Dulles, Kennedy-Johnson-Rusk, Nixon-Kissinger war on commies at home and abroad was thrilling to the military. For one thing the ideals of socialism are anathema to them even though, paradoxically, the West Pointer is entirely cared for by the state from his birth in any army hospital (if he is born into a military family) to taps at government expense in a federal bone-yard. Yet the West Pointer takes this coddling as his due and does not believe that a steel worker, say, ought to enjoy privileges that belong rightfully to the military elite. Retired officers are particularly articulate on this point, and their passionate letters supporting the AMA's stand against socialized medicine are often as not written from government-paid private rooms at Walter Reed.

The cold war also meant vast military appropriations for weapons. One of the few American traditions (almost as venerable as the Warner Brothers Christmas layoff) is the secretary of defense's annual warning to Congress at budget time. Since his last request for money, the diabolical Reds are once again about to pass us—or have passed us—in atomic warheads, cutlery, missiles, saddles, disposable tissues. Distraught, Congress immediately responds to this threat with as many billions of dollars as the military feel they need to defend freedom and human dignity for all men everywhere regardless of color or creed—with the small proviso that important military installations and contracts be located in those areas whose representatives enjoy seniority in Congress.

In this fashion, more than a third of the nation's federal income has been spent for more than a generation in order that the congressmen who give the generals the money they ask for will then be re-elected with money given *them* by the corporations that were awarded federal money by generals who, when they retire, will go to work for those same corporations. Beautifully, both nation and self are served because the commies are rats, aren't they? Particularly the home-grown ones.

Just before the Second War, I listened several times to Air Force generals discuss with a humor that soon turned into obsession the ease with which the White House could be seized, the Congress sent home, and the nation kept out of the war that the Jew Franklin D. Rosenfeld was trying to start against Hitler. Although Hitler was a miserable joker (and probably a crypto-Jew), he was doing our work for us by killing commies. I do not think this sort of thinking is by any means dead today. I once asked Fletcher Knebel what gave him his idea for *Seven Days in May*, a lively and popular thriller about the possibility of a military coup in Washington. "Talking to Admiral Radford," he told me. "He scared me to death. I could just see the Joint Chiefs kicking Kennedy out."

The United States has now been a garrison state for thirty-two years. To justify all those billions of dollars spent, the military likes to have a small war going on somewhere in the world. Or as General Van Fleet (W.P. 1915) said with some satisfaction, "Korea has been a blessing. There has to be a Korea either here or some place in the world." And so these blessings continued to shower upon us until August 15. Has peace at last come to our restless empire? Well, several weeks ago the new secretary of defense warned Congress that the Soviet's iron fist is still powerful within that velvet glove. If this striking image does not get the money out of Congress, a military crisis in the Middle East, or a small war in Chile, say, ought to keep the money flowing in the right direction.

Galloway and Johnson are, I think, too hard on the individual shortcomings of the West Pointers. After all, if we didn't want them to be the way they are (militantly, anti-communist, anti-politician, anti-dissenter) they would be different. A class of this sort is made not born. I have known a good many West Pointers of the imperial generation and found them to be men of considerable virtue though none had, I should say, much sense of the civilian world. But then how could they? Their education was fifth-rate; their lives remote from everyday cares; their duty and honor directed not toward the republic but toward one another.

For a half century now West Pointers have been taught that communism is America's number one enemy without ever being told what communism is. Paradoxically, fascist-minded Americans tend to admire the communist societies once they actually visit them. The Nixons and the Agnews particularly delight in the absence of dissent; not to mention the finality of all social arrangements. Certainly the world of Mao (less some of his subtler thoughts) is nothing but the civilian world as West Point would like it to be. And if Mao is not an admirer of elites—well, neither (officially) were the founders of the American republic and just look what we have created! Anomalies are the stuff of political systems.

Certainly the West Pointers would approve the puritanism of the communist societies. Galloway and Johnson give a grim picture of the sexual deprivation of the cadets which, they maintain, makes for a lifetime of uneasy relations with women—not to mention "the entire company [that] once masturbated together in the showers." Life on the Hudson was even more austere in my father's day. But there were occasional mavericks. Although G.V. never much liked Eisenhower ("a sour cuss, always on the make"), he did give Ike credit for having managed, under the most perilous conditions, to lay the wife of the post dentist. Obviously *supreme* commanders are made early.

The military-industrial-West Point complex is more than a century old. One of the first functions of the Academy was to supply engineers to the nation. West Pointers built the first railroads as well as many roads and dams. Working as engineers for the early tycoons, West Pointers were brought into close contact with the business elite of the country and the result has been a long and happy marriage.

The military was also used to protect American business interests overseas. On at least one occasion the business interests tried to get the military to overthrow a president. In 1933 the Liberty League secretly approached Major General Smedley Butler and asked him to help them remove President Roosevelt. Butler turned them down flat. He also launched the most devastating attack ever made on American capitalism. Of his thirty-three years in the Marine Corps, he declared,

I spent most of my time being a high-class muscle-man for Big Business, for Wall Street, and for the Bankers. In short, I was a racketeer, a gangster for capitalism. . . . Like all members of the military profession, I never had an original thought until I left the service. . . . I helped make Mexico—and especially Tampico—safe for

American oil interests in 1914. I decided to make Haiti and Cuba a decent place for the National City Bank boys to collect revenues in. . . .

He also lists among his field of operations Nicaragua, the Dominican Republic, China (where the Marines protected Standard Oil's interests in 1927). Butler summed up, "Looking back on it, I feel that I might have given Al Capone a few hints. The best he could do was operate his racket in three districts. I operated on three continents."

Our military today operates on all five continents with results that no longer please anyone except those businesses that make weapons and pay for presidential elections. The final irony is that despite all the money we pour into our military establishment it probably could not win a war against anyone—except perhaps the American people. The disaster in Vietnam showed that the services could not fight a war in a primitive country against a "highly motivated" enemy. Naturally, the West Pointers blame this defeat on the commie-weirdo-fags (and/or politicians) who forced them in the President's elegant phrase, "to fight with one arm tied behind them." Whatever that meant: after all, the military were given a half-million American troops and more than 100 billion dollars to play with. Admittedly there were a few targets they were told not to bomb, like hospitals in Hanoi—or Peking or Moscow—but secretly president and generals bombed pretty much whatever they wanted to. Perhaps the generals felt betrayed because they could not use hydrogen bombs on the jungles and dikes of North Vietnam, or attack China. Yet even the blood-thirstiest of the Pentagon hawks did not want another go 'round with Chinese ground troops after the rout we suffered in Korea.

It should be noted that the American fighting man has been pretty lousy from the beginning of the republic, and more power to him. He has no desire to kill strangers or get hurt himself. He does not like to be told what to do. For him, there is neither duty nor honor; his country is his skin. This does not make for a world conqueror. In fact, according to a 1968 study of American performance in World War II and Korea, "the US side never won unless it had a 2-to-1 superiority of forces over the other side."* Shades of George Washington, who disliked taking on the British unless he was certain to outnumber them, preferably five to one. Even then, Washington's troops were usually beaten. Like the Italians, we Americans are killers for personal profit or revenge; the large-scale stuff doesn't really grip us.

Stuart H. Loory's *Defeated: Inside America's Military Machine* is an

*From "Ideology and Primary Group," a paper delivered by John Helmer to the annual meeting of the American Sociological Association on August 27, 1973. The material in this paper will be included in the *Deadly Simple Mechanics of Society*, to be published by the Seabury Press early next year.

analysis of the state of the armed forces today. If his report is true, let us hope that the Soviet military machine is in just as big a mess as ours. Loory begins with the usual but always staggering statistics. Between 1946 and 1972 five million citizens of a free republic were drafted into the "peacetime" [sic] armed forces. Year in, year out, 37 percent of the national budget goes to the military. Of all military expenditures by every nation in the world, the United States accounts for 27.6 percent. The army's PX system is America's third largest retailer. The Defense Department owns land equivalent in area to the state of Ohio. And so on.

But what are we getting in exchange for all this money spent? A fifth-rate "ticket punching" officer corps, according to Loory. Apparently no officer is allowed to stay in any job long enough to learn to do anything well. In order to be promoted, he must get his ticket punched: a brief time in the field, then to command school, to the Pentagon, etc. This moving about ("personnel turbulence" is the army's nice phrase) has resulted in what appears to be a near-total demoralization of the basic units of the army. Officers are shipped out just as they get to know the names of the men in their outfits while the problems of drugs and race occupy most of the time of the commanders, particularly in Europe. Even the nuclear forces of SAC, forever guarding the free world, are in disarray. Obviously the second law of thermodynamics is in operation, and irreversible.

Mr. Loory contrasts American troops in Germany unfavorably to the soldiers of the Bundwehr. Apparently American troops are assigned to broken-down barracks and constantly oppressed with that mindless chicken shit which so appeals to the traditional "West Point mind": if you have nothing to do, police the area. The Germans, on the other hand, have modern barracks, interesting training, a good deal of freedom, and of course a stronger currency. In a nice reversal of history, the Americans are now the Prussians—in a sloppy sort of way—while the Prussians behave as if the private soldier is actually an intelligent member of the same race as his officers.

In the wake of the defeat of the American military machine in Asia and the resulting shocks to our institutions at home, a good many questions are bound to be asked about what sort of a country we want. Fatigue and lack of resources have stopped the long march from the Atlantic to the borders of China. The West Point elite have not served us well even though they have never disguised the fact that we are number three on their list of priorities. Yet even when they try to work peacefully for the country, they are often a menace. The Army Corps of Engineers has made such an ecological mess of our rivers and lakes that Justice Douglas has termed them "public enemy number one."

Not unnaturally, the West Pointers are most successful at creating miniature West Points, particularly in Latin America (though Ethiopia and several other exotic countries have been seeded with Duty, Honor, Country academies). All around the world West Pointers are turning out military elites trained to fight not wars but those who would extend democracy at home. Galloway and Johnson have a particularly fascinating chapter on the links between West Pointers and their opposite numbers in Latin America, particularly with the dictator of Nicaragua, Tachito Somoza (W.P. 1946).

Galloway and Johnson favor placing the Academy's four regiments in four different cities, making them closer to the grass roots of, say, Harlem or of San Francisco. They feel that this would in some way acquaint the cadet corps with their third loyalty. I doubt it. I agree with Davy Crockett and Senator Wade: an aristocratic military elite is deeply contrary to the idea of this republic and its constitution. Since the next great war will be fought by computers and by highly trained technicians, we have no need of a peacetime army of two million or even of two hundred thousand. Certainly a large army controlled by the West Point elite will continue, as it has done for nearly a quarter century, to squander money and create wars.

Forgetting the morality of a republic trying to be an empire, we now lack the material resources to carry on in the old way (LBJ ran out of bombs one afternoon downstairs in his war room; later, Nixon was to run out of kerosene for his bombers). What money we have would be better used for internal improvements, in Henry Clay's phrase. After all, the two most successful nations in the world today are Japan and Germany—and neither has much of a military establishment. This simple lesson ought to be plain to America's capitalists; yet many of our magnates are as bemused by military grandeur as any plebe, misty-eyed at the thought of the Long Gray Line and by the resonant self-aggrandizing horseshit the late Douglas MacArthur used so successfully to peddle.

Self-delusion is a constant in human affairs. Certainly without self-delusion on the grandest scale we could never have got into our present situation; and West Point has certainly made its contribution. But reality has never been West Point's bag. According to George A. Custer (W.P. 1861), "The Army is the Indian's best friend." While according to West Point's current version of what happened in Vietnam, "The War . . . ended in August of 1968 when sorely battered Communist troops were unable to engage the allied war machine." With historians like that who needs generals?

There is also mounting evidence that today's soldier will not endure much longer West Point's traditional oppression. John Helmer's thesis in "Ideology and Primary Group" makes this pretty plain. According to Helmer, the division between the West Point officer class and today's working-class soldier is now almost unbridgeable. Since middle-class men were able to stay out of the worst of the Vietnam war, the working class provided the combat troops. They quickly got the point that "in the search and destroy tactics most commonly used [the infantryman] was, strictly speaking, the bait to catch the enemy. According to the plan he was intended to be a target, a sitting duck for the other side to attack at its ultimate cost."

The same cynical use of men is at work in Europe, where working-class American troops are, if not exactly bait, political hostages to ensure a "proper" American response in case of a Soviet strike. These men don't have to be good soldiers; they don't have to be anything but on the spot. It does not take great prescience, however, to know that should a Soviet army ever occupy Paris, the United States would abandon its own troops as swiftly as it would its allies. The American empire is not about to lose a single of its cities to save all Europe—much less three hundred thousand fuck-ups (in the eyes of the West Point elite) with their drugs, their brawling, their fragging of officers whom they regard as an alien and hostile class.

Today the first order of business in the United States is the dismantling of the military machine. Obviously, we must continue to make it disagreeable for anyone who might decide to attack us (this could be done of course by not provoking other nations but that is too much to ask). Nevertheless the military budget must be cut by two thirds; and the service academies phased out.

What to do with the officer corps? That is a delicate point. West Pointers are now more and more into politics and, as always, they are on the side of reaction. Their web of connections with the military academies they have created in Latin America, Asia, and Africa makes them truly international. Also their creations may give them dangerous ideas. It is not inconceivable that a coup of the sort that General Butler refused to lead might one day prove attractive to a group of the Honor, Duty, Country boys. Let us hope that Richard Nixon never asks General Haig (W.P. 1947) to send home Congress and Supreme Court so that the sovereign might get on with the country's true business, which is the making of armaments and small wars. Finding suitable employment for our officer caste will be, as they say, a challenge.

I look guiltily at the silver cup, and think of the generals who gave it to me. On a bright day in May four years ago I stood beside my uncle, General F. L. Vidal (W.P. 1933), at the edge of an Air Force runway near Washington, D.C. Awkwardly, my uncle held what looked to be a shoebox. "It's *heavy*," he muttered in my ear. I shuddered. Like the contents of the box (my father's ashes), I am a lifelong thanatophobe. Behind us stood a dozen of G.V.'s classmates. Among them the solemn, pompous, haggard Leslie Groves—himself to die a few months later; and that handsome figure of the right wing, General Wedemeyer.

After the helicopter departed on its mission, the old generals of the empire commiserated with one another. The icon of their generation, the lovely athlete of a half century before, was now entirely gone, ashes settling upon the Virgina countryside. The generals looked dazed; not so much with grief as with a sense of hurt at what time does to men, and to their particular innocence. Although I have always found poignant (yes, even honorable) the loyalty of West Pointers to one another, I could not help thinking as I walked away from them for the last time that the harm they have done to this republic and to the world elsewhere far outweighs their personal excellence, their duty, their honor. But then the country that they never understood was always last in their affections and so the first of their loyalties to be betrayed.

White Pelicans

lake level: 4209.90'

The Refuge is subdued, unusually quiet. The spring frenzy of court-ship and nesting is absent, because there is little food and habitat avail-able. Although the species count remains about the same, individual numbers are down. Way down. This afternoon, I watched a white-faced ibis nest float alongside a drowned cottonwood tree. Three eggs had been abandoned. I did not see the adults.

A colony-nesting bird survey has been initiated this spring by the Utah Division of Wildlife Resources to monitor changes in population and habitat use of selected species affected by the rising Great Salt Lake. The historical nesting grounds on the islands of Great Salt Lake are gone, with the exception of a California gull colony on Antelope Island and the white pelicans on Gunnison. This means colony nesters are now dependent upon the vegetation surrounding the lake for their livelihood.

Great blue herons, snowy egrets, cattle egrets, and double-crested cormorants use trees, tall shrubs, or man-made structures for nesting.

Franklin gulls, black-crowned night herons, and white-faced ibises nest in emergent vegetation such as bulrushes and cattails.

American avocets, black-necked stilts, and other shorebirds are ground nesters who usually scrape together a few sticks around clumps of low-lying vegetation such as salt grass and pickleweed.

Don Paul, waterfowl biologist for the Division of Wildlife Resources, anticipates that the white-faced ibis and Franklin gull populations will be the hardest hit by the flood.

"Look around and tell me how many stands of bulrush you see?" He waves his hand over the Refuge. "It's gone, and I suspect, so are they. We should have our data compiled by the end of the summer."

I turn around three hundred and sixty degrees: water as far as I can see. The echo of Lake Bonneville lapping against the mountains returns. The birds of Bear River have been displaced; so have I.

Nothing is familiar to me any more. I just returned home from the hospital, having had a small cyst removed from my right breast. Second time. It was benign. But I suffered the uncertainty of not knowing for days. My scars portend my lineage. I look at Mother and I see myself. Is cancer my path, too?

As a child, I was aware that my grandmother, Lettie, had only one breast. It was not a shocking sight. It was her body. She loved to soak in steaming, hot baths, and I would sit beside the tub and read her my favorite fairy tales.

"One more," she would say, completely relaxed. "You read so well."

What I remember is my grandmother's beauty—her moist, translucent skin, the way her body responded to the slow squeeze of her sponge, which sent hot water trickling over her shoulders. And I loved how she smelled like lavender.

Seeing Mother's scar did not surprise me either. It was not radical like her mother's. Her skin was stretched smooth and taut across her chest, with the muscles intact.

"It is an inconvenience," Mother said. "That's all."

When I look in the mirror and Brooke stands behind me and kisses my neck, I whisper in his ear, "Hold my breasts."

Hundreds of white pelicans stand shoulder to shoulder on an asphalt spit that eventually disappears into Great Salt Lake. They do not look displaced as they engage in head-bobbing, bill-snapping, and panting; their large, orange gular sacs fanning back and forth act as a cooling device. Some preen. Some pump their wings. Others stand, take a few steps forward, tip their bodies down, and then slide into the water, popping up like corks. Their immaculate white forms with carrotlike bills render them surreal in a desert landscape.

Home to the American white pelicans of Great Salt Lake is Gunnison Island, one hundred sixty-four acres of bare-boned terrain. Located in the northwest arm of the lake, it is nearly one mile long and a halfmile wide, rising approximately two hundred seventy-eight feet above the water.

So far, the flooding of Great Salt Lake has favored pelicans. The railroad trestle connecting the southern tip of the Promontory peninsula with the eastern shore of the lake slowed the rate of salt water intrusion into Bear River Bay. The high levels of stream inflow help to keep much of Bear River Bay fresh, so fish populations are flourishing. So are the pelicans.

Like the California gulls, the pelicans of Gunnison Island must make daily pilgrimages to freshwater sites to forage on carp or chub. Many pelican colonies fly by day and forage by night, to take advantage of desert thermals. The isolation of Gunnison Island offers protection to young pelicans, because there are no predators aside from heat and relentless gulls. Bear River Bay remains their only feeding site on Great Salt Lake.

So are their social skills. White pelicans are gregarious. What one does, they all do. Take fishing for example: four, five, six, as many as a dozen or more forage as a group, forming a circle to corrall and then to herd fish, almost like a cattle drive, toward shallower water where they can more efficiently scoop them up in their pouches.

Cooperative fishing has advantages. It concentrates their food source, conserves their energy, and yields results: the pelicans eat. They return to Gunnison Island with fish in their bellies (not in their pouches) and invite their young to reach deep inside their throats as they regurgitate morsels of fish.

It's not a bad model, cooperation in the name of community. Brigham Young tried it. He called it the United Order.

The United Order was a heavenly scheme for a totally self-sufficient society based on the framework of the Mormon Church. It was a seed of socialism planted by a conservative people. So committed was this "American Moses" to the local production of every needful thing that he even initiated a silkworm industry to wean the Saints from their dependence on the Orient for fine cloth.

Brigham Young, the pragmatist, received his inspiration for the United Order not so much from God as from Lorenzo Snow, a Mormon apostle, who in 1864 established a mercantile cooperative in the northern Utah community named after the prophet. Brigham City became the model of people working on behalf of one another.

The town, situated on Box Elder Creek at the base of the Wasatch Mountains, sixty miles north of Salt Lake City, was founded in 1851. It consisted of some six families until 1854, when Lorenzo Snow moved to Brigham City with fifty additional families. He had been called by Brother Brigham to settle there and preside over the Latter-day Saints in that region.

The families that settled Brigham City were carefully chosen by the church leadership. Members included a schoolteacher, a mason, carpenter, blacksmith, shoemaker, and other skilled craftsmen and tradesmen who would ensure the economic and social vitality of the community.

Lorenzo Snow was creating a community based on an ecological model: cooperation among individuals within a set of defined interactions. Each person was operating within their own "ecological niche," strengthening and sustaining the overall structure or "ecosystem."

Apostle Snow, with a population of almost sixteen hundred inhabitants to provide for, organized a cooperative general store. Mormon historian Leonard J. Arrington explains, "It was his intention to use this mercantile cooperative as the basis for the organization of the entire economic life of the community and the development of the industries needed to make the community self-sufficient."

A tannery, a dairy, a woolen factory, sheep herds, and hogs were added to the Brigham City Cooperative. Other enterprises included a tin shop, rope factory, cooperage, greenhouse and nursery, brush factory, and a wagon and carriage repair shop. An education department supervised the school and seminary.

The community even made provisions for transients, declaring a "tramp department" which enlisted their labor for chopping wood in exchange for a good meal.

After the Brigham City Cooperative was incorporated into Brigham Young's United Order, members were told,

If brethren should be so unfortunate as to have any of their property destroyed by fire, or otherwise, the United Order will rebuild or replace such property for them. When these brethren, or any other members of the United Order die, the directors become the guardians of the family, caring for the interests and inheritances of the deceased for the benefit and maintenance of the wives and children, and when the sons are married, giving them a house and stewardship, as the father would have done for them. Like care will be taken of their interests if they are sent on missions or taken sick.

By 1874, the entire economic life of this community of four hundred families was owned and directed by the cooperative association. There was no other store in town. Fifteen departments (later to expand to forty) produced the goods and services needed by the community; each household obtained its food, clothing, furniture, and other necessities from these sources.

In 1877, the secretary of the association filed the total capital stock as $191,000 held among 585 shareholders. The total income paid by the various departments to some 340 employees was in excess of $260,000.

Brigham Young's ideal society where "all members would be tending to their own specialty" appeared to be in full bloom. The Brigham City Cooperative even caught the eye of British social reformer Brontier O'Brien. He noted that the Mormons had "created a soul under the ribs of death." Edward Bellamy spent a week in Brigham City researching Looking Backward, a Utopian novel prophesying a new social and economic order.

Home industry was proving to be solid economics.

But signs of inevitable decay began to show. A descendant of a Brigham City man told Arrington that his grandfather formed a partnership with another prominent Brigham City citizen in the late 1860s.

Their haberdashery was the only place in town where material other than homespun could be purchased. When they succeeded beyond their dreams, they were asked to join the association. They declined, and townfolk were immediately instructed not to trade with them. When some of the community persisted in trading with these men, despite orders from Church officials, members of the Church were placed at the door of the shop to record the names of all persons who did business inside, even though the men in partnership were Mormons in good standing. As a result of this tactic, the business soon failed and the men were forced to set up shop elsewhere.

The ecological model of the Brigham City Cooperative began to crumble. They were forgetting one critical component: diversity.

The United Order of Minutes, taken on July 20, 1880, states, "It was moved and carried unanimously that the council disapprove, discountenance, and disfellowship all persons who would start an opposition store or who would assist to erect a building for that purpose."

History has shown us that exclusivity in the name of empire building eventually fails. Fear of discord undermines creativity. And creativity lies at the heart of adaptive evolution.

Lorenzo Snow's fears that the Brigham City Cooperative would not adapt and respond quickly enough to the needs of a growing population materialized. Fire, debt, taxes, and fines befell the Order. In 1885, Apostle Snow was indicted on a charge of unlawful cohabitation (polygamy). He served eleven months in the Utah State Penitentiary before his conviction was set aside by the United States Supreme Court. Finally, as a result of the 1890s depression, the cooperative store went bankrupt. By 1896, all that remained of Brigham City's hive of industry was the unused honey stored on the shelves of the new general store.

Fifteen years of United Order graced Brigham City, Utah. A model for community cooperation? In part. But there is an organic difference between a system of self-sufficiency and a self-sustaining system. One precludes diversity, the other necessitates it. Brigham Young's United Order wanted to be independent from the outside world. The Infinite Order of Pelicans suggests there is no such thing.

"Can you count?" Don Paul asks me one morning at the Ogden airport.

"1, 2, 3 . . ." I joke.

"Get in, you'll do fine."

We board *Skywagon II* for Gunnison Island for the Division of Wildlife Resources annual count of breeding pelicans.

We are cleared and begin taxiing down the runway. In a few seconds we are airborne, flying over farmlands. The checkerboards of crops, so familiar to rural communities, become submerged and suddenly we are flying over water. To see how much Great Salt Lake dominates the landscape from the air is to adopt a radical respect for its geography.

"I had no idea . . ." I mused.

"Nobody does," answers Don. "Except for the birds."

Images of the Utah poet Alfred Lambourne come to mind as we look out over his "inland sea."

In outline the sea is peculiar, resembling somewhat a human hand. The fingers are pressed together and point north, northwest. The stretch of water forming the thumb is known as Bear River Bay, and the dividing mountains between thumb and fingers is Promontory Range. In the palm of the hand are four large islands— Stansbury, Antelope, Carrington, and Fremont. Three which are smaller lie away to the north—Strong's Knob, Gunnison, and Dolphin.

While Lorenzo Snow was maintaining the United Order, Lambourne was living out his own order of solitude on Gunnison Island. Lambourne inhabited the island for one year in 1895, with the hope of homesteading seventy-five acres. But his application was denied, the rationale being that the island was more suitable for mineral interests than agriculture. Given the Mormon Church's religious doctrine against the drinking of alcohol, his carefully tended vineyard did not do much to bolster his request for residency.

I can see the flooded offices of the Bear River Migratory Bird Refuge on my right. Herons and cormorants are nesting on the roofs. Fremont Island, on our left, looks like a piece of worked flint.

"No colony nesters down there," says Paul. "No native grasses. No nothing. Only Welsh ponies and sheep. That island has been beaten to death. It's privately owned now. Kit Carson painted a cross on one of those rock outcrops, but darned if I can find it. I've tried."

The pilot, Val, banks the plane to the left. Three more islands come into view.

"There's Stansbury, Carrington, and the tiny island beyond is Hat, formerly known as Bird Island. It used to be covered with nesting pelicans, herons, gulls, terns, and cormorants. As you can see now, it's almost underwater."

Below us, rust ribbons of brine oscillate with the currents. Gulls, grebes, and phalaropes feed along the shrimp lines.

"There's practically no brine left in the south arm," Paul says. "As a result, most of the phalaropes and grebes have moved up here."

"Up ahead, Gunnison Island," the pilot reports. Lambourne's description is accurate:

It is a rock, a rising of the partially submerged Desert Range of mountains, a summit of black limestone with longitudinal traversements of coarse conglomerates.

The plane circles the island rounding the west shore. The pilot banks hard to the right so Don Paul can get a solid counting. He begins charting the nesting pelicans. The island is beaded with them.

"Most of these birds are young," he explains. "The adults are feeding at Bear River Bay. I saw them feeding as we flew over."

We circle the island once again, while he continues counting, marking dots on his map of Gunnison.

"The colonies look like they're all synchros."

"Synchros?" I ask.

The plane crosses over to the east shore, which appears rockier. I see no pelicans nesting on this side.

"The reproductive activities of pelicans within a specific colony are highly synchronized. Egg-laying, hatching, and fledging of chicks in any given colony usually occurs within a five- to nine-day period."

We swing around the west shore of the island. He asks Val to bank right again and fly as low as he can.

"But the interesting part of this environmental story is that the reproductive activities of the pelican population on Gunnison Island as a whole is asynchronous. The reproductive-cycle stages between colonies may differ by as much as four to eight weeks."

"What's the advantage?" I ask.

"Scientists hypothesize that coloniality increases an individual's chance of successfully finding food, either by an exchange of information within a colony about where food is particularly abundant, or by enabling pelicans to form groups, leaving the island in flocks so they can take advantage of the thermals. Then, when they find their foraging grounds, they will fish cooperatively."

"Colonial economics," Don Paul continues, "would not be advantageous if every colony was on the same breeding and feeding schedule. The competition for food would not only diminish the resource but also result in pelican mortality. Whereas, a month later, it's a different ballgame: there's plenty of food to go around. The staggering of intercolony development on Gunnison Island makes good ecological sense."

"We'll catch them one more time," says Val. "There's the triangulation post set up by Stansbury in 1850."

I can see three sticks on top of one of the peaks. I try to locate Lambourne's cabin but can only find the guano miner's shack. As we circle the island for the last time, I recognize the northern cliffs, which Lambourne describes as "a couchant lion. His massive head turned eastward, his monstrous paws rest on the lower shelves."

Not much has changed.

"That's it . . ." says Paul as *Skywagon II* levels and straightens for home.

"And the count?" I ask.

Don Paul looks over his papers. "Ten thousand breeding adults."

Water. Rock. Bird. I don't know if Brigham Young ever ventured to Gunnison Island or observed the finely tuned society of pelicans. But had his attention been focused more on Earth than "heaven on earth" his vision for managing the Saints in the Great Basin might have been altered.

Today, a Woman Went Mad
in the Supermarket

E ven now, saying it aloud or, later, repeating that sentence to my husband, I will see that it is meant to amuse, to attract interest, to get attention. Of course, I am too sophisticated in things psychological (isn't everyone today?) to think that one goes mad at a moment's notice. There are insipid beginnings to a nervous breakdown. There is lonely crying in the bathroom, balanced on the edge of the tub, and in the kitchen, weeping into the dishwater, tears breaking the surface of the suds. There is forgetting, or wishing to forget, the names of the children, the way to the local bank, the reason for getting up in the morning. There is loss of vanity—toenails growing long and dirty into prehensile claws, hair uncombed, eyebrows unplucked. Yet, somehow there seems to me something very right about going mad in a supermarket: painted oranges, threatening to burst at the navel; formations of cans, armored with labels and prices and weights; cuts of meat, aggressively bloody; and crafty peaches and apples, showing only their glowing perfect faces, hiding the rot and soft spots on their undersides.

Nevertheless, this woman did not go trundling her cart through the ordered chaos. She stood transfixed, as if caught in some great thought. She was blocking the aisle.

"Excuse me," I said tentatively, hesitant and self-protective as only a woman expecting her first child can be. "Pardon me, could I just get through?"

She turned slowly, and the two small children clinging to her skirt held on and tightened the cloth across her hips. Perhaps for the glory of the retelling, I might say that she was a great beauty, that her beauty was marred (or enhanced) only by her wild expression. In truth, she was pretty in a common sort of way, with conventional hair and eyes and nose. Only what she said then stopped me from clearing my throat and asking again if she would move and let me through.

She gripped the handle of her empty cart and said, "There is no end to it." It was said so simply and undramatically, but with great honest conviction, that for a moment I thought she was referring to the aisle of the supermarket. Perhaps it was blocked ahead of us, and she could not move up farther. But then she said, "I have tried and I have tried, and there is no end to it. Ask Harold. Ask anybody, ask my mother."

"Do you feel all right?" I asked. "Can I help you?"

Her knuckles were white and hard as she clung to the cart. She did not answer.

I looked around me self-consciously, and then I leaned toward her and said, "Would you like to go home?"

"You know," she said severely, "that I can't go *there*."

Then a woman rattled her cart toward us from the other end of the aisle. "Excuse me," she called out cheerfully. "Coming through!"

"Could you go the other way?" I asked her.

"Why should I go the other way?" she demanded.

"Because this aisle is blocked," I answered, grimacing and rolling my eyes. She looked at me suspiciously and walked briskly back in the other direction. A chain of voices began in the back of the store. I heard the last one call, "Mr. A.! Mr. A.!"

Then for a few minutes we were alone, the woman and her children and myself. We stood in the supermarket as if primed for a television commercial in which the magical product would come winging from the shelves, where brand X would forever stay, unwanted and untried. The manager, Mr. A., came eagerly toward us. He is a kindly fellow with dull eyes, who perhaps could seem even kinder in a small, intimate grocery store. He will sprint off on a given signal and bring back the bread crumbs or the baking soda or the canned crab meat that you cannot seem to find anywhere. He rubbed his hands nervously.

"How can I bear it?" the woman cried in grief.

Mr. A. looked at her questioningly. "Can I get you some water?" he asked.

She did not answer him, but covered her mouth with her hand, so that all her anguish was concentrated in her eyes. I began to tremble, and I worried that my concern for her would somehow affect the child I was carrying. Didn't I worry two aisles back, if, when the time came, I would choose the right baby food, that my milk would flow, that I would be a wise mother? All this time, the two small children did not release their grip on their mother's skirt.

"She's very ill," I told Mr. A.

"Shall I call the police?" he asked. The woman began to weep big flowing tears, and I thought then that all the priests and plumbers and policemen of the world could not stay them.

"No, no," I said quickly, looking at the children. Bending at the knees, I leaned toward the taller child. "What's your name?" I asked him. I was close enough to smell his milky breath and to see that his nose was running onto a crusty sore right under it. He turned his face away from mine and did not answer. Feeling bolder, I took the handbag that was looped over the woman's wrist, and she did not resist me. She did not seem to notice.

"There must be something, if only I could remember," she said vaguely. The pocketbook creaked open, as if from long disuse, or like the mouth of a nervous child at the dentist's. Mr. A. peered over my shoulder. There was a sweet, hair-tonic smell. The pocketbook was empty. We peered into it, unbelieving. It was the saddest thing I had ever seen, that empty pocketbook.

"Jeez," Mr. A. whispered. But then he brightened. "Say," he said, "say, if her pocketbook's empty, then she doesn't have any car keys. She must have walked here. If she walked here, then she can't live too far."

I looked at him coldly. "Maybe she left them in the car," I said. "Or maybe she cleaned out her purse somewhere, or left home with it empty."

This deflated him for only a moment. He looked thoughtful, then called to a stock boy who had been staring at us. Mr. A. sent him out into the parking lot and told him to look at the ignitions of all the cars.

"Pee-pee," said the smaller child suddenly, tugging at his mother's skirt.

"Oh," I said. "He has to go to the bathroom." I took his fist and tried to detach it from his mother's skirt. He held fast with the tenacity of a tick in a dog's coat.

"*Mama*, pee-pee," the child insisted.

"He only wants his mother to take him," I told Mr. A., and he nodded as if I was translating from a foreign language. The child stuck his thumb into his mouth and sucked greedily. Then the stock boy came back and said that there was no car with a key in it.

A small group of women had gathered at the end of the aisle, curiosity drawing them close, fear keeping them distant. "Do any of you know this woman?" I shouted to them.

They mumbled among themselves, and then a tall, rawboned woman in a Girl Scout uniform walked closer. "I don't *know* her—" she began, and from the rear someone called, "Why don't you look in her pocketbook?"

"I don't *know* her," the tall woman repeated, "but I know who she is." She ducked her head and then glanced up guiltily. "Her name is Shirley Lewis. Mrs. Harold Lewis," she whispered, and then fell back into the crowd of women like a frightened informer.

"But where does she live?" I asked irritably.

"Oh-oh, pee-pee," sighed the little boy, and a stream of urine, tentatively begun, ran down his leg.

"Never rush into *anything*," his mother stated. And then nostalgically, "How nice it was to be children!"

"Where? Where?" I snapped at the woman in the Girl Scout uniform. I knew that I was vying with Mr. A. We were playing detective, saviour, twenty questions, God. Who would win this terrible contest and solve the mystery and set things right again? I had a good lead. All-powerful, matriarchal, replete with swollen belly.

The woman came forward again. She mumbled an address and stepped back into the group of women. Mr. A. scribbled the information in a little notebook and went to the telephone in his office. One point for Mr. A.

"Where is Harold?" I asked slyly when Mr. A. had gone. Shirley Lewis looked at me with real interest. "Ha, ha," she said, and smirked, squinting her eyes, as if I had said something vulgar but worth noting. The little boy stood, straddling his puddle, miserable with his public act. I looked into my shopping cart and saw that the frozen things had begun to sweat and thaw. I was very tired. My legs were singing with fatigue. I wanted to sit down. I wanted to go home and take a bath. The woman was tiresome, the game was tedious, the supermarket was boring.

"We sat at the table," Shirley Lewis began. "My grandmother brought in the soup. It was so heavy, her hands trembled. Uncle Al brought everybody in the car. He had a Pontiac."

Mr. A. came back. He was smiling. The game was over. "Her husband is home! He was sleeping; he didn't even know she was out."

"Ahhhhh," moaned the crowd of women, like a Greek chorus.

Soon, the husband came. He had the car, after all. The children rushed from their mother to him. Fair-weather friends, I thought. He was tall and heavy. He was wearing work clothes, and his shoes were untied. There were sleep creases down the side of one cheek. He ignored everyone else, although we looked eagerly to him as we might to the comedy relief in a melodrama. Incredibly, he scolded the small boy for wetting his pants. To his wife, he said, "What's the *matter* with you?", and he took her arm. She went with him, and then it was all over. Several women broke away from the crowd and went to the window. They watched Harold and Shirley and the children get into the car.

I looked dully into my shopping cart. It was impossible to remember the other things I had wanted to buy. Shirley Lewis's pocketbook lay gaping on top of my own. I wondered if it would be returned to her. I thought, whimsically, that we would not be hearing from her. Harold had not said thank you to anyone. I imagined, giddily, an engraved card coming in the mail: "Mr. Harold Lewis and family thank you for the kindness extended to Mrs. Lewis in her time of need."

Mr. A. was extremely gracious. He guided me to an unopened checkout counter and personally rang up the few items in my cart. "Some fun," he said, clucking his tongue. "You were swell." He was the master detective congratulating the cop on the beat. His glory knew no bounds. He offered to take my package to the car.

"No, no," I said, yawning in his face. I left the pocketbook on his counter, sneakily, as one leaves a litter of kittens in a vacant lot.

"Good-bye," some of the women called to me. I had proved myself after all, and someday they would ask me to join committees and PTA's and protest groups. I went home. My matriarchal stature had changed to a pregnant waddle. When my husband came home from work, I was sitting in the bathtub and weeping.

"What—what is it?" he cried, primed for catastrophe.

"Everything," I said, gesturing at the swelling that rose above the water level. "Everything. The human condition. The world."

His face relaxed slightly, and he waited for me to go on.

I rose, the water spiraling from my belly. "A woman went mad in the supermarket today."

He managed to look both compassionate and questioning. "What did you do?"

I waved the towel as if it were a banner, a piece of evidence. "There was nothing I could do. Nothing at all. I mean, I tried, but there was simply no way that I could help her."

He took the towel and began to dry my back. "I think I know how you feel," he said, "but you can't mother the whole world."

"No," I said. "I guess I can't, can I?" I turned around and threw myself awkwardly into his arms.

Autobiography of a Family Photo

Accidents

M y big brother assures me I wasn't an accident. He says I was a plan, a sneaky-woman plan my mother devised to get my father to stay. "That's how women are," my big brother says. "They plan stuff behind your back."

My brother peers into the mirror above our dresser. "My eyes are baby blue," he says. "Wonder how I got baby blue eyes."

I tell him his eyes are brown, dark brown like everyone else in the family. I tell him I don't care about accidents, don't care about anything. I say this while I twirl a piece of string uncertainly between my stumbling seven-year-old fingers. I say this as if I really don't care.

The house is empty, tight and empty as the inside of somebody's shoe.

My big brother squints into the mirror then opens his eyes wide. "Baby blue. Dark, dark blue. Sometimes that color looks brown you know. It's hard to tell." He turns away from the mirror and gives me a long look. I am sitting on the edge of my little brother's bed—a bunkbed. The top belongs to my big brother. The top bunk sags. My big brother is chubby, dark brown. He and my big sister have the same hair—more curly than nappy, soft blue-black hair that shines without oil. I have my mother's kinky hair, my father's slitted eyes.

"Mama wanted him to stay. She figured if she had one more kid, that would do it. He stayed. Least for now. But he'll be gone soon."

"I don't care." My voice wavers.

My big brother touches my shoulder. His hand slips down, grazes my chest, pauses. This summer my mother made a mistake and bought him a t-shirt with a man's face on it. Only the man's eyes were breasts. My big sister noticed this. "Those eyes are titties," she said, pointing. My brother looked down at his shirt. He stared at the breasts for a long time until my mother made him take the shirt off. The breasts were pale with pinkish nipples. "It was on sale," my mother said. "Maybe that's why it was so cheap."

His hand slips down further and comes to rest at the place where a breast would be if I had any. I can hear his breath, coming fast. Heavy ten-year-old breath hovering above my fear. Otherwise, there is silence, emptiness and silence. "Titties are cheap," he says. "You can get them on sale."

Maybe he is lying.

Getting Stoned

"What's 'getting stoned'?" I ask.

We are sitting in a circle with my sister in the center rolling pot she has just bought from the boy who paces the corner of our block whispering "Sess! Sess! I got your Sess! Joints and nickel bags." The boy has the greasy black hands of a mechanic that contrast strangely to the thin white sticks of pot and squares of yellow bags he produces for the approval of passersby.

My sister cocks an eyebrow at me. "It's when people throw rocks at you." Then she and my big brother exchange looks and laugh.

My older brother stares wide-eyed as she expertly twists the pot into tissue-like paper, licks it and holds it up in front of her face to admire.

"Where'd you learn how to do that?" he asks.

"From wherever."

"Is it dope?" This is my baby brother asking—his soft brown eyes wide with fear.

My sister glares at him. "No, it's not dope, stupid, but you still can't have any. And if you breathe one word to anybody, I'll kick your ass around the block and back again."

My baby brother's face folds into something between anger and humiliation—a frown maybe, or the beginning of a hard cry. "I'm a tell Mama you cursed."

"Shut up," my sister and big brother say at the same time.

I take my baby brother's hand in my own. "I don't want any either," I whisper.

"You're such a coward," my sister says, lighting the joint and sucking the smoke deep into her chest. She squints when she does this. After a moment, she passes the joint to my big brother and exhales. "Just suck on it and hold it."

"Just suck on it and hold," I mock, for the sake of being mean, reestablishing my presence.

They ignore me, passing the joint back and forth until the room is filled with a yellow haze of sweet-smelling smoke and the joint is no more than a spot of paper burning the tip of my big sister's fingers.

"Now what happens?" I ask.

My big sister and brother exchange looks and start laughing as though they are being tickled.

"Look at her ears," my big sister coughs between peals of laughter. "Look at *his*!"

My little brother puts his head down, covers his ears with his hands.

"They are so stupid looking."

The laughter grows louder. Then my sister is coughing and tearing. "They're so weird. I need water."

She stumbles to the kitchen, returns with a tall glass of water and a bag of popcorn.

"You want some?"

My big brother nods, takes the bag from her and tilts it up, pouring popcorn into his mouth.

"I want some," I say, holding out my cupped hands.

They look at me, my sister's eyes bright. She takes a kernel from the bag and hands it to me. This sends them both into another fit of laughter.

I roll my eyes, look away as though I could care less about being in the same room with them. My little brother is crying.

"I'm telling," he says, sniffing back snot.

"Don't be a crybaby," I whisper. "It's not anything."

But the distance in their eyes scares me. There is an apathy behind it I don't yet understand.

My sister leans back on her elbows and looks at us as though taking us in from a distance.

"You both . . ." she begins. "You two . . ."

Then she is laughing again and my big brother is laughing with her. "I don't even know what I was gonna say!"

"You both . . . are so stupid," my big brother laughs. "How could we even be related?"

"What is somebody comes home?" I say, scared of their hysteria, groping for the sanity a parent provides but afraid still to be caught, knowing that my presence here is in itself incriminating.

Years later, when I sit against the wall in this room folding pot into tissue for my own private consumption, I will stop, mid-roll, and remember that this day—with the two of them getting high—was the beginning of an absence of grownups, a beginning of the four of us alone because our parents had begun to hate each other—had begun to hate the space four children could not put between them. I would remember that this was our first lesson in filling space, our first realization that there were ways we could fill up the air of their absence.

"Nobody's coming," my sister mumbles. Behind her eyes there is so much distance that I want to ask her *What happened to your other eyes?* She glares at me and says, "It's like everybody just ran away."

My Oldest Brother

When I am sixteen, my sister pulls me aside. "Deconstruct," she says, whispering, as though we are children again and she is teaching me a dirty word. "Pull the world apart syllable by syllable, word by word. Break it down." Then she is gone, off again, into a stony pot-induced haze.

But now I am eight and as of yet, don't know this word. Now I am sitting in the bathtub, counting the stages of my growing, three new public hairs, a soreness behind my nipples that may mean the beginning of breasts. Now I am nowhere but here, in the bathtub with my body, thinking, thinking *This is mine. This all belongs to me.*

Precarious. The door that shelters me in this privacy is held on by rusted hinges and a latch carelessly drilled into a rotting wall. This privacy, this growing, this shelter behind the door beneath the water can so suddenly be destroyed. This is what means to be eight and naked, perched though unbalanced in a small space. All of this happening in the tiny room that is only a sink, a claw-foot tub, and the blue-white porcelain toilet.

"Toilet," I whisper.

From the other side of the door, my big brother calls my name, softly at first, then louder and louder. I splash my washrag into the bath water, squeeze it against my chest, let the lukewarm water drip down.

"Let me in," my brother says softly, although no one else is home. "I have to go."

"I'm almost finished," I call through the door. Then whisper again, "toilet."

"I have to go now, please. I want to show you something."

"No."

"Please . . ."

"No."

Then there is quiet. Almost quiet, except for the word. "Toilet" beating out its own rhythm against the back of my throat. "To—i—Let."

If I change it, the first T to a D, then the word would be different, would take over itself, this moment, me.

My brother is back again. My stomach moves beneath the washrag I have covered myself with.

"Go away. Let me take a bath."

"I have to go."

I hear the sound of scraping, see the beginning of the flat silver blade of the knife moving underneath the latch, then up, until it is flipping the latch from its eye and the door is opening and my big brother is slipping inside the bathroom, relatching it, turning, his thing hanging from his zipper, dark, wrinkled, hanging still as death.

Do—I—let.

"Get out of here, I'm taking a bath."

"Stop being stupid. Just let me do the thing and I'll let you finish being by yourself. You been in here too long anyway."

Then I am standing, a million miles away but there, above the still, half-cold bathwater, my legs spread, shoulders, arms, hands dripping waiting for him to finish rubbing his thing between the space there. Waiting, waiting, dripping, staring off.

There are places you can go to when it happens to you.

When I try to tell my friends about it, they don't let me say who it is. They say there are places you can go to and in a sense it's the same as saying it happens to everybody, including boys, that no one's immune.

My friends gather quietly around me. One says, looking down at her new breasts "My mom says we're all in stages of decay" and her voice sounds old when she says this. It sounds as though it's a hundred million miles away.

"If you don't breathe, you won't smell," another friend advises. "If you shut your eyes real tight, you can be in that other place in less than a minute. Don't even think or feel and boom!, you're not even anywhere anymore."

Do—I—let. Allow. Toilet. Let. You must have let him. Why did you let him? You shouldn't have let him.

Toilet.

I look up places in books and imagine the ones with beautiful names; Senegal, The Fijis, Scituate, Mattawan, Indonesia, Fair Isle.

"Sometimes," another friend says, "it's like you can keep right on looking and see through mirrors and walls."

"Maybe mothers do it to their sons when they're nursing them and even probably, after."

Without saying who or when or how. Without even knowing that maybe we can question why, we talk in whispers, embracing ourselves with our own fear, afraid of what more might happen, what it might mean, afraid even to picture ourselves; little girls with our legs spread like those dirty women in the pages of our father's magazines, like those women walking back and forth along the same patch of sidewalk at night chewing gum loud, showing too much leg on too cold a day, running up to cars, looking left and right before whispering "Hey Mister" in those voices too full of sugar to be sweet. Little girls we are, little nasty girls who don't scream at the sight of those things coming toward us, who don't look up at those faces smiling down at us, who swallow, go blank as sky, don't cry out, just wait wait wait and it'll be over soon.

"Sometimes," one of my friends whispers, "my father gives me a dollar and then I go to the store and buy whatever I want."

"Once," another says, chewing on the rubber band keeping the edge of her braid together, "my mother's boyfriend gave me two subway tokens. I cashed them in and got a slice of pizza."

We can't say it. We don't know if this is what dirty boys write about on subway walls, the words that would make us anything else but a bunch of little girls. How can we dare, at eight, nine, ten, think of ever being anything other than little girls?

Across the Street

Maria's mother's arms are flabby, Puerto Rican tan. When you are close, you can see the stretch marks near her shoulders and the tiny dimples at her elbow. Maria is afraid she'll get shaky meat, the layer of flab that hangs down when her mother lifts her arm to wave.

I don't want shaky meat, Maria says, pulling the tight skin beneath her biceps. *My mother even has shaky meat on her ass.*

You know what I don't want? Maria asks, her eyes squinting into dashes. *I don't want anything that my mother got.*

Across the street a lady is screaming that her baby is drowning. Maria and I run, our double dutch game forgotten for the moment.

A baby is drowning, my friend Maria yells to her mother. But her mother doesn't leave her pillow in the window and Maria runs on, without her. There are other mothers leaning on pillows in windows. Maybe because it is so hot. Maybe they are tired. The pillows are flat and gray.

The woman screams again and when we run into her apartment we find her baby asleep in the center of a pee-stained mattress. The baby has her thumb in her mouth and Maria, because she is older, leans over the baby and kisses it. The baby's name is Cassandra. Her cheeks are brown like the color of a hershey bar. Her hair is brown too. When Cassandra grows up she will have a baby and learn to scream. Maria and I, perched in windows the way our mothers are now, will watch her standing in the middle of the street, her legs spread, her head thrown back in fear, screaming *Help me. My baby is drowning*, without running downstairs. We will watch the tears move slowly down Cassandra's cheeks without blinking. We won't remember this baby, so quiet with her thumb in her mouth, her eyelids fluttering, her lips curving into a dreamer's smile.

Outside, Cassandra's mother keeps screaming. Maria says it is because when Cassandra was born, her mother lost her mind. *She still feels the pains*, Maria says. *The pains*, Maria says, *Sometimes they don't go away.*

Pantyhose

I want pantyhose like the ones my mother buys my sister. The ones in the brown paper bag she carries into the bathroom. *I want pantyhose,* I scream through the thin sheath of wood keeping my sister at such a distance. But my sister emerges from the bathroom bare-legged, her face gray and drawn as a dead person's.

"How does it feel?" My mother asks, touching my sister's hair.

"Fine."

"I want pantyhose. Where are your pantyhose?"

My sister glares at me, calls me stupid then goes to lie down on the couch. When my mother leaves for work, my sister clutches her stomach and starts to cry, softly at first then louder and louder.

Leave me alone, she screams. *Everybody just leave me alone.*

My brothers and I watch her silently, afraid to get too close. Later, when my mother calls for my sister, they speak in whispers. Crouched in the corner of the livingroom behind a chair listening, I feel myself growing smaller and smaller. Maybe I will disappear.

"It's going to happen to you, too," my big brother warns me. "It happens to every lady. Then you have to watch your back."

At night I hear my sister in the bathroom, water trickling into the tub. When she climbs back into the high riser beside mine, she seems to be surrounded by dampness, her eyes wide. Lying beside her, I watch, half-asleep as her hands creep up to the new breasts. Her sudden intake of breath, an indication that this growing is painful.

In the morning, her spotted gown hangs drying over the shower curtain. But there are no pantyhose, only toilet paper wadded in the waste basket stained red with blood for days until my mother yells at her *don't be so nasty* and I realize that getting your first pair of pantyhose is nasty. But it happens to every girl. Then every girl has to get up in the middle of the night to wash her gown. And watch her back.

Autobiography of a Family Photo

My big sister wants to wear black stockings but my mother says no, matter of fact as if it is that easy, and continues to apply eyeliner, her lips turned downward as though this helps the horizontal motion.

"Not with a white dress," she says. "You'll look like a whore."

The stockings hang from my sister's right hand like the murky slaughtered estuaries of horror movies. In her other hand, she is fingering a garter belt that my mother has given her and shown her how to manipulate.

"Wonder where I learned it," my sister mumbles, out of earshot of my mother.

I am dressed in my favorite outfit—a brown suede miniskirt with strips of a darker brown leather running horizontally from waist to hem, a white sweater, black tights and patent leather shoes. Cornrows travel down the back of my head and dangle entwined in colored rubber bands at my shoulders.

"Your mama's girl outfit," my sister sneers, kicking me as she passes.

My mother doesn't see this and I am trying to control my tattling.

I stand beside my mother, watch her put on makeup in the tarnished mirror that hangs above a dresser at the foot of her bed. "How can we take a picture without daddy?"

"We just can."

"But how? Then it's not even a family."

"People do it," my mother says. "People survive."

"It's not the same. It's not a family. It's like our family is fake."

When my sister reenters, she is wearing the black stockings.

In the photo, my sister is wearing black stockings. My brothers are dressed in jackets and ties. They are standing behind us, in front of my mother. No one is smiling. In the photo, I am looking up at my sister, my face turned away from the camera so that one side is shadowed in darkness. It is as though the picture is fading even as the camera flashes, its edges curling up like paper on fire.

My sister grows up to marry a Jehovah's Witness and writes me often. *There will come an end to this system of things*, her letters warn. *God has had enough.*

In the picture it is as though I already know this, as though the words are there already, festering inside my sister's brain, waiting to explode. My baby brother looks frightened. Maybe there are things he knows too—that one day he will discover heroin and he too will begin to fade. And my older brother—that he will have daughters who grow up afraid of his presence.

When I visit my mother years later, the picture is framed still, on the mantlepiece in her livingroom, yellowing, shrinking with age, my baby brother's gold skin turning green. *Are you ever going to get rid of that dumb picture?* I ask.

She shakes her gray head slowly, mouths *Never* because she has lost the ability to speak out loud. *Never* she mouths again as if she cannot see the picture, as if she doesn't remember why none of us are smiling, why there is still a faint dark ring and puffiness circling my sister's eye.

Later

I am kissing Dennis Victor inside my vestibule when the lights go out. "The fuse," I say, pushing him away from me. "My mother will come down to change the fuse." But Dennis pulls me close to him again, and sucks my lips into his own. He is so beautiful he is almost white and that is so beautiful because I am almost thirteen and there is only white that's so beautiful anymore. The day before my mother tells me *the more coffee you drink, the blacker you get* and I push my coffee cup away from me, afraid that I will get darker than I already am, afraid the kids at school will stop picking on Valroy—blackie, blackie Valroy, Hurry on down to Hardies, where the Valroys are charcoal broiled Valroy, and turn on me. I push my coffee away from me, go outside where light-bright Dennis Victor is spinning a top and touch his arm. *You want to make it with me, later, Dennis?* Later the other boys will call me a ho and say I'm easy as pie, kiss the boys and make them cry. But Dennis nods, says, "I gotta go home tonight but how about tomorrow in your hallway and I say okay. I know Barry told him I kiss good and if he says he loves me I'll let him touch my breasts but not inside my blouse even if he says it. I know Barry told him he can probably get a little bit from me if my mother isn't around but I don't care. I really don't. If he loves me that's okay too. It's nice to be loved even if deep inside I know it's not for real.

But it isn't a fuse. It's a blackout and people are running up and down the street when we come out of the vestibule, our lips swollen, my breasts sore where Dennis pinched them too hard trying to feel underneath my t-shirt and bra. Shadows run up and down the block screaming "Blackout! Blackout! Everywhere is dark!"

Then my friend Maria is running past. "I'm going to Broadway. Everybody's going to Broadway cause all the stores, the alarms don't work."

My mother brings a pillow to the window and watches the people. "I don't want none of you leaving the gate," she says to us. My sister and brother beg but my mother just shakes her head watching the people run up and down the block.

I see Maria again and make her promise to bring me something back. Later, she returns with boxes from Shoe Town. *I couldn't find your size,* she says.

"You two go find some soda and a bag of ice," my mother says to my big sister and brother, throwing down a sock with money in it. "Come right back."

But they don't come right back. They come back later with shoes and shirts from Buy Rite. My mother cries and screams when she sees the stuff but my sister keeps saying over and over, "But we got it for free. The store was wide open." My mother takes the stuff to the front gate, pours Mazola oil over it and lights a match. When the fire goes up, there is much light that for a moment, people stop and watch.

"No child of mine . . ." my mother keeps saying. "Never, no child of mine . . ."

But my sister is hiding a shirt behind her back. Later, she will put it on.

CLARA YU

Virgin River Bride

*(It is said that, in ancient China, virgins were
regularly tossed into rivers as part of the
sacrificial ceremony to appease the river gods,
and to insure against floods. They were
known as virgin river brides.)*

On the day of the wedding,
The cicadas were especially restless;
Their droning drowned all words.

This was going to be a western-style everything—
The men came up from the city in formal attire;
Like ravens they gathered at the church.

Ladies stayed in the shade,
Cooling themselves with sandalwood fans,
Patting their foreheads with silk handkerchiefs.

The groom was alone in the afternoon garden.
He stood hard.
Looking at nothing.

Then there came a gasp.
You think you blinked but you didn't—
And there she was,

Running toward him like the wind,
Black hair flowing,
White, long skirt kicking up the air.

As she neared him
The groom moved back, stiffening.
She took another step, said something to him.

He made a half turn to avoid her eyes.
Yes I do but I must obey my parents,
He must have said.

Suddenly, the full skirt flew up high,
Over her head,
As if she were about to take it off,

But instead she buried her face in it—
A weeping water lily
Folding up at dusk.

Her thighs, unkissed by sun,
Untouched by sight,
Blinded like new snow.

The stunned men stared;
The ladies cried out, some looked away,
Others covered their mouths.

Before they realized what was going on,
Again she flew, swift as fury,
Leaving behind a sea of bobbing heads.

The guests were herded into the church,
In their stiff seats they squirmed—
Something unsettling was in the wedding march.

Next morning she was nowhere to be found;
They dragged the modern reservoir.
She came up reluctantly, slightly puffy,

The white skirt gathered modestly round her legs—
Sleeping lily, my Sister,
Virgin river bride.

June Elegy

(In honor of a Chinese student)

I

Last year's calendar shows June in a pastoral dress,
Holsteins quilting a bright deep green,
Red barn lazy, behind a willowed breeze.

This June, a Matisse still life—
Four yellow apples with a lime, on a table cloth of pink,
Blue floral wallpaper encroaching on the scene.

Four years have gone and come,
And I have come to remember June,
While the eleven other months go
Unmarked, unmourned.

II

How many of us still remember you,
"A Chinese student."
You had your back turned against us,
Not out of scorn, but indifference.

Under the worlds' unsleeping camera eye,
Faceless, nameless, white shirt, black trousers,
Hair grown long for lack of care?
You stood alone—

Before the bestial tank convoy in Tiananmen,
Forcing it to wag this way and that:
A deadly dragon dance.

My neighbor's boy dropped by and glanced at my TV.
Blue eyes sparkling innocent,
Broad smile on his face, he asked,
"Wow, what's that? A parade?"

As an older, wiser, Chinese, I cried out to you:
"Turn around, you fool! Show your face!
Let them zoom in on you; make yourself known!"

III

End of parade—the usual debris
Surprised us all with roasted flesh, dark blood.
The massacre drew furious coverage, and then,
Like all news, disappeared.

I asked connected friends:
"Who was that student? Is he all right?"
"He's dead," a western journalist said,
"Or we'd have smelled him out a long time ago.
He would've made a human interest piece like . . .
TNT!"

My Chinese sources shook their heads.
Using psychology, rules of politics,
They said you wouldn't want to live,
Nor be allowed.
One even produced a name for you as proof—
A name that I promptly shut out of my mind.

IV

My mind plays flashback all the time:
One glance at us,
At the CNN lens focused on your neck,
And you'd have saved yourself from the cruel plot . . .
Yet in the end you never turned around,
Nor flinched in that joust of soul with beast.

So here June comes again,
With maddening, monumental regularity.
As the sun beats down on the yellow earth,
On people's heads bowed low,
I can almost hear them mumble,
Making their apology:

"This, this too, we shall let pass."

Skull

(Sculpture by Cao Guanlong)

A human skull sits glum in slanted light.
Its solemn expression comes
From a slightly forward
Tilt—
As if the space that used to house a brain
Is still capable of contemplation.

The smooth surface of the skull
Is broken in its center
By a foot,
With five toes showing
As they rupture fontanel
Long since closed over,
Kicking the inside out.

The size of the foot tells
That it belongs to a small child:
Chubby, fleshy, happy—
Its big digit bending backward
In the gesture of an upturned thumb:

Freedom!

Swallows of Xi'an

These must be yesterday's swallows—
Look how they dart around,
Scissoring the sky,
In what looks
Like frenzy,
As if they have just been
Released from another
Time.

Below this lofty city tower,
On a wide brick walk
That was the ancient city wall—
Twenty horse-drawn carriages rode side by side,
Through the grandest capital in the world.
Now the music I hear
Comes from the Square down below—
Big Band, broadcast too loud, too distorted,
For ballroom dancers of the neighborhood.

I lift my head skyward
Searching for my swallows—
There they go again, blowing over, dipping in the same air
That resounded with songs of the Tang,
Remembering the likes of Li Bo and Tu Fu,
Who eulogized them—
Nimble fliers from noble households,
Now nesting under souvenir venders' eaves.

CONTRIBUTORS

JULIA ALVAREZ teaches English at Middlebury College. She is the author of *Homecoming* and *How the Garcia Girls Lost Their Accents*.

JAMES ATLAS is the author of biographies of Delmore Schwartz and Saul Bellow. He has written a novel called *The Great Pretender*.

PINCKNEY BENEDICT lives on his family's dairy farm just north of Lewisburg, West Virginia. He was educated at Princeton University and at the Writers' Workshop of the University of Iowa. He has received the *Chicago Tribune*'s Nelson Algren Award and the Writers' Workshop's Michener Fellowship. His books include *Town Smokes*, *The Wrecking Yard*, and *Dogs of God* (forthcoming).

LARRY BROWN was born in Oxford, Mississippi, in 1951, served in the U.S. Marine Corps from 1970 to 1972, joined the Oxford Fire Department in December 1973 and served sixteen years, and left in January 1990 to write full time. His most recent books are *Big, Bad Love*, *Joe*, and *On Fire* (forthcoming).

JUDITH ORTIZ COFER is the author of a novel, *The Line of the Sun*, *Silent Dancing*, a collection of essays and poetry, and two books of poetry, *Terms of Survival* and *Reaching for the Mainland*. She has received fellowships from the NEA, The Witter Bynner Foundation for Poetry, and the Bread Loaf Writers' Conference. *The Latin Deli*, a collection of prose and poetry, is forthcoming in 1993 from the University of Georgia Press. She is on the English and writing faculty at the University of Georgia.

WILLIAM C. COOK is Professor of English at Dartmouth and the author of *Flight to Canada* (a play) and *Hudson Hornet* (poems).

MELVIN DIXON was a poet, fiction writer, and professor of English and African American Studies at City University of New York. His first novel, *Trouble the Water*, won the 1989 Excellence in Minority Fiction Award from the University of Colorado. He also wrote the novel *Vanishing Rooms* and a collection of poems entitled *Change of Territory*, as well as volumes of literary criticism and translation. He died from complications related to AIDS in 1992.

MICHAEL DORRIS is the author of *The Broken Cord, A Yellow Raft in Blue Water*, and, most recently, *Working Men*.

LOUISE ERDRICH is the author of many novels, including *Love Medicine, The Beet Queen*, and, most recently, *The Bingo Palace*.

GARRETT HONGO was educated at Pomona College, the University of Michigan, and UC Irvine, where he received an M.F.A. in English. He is author of *Yellow Light* (UPNE/Wesleyan, 1982) and *The River of Heaven* (Knopf, 1988), which was the Lamont Poetry Selection of the Academy of American Poets in 1987 and a Finalist for the Pulitzer Prize in 1988. He is currently Professor of Creative Writing at the University of Oregon.

ROBERT HOUSTON has published ten novels, including *Bisbee '17, The Nation Thief*, and *The Fourth Codex*. He was editor of and contributor to a volume of translations of the Spanish/Mexican poet Leon Felipe. His articles and reviews have appeared in such publications as *The Nation, The New York Times, Mother Jones*, and *Newsday*. He is a professor in Creative Writing Program at the University of Arizona in Tucson.

ERICA JONG is the author of many novels and, most recently, a biographical memoir of Henry Miller.

YUSEF KOMUNYAKAA served in Vietnam as a correspondent and editor of *The Southern Cross*. Afterward, he earned a B.A. (1975) from the University of Colorado, an M.A. (1979) from Colorado State, and an M.F.A. (1980) from the University of California, Irvine. He is professor of English at Indiana University. His books include *Copacetic, I Apologize for the Eyes in My Head* (winner of the San Francisco Poetry Center Award), *Diem Cai Dau*, and *Magic City*. He has won the Pulitzer Prize and Kingsley Tufts Award for *Neon Vernacular*.

MICHAEL KRAUS, professor of political science at Middlebury College, received his M.A. and Ph.D. in Politics from Princeton University. A recipient of grants from the Ford Foundation and the American Council of Learned Societies, he was a lecturer at Princeton and a visiting scholar at Harvard, Columbia, and George Washington University. His research and writings focus on Russian and East European politics and history and include translations of poetry. His most recent publication (with Ronald

Liebowitz) is *Perestroika and East-West Economic Relations: Prospects for the 1990s.*

LESLIE LI was born in New York City of Chinese and Polish parents, lived in China as a small child, and was educated in Hong Kong, Europe, and the United States. A graduate of the University of Michigan with a degree in English, she has written travel and feature articles for a number of American and East Asian publications. Her grandfather Li Zongren was vice president and acting president of China in 1948 and 1949.

NANCY MAIRS is the author of *In All the Rooms in the Yellow House* and *Remembering the Bone House.*

PAUL MARIANI's latest books are *Salvage Operations: New & Selected Poems* (Norton, 1990) and *Lost Puritan: A Life of Robert Lowell* (Norton, 1994). He is Distinguished University Professor at the University of Massachusetts/Amherst.

ROBERT PACK teaches at Middlebury College and is director of the Bread Loaf Writers' Conference. His most recent books are *The Long View: Essays on the Discipline and Hope of Poetic Craft* and *Fathering the Map: New and Selected Later Poems.*

JAY PARINI teaches at Middlebury College. His most recent books are *The Last Station* and *Bay of Arrows.*

LINDA PASTAN has published eight volumes of poetry, most recently *Heroes in Disguise.* She is currently serving as poet laureate of Maryland and lives in Potomac, Maryland, with her husband.

TED PERRY is professor of Theatre and Art, and also director of the Film/Video Program at Middlebury College. A writer and director of plays, and of books and essays on film, he has taught at the University of Iowa and New York University and was the director of the Film Department at New York's Museum of Modern Art.

SAMUEL F. PICKERING's sixth collection of familial essays, *Trespassing,* has been published by University of Press of New England. He is spending this year at the University of Western Australia in Perth and is writing about Australia.

RON POWERS is a novelist and journalist, and was the media correspondent for CBS News *Sunday Morning.* His most recent books are *White Town Drowsing* and *Far From Home*; a biography of Jim Henson is forthcoming.

JOHN PRESTON is the former editor of *The Advocate.* He has produced more than forty books, including the novels *Franny The Queen of*

Provincetown and *The Arena* and the anthologies *Hometowns: Gay Men Write About Where They Belong* and *Flesh and The Word: An Erotic Anthology.*

WILLIAM H. PRITCHARD is Henry Clay Folger Professor of English at Amherst College and the author of various books on modern writers including, most recently, Robert Frost and Randall Jarrell. He writes regularly for *The Hudson Review* and for other magazines and newspapers.

LEV RAPHAEL holds an M.F.A. in Creative Writing from the University of Massachusetts at Amherst, where Martha Foley awarded him the Harvey Swados Fiction Prize, and a Ph.D. in American Studies from Michigan State University. His first collection, *Dancing on Tisha B'Av*, won a 1990 Lambda Literary Award. Raphael is also the author of *Edith Wharton's Prisoners of Shame* and *Winter Eyes.*

ISHMAEL REED is the author of many novels and collections of essays, including *Mumbo Jumbo, Flight to Canada,* and *The Terrible Twos.*

RICHARD RODRIGUEZ is the author of *Hunger of Memory* and *Days of Obligation*, which was a finalist for the Pulitzer Prize. He works as an editor at Pacific News Service in San Francisco and is a contributing editor for *Harper's* and the Sunday "Opinion" section of the *Los Angeles Times.*

LEE ANN RORIPAUGH was born and raised in Laramie, Wyoming. She received a B.M. in Piano Performance and a M.M. in Musicology from Indiana University, and she currently resides in Bloomington, Indiana, where she is working on an M.F.A. in Creative Writing. Her work has appeared in the *Louisville Review, Poet Lore*, and the Dell anthology *Waltzing on Water: Poetry by Women.*

SARAH SCHULMAN was born in New York City in 1958. She is the author of six novels and one nonfiction book. She was awarded The American Library Association Lesbian/Gay Book Award in 1989 for *After Delores* and The Gregory Kolovakos Memorial Prize for AIDS Writing in 1990 for *People in Trouble*. Sarah is a cofounder of both The New York Lesbian and Gay Experimental Film Festival (since 1986) and The Lesbian Avengers, a lesbian direct action group.

LYNNE SHARON SCHWARTZ has written four novels, *Rough Strife, Balancing Acts, Disturbances in the Field*, and *Leaving Brooklyn*. Her translation from Italian of Liana Millu's *Smoke Over Birkenau* received the 1991 PEN Renato Poggioli Translation Award. She has also published two story collections. Her fiction, essays, and poems are collected in *A Lynne Sharon Schwartz Reader* (UPNE/Middlebury, 1992).

GARY SOTO was born and raised in Fresno, California, and now lives in Berkeley. He has written numerous books for adults and young adults, including *Living Up the Street, A Summer Life,* and *Home Course in Religion.* His film, "The Pool Party," received the 1993 Andrew Carnegie Medal for video excellence from the American Library Association.

ROBERT B. STEPTO has taught American literature at Yale since 1974 and at The Bread Loaf School of English since 1990. He is the author of *From Behind the Veil: A Study of Afro-American Narrative* (1979), the editor of the *Selected Poems of Jay Wright* (1987), and the co-editor most recently of *The Harper American Literature,* second edition (1993).

MICHELLE TAIGUE is an assistant professor of American Indian Studies and English at the University of Arizona. She is currently completing her book, *Between Silence & Sanction,* which deals with the history and the oral tradition of the Pascua Yqui Indians.

GAY TALESE has written *Unto the Sons* and many other books on Italian-American subjects.

GORE VIDAL's collected essays, *United States,* recently won the National Book Award. He has written twenty-five novels.

TERRY TEMPEST WILLIAMS is Naturalist in Residence at the Utah Museum of Natural History. Her books are *Pieces of Shell: A Journey to Navajo-land, Coyote's Canyon,* and *Refuge: An Unnatural History of Family and Place.*

HILMA WOLITZER is a novelist and short story writer. She has taught at the University of Iowa, Columbia University, and New York University. Her most recent books include *Silver* and *In the Palomar Arms;* a new novel, *Tunnel of Love,* is forthcoming.

JACQUELINE WOODSON is the author of a number of books for young adults and a recipient of *The Kenyon Review* Award for Literary Excellence in Fiction. Her first adult novel, *Autobiography of A Family Photo,* will be published by Dutton in 1994. She lives in Brooklyn.

CLARA YU, associate professor of Chinese and Chinese Literature at Middlebury College, was born in Nanjing, China, and grew up in Taiwan. She edited two literary magazines, *Chung-wai Literature* and *Modern Literature,* before coming to the United States as a graduate student. She now serves as vice president for Languages and director of the Language Schools at Middlebury College. She published her first collection of poetry, *To the Interior,* in 1992.

ACKNOWLEDGMENTS

"Homecoming" by Julia Alvarez is reprinted from *Homecoming*, Grove, 1984. © 1984 Julia Alvarez.

"Chicago Highbrow" by James Atlas originally appeared in *The Atlantic Monthly*, April 1982. © 1982 The Atlantic Monthly Company.

"Bank Examiners" by Pinckney Benedict appeared in *Wig-Wag*, October 1989. © 1989 by Pinckney Benedict.

"Advanced Biology" by Judith Ortiz Cofer is reprinted from *The Latin Deli: Prose and Poetry*, University of Georgia Press, 1993. © 1993 by Judith Ortiz Cofer.

"Hudson Hornet," "Maternity," "Translations," "Times Square Hotel," and "First Baptist Church" by William C. Cook, are reprinted from *Hudson Hornet*, Reed & Cannon, 1989. © 1989 by William C. Cook.

"The Boy with Beer" by Melvin Dixon appeared in *Breaking Ice: An Anthology of Contemporary African-American Fiction* (ed. Terry McMillan), Viking, 1990. ©

"Home" by Michael Dorris originally appeared in *Threepenny Review*, Summer 1993. © 1993 by Michael Dorris.

"Conversions" by Louise Erdrich appeared in *Day In, Day Out: Women's Lives in North Dakota* (ed. Bjorn Benson, Elizabeth Hamsten, and Kathryn Sweeney), University of North Dakota Press, 1988. © 1988 by Louise Erdrich.

"Kubota" by Garrett Hongo originally appeared in *Ploughshares* 16:2–3, and was included in *Best American Essays 1991* (ed. Joyce Carol Oates). © 1990 by Garrett Hongo.

"Monticello," "Rendezvous," "Anthony, Isabella . . . ," "Henry the Navigator," and "Other Worlds" by Yusef Komunyakaa are reprinted from *Neon Vernacular*, University Press of New England, 1993. © 1993 by University Press of New England.

"The Gospel According to Walter," "Fog Warning," and "The Conning Towers of My Father's War" by Paul Mariani are reprinted from *Salvage Operations*, Norton, 1990. © 1990 by Paul Mariani. "Class" appeared originally in *New England Review* 15:2. © 1993 by Paul Mariani.

"South Bronx, 1939" by Robert Pack is reprinted from *Fathering the Map*, Chicago, 1993. © 1993 by Robert Pack. "Clayfeld Prunes His Apple Trees" by Robert Pack appeared in *Clayfeld Rejoices, Clayfeld Laments*, Godine, 1987. © 1987 by Robert Pack.

"Anthracite Country," "Playing in Mines," "1913," "The Miner's Wake," and "Coal Train" by Jay Parini are reprinted from *Anthracite Country*, Random House, 1982.

"It is Raining on the House of Anne Frank," "A Real Story," "Rachael (a ewe)," and "A Short History of Judaic Thought in the Twentieth Century" by Linda Pastan are reprinted from *PM/AM*, Norton, 1982. © 1982 by Linda Pastan. "Grudnow" appeared in *The Imperfect Paradise*, Norton, 1988. © 1988 by Linda Pastan.

"Losing the Aristocratic Taint" by Ron Powers is reprinted from *New England Review* 15:2. © 1993 by Ron Powers.

"Ear Training" by William Pritchard originally appeared in *Teaching What We Do: Essays by Amherst College Faculty*, Amherst College Press, 1991. © 1991 by Trustees of Amherst College.

"History (with Dreams)" by Lev Raphael is reprinted from *Dancing on Tisha b'Av*, St. Martin's, 1990.

"Distant Cousins" by Ishmael Reed originally appeared in *Airing Dirty Laundry* by Ishmael Reed. © 1993 by Ishmael Reed. Reprinted by permission of Addison-Wesley Publishing Co., Inc.

"Family Values" by Richard Rodriguez was first published in *The Los Angeles Times Magazine* as "Huck Finn, Dan Quayle and the Value of Acceptance," and is reprinted by permission of Georges Borchardt, Inc. © 1992 by Richard Rodriguez.

"Rat Bohemia" by Susan Schulman is excerpted from her forthcoming novel of the same title, to be published by Dutton in 1995.

"Being There" by Lynne Sharon Schwartz is adapted from *We Are Talking About Homes*, Harper & Row, 1985. © 1985 by Lynne Sharon Schwartz.

"One Last Time" by Gary Soto is reprinted from *Living Up the Street*, Strawberry Hill Press, 1985. © 1985 by Gary Soto.

"Idlewild" by Robert B. Stepto appeared in *Callaloo* 14:1. © 1991 by Robert B. Stepto.

"The Italian-American Voice: Where Is It?" by Gay Talese appeared in *The New York Times Book Review*, March 14, 1993. © 1993 by The New York Times Company.

"West Point" by Gore Vidal originally published in *The New York*

UNIVERSITY PRESS OF NEW ENGLAND
publishes books under its own imprint and is the publisher for Brandeis University
Press, Brown University Press, University of Connecticut, Dartmouth College,
Middlebury College Press, University of New Hampshire, University of Rhode
Island, Tufts University, University of Vermont, Wesleyan University Press, and
Salzburg Seminar.

Library of Congress Cataloging-in-Publication Data
American identities : contemporary multicultural voices / edited by
Robert Pack and Jay Parini.
p.   cm. — (A Bread Loaf anthology)
ISBN 0–87451–641–2
1. American literature—Minority authors.   2. Ethnic groups—
United States—Literary collections.   3. Pluralism (Social
sciences)—Literary collections.   4. Minorities—United States—
Literary collections.   5. American literature—20th century.
I. Pack, Robert, 1929–   . II. Parini, Jay. III. Series.
PS508.M54A43   1994
810.8'0920693—dc20   94–8809